W9-BKV-024

Showa
The Japan of Hirohito

Essays by

Carol Gluck
Masataka Kosaka
John W. Dower
Chalmers Johnson
Makoto Iokibe
Herbert Passin
Chikashi Moriguchi
Michio Muramatsu
Shinichi Kitaoka
Shoichi Royama
Edward J. Lincoln
William W. Kelly
David W. Plath
Masakazu Yamazaki
J. Thomas Rimer
Edward Seidensticker

Showa

The Japan of Hirohito

CAROL GLUCK *and* STEPHEN R. GRAUBARD,
Editors

W·W·NORTON & COMPANY
New York · London

Printed in the United States of America

The text of this book is composed in Sabon.
Manufacturing by the Maple-Vail Manufacturing Group.

ISBN 0-393-02984-0

W. W. Norton & Company, Inc., 500 Fifth Avenue, New York, N.Y. 10110
W. W. Norton & Company Ltd., 10 Coptic Street, London WC1A 1PU

1 2 3 4 5 6 7 8 9 0

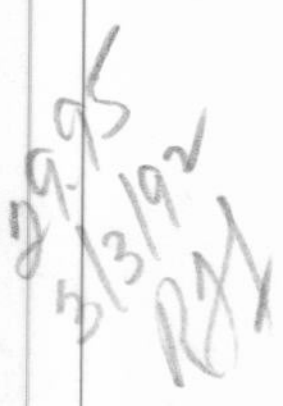

Contents

Preface

THIS BOOK ON SHOWA, the Japan of Hirohito, may be read as an expression of certain promising tendencies in twentieth-century learning and scholarship. A book of this kind would have been inconceivable sixty-five years ago when Hirohito came to the throne of Japan, because it speaks of an intellectual and institutional collaboration that would have been impossible then. Now scholars in much greater numbers make the study of other civilizations their subject. And yet the effective translation of Japanese scholarship into English is still rare, allowing little access to Japanese analyses for those who lack the language. Thus the effort here to bring Japanese and American scholars together, to show how they argue, how they see the past, what they deem important. This volume is as significant then for its many voices as for its particular observations and arguments.

The contributors to this volume seek explanations of how Japan came to be the society it is today, how it experienced the twentieth century in war and in peace, why it is so seemingly successful as an economic power, what its prospects are, and what kinds of challenges and contributions it is likely to make to the United States and the world in the 1990s. On the controversial question of Japanese "exceptionalism," these writers deny claims of cultural uniqueness even as they explore the ways in which Japan differs from societies in the West. They offer a multi-faceted portrait of contemporary Japan and of present relations between Japan and the United States.

This edition consists of essays that appeared originally in the Summer 1990 issue of *Daedalus,* the Journal of the American Academy of Arts and Sciences. *Daedalus,* in collaboration with *Asteion,* a Japanese quarterly, agreed to bring out simultaneously, though not in identical form, essays expressly commissioned to suggest what such transnational communication might produce. A great debt is owed the Suntory Foundation, which provided the funds that made the enterprise possible. It is a pleasure to express the gratitude of the American Academy of Arts and Sciences to Keizo Saji, president of Suntory, and Messrs. Minoru Iki and Tetsuji Katsuta of the Suntory Foundation. We are also indebted to Professor Henry Smith and the Mainichi Newspapers for providing the photographs that appear on the jacket cover.

Thanks are due to Professor Daniel Bell who helped conceive the project and who was so instrumental in moving it forward. All the authors, Japanese and American, showed rare patience in responding to persistent demands (which must at times have seemed peremptory commands) of a small army of translators and editors. Producing this volume, in its Japanese and English editions, was never easy. Professor Herbert Passin helped in so many ways that some note must be taken of his many contributions. And it is a pleasure to acknowledge the help of the co-editor of the book, Professor Carol Gluck, who was so generous with her time, confident that all would work out well in the end.

Stephen R. Graubard
Editor of *Daedalus*

Introduction

Carol Gluck

FOR JAPAN, "Showa" is the name of an emperor and an era. From 1926 to 1989, during the reign of the emperor known to the world as Hirohito, Japanese counted the calendar of years from Showa 1 to Showa 64. It was a long period, long enough to encompass the lives of most Japanese alive today and long enough to witness a dramatic wave of history that swept Japan down to imperial defeat in the Second World War and up to economic power in the present. Such is one view of the period the Japanese call "turbulent Showa." Another sees Japan as having engulfed itself, Asia, and the United States in war, then riding the curl of America's cold war to "high growth." Still another has Japan helplessly borne along to war by the military, but cleverly navigating its bureaucratic hard-working way to postindustrial prosperity. All these views, in different hybrid variations, are represented in this book.

For Showa is most of Japan's twentieth century, and the two preoccupying issues are how Japan came to aggressive war and then to macroeconomic might. Without agreeing beforehand, the Japanese and American writers here address the same questions. They then answer them differently, but the differences fall not so much along national lines as along a kind of San Andreas fault of opinion about the way Japan looked at Showa's end. Critics, celebrants, and sobersides—their analyses of Showa reflect differing assessments of the outcome of Japan's twentieth-century history, which is to say, Japan today. Since these fault-lines often lie beneath the surface of the essays, some introductory exploration is in order. The Showa presented by this bi-national group of historians, economists, political scientists, anthropologists, and literary scholars is as complex and contradictory as their own feelings about the past and future of Japan.

Another theme, the nature of the relations between Japan and America, runs through the book, and it runs no more smoothly here than it did in the course of twentieth-century history. What is striking is how much of the discussion depends on America to explain Japan and on Japan to explain America. Of course the mere, if not so simple, deed of joining Japanese and Americans together to dissect Showa leads naturally to transpacific reflection and even recrimination. In its Japanese-language edition, this book is entitled "Japan-American Showa," suggesting the collaborative production of a Showa with a distinctively bi-national flavor.[1] But it is also true that the relationship between the two countries was central to the past six decades of Japan's history. Fluctuating cycles of influence, amity, and hostility reached extremes of dominance, alliance, and conflict. No wonder that these writers pin so much on the United States, for better and for worse. And no wonder that Japan looms increasingly large in their remarks about America as the postwar years passed. Again, one needs to do some digging to reveal the subterranean strata of feelings that determine the writers' views but do not always show in the text. Not far below the surface, admiration vies with resentment, pride with ruefulness. The Japanese disagree among themselves, as do the Americans, about the nature of "Japan-American Showa." And in the deepest vein of all resides a palpable ambivalence.

CAUSES OF WAR

People speak of "prewar" Showa, which lasted nearly two decades. Yet a full three-quarters of those years corresponded to Japan's "Fifteen-Year War" against China, which began with the Manchurian Incident of 1931 and did not end until the Pacific War did in 1945. Odd that such a period is considered "before" the war, when, if not in 1931, then at least by the beginning of all-out war against China in 1937, Showa Japan was already Japan at war. It is a matter of perspective. The twenties and thirties in Europe are now called the interwar years, respecting the importance of the two world wars as parts of a connected conflict in twentieth-century European history. The First World War did not affect Japan (or America, for that matter) to anywhere near the same profound degree it did Europe. For Japan (as for America) the conflict of greatest consequence was the Second World War, and greater for Japan because of the profundity of defeat. The main agent of Japan's defeat in the Pacific War was the United States, which then placed Japan under foreign occupation for the first time in its history. This experience was traumatic for the Japanese and triumphant for the Americans, but it mutilated the memory of Showa on both sides. Americans and Japanese—quite unlike, for example, Chinese or Koreans—have to this day used pre- and postwar as the marker that divides both Showa and the century at 1945.

Using the term "prewar" in no way diminishes the importance of the war, since everything that happened before the war is often seen as leading to it, as if the so-called Road to Pearl Harbor had been the only highway traversed, or traversible, in the preceding decades. This kind of inevitabilism makes poor history-writing because it ignores contingency and the possibility of other outcomes. The writers here avoid the extremes of inevitability by suggesting possible turning points, when something might have been done to avert war. But—inevitably, one might say—they mostly approach the war as a great gash, a gigantic crater in the historical landscape, which the historian or political scientist walks around, measures, explains, judges, but accepts as a given of the Showa terrain.

However did it happen? The essays offer several axes of explanation: international as against domestic factors, economic as against political causes, systemic as against aberrational patterns. Kitaoka and Iokibe emphasize the international context. Kitaoka describes a vulnerable Japan surrounded by empires, most powerfully that of America, which continually denied Japan's national interests on the Asian mainland. The war was fought for reasons of security and self-defense, as "Japan tried to become an empire that could uphold its own values vis-à-vis the United States, the Soviet Union, and China, but failed in the attempt."[2] This seemingly recidivist view resembles that of Japanese leaders of the thirties and forties more than it does either the view of Japanese historians, who have long stressed Japan's own imperialism, or the view of most Japanese, who have fastened on the fact of the failure rather than the reasons for the attempt. Still, the keywords here are vulnerability, big-power international politics, and reactive but mistaken confrontation, all of which Kitaoka links to Japan's present situation. It is a sign of the times that we must be reminded how governments react when they feel cornered on the playing fields of international politics.

Other writers focus on domestic causes for the war. In economic terms, they reflect a recent argument that Japan's imperialist aggression in the 1930s should not be attributed overmuch to effects of the world depression. Kosaka and Dower both point out the high rate of macroeconomic growth in the period that Dower calls Japan's "second Industrial Revolution" from 1931 to 1945.[3] Lincoln, an economist, agrees. Through the fiscal policies of Finance Minister Takahashi, "the Keynes of Japan," and the expansion of export markets, the GNP had recovered to its pre-Depression levels by 1934, a feat that America, whose GNP in the twenties had of course been much higher, nonetheless did not permanently reach until 1941.[4]

Few would assert however that such national economic indicators suffice to express the suffering of the vast numbers of people who received a paltry slice, or no slice at all, of the growing military-industrial pie. It is commonplace to say, as Kosaka and Passin remind us, that most of them lived in the countryside and to attribute the rise of the radical right wing to agrarian distress. But the villages had no monopoly on economic hardship during the Depression. Not only farmers but workers, shopkeepers, the new educated salaried class, even the unemployed intellectuals that Yamazaki mentions found the times tough-going. And the hundreds of thousands in the thirties who left for the puppet state of Manchuria lured by inflated promises of a "new world" were living socioeconomic proof of the link between depression and imperialism, economics and war.

Nor would anyone deny the consequences of the economic nationalism practiced around the world during the Depression or of the effort to create independent economic blocs as Japan sought in its inaptly named Greater East Asia Co-Prosperity Sphere. And there is small doubt that the need for raw materials drove Japan in its long and futile quest for economic security, and, in 1941, with the American embargo on oil, helped decisively to move Japan in the direction of Pearl Harbor.[5] The authors here have no quarrel with the importance of these economic factors. Rather they de-emphasize the Depression for reasons that have less to do with the "pre-" than with the "post-"war part of Showa. They seek to correct the standard assumption that Japan's postwar economic success was built from scratch out of the rubble of 1945. Kosaka is more a celebrant and Dower more a critic of the shape of Japan's political economy today. Yet both explain the postwar period in terms of prewar legacies, and to neither is it fair to look for a comprehensive economic analysis of the road to war.

As for the three economists in the volume, Moriguchi, Royama, and Lincoln, the war makes but a slight dent in their accounts of Showa. They suggest none of the economic scenarios that led Japan to imperialism and war. Lincoln tells us that "the war years are often ignored by economists," so they may have been professionally mesmerized to leave the subject to the historians.[6] But it also seems probable that for these three analysts, who like many in their trade are a mix of celebrant and sobersides when it comes to present-day Japan, the stunning postwar economic performance absorbs all available attention.

Little is said about the war as the product of social forces. Johnson evokes the link between economic late-development and imperialism, the Bismarckian sleight of hand that staged imperialist adventures to divert the nation from the social costs of rapid industrialization and the threat to those in power posed by social protest. German historians once called these diversionary tactics "social imperialism." Kosaka makes a related point when he says that "the rise of Japan's military during the 1920s was a social and political phenomenon that accompanied the modernization process."[7] This is a Japanese version of what one might call "the theory of the inadvertencies of modernization." That is, economic industrialization, nation-state building, and other such changes that characterized modernization all over the twentieth-century world produced social and political consequences that were frequently unintended, often uncontrollable, and sometimes unholy.

Johnson sees the sleight-of-hand response of the prewar state as systemic, with the postwar version of the system substituting export growth for empire as a diversionary tactic to keep Japanese society performing smoothly in the service of the nation. The historical context was different but the state operated in much the same way. In the 1930s the result was war, in the 1960s high growth, but those in power remained there by controlling any social opposition—Johnson mentions the labor movement—that would threaten the political status quo. Kosaka, to the contrary, presents the "stumble theory," as it appears in my essay, which sees fascism and war as an aberration, explicable as an unfortunate episode in the process of modernization.[8] This view suggests that once the episode passed, the postwar reforms changed the constitutional basis of the state and with it the relationship between the government and the people. Although with good reason both authors focus on the state's control of society, the result is that society itself appears as passive, inert, and powerless.

Yet even "fascism from above" (a famous interpretation from 1946) required and in fact possessed its counterpart in "grass-roots fascism" (an innovative interpretation from 1987) at the popular level.[9] Yamazaki offers a glimpse of those intellectuals who, while not grass-roots themselves, at least wrote for the mass press, "which loudly argued for an unrestrained military, and at times gratuitously goaded the nation to military adventurism." Like Kosaka, he describes the intellectuals as "shaken emotionally by the avalanche of modernization" to which they responded by digging themselves out with shovelfuls of chauvinism, imperialism, antimodernism, and anti-Americanism.[10] His is a variant of the stumble theory, in which the intellectuals were buried rather than tripped by the force of modernization. As one would imagine, the widespread wartime support among Japanese intellectuals for Asian empire and anti-Western war has long been a besetting problem for postwar Japanese intellectuals. Japan had no Resistance, no stream of exiles, no martyrs except on the Left—and only a few of them, the majority having "recanted" in the early thirties and gone over to patriotism by the time of the Pacific War. Some wielded the weapons of silence and nonenthusiasm, but these do not, by definition, stand out. Thus it will take more than an avalanche of modernization to explain the breadth and vigor of their wartime support.

And what of the ordinary Japanese, as they are vaguely called, who inhabited the fabled grass-roots? They are hazily invoked here as having been brought to war by the state, but did they play no role in bringing themselves to war? The experience of other societies, whether German, Austrian, Italian, or French, suggests that ordinary people, too, played such a role, even in the strongest of states. It is a measure of the postwar concern with the strength of the prewar state that there is far less written, not only in this book but anywhere, about the social history of Japan in the period leading to the war, both the protest and the complicity, the victims and the accomplices, the bystanders and those who stood by the cause. The protagonist of prewar history still remains the state.

In these essays, too, the war is seen as a failure of internal politics. Since the three writers most concerned with the question are the political scientists, Kosaka, Johnson, and Muramatsu, professional inclination may figure here as well. Yet their discussion represents the accepted view of prewar Japanese political history, which has long traced the war to a profound failure of the system, although not always from the same stance as these writers. All here take the military domination of politics in the 1930s as a given and then proceed to examine the political system and practices that enabled the military to dominate. They stress the lack of political leadership on the one hand and the flawed institutional, or constitutional, structure of the state on the other, together presented as a fatal combination.

Imperial Japan was a constitutional monarchy, but of a curious kind. Parliament was weaker than the bureaucracy, and neither was a match for the military, which could exert its will in the name of an emperor who—though constitutionally sovereign, in supreme command of the military, and "sacred and inviolable"—is said to have been "by custom prevented from expressing his personal opinion."[11] And through it all—and in the end—no one was in charge. The "system of irresponsibility" described by Maruyama decades ago is here intact.[12] But of course someone must have been in charge; how else to explain the survival of what Johnson calls "the conservative alliance that keeps the elite establishment in power" and kept it in power through the prewar years?[13] What he means was that no one could be held *ultimately accountable*. The diffusion of decision-making left accountability, and hence responsibility, undefined.

Perhaps the reader now sees why so much is made of the emperor system in Japan, and why the question of the "war responsibility" of the Showa emperor, Hirohito, is still so controversial an issue. Johnson and Muramatsu, both methodologically trained in American-style political science, tell the political story through parties and bureaucracies, army and navy, political and economic elites. But Kosaka tells it with the emperor system as "the key to the problems of the first two decades of Showa,"[14] and with the emperor himself in his orthodox role, the same role presented on national television after Hirohito died in 1989, as discussed in my essay. Because Kosaka's explanation so closely echoes the view now seemingly dominant in Japanese national memory, it is worth outlining the causes of the war as he describes them here.

The order of argument is as follows: Economic factors are adduced in some detail, but the Depression is seen as only a partial explanation for the rise of the military. For that the longer-term maladjustments of modernization are blamed, but those, too, recede in the face of the difficulties placed in Japan's way by the international environment after the First World War. The suddenly powerful antiimperialism of both the United States and the Soviet Union threatened Japan's newly gained position among the Great Powers. Japanese pan-Asian racism directed against the Anglo-American powers and American racism directed against the Japanese compounded the "difficulty." And the failure of international economic diplomacy in the context of world depression played right into the hands of the military. Hence the Manchurian Incident of 1931—which however is not to be considered "the sole determinant of the tragedy." The following decade of "a rising madness" in the form of right-wing assassinations and extremism led to further military expansion and then the clash in the Pacific. But not by themselves, for at this point Kosaka indicts the politicians first for failing to restrain the right wing and next for Machiavellian maneuvering with the military. Along with leaders like the "basically irresponsible" and twice prime minister Konoe, these were the men "most to blame for what happened." Still, since Kosaka judges it too simplistic to blame "a handful of men" for the tragedy, he adds that many Japanese cooperated and even welcomed the fruits of military aggression.

And the reason for the overwhelming failure of responsible leadership lay in "the whole political structure . . . epitomized in the person of the emperor." The Meiji Constitution of 1890 had established an emperor system beset by contradictions. The so-called direct imperial rule was in fact "up for grabs" among those who claimed the right to act in the emperor's name. The powers of government were fragmented and in contention among themselves, but the bureaucratic-parliamentary hybrid worked as long as the elder statesmen survived to manipulate the system they had created. Here one finds a positive appraisal of Meiji statesmanship as well as the myth of "the last *genrō,*" Yamagata, the sole surviving Meiji "elder statesman," who died in 1922. This suggests that with the right kind of extraconstitutional leadership, or puppeteering, the flawed constitution could perform. By Showa, writes Kosaka, such leaders were gone, power rivalries overtook constitutional limits, and ultranationalists laid claim to the imperial name.

This analysis resembles one view of Wilhelmine Germany—an era of political modernization similar to Meiji Japan—which sees Bismarck's dismissal as having left the German "pyramid of power" without a peak and beneath it "a polycracy of rival centers of power" that resulted in a "permanent crisis of the state" and "polycratic, but uncoordinated authoritarianism."[15] Among the rival centers of contending power in Japan, the military, which was constitutionally independent, won out. And unlike Germany's Kaiser Wilhelm II, who had tried, unsuccessfully, to fill the vacuum of power left by Bismarck, the Japanese emperor was himself a power vacuum that he alone could fill but was constitutionally incapable of doing so. Here for Kosaka lies the key: The emperor had "no choice" but to approve the policies agreed upon by the government and the military. This is what made Hirohito's life so "trying" and the war so "tragic."

On the causes of the war, Kosaka doubles back each time to conclude that none alone was decisive, yet in the end the Pacific War was a "necessity" to secure the survival of the nation. On the question of ultimate responsibility, it rested in no one place, and the emperor, prevented from acting by the constitution, was not responsible for the actions committed in his name. This view exonerates not only the emperor but the people, since "his anguish mirrored the distress of the whole country." All helpless together—this partly explains the appeal to older Japanese of the image of Hirohito as "the Good Showa Emperor." Moreover this view also reflects a satisfaction with the present day, a sense of "the Good Nation Japan," which has surmounted the trials of Showa foisted upon it by situations where there had been "no choice."

It is important to realize that the dominance of this view of the war is very recent, a product of post–high-growth national memory, and that it is by no means universal. Missing here are the historians, intellectuals, and others—mostly progressives and mostly on the Left—whose voices strongly influenced the way the war was viewed from 1945 until the 1970s, and who have not yet fallen silent, even as their authority waned in the increasingly conservative atmosphere of recent years. They regard the causes of the war as thoroughly systemic, involving not only the state but society, not only Showa but Meiji, imperialism not only reactive but aggressive, and an emperor system not exempt from responsibility but exemplifying it.[16] As steadfast critics of present-day Japan, they see the Showa emperor, who reigned before, during, and after the war, as the symbol of all the wrong kinds of institutional and ideological continuity. For them, as for the Mayor of Nagasaki and those "ordinary Japanese" who in the polls have publicly assigned war responsibility to Hirohito, the emperor was at least morally responsible for his inaction and should be charged as such.[17]

Their charge of repeated imperial inaction gains saliency because the image of what I call "the Good Showa Emperor" gives Hirohito the credit for finally deciding to accept surrender in 1945. Like Kosaka, Iokibe describes Hirohito as "unexpectedly masterful" in making the so-called sacred decision to end the war, adding that any "opposition to his sacred will was treason."[18] Those of us outside the debate may recognize both sides of the paradox: that the emperor long acted the role of a constitutional monarch by not interfering with the decision of his ministers, but also that the same constitution that established the system of ministers and parliament gave the emperor supreme and inviolable authority, which in moments of prewar crisis he nearly always declined to use. When he "departed from customary practice under constitutional government" and used that authority in 1945, the decision stood, despite the mutinous opposition of army stalwarts.

Thus if one were to conceive an image of a "Responsible Showa Emperor," it would lodge somewhere between the exercise of constitutional power in restraint and the exercise of moral authority in extremity. Such an imperial dilemma surely complicates, rather than precludes, historical questions of responsibility. Similarly, of Kosaka's "conscientious and sensible leaders who could not say no," it may as well be said that they *did* not do so.[19]

Again the point with the emperor, as with the state, is not responsibility but the *assigning* and *assuming* of it. It cannot be that no one was responsible for the war, or it would not have happened. But it can be that people all along the scale of power, up to and including the emperor, can have come to feel and act that way. The difficulty the reader may have here in locating the causes of the war with any satisfying precision reflects this sense of elusiveness: the military, the bureaucracy, the economically depressed, the capitalistically advantaged, the terrorists of the radical right, the ineffectual leaders, the international climate, the emperor system, the chauvinists, the imperialists, everything but the cycles of the moon. All involved—and all, I think, responsible.

REASONS FOR GROWTH

Judging from the range of explanations presented here, and nearly everywhere else in contemporary comment, the reasons for postwar Japan's rise to economic power are no easier to agree upon than the causes for prewar Japan's descent to war. What is the secret, if there is one, of what Lincoln calls the "epic success" of the Showa economy? He alludes to "the magical combination of government policy, aggressive entrepreneurship, education, social behavior norms, labor-management relations, and dedicated hard work" that produced Japan's "remarkably successful advanced industrial society."[20] Johnson sees no magic in it. He pictures instead the machinations of a "capitalist developmental state," which "combines private ownership of property with state goal setting" and is based on a "covert conservative alliance to keep the people docile and preoccupied with nonessential matters."[21]

Here the reader has two poles of contemporary American opinion on the subject. One is impressed and intrigued by Japan's economic performance, the other impressed but critical of the means by which it has been achieved. They represent positions that differ in their assessment of the role of the state in the political economy, an issue that is central to all interpretations of Japan's economic development. They also differ on the relation of social cost to economic benefit for the Japanese people, whose experience does not necessarily align with the balance sheet of the national macroeconomy. They differ, too, on the nature and degree of democracy that they see in Japan today. They further differ in the importance they assign to the international context, particularly the role of the United States, in Japan's postwar growth. And needless to say, they differ in their prescriptions for the proper handling of U.S.-Japanese relations in the 1990s.

Japanese opinion also has two poles and, like its American counterpart, much in between as well. This book does not include the extreme poles of Japanese opinion, though its "in between" positions lie much closer to the positive appraisal of the Showa economy than to the negative critique. A caricature of the positive pole appeared in the controversial book of 1989, *The Japan that Can Say No,* by the politician Ishihara Shintarō and Morita Akio, the chairman of Sony and recent purchaser of Columbia Pictures.[22] With a swaggering nationalism in Ishihara's case and a proud productionism in Morita's, this sort of view tends to attribute Japan's success to its native traditions and culture, its willingness to sacrifice self for society, short-term for long-term, personal gratification for hard work, and the rest of the package of cultural stereotypes. Americans who have been attending to their own media in recent months will find this cultural argument fully familiar, though here the nationalism comes from the other side. Notable in many popular versions is the absence of economic analysis to explain economic development.

The authors in this book, both Japanese and American, are unanimous in rejecting any wholehearted reliance on cultural explanations, even those who like Kosaka and Yamazaki are generally partisans rather than critics of their culture. They, too, deny Japan's "uniqueness," for this is the keyword that marks the place in the text where cultural exceptionalism is summarily dismissed as an explanation for high growth. The economists are at particular pains to discuss the Showa economy in universally applicable terms. Royama calls for an "analysis of the rational behavior of various economic entities" that operates in Japan the same way as anywhere else.[23] Moriguchi manages to make even the Japanese obsession with (Japanese) rice seem socially rational. Lincoln disallows "Japaneseness" as a reason for economic behavior in everything from woefully small houses to workaholism and the protection of rice. There is nothing "natural," he pointedly states, about these allegedly "cultural" outcomes; they are the product of "deliberate government policy."[24]

Dower scuttles the "deep, peculiar cultural explanations" for the so-called Japanese employment system, allegedly based on age-old Confucian or familial values of harmony and hierarchy.[25] These age-old values, it turns out, are twentieth-century creations. Born of long contention between labor and management, the system of industrial relations was subsequently ideologized to appear as if it were based on values that had always been there. Kelly shows a similar reinvention of tradition in the contemporary countryside, where rural Japan, the mythic repository of all that is naturally, culturally Japanese, has been reconceived to create a new "farm family," a new "farm crisis," even a new "rural nostalgia" for the old Japan. Follow his unfolding of the social and historical process by which "the chains of blind custom became the roots of authentic tradition" and you will see why Japanese culture, as if some unchanging substrate, is not in itself the singular secret to Japan's economic success.[26]

As with the history of the war, the opposite pole of Japanese opinion on the Showa economy originally came from the Left, unrepresented here except indirectly. Yamazaki recounts the rise of Marxism after the war and its decline since 1955, when "it virtually ceased to be accepted as the guiding principle of the intellectual community."[27] Here he means the Marxist orthodoxy that was tightly tied to the Japan Communist Party, which indeed faced an ideological crisis in the years of engulfing economic growth. But marxism—perhaps a small "m" would help here—and a blended spectrum of progressive orientation that included old Marxists, postmarxists, lapsed marxists, and even left-liberals, remained common intellectual currency among Japanese intellectuals. And because marxists and progressives were so important as academics and public intellectuals, their critical views were well known in postwar Japan, not least through the press and broadcast media, which have continued to present their views along with those of the "pragmatic . . . new intelligentsia" of which Yamazaki speaks.

If the progressives are less accessible in English, the fault lies partly with the general Anglo-American aversion to marxist-sounding interpretation. This gap is particularly unrepresentative in the case of the economists, who over the postwar years evolved several useful hybrids of marxist and neoclassical economic analysis to explain Japan's economic development.[28]

In a more general sense, prominent progressive social critics like Hidaka, briefly quoted here by Johnson, have long fastened on the costs of what Hidaka calls the rampant "economism" of the high-growth period.[29] Others label it GNP-ism, and most refer to such examples as the extremes of environmental pollution in the early seventies, the long-term political disenfranchisement of labor, the inequities of social status despite the myth of all Japanese as one happy, prosperous middle class, and other social accompaniments of industrial capitalism in high gear. The closest the reader comes to this pole of postwar Japanese opinion is Johnson's essay, an instance of somewhat strange bedfellows. Unlike the Japanese progressives, Johnson does not dispute the goal of the postwar political economy so much as its methods and outcome. And unlike Johnson, the Japanese progressives are as critical of the American-style "capitalist regulatory state" as they are of the Japanese "capitalist developmental state" that Johnson contrasts with it. The wellsprings of the respective criticisms are clearly different.

Among the authors represented here, critics and celebrants alike stress the importance of international factors in explaining Japan's economic success. The world, primarily in the form of the United States, presented postwar Japan with what one might think of as the four Bs: blessings, brass rings, banes, and burdens. The first blessing was defeat, which brought the dual "dissolution of the empire and the military structure" at a single stroke of demilitarization under the occupation. Japan was thus free "to spend little on defense and the remainder on economic reconstruction."[30] But the greater blessing, in Kosaka's words, was bipolarity and the cold war. Allied to and protected by the military power of the United States, Japan prospered under the Pax Americana, a term the Japanese use more frequently than other Asians for whom the cold war was less than peaceful.[31] Japan also benefited directly from the superpower conflict. Not only did the United States want its Pacific ally to become economically strong, but Japan's profits from the Korean War propelled recovery with a momentum that occupation policy alone had never managed to achieve.

The defeat and occupation are credited here with one further blessing: the integration of Japan into the world economy, redefined in terms of American-style free trade and international economic agreements. Japanese commentators often speak of the early postwar years as a second "opening" of Japan to the world. The first opening in the nineteenth century ended two centuries of isolation and began a period of rapid modernizing change. This inviting comparison can be used in various ways. American textbooks, for example, once recounted modern Japanese history in a satisfyingly American mode, beginning with Commodore Perry, who was credited with initiating Japan's modernization, and ending with General MacArthur, who credited himself with having completed the democratization of Japan. Here Dower uses the comparison to make the opposite point. No matter the external provocation or the sudden change in response to it, both Meiji and postwar Japan were built of internal continuities and influences. More important than the Commodore and the General was the Japan that was there when they arrived.

Several Japanese writers here take a different, and in Japan, more common, tack. They say that Japan emerged from the "claustrophobic" insularity of wartime into an open field of international trade. Military dependence on the United States freed Japan from what Kosaka calls the distractions of diplomacy at the same time that American patronage helped Japan reenter the world order. This represents the view of the establishment, which has gladly nestled in the U.S. alliance while the opposition bristled at the price of what it used to call "subordinate independence." Nonetheless, "the great irony was that through defeat, Japan gained admission to the IMF-GATT system, which allowed it to export its products everywhere in the world. . . . a world freer than it had ever been since the Meiji period."[32] Between the postwar trading system, the stabilization of international currency, and access to cheap oil, the Japanese share of postwar global economic growth grew apace through the fifties and sixties. And so we have a happy picture of Japan becoming "a commercial state busy carrying on industrial production and international trade under U.S. protection."[33]

To Americans today this may seem more like the satirical caption to a political cartoon showing both Japan and Germany having prospered beyond Uncle Sam's wildest projections and to his ultimately embittering disadvantage. But that is not fair to the United States, Japan, or history. Remember that one lesson of World War II had been the damaging effect of the economic nationalisms of the 1930s. The postwar international order was partly conceived as an antidote to the past. When that order was swallowed whole by the cold war, it continued more or less on its now divided but still multilateral course. And if Japan and Germany gained from it, none gained more than the United States. The second "opening" of Japan, like the first, had its international ironies. "The United States," says Iokibe, "has no cause to regret such commendable behavior. On the contrary, Japan should model its behavior on America's good example."[34]

Such were the economic blessings of the international context. The brass rings, too, were proffered primarily by the United States. Postwar Japan embarked on the last phase of its "catch-up" development, the home stretch of late-comer industrialization. The United States was the technological leader for all economies engaged in the advanced industrial catch-up game, and Japan's rapid growth, Lincoln tells us, was based on aggressive adaptation of borrowed technology. The growth was export-fed, and the largest external market in the period of high growth remained the United States. The countries on the advanced industrial merry-go-round all reached for the brass rings of American technology, capital, markets, and the like. As they did the carousel turned faster, and again America prospered. Because of Japan's position as a U.S. client, it had a shorter distance to reach than some other countries, but like the others it worked to grab the prize. Many of course had little chance at all. It was a fact of international life, not only for Japan but for much of the world, that the United States initially set the pace in the postwar global economy.

In the early seventies, however, the international context for Japan's economic growth turned from blessing to bane. Kitaoka lists the catalogue of events. The textile issue signalled the beginning of a series of bilateral trade frictions with the United States that has not ended yet. The Nixon shocks of 1971, in addition to suddenly normalizing relations with China, released the dollar from fixed convertibility to gold, leading to an ever rising appreciation of the yen that many say is likely still to continue. The oil shock of 1973 not only drove production costs up and export competitiveness down, but also reconfirmed the degree of Japan's dependence on volatile areas of the world political economy. This point has lost no relevance, as events in the Middle East proved in 1990. And although Kitaoka does not mention it, the early seventies also saw rising criticism in Southeast Asia of Japan's new economic penetration, which has since grown vastly in proportion, and with it the ambivalent combination of open-armed reception and local leeriness on the part of the Southeast Asian countries.

This parcel of international perturbations is often associated in Japan with the "end of high growth." By this is meant the end of double-digit rates of expansion, not the decline and fall of the Japanese economy, which did not occur, high yen, rising labor costs, and expensive oil notwithstanding. What the Japanese are really saying is that the international context that had earlier blessed the gods of growth had turned prickly. There was a sharpening in the proverbial "foreign pressure" *(gaiatsu),* which Johnson alleges to be the Japanese counterpart of public opinion elsewhere in its ability to move the political system to action. Action was indeed called for in the seventies and eighties, most frequently but not exclusively by the United States. Voluntary export restraints, removal of nontariff barriers, initiation of direct foreign investment, deregulation, liberalization, cessation of direct foreign investment—the list of demands shifted and grew. Recent items on the list appear throughout this book, but especially in the Japanese essays, which echo the sincere but formulaic call for "internationalization" without sounding either specific or optimistic about the prospects.

Seldom in the past two decades was the (re)action of Japan's political system deemed sufficient by pressuring foreign governments. And seldom did the Japanese cease to be amazed when their efforts were belittled. As Seidensticker satirizes in his imaginary debate with the expert, "the truth of the matter is that the problem of Japanese economic power and what to do about it is a devilishly complicated one."[35] For the Japanese, conditioned by a quarter-century of postwar experience to economically favorable international conditions, the change from blessing to bane came as something of a shock. This was the Japanese counterpart of what was felt in other countries, the United States included, when their seemingly permanent postwar prosperity faltered in the seventies. To the Nixon and oil shocks, one might as well add the "success shock." Japan managed to pay the price of investment, resources, and labor in good and even bad international times. But the price of success came harder.

In the eighties the price of success began more pressingly to include shouldering the international burden commensurate with Japanese economic power. America argued that it was now Japan's turn to contribute to its own defense, to the multilateral organizations, the UN, IMF, World Bank, and the rest, to Third World aid, to securing oil supplies, to the gamut of world responsibilities that economic superpowers are heir to—or at least, as the United States had construed the inheritance. There are no writers in this book, or perhaps anywhere, who do not agree with the spirit, if not the details, of this charge to international responsibility. It is part of the rhetoric of "internationalization," which is now standard fare in Japan. But judging from the commentary, there is not yet much to celebrate in the way of concrete accomplishments.

Kitaoka is more positive than most when he calls the determination to join the boycott of the 1980 Moscow Olympics "a bold decision" and dates "enormous changes" in Japan's foreign policy to Nakasone's premiership in the mid-eighties. As evidence of the new task of contributing to world peace, he tells us that "in 1988 Japan did send two civilian officials to join a United Nations military surveillance team."[36] If in the context of the Gulf Crisis of 1990 this action dwindled in significance, the example is nonetheless edifying. For it shows how even small excursions into world responsibility run against the grain of postwar Japanese experience. As with the banes so with the burdens: Decades of postwar history had conditioned Japan to stay out of the international arena. Dower alludes to the sincerity of the popular commitment to peace and peaceableness. America was in charge of Japan's world affairs anyway, say others. Japan prospered at home and gained stature abroad by producing and selling goods, not policy. And as I say in my essay, the lessons of the wartime past directed Japan toward the wings, not the center, of the international stage.

From this perspective one can see that the notion of a second opening of an insular Japan after 1945 works better in one direction than the other. Receiving international influence and joining international markets opened Japan to the world and the world to Japan. But it did not imply Japan's turning outward to help shape the world it had opened itself to. This was true in the Meiji period and true again after the war. As the original Japanese word suggests, "opening the country" *(kaikoku)* locates the action *within* Japan. It is a national not an international perspective. Moreover its opposite is isolation, often appearing as the old metaphor of seclusion, or "the closed-off country" *(sakoku)* of the two centuries before Commodore Perry. This is both a national term and, considering the globalized interdependence of the late twentieth century, an impossible one. Some conservatives have waxed nostalgic for the age of seclusion, when Japan was able to tend its cultural garden without outside interference. In the stressful international atmospherics of the eighties, perhaps national seclusion had its appeal. But no one suggests locking Japan away from the world. The notion of opening and closing the country belongs to another age as surely as does Xanadu.

Yet several writers here, Dower and myself among them, warn of the cultural and economic nationalism that arose in response to the international tensions of the eighties. Others have pointed out that the flip side of all the talk of "internationalization" is in fact *Nihonjinron,* the voluminous and defensive discourse on what it means to be Japanese, as in "how different we Japanese are from the rest of the world."[37] This infernal "navel gazing," as Johnson calls it, is now reaping what it has sown. In the present mood of hostility toward Japan, the successful but ungenerous economic superpower, the world is beginning to believe that the Japanese *are* different. This only feeds nationalism on every side and moves Japan no further toward shouldering the much-discussed burdens of international responsibility.

The international context receives substantial attention here partly because the Japanese themselves have been so concerned with external models, expectations, and responses and partly because Japanese and Americans are reflecting on their respective situations vis-à-vis one another. But international factors go only so far toward explaining Japan's postwar economic growth. Indeed several authors particularly admonish those who would belittle the legacies of the prewar and wartime political economy. This may mean that the "phoenix-from-the-ashes" school will finally go out of fashion.

Moreover, the active economic ingredients listed in these essays are largely domestic. The international environment, including the alliance with the United States, was a crucial enabling condition, but not the driving cause, of Japan's success. This may help discredit the "America-rebuilt-Japan" fable, which Americans once told proudly and now tell with some acrimony, but never told with great historical accuracy. From this book it is clear both that Japan rebuilt itself—and that it could not have done so with such success had America acted differently.

An additional Japan-America factor affects the analysis here as in many other works. In defining the elements of Japan's domestic political economy, the basis for comparison is often the United States. It is hard to think of a poorer choice. America and Japan are both "outliers": They lie outside the main statistical middle, each in its way an extreme of its own type—and proud of it. Comparing Japanese to European political economies, for example, makes more sense, since Japan is closer to some continental European patterns than to the American, as Lincoln suggests. Or comparing Japan with other Asian nations sheds light on important commonalities, as Johnson implies by stressing the patterns of late-development. Any place, one is tempted to say, but America, which itself is different and from whose vantage point Japan becomes the extremity of difference. But history brought the two together, and together they remain in their descriptions of one another. Thus the economic and political definitions in use here often reflect the mutual mirages of this long transpacific relationship.

The interpretations of the nature and role of the state, for example, emphasize "the practice and ideology of technocratic control" by the bureaucracy over the market. Adam Smith is evoked on one end and state socialism on the other. Resembling neither, Japan becomes "laissez-faire in a box," with "many visible hands" and an "economic general staff," or "a managerial pattern of state governance." What Johnson terms the "capitalist developmental state," Dower calls "brokered capitalism," which "retains the market while controlling 'excessive' competition and promoting nationalistic goals." Several authors refer to Johnson's work on MITI, the Ministry of International Trade and Industry, as the locus classicus of the current emphasis on the role of the bureaucracy in steering the Japanese economy toward success.[38] Indeed the strongest statements here are made by Johnson: Until the early seventies "the official bureaucracy made all the policies and actually supervised the government," and still today "the politicians reign but the bureaucrats rule." Moreover, when it comes to the role of big business in politics, "the two are indistinguishable," a statement that recalls the once popular term "Japan, Inc."[39]

The third member in that alleged corporation of business, bureaucracy, and politicians is the ruling Liberal Democratic Party (LDP), which figures prominently in Muramatsu's discussion of postwar economic policy. He argues against those who assert bureaucratic dominance, saying that "while the system may have initially fostered dependence on the bureaucracy, it underwent a transformation that changed all this" and centered policymaking in the Diet. His "visible hands" belonged to prime ministers like Yoshida and Ikeda, who practiced active economic management as part of the "Conservative Policy Line" ("CPL") that kept the LDP in power for decades.[40] Yoshida made economic reconstruction a national priority in the early fifties, and Ikeda followed a decade later with a high growth policy based on his famous "income-doubling plan." Both policies were consciously apolitical strategies designed to preserve order against the protests of the political opposition and labor. But where Johnson describes Ikeda's settlement of the violent Miike coal mine strike of 1960 as paving the way for easier government control of industrial policy, Muramatsu sees it as the beginning of "a new era of reconciliation" and communication between the ruling LDP and the political opposition. Muramatsu stresses a "political" management of economic policy that gradually incorporated demands of outside interest groups as well.

There seems to be a sharp difference between interpretations like Johnson's, which emphasize bureaucratic guidance, control, planning, and protection of the postwar economy, and those like Muramatsu's, which stress the expanding role of party politicians, interest groups, and "politics" in general in contesting and guiding the direction of the national economy. We may think of it, in shorthand, as "the MITI model" versus "the CPL model." Neither denies the importance of the other, since the career bureaucracy and the ruling conservative party are both seemingly permanent fixtures of the postwar Japanese political economy. It is rather a difference of emphasis—and of perspective.

In recent American opinion, for example, those who emphasize the role of the state in Japan's economy tend to stress the ways in which Japan is different from the United States. In 1979 when Ezra Vogel published his *Japan as Number One,* a book the Japanese cherished and made a huge best seller, he suggested that America could usefully learn from the difference in such bureaucratic Japanese practices as industrial planning.[41] In 1989 when James Fallows published his "Containing Japan," an article the Japanese did not cherish but made a huge fuss over anyway, he suggested that America should recognize that Japan's capitalist developmental state operates differently from an open free-trading nation like the United States and that the United States should defend both itself and free trade by acting to contain Japanese expansion.[42] Clearly both authors were as concerned about the situation of their own country as they were about the lessons of difference they learned from Japan. Their points of view were, quite reasonably, "made in America," where the state does not play such an interventionist role in the economy or, perhaps more important, where people at least believe it does not and should not do so.

Those Japanese and Americans who stress the political rather than the bureaucratic brokering of the economy tend to think of Japan in the same terms of analysis as other contemporary industrialized democracies. Few subscribe to the old mythology of convergence, according to which all industrialized countries would eventually come to look more or less alike, or rather, to look more or less like us. But they do see Japan less in terms of difference than of similarity, or commonality, with other postindustrial political economies, including the United States. In a recent book entitled *The Japanese Way of Politics,* Gerald L. Curtis concludes an argument that resembles Muramatsu's by describing expanded LDP involvement in policy making in a "political system that echoes universal values and behavior while at the same time being utterly unique."[43] Although this remark could apply to any country one might name, here it refers particularly to the democratic process of electoral politics that operates in Japan as it does elsewhere.

Although that "elsewhere" is not necessarily the United States, the concepts that underlie these interpretations often originated in analyses of politics in America, where people believe that political parties represent their interests rather than those of the state.

To some extent, then, whether one stresses the MITI model, which focuses on the state, or the CPL model, which focuses on the politicians, is a matter of personal stance. Both are only partly correct, and neither alone is entirely sufficient. The bureaucracy never had the degree of economic prescience or control that is sometimes imputed to it. Debunkers show how MITI made mistakes, for example, in targeting the petrochemical industry not long before the oil shock and in trying, unsuccessfully, to dissuade Sony from committing its resources to an invention called the transistor. In his book *The Business of the Japanese State,* Richard J. Samuels argues that "although the Japanese state pervades the market, it does not lead, guide, or supervise private interests." Instead it negotiates with them, and they with it. In his study of the historical transformation of energy markets, Samuels concludes that "in *no* case did the state prevail against private interests." Instead he portrays an ongoing process of negotiating a "reciprocal consent."[44] This is similar to the "network state" or "societal state" that Daniel I. Okimoto describes as "a complex process of public-private sector interaction, involving subtle give-and-take, not frontal confrontations which would result in the forcible imposition of one side's will on the other."[45] Without disputing the importance of the state, these writers deny its dominance by emphasizing the process of interaction by which government and business agree to wrangle and wrangle to agree.

Recent descriptions of the relations between the bureaucracy and the LDP also emphasize processes of interaction and contention rather than simple dominance, either by the state or the "conservative policy line." Here Kelly shows how the much discussed issue of "local development" depends on an interaction among local politics, national party brokerage by the LDP, and the bureaucracy, with costs and benefits for each. He argues that "both ideological disposition and electoral interests reinforce a pattern of regional development through extensive subsidies."[46] The commitment of politicians and bureaucrats to centralized planning is as much a shared as an imposed one. This is "reciprocal consent" operating on the level of relations between the state and the local political economy.

Scholarly efforts to describe the Japanese political economy have resulted in flights of terminological creativity, as shown in Dower's listing of the various names for the system: from "corporatism without labor" to "bureaucracy-led mass-inclusionary pluralism."[47] The point in all this—which even the most ardent advocate of one model or another would agree upon—is that no single model does the trick. Just as late–twentieth-century analysts would not explain the U.S. political economy wholly in terms of market forces, one cannot explain the Japanese political economy wholly in terms of state dominance. Nor can one make conservative party politics the whole story either. Hence while political scientists and economists conduct their quest for the perfect term to describe the processes of interaction between state and society, state and economy, the rest of us may as well refrain from taking to the cliffs so clearly demarcated on one side or the other and stand instead in the muddy middle, where most of the action takes place anyway. If there is less muddy middle in this book than there might be, it is probably because the Japan-America comparison so easily drives writers to the opposing cliffs of bureaucratic state control versus pluralistic political process. In reality the process of policymaking largely occurs in the routes that lie between and link the two.

On the more strictly economic front, Royama discusses the contribution of financial management to growth. Keeping interest rates artificially low and restricting capital flow in and out of the country set the stage for four distinctive—but not, Royama insists, unique—characteristics of Japanese finance: indirect financing, overborrowing, overloaning, and a system of banks with uneven availability of funds.[48] Within a "controlled financial system which avoided the guiding hand of free markets," Royama assures us that Japanese firms and individuals acted no differently from profit-maximizers anywhere. He then suggests that the most important change in recent years was not the deregulation or internationalization of Japanese finance but its "securitization." Expanded securities markets, secondary markets for government bonds, and new kinds of financial services operating on the open market meant that "the price mechanism therefore began to work throughout the Japanese financial system."[49] Whether or not the price mechanism operates as freely as this description suggests, Royama fears that financial speculation may result from the new freedom of choice to manipulate "money for money's sake." Pondering the growing enthusiasm for the stock market, he asks "Will Japan turn into a nation of coupon clippers and degenerate?"[50] Here again one knows from what country such fearsome images derive.

The nation of coupon clippers may yet materialize, but for the present Japan is still a nation of household savers, a fact that is always stressed in explaining where the capital for high growth came from. Postwar Japan had an extremely high level of household savings, as Lincoln recounts, and even now its rate remains high among the advanced industrial countries. (Toward the other end of the spectrum, as usual, is the United States.) The two questions commonly asked about Japanese savings rates are why do the Japanese save, and will they continue to do so "post-high growth"? To the first, the answers range from the econo-rational, such as income rising faster than consumption or the desire to increase family assets, to the psychocultural, such as a reflexive or Confucian-induced frugality. Remaining noncommittal, Lincoln comments that considering the abiding low interest on savings accounts, the recent opportunities for speculators and coupon clippers, and the absence of a capital gains tax, postwar Japanese households have demonstrated what to Americans appears as "an astounding financial conservatism."[51] As to whether Japanese savings rates will "converge" downward toward U.S. levels as consumption increases, this is an economist's equivalent of the Zen question about the sound of one hand clapping. Some say yes, some say no, but most agree in recognizing that dramatic increases in consumption levels occurred during the same postwar years that saw the high savings rates. During high growth the Japanese both consumed more and saved more than they had before, a phenomenon that is unlikely to continue in similar proportion in the future as the population ages rapidly and social security benefits fall behind.[52]

To sum up the reasons for growth, we may refer to Lincoln's essay, which represents the views of many mainstream professional economists drawn to the magnetic topic of Japan's macroeconomic success. Lincoln arranges his answers around the question of why investment levels were so high that they propelled rapid economic growth. The first answer is a variant of the late-developer thesis, in that catch-up industrialization proceeded by adopting and adapting Western technology. By the early years of Showa, the development of modern heavy industry was underway, taking advantage of the supply of inexpensive labor from the countryside. The isolation of the war years widened the technology gap, and the expectation of the profits to be made from closing it again spurred the extremely high investment of the fifties and sixties. But, Lincoln says, technological lag and ample labor supplies existed in many places and are not enough to explain such "high profit expectations" and "high levels of investment."

Next on the list is high domestic savings, the reasons for which, Lincoln agrees, are only poorly understood. Also, he adds that savings alone do not produce growth. Further explanation is needed as to why those savings were so efficiently and productively invested. On the contribution of the occupation reforms to the postwar economy, Lincoln sits the fence of the argument, leaning somewhat toward the side that credits the reforms with helping to create a stable and competitive economic environment. He writes that land reform may have contributed to political stability and to entrepreneurial investment by the new landowners, but its effects on agricultural productivity remain ambiguous. Disbanding (or better said, restructuring) of the large industrial combines *(zaibatsu)* like Mitsui and Mitsubishi may have fostered more competition and vigorous investment, but even here the verbs in Lincoln's sentences are never stronger than "may."

The organization and behavior of the firm are offered as more important factors in Showa economic history. Indeed Lincoln suggests that we may see "the forging of a new set of corporate behavior patterns as the outstanding legacy of the era." These include the so-called Japanese employment system, management innovations, worker participation, quality control, and the evolution of what has been termed "lean production" in industries like automobile manufacturing. These amount, in Lincoln's words, to "an indigenous revolution in production practices." Here the analytic dilemma is not ambiguity of impact, but debate over derivation. Which, if any, of these corporate practices are "bound up in distinctive Japanese social behavior patterns" that cannot be transported overseas? asks Lincoln. This version of the uniqueness argument has been used both ways: to justify Japanese reluctance to build plants in the United States, which means Japanese production methods depend on having grown up Japanese, and to justify Japanese practices in American plants when the Japanese do build them, which means the assembly line secrets are due to organization, not culture. Lincoln says we do not yet know how much of Japanese manufacturing practice will travel or with what effect.

That brings us to the role of the state. Lincoln recapitulates the debate over the role of government industrial policy in Showa economic growth, concluding that the argument over planning versus market forces remains far from resolution. He acknowledges the American objections to the import barriers that protect domestic products from foreign competition until they can meet it successfully. He contrasts Japan's industrial policy to Europe's, where there is government ownership or sponsorship rather than the structuring of a circumscribed arena in which a small number of firms engage in "ferocious competition" over product development and market share. He says that the heyday of government planning is now over in Japan, but that industrial policy has by no means disappeared. He concludes that the debate over its desirability will continue.

The next entry on Lincoln's list is the national bias toward the corporate sector and the concomitant disregard of public welfare, or "social infrastructure," which includes everything from sewers to libraries. Until the seventies Japan's GNP grew at the expense of the environment, public services, social welfare, and consumer interests. Since then, often under considerable pressure, the government has paid increasing, if still uneven, attention to these matters. From a different perspective, Lincoln commends Japan's "general success in organizing an industrial society" in terms of such things as low crime rates and high educational achievement. He also judges it "ironic that a nation of financial conservatives should become major international financiers," now that Japan has replaced the United States as the world's largest creditor. He concludes the list of ingredients in Showa's economic success with "insularity." Postwar Japan saved and invested at home, minded its own production, and limited the exposure of its people and markets to the world. But by the end of Showa the "transition to advanced industrial status was over," and Japan had to face the increasing demands of international power.

To complement this professional view by an American economist, the reader may turn to "A Cartoon Introduction to the Japanese Economy," a bestselling comic book version of an introductory economics text, both published by the Japanese newspaper counterpart of *The Wall Street Journal* in 1986.[53] The story is familiar, but the Japanese perspective is different. Follow the fortunes of the Mitsutomo Trading Company, with a complete cast of characters, both good guys and bad guys, in such thrilling (and true) episodes as trade frictions with the United States, ill-fated oil ventures in the Middle East, a "fi-tech" scheme involving the Vatican, an exposé of old folks' welfare facilities, and the like. Americans will recognize President Ironcoke of Chrysky Motors and the White House chief executive who says, "They should buy more U.S. beef and rice!" and, sleepily, "Enough! I'm getting tired." More surprising perhaps are the scorn heaped on Japanese politicians and bureaucrats, the stress on corporate social responsibility, and the sense of inexorability of industrial restructuring after the oil crisis in the seventies and of securitization in the wake of the financial liberalization of the eighties. The comic book ends as Lincoln does, with Japan's choices having "great meaning for the world of the future." But where Lincoln stresses the reasons for economic success, the cartoon version suggests an almost Darwinian struggle for macroeconomic survival along with an individual crusade for social decency on the corporate battlefield.

In his comprehensive presentation of the factors that produced Japan the economic superpower, Lincoln judges each explanation insufficient in itself, much as Kosaka did in listing the causes of war. Perhaps we are to add all the factors together. Or perhaps we should infer that they "worked" because Japan was able to carry on largely in isolation from the interference of other economic systems. Or perhaps the stars were in the right house and Japan in the right place for concerted socioeconomic achievement. Whatever the reasons, or combination of reasons, we spy no particular "secret" to Japanese success. In that alone there is a useful lesson.

POSTWAR PARADOXES

Let us conclude with our own list, a list of five paradoxes and ironies that contemporary Japan exhibits and this book presents. First, the paradox of well-being. Leaving the realm of national politics and macroeconomics, how does postwar Japan feel on the ground? Kelly takes us to the home of the Satos in a rural area well north of Tokyo. There we find three generations in the household, three hectares of land in the ricefields, and three vehicles in the driveway. The Sato family represents the Japanese farmer, politically much discussed but socioeconomically on the way to extinction.

The "politics of rice" continues to absorb attention on a national and international level. It is linked to the legendary but now mythical notion of the LDP as a party of rice farmers and to the increasingly untenable but tenacious defense of the homegrown grain that is "Japan's soul" against foreign rice, though it be grown under Japanese ownership in California. To Americans, who are no strangers to the often curious effects of a strong farm lobby in a postindustrial economy, this political phenomenon should not seem peculiar. And in Japan, as in America, neither the political defense of agriculture nor the cultural sentimentalization of rural life—what Moriguchi calls Japan's "agrarian idealism"—speaks to the enormous changes that have occurred in the real lives of all these idealized down-home, hometown "farmers."

First, as Moriguchi and Kelly show, most of them do not farm anymore, or, rather, they farm only around the edges of their lives, which are spent as salaried workers in factories, offices, and service jobs. Kelly calls it the metropolitanization of the countryside. He portrays the ways in which the "new middle-class" consciousness has seeped into the nooks and crannies of what used to be rural Japan. Now the ideal *raifu-sutairu* (lifestyle) includes "career employment in large organizations, meritocratic educational credentialing, and a nuclear household division of labor between the outside 'working' husband and the inside domestic wife."[54] Second, these ideals, like those of the mythical rice farmer, are not so easily realized. Mrs. Sato works full-time as an accountant, her university-educated husband is employed by a small firm without the security offered by the idealized large organization, and their children's education is unlikely to gain them entrance to a prestigious national university. Provincial life has never been so prosperous, but the Satos, who appreciate that fact, do not feel particularly well-off.

This is a rural expression of the paradox of "rich Japan, poor Japanese" that Johnson alludes to here and that we hear so often mentioned. Even as the GNP and Japan's economic power grow, Japanese complain with reason of high food prices, absurdly high land prices, and difficulty in making family ends meet, especially in terms of housing and caring for older people. The situation is far worse in the cities, which is where most Japanese live. That urbanites are largely absent from this book may reflect that agrarian-mindedness that pays more analytic attention to rice and melons than to two-and-a-half-hour commutes and housing so cramped that a recent film shows the husband and wife convening in the closet to watch television while one child sleeps and the other studies.

The family car, as Plath attests, offers city dwellers a similar privacy or escape.[55] His portrait of automobilized Japan suggests a rural image of landless, carless tenants having first become owner-farmers as a result of the postwar land reform and then a society of owner-drivers as the automobile became a consumer necessity. But the Satos at least have a driveway for their triad of vehicles. In the cities, Plath points out, people have virtually to shoehorn their cars into a space that was once or might have been their living room, and when they manage to extricate it for a holiday *doraibu* (drive), they may sit in highway traffic jams that stretch for kilometers.

As with the car, so with other aspects of what Tokyo advertisements would call the good *aaban raifu* (urban life). For many, it is good, or at least worlds better than when the postwar era began. Polls repeatedly reveal that most Japanese, urban and rural, think of postwar history as a chronology of improving livelihood and lifestyle, often defined as a progression of consumer items. No popular account of postwar life is complete without an enumeration of the coveted three treasures of the fifties—the washing machine, refrigerator, and vacuum cleaner (or television set)—which, once acquired, gave way to the desired three Cs of the sixties, the cooler (air conditioner), car, and color TV. These were then superceded by the luxurious three Vs of the early seventies, the villa, *vacansu,* and the visit (vacation house, foreign travel, and guests at home for dinner). After that, post–oil-shock and post–high-growth, the triplets ceased to multiply, but the consumption continued and the eighties saw middle-class Japanese feeling that they were both living better and not living well at one and the same time.

Much of the contemporary complaint focuses on housing, which has grown so prohibitively expensive in Tokyo that it is sometimes possible, and necessary, to take out a "three-generation mortgage" to be paid back within a century. Much of the future worry centers on whether the social welfare system will manage to support the postindustrial world's most rapidly aging population. Moreover, despite the social myth of the middle class, disparities of net wealth, employment security, and social equality affect the lives of those 95 out of 100 Japanese who identify themselves in that category. It is of course worse for those who by virtue of poverty, gender, or minority status find themselves outside both the ideal and the real characterization of a "homogeneous, egalitarian, middle-class Japan." For non-Japanese, whether they are workers newly arrived from Asia or third-generation Japan-born Koreans, for *burakumin,* the former outcaste class that was legally abolished over a century ago, or for women working in an employment context of entrenched discrimination of wage and status, the gap between gross national wealth and individual social well-being can yawn wide indeed.

Second, there is the paradox of democracy. As several writers here state, postwar Japan offers a remarkable example of political stability. Not only is the system stable, but as of 1991, the Liberal Democratic Party had been in power since 1955. A ruling party electorally dominant for thirty-six years represents stability from nearly any definitional point of view. The contributors disagree, however, over whether such stable politics merits the name of democracy as they understand the meaning of the term.

Johnson argues that the conservative elite distrusts democracy as socially disruptive and works to deflect mass action away from the arena of politics to the safer ground of economic growth. For him the opposition parties let themselves become "ornaments to give citizens and the outside world the impression that Japan was a multiparty democracy." In reality, he writes, the politicians and the bureaucrats—the "pols" and the "crats," one might say—rule Japan together. The last moment of mass democracy occurred in the Security Treaty protests of 1960, when a broad-based opposition took to the streets to protect democracy from autocratic LDP manipulation.

Thirty years later, the LDP still in power, Johnson sees a possible breakthrough as a result of the Socialist Party gains in the July 1989 elections, which "opened up the possibility that Japan might resume its development toward democracy, a process that has been more or less on hold since the 1960s." Since by 1991 no further gains for the opposition parties were yet in sight, one guesses that Johnson would still judge democracy to be "on hold." Hence his description here of "great economic development, significant social development, and serious political underdevelopment," what he has elsewhere evoked in the scarcely milquetoast image of "Japan as economic giant and political dwarf."[56] Until the people speak out and interject their voice into the deaf-eared coalition of ruling pols and crats, for Johnson, who sometimes seems to evoke our own throw-the-bums-out principle of political change, Japan is a democracy only by another name.

Dower's view is milder but he, too, describes a democracy "brokered" by the same pols and crats "in ways that respect the form but frequently kill the spirit of democracy." Quite like the progressive critics in Japan, he sees the forceful democratizing movement of the early postwar years as having been short-circuited by the conservative elite. He then recognizes and commends the authentic popular support for the democratic ideals embodied in what most Japanese call their "peace constitution." But he adds the same charge that had so animated the 1960 Security Treaty protests: Genuine democracy is not conferred from above; it must be defined and won by the people.[57] In his case the principle of active participation, as opposed to passive resignation, is the earmark of democracy that he finds weak in Japan today.

In postwar Japan it was felt that the people had to win active participation ex post facto, since democracy in its postwar constitutional form had indeed come from on high, from the occupation authorities who drafted the new constitution. If those in the occupation saw the process differently, it was partly because they were comparing postwar Japan, as Passin does here, to its immediate prewar predecessor, "a militaristic, ultranationalist, fascist, imperial state." Passin, who was a member of the occupation (though not of the section concerned with political reform), praises the postwar transformation to "a peacefully inclined, democratic, and economically healthy nation." He speaks of freedom of dissent, opposition parties that regularly take nearly half the vote, and the common people of Japan having been brought into "the mainstream of citizenship, both politically and economically, in a way they had never been before."[58] For him the democratization of the political process makes Japan a democracy like others.

Muramatsu says something similar but in different terms. He credits the new parliamentary democracy with a continuously expanding "accommodation of more social forces in the political system." Not only did the pols become more important than the crats, as the postwar Diet became the highest policy-making authority, but the LDP also practiced "a new politics of inclusion" in the "pluralist political dynamics" that increasingly took contending interest groups and public opinion into account.[59] Public opinion refers to the views of what is sometimes known as "the new middle mass," a supposedly vast social center composed of middle and working classes that merged during the high growth years of the sixties. Because the new middle mass was "pro-system," it supported the Conservative Policy Line but also influenced and directed it.[60] LDP dominance suited the inclination of the new middle mass toward stability and support of the status quo. In this light Japan is an example, along with Italy, Sweden, and Israel of the "one-party dominant regimes" that T. J. Pempel labels "uncommon democracies," uncommon perhaps but democracies nonetheless.[61]

Whether pro or con in the argument, democracy in all such views is defined politically, in terms of participation in the processes of government through parliamentary representation or mass action. Political parties are central to some definitions, participatory activism to others. But the locus of democracy is politics, and its essential meaning is engagement of the governed in the process of their governance. It is essential to emphasize that this definition is not new to Japan, which saw its first modern democratic politics over a hundred years ago in the Freedom and Popular Rights Movement of the Meiji period. The widely spread and deeply accepted definition of constitutional democracy in Japan today derives from the past thrice over: from the long modern tradition of representation in political parties and social protest, from the negative experience of the prewar suppression of all politics outside the imperial state, and from the nearly half-century of postwar constitutional and parliamentary practice. This last is the reason why the polls reveal that Japanese today think they live in a political democracy, which they approve of, however little they like the politicians who run it.

There is, however, another definition of democracy that became very important in the postwar period, and it is social rather than political in emphasis. It held that democracy means open and more equal access to social and economic goods, whether education, civil rights, wages, or consumer products. It is a democracy of daily life, of livelihood, of private rather than public value. Indeed the popular retrospectives of Showa history that I discuss in my essay made the improvement in livelihood the central domestic story of postwar Japan. It was doubly domestic, counting both as the main achievement within Japan (as opposed to developments in foreign relations) and as the main experience in the private lives of most Japanese, having happened, as it were, at home.

Immediately after the war the goods in question were elemental, both materially in terms of food, shelter, and work, and intangibly in the assertion of the right to private life freed from the demands of the state. The high growth years of the 1960s brought Japan close to the top of the list of industrial democracies in equality of income distribution, ranking after Sweden, Norway, and Australia. However brokered the capitalism by elitist pols and crats who cared more for industrial than social planning, postwar Japanese households in fact experienced the egalitarian income distribution of a social democracy. This is part of the reason for the widespread feeling of middle-classness and for what one Japanese scholar called "a virtuous cycle in which economic development (growth) promotes economic equality, which promotes supportive or enthusiastic participation in favor of the dominant party (which happens to be conservative), which in turn increases government stability and provides an encouraging environment for still more economic growth."[62] Japanese support for the political status quo was as much, or more, a support for the socioeconomic status quo that postwar democracy had brought.

The nature of social goods gradually expanded. Yamazaki writes here of "the age of the learning society" and elsewhere of "the age of flexible individualism" that characterized postindustrial Japan since the seventies.[63] The notion that one could become what one wanted to be came to seem part of the inalienable social property. In recent years the frequent promises of the futuristic benefit to come from the "information society" suggest to Plath, only half humorously, that "software individualism" may be the moral challenge of the future.[64] Whether *maikaa* (my car) or *maikon* (my computer), consumer culture envisions one in every *maihomu* (my home), where as a result of a *betaa uiiku* (better week) of only five working days, the whole family will have more time for self-improvement and *rejaa* (leisure). This caricature proves that it is just as easy to make fun of contemporary Japanese society as of our own. It also suggests that as in other postindustrial societies, the Japanese regard individual (rather than collective) quality of life as a democratic entitlement.

Dore here bemoans the loss of intellectual and political excitement that characterized "the great postwar renaissance. . . . Today's Japan is much more sophisticated—and duller."[65] A considerable number of Japanese intellectuals would agree with him. But the fact is that in postwar Japan peace and democracy were early conjoined in the realm of private life, and to many Japanese, democracy remains less a matter of politics or the ballot box than of the cycles of personal and family life. If this is democracy in a form the Athenians would not recognize, the paradox is not confined to Japan alone.

Third, there are the ironies of Showa history. As I write in my essay, postwar Japan has long presented itself in terms of radical discontinuity. It was as if history stopped and began anew with the defeat in 1945, which severed war from peace, the prewar from the postwar, the imperial state from the democratic society, the besmirched old from the reborn new Japan. This is what I call the founding myth of postwar Japan, what people wanted and willed themselves to believe. The tenacity of this belief has created "the long postwar" that I describe in my account. It has also created problems for Showa history, which has been particularly beset by the perennial historical difficulty of balancing continuity against change. What is the relationship between the two parts of Showa, one prewar, the other postwar; between the two Hirohitos, one divine sovereign, the other human symbol; between the two constitutional states, one imperial, the other democratic? The list is long, but the question may be wrong. Common sense tells us that history does not stop and begin again, that institutional, social, and psychological practices do not alter overnight, even in the crucible of radical change. Everyone knows this, but Showa "mythistory" still remains powerful enough to frame the general debate in terms of disjunctive change between prewar and postwar Japan.

In this book several authors present arguments for transwar continuity that in other national contexts would be quite commonplace now that a half century has passed since the events, no matter how momentous they may have been. Dower writes of the legacies of war, Lincoln and Kosaka of the importance of the industrialization in the earlier part of the century, Johnson and Muramatsu of abiding forms of political practice. In each case they make the point that contemporary Japan is a product of both its prewar past and its postwar present. Having said that, however, the overall impression is still of a comparison between the two. Take the state as an example. What are the continuities between the imperial state that brought Japan to war and the democratic state that brought Japan to economic superpowerdom? One might combine several essays here to conclude that the continuity lay in lack of leadership and absence of an identifiable site of ultimate accountability. No one here gives the political leaders of the 1930s high marks, and the entire system is described in terms of collective irresponsibility. Except for the military, which more or less knew what it wanted, everyone, the emperor included, appears to have been helpless before the currents pushing Japan toward war.

In the postwar period, several essays refer to lack of leadership in the LDP, with only Yoshida, decades ago, and Nakasone, in the eighties, receiving honorable mention for statesmanship from some Japanese authors. In comparison to what Kitaoka calls the passivity of other prime ministers, Nakasone appears to Muramatsu to have displayed "leadership of presidential proportions."[66] But such proportions, he implies, are exceptions to the rule, and Johnson states flatly, "Japan currently lacks the capacity for true political leadership." Then there are the references to the "decapitated state," the "headless monster," and the "truncated pyramid" in Dower and Johnson, evoking the frustration of foreign governments, especially that of the U.S., when they cannot find that legendary place where the buck stops.[67] This sounds like the prewar system of irresponsibility in postwar clothing. But in this case rather than being carried helplessly along by the currents, the headless monster is depicted in aggressive technocratic control of the political economy, driving the nation toward high growth. One is only left to imagine what might happen if the monster had a head.

There is something wrong with this picture, just as there is with analyses that postulate nearly total transformation between the prewar and postwar state. Not only is history skewed by overdrawing the comparison between the two, whether in the direction of continuity or of change, but it is also marked by strong and distinctive postures in relation to the present. In the essays here the Americans offer harsher descriptions of the present political system than the Japanese, who, it is true, do not rank in Japan as critics of the system. But even those Japanese who are known to be extremely critical would be less likely to talk about the state as a headless monster than about its abuse of power and the need for concerted popular action against it. During the many years when Japan was a dependent economy and a client who followed the political lead of the United States, American commentators did not so much fasten on the lack of Japanese political leadership or a buck-stopping place. Now that the historical relationship between the two countries is changing, there is a tendency on both sides to focus on the differences between them, each applying its own standards or preferences to the other. This, too, is nothing new, since the initial definitions of continuity and change in postwar Japan were a product of Japanese-American debate even as "the present began" in August, 1945.

Fourth, then, is the irony of Japan-America, or as Japanese wordsmiths have put it, *Japamerika* or *Amerinippon*. The two countries have now been involved with one another for nearly 140 years. Iokibe may go further than most when he writes, "In a sense, the United States determined the destiny of modern Japan."[68] Yet all would agree that during Showa the involvement became closer than ever before.

The era began as it would end, with Japan simultaneously attracted to and repelled by the culture and the power of the United States. Yamazaki reminds us that in the 1920s America stood for the modern, and Japan, like Europe, was swept by a wave of social fashion that the Japanese called *Amerikanizumu* (Americanism). For high culture, Rimer reminds us, the Japanese, much like the Americans, had always turned toward Europe, but America was the mecca of the *modan* (modern) in popular culture.[69] Seidensticker and Kosaka give a glimpse of the other side in the resentment aroused in Japan by the immigration exclusion act of 1924, which barred Japanese immigrants from the United States. Few Japanese accounts of the period fail to mention the shock Japanese felt at this action and the racism that lay behind it. Seidensticker also gives us Hector Bywater's popular novel of 1925 about a coming Pacific war, which the Japanese would start by sabotaging the Panama Canal.[70] And while war-scare literature flourished in Japan as well, it was customary for diplomats of both countries to declare permanent amity, as they called it, between Japan and the United States.

Amity did not bring the two together, but war did. In the style of an operatic plot summary, the story would read like this: During the overture, the United States and Japan fought a brutal war in the Pacific, with great mutual racism and destruction. America then occupied Japan, and the hostility seemed to have vanished overnight. The vanquished welcomed the victor, the victor sought to remake the vanquished, and together they built "the new Japan." The United States, which, as Seidensticker says, could manage either China or Japan in its affections at any one time, but never both, had fought to save China from Japan but, having "lost" China to Communism in 1949, promised undying protection of Japan, provided Japan promised to reconstruct itself economically and become "a bulwark against Communism in East Asia." Act I ends in 1952 with Japan's independence and the security alliance with the United States.

In Act II America carried on its cold war, while Japan rebuilt itself, made things, and sold them to the United States. In 1960 Japanese demonstrators protested the renewal of the Security Treaty and Japan's role as cold war ally, but the treaty was renewed. At first Japan made cheap things, but after a decade of high growth, the things became quite sophisticated, until by the seventies the famous Frictions entered the scene. Soon, as Plath recounts, the direction of automotive invasion was reversed. American plans for invading Japan in 1945 had coded Japanese beaches with the names of American cars, but now Japanese cars were advancing on American roads.[71] In 1971 the Shocks occurred, and the Frictions continued. By 1985, forty years after the end of the war, it was back to the spirit of Hector Bywater, only this time the Americans were writing rhetorically of transpacific warfare that was economic.

The Japanese and Americans now remembered their common history differently. In a 1985 poll on the benefits America had brought to Japan during the occupation, the largest number of Japanese, 25 percent, attributed their "democracy, freedom, and liberty" to the American occupiers. Only 3 percent of the Americans thought that, but nearly half, 46 percent, said the United States had "rebuilt Japan's country and economy," while a mere 7 percent of the Japanese agreed.[72] Japanese memory was more accurate, but Americans were more angry. Japan, they now said, had won the war. As Japan's economic power waxed and America's waned, it seemed to some that the two were changing places. Bashing began, first by America of Japan, then, eye for an eye, by Japan of America. Each called the other names, while the two economies grew more intertwined than ever before. Japan's long obsession with America was now repaid with an American obsession with Japan. Seidensticker says "the Japanese image of America continues to be clearer than the American image of Japan," but what there is of the latter is clearly souring.[73] At a standoff in 1990, the curtain falls.

And this book opens. The postwar history of the Japanese-American relationship is of course far more complicated than a parade of pasteboard images suggests. But images underlie much of the contemporary comment in the two countries and explain some of the positions taken in the essays here. The authors tend to agree on the facts of Japanese-American relations but disagree about when and which country to credit or to blame for them.

Few doubt the importance of America in postwar Japan, which was affected not only by American foreign policy but also by domestic developments in the United States. One cannot explain the early occupation reforms without the New Deal or the American belief in town-meeting democracy, or the later change in occupation policy without American mistrust of political unions or fear of communist infiltrators. Passin writes of the American models for the occupation reforms and of the results that came from seeing "everything through American eyes." The mission sent to "defeudalize the bureaucracy," for example, carefully laid plans to eliminate a spoils system, which the Americans suffered from but the Japanese had never had. One member of the occupation later wrote, "I sometimes thought that if the Mission had been sent to the Arctic Circle instead, it would have come up with the same prescription for the Eskimos, seals, and seagulls." And in its American single-mindedness, the mission entirely overlooked the "old school tie" elitism, which created the tightly knit bureaucratic cliques that the mission was trying to break up.[74]

In fact, one of the oddities of an occupation determined to leave scarcely a stone unturned in the demilitarization and democratization of Japan was that it did very little to the structure and personnel of the bureaucracy.[75] Some praise the occupation for working through the bureaucracy instead of establishing a direct occupation regime as in Germany or Okinawa. Others, like Dower and Johnson, blame the occupation for modernizing and rationalizing—in a word, strengthening—the centralized bureaucracy of prewar times. Iokibe judges the abolition of the prewar Home Ministry, the seat of the secret police and domestic social control, an example of the "unfortunate use" of MacArthur's broad authority. It is not, one presumes, because of any nostalgia for the Home Ministry but to emphasize how free the occupation was to interpret the terse text of the Potsdam Declaration, which was the legal international basis of the occupation.

There are many such examples of Japanese and Americans' judging specific occupation reforms in terms of larger national issues: the Americans as well-intentioned or self-interested, the Japanese as protagonists of reform or the coerced objects of American plans, the occupation as a successful international collaboration or an imposed intervention by one country in the intimate national affairs of another. That it was both collaboration and intervention resulted in what I have called "entangling illusions" on the part of both parties.[76]

Most here judge the reforms a task that Japanese and Americans performed in common, even if sometimes at cross purposes. The land reform receives nearly universal kudos, and for good reason. In a sense it was the perfect reform, in that it had been initially conceived by the Japanese bureaucracy before the war, but as Iokibe points out, the authority of the occupation made it possible to implement it over any objections the landlords might offer. Yet the Japanese government executed the reform, and best of all, the reform worked, ridding the country of tenancy and establishing a basis in landownership for the rice farmer whose postwar political importance has already been mentioned.

Interestingly, the constitution also rates high on the authors' list of occupation successes. For years the constitution was the focus of political debates between those who wanted to jettison the foreign-made law and those who defended it, as I discuss in my essay.[77] It is something of an anomaly that a constitution initially drafted in a week by a group of Americans who were, not surprisingly, amateurs at the task should have become the stable basis of the political system of postwar Japan. It did so because the Japanese implemented it through decades of constitutional practice and in the process made it real and made it their own. Conservative voices still call for revision, especially in relation to Article 9, the famous no-war clause that was responsible for the name of the peace constitution. This issue may gain saliency in a post-cold war world, but it will be no easier to resolve now than it has been in the past, perhaps even harder in the changed international milieu. And according to Iokibe, "If reforms were welcomed by the people, especially if they created a new class of beneficiaries, it was impossible for anyone to undo them even after the occupying powers had returned home."[78] Popular support for the constitution suggests that the decades of postwar experience have created constitutional beneficiaries out of the majority of the population, who clearly do not want the system to be undone.

On the contribution of the occupation to Japan's subsequent economic growth, however, there is dispute. Kitaoka chastizes prewar America for its unwillingness to take responsibility in the world and, while recognizing that postwar America was indeed willing to bear the cost of the world it created, he adds that for Japan it was "not pleasant, however, to be continually on one's knees before the overwhelmingly dominant power of other countries."[79] This suggests that he is not soft on America. Yet he states that "the American Occupation of Japan was probably the most magnanimous occupation in human history from the economic and humanitarian point of view." And Iokibe writes that "the American Occupation of Japan as well as the Marshall Plan will always be regarded as America's highest achievements."[80] For a long time this was a fairly standard view in Japan, except on the extremes of the Right and Left. Here it seems like something of a thank-you note, which has an unstated P. S. to the effect that America in recent decades has been less worthy an international partner.

Other Japanese scholars have begun to downplay the overall contribution of the occupation to Japanese economic development. They do this partly to recognize the legacies of the prewar and wartime economy and partly, as Lincoln says, out of national pride, to give Japan, not America, credit for the postwar miracle.[81] Dower does the same thing here (as do I in this introduction), but for opposite reasons. In a sense he is returning Japan's postwar history to the Japanese, stressing continuities and diminishing America's role, which at times has seemed to usurp the entire stage.

Even Passin, who was part of the heroic phase when it seemed that America was indeed remaking Japan, is measured in his assessment of the occupation's impact on the economy. Perhaps, he says, the miracle was in fact a case of "deferred growth" after the cataclysm of war. His concluding metaphor sees "the social history of any great people . . . as a majestic flowing stream," into which outside influences enter and merge with the currents, some left behind "in the gravelly riverbed."[82] This is a far cry from MacArthur's view, which would have been more comfortable thinking that he had completely changed the course of the river. The present American public might agree with the General, resenting the economic power that is overflowing Japan's banks in its direction. But most of the Americans here are both more respectful of Japan's prowess and less beguiled by America's. Almost a half century has passed, and Japan-American times have changed.

The discussions of the emperor present a different case. At the end of the war Americans decided to retain both the imperial institution and the Showa emperor. Against vociferous opposition from the allies and negative public opinion in the United States, the occupation struck Hirohito's name from the list of suspected war criminals. Instead of trying the emperor at the war crimes tribunal, the Americans, and MacArthur in particular, chose instead to democratize him and transform his role from sovereign to symbol. This suited Japan's conservative leadership and outraged its leftist opposition. Years passed, and as I say in my essay, the Showa emperor was again controversial at the end of the era that bore his name.[83] The reader will see that I think there was good reason for the controversy, considering the relation of the "two Hirohitos" to the war and of the imperial institution to Japanese nationalism.

The Japanese authors who mention the emperor here take a different view. They link the success of the postwar reforms to the retention of the emperor system. Kosaka writes, "For those for whom the identity of the nation is important—this author included—the success of the postwar reforms stems from the historical continuity maintained."[84] Iokibe argues for its influence on the entire course of postwar Japanese-American relations: "Had the Japanese monarchy been abolished by the Occupation authority, postwar history would have witnessed traditional nationalists joining the ranks of America's enemies and both extremes of the political spectrum forming anti-American movements." Instead only the Left turned against America in the cold war years, while the conservatives and the majority of the Japanese "regarded the U.S. as a friend." Yamazaki writes of prewar nationalism that "the ideal system of imperial rule it envisioned had nothing to do with the traditional institution of emperorship in Japan."[85] Once the postwar reforms returned the emperor to reigning rather than ruling, the imperial institution once again performed its traditional function of providing cultural continuity and identity.

These views represent what I describe as the cultural interpretation of the imperial institution. Muramatsu presents a rather categorical form of what I call the constitutional view, when he states that "the emperor's ideological importance had been destroyed" by the postwar reforms and leaves the subject at that. Most of the Americans do not mention the emperor at all in their accounts of postwar politics, economics, society, and international relations. The contrast is instructive.

In most of these essays there is an undertone of ambivalence about the present relationship between Japan and the United States. Seidensticker recounts his childhood memory of indignation at learning that Tokyo was about to expand and become the second largest city in the world, perhaps soon the largest, overtaking New York. "We were particularly indignant at the way this was happening, a characteristically Japanese way, underhanded and deceitful. A good honest city grew gradually as it accumulated people. A dishonest city expanded its city limits and announced that its population had doubled overnight. . . . there were a few calls that day that we go to war immediately, and show them." He worries that once again indignant Americans might now be "returning to something we had hoped would be forever in the past."[86]

Royama follows his depiction of Japan as a nation of stock market speculators and coupon clippers with the warning that such a scenario "is certain to change the Japanese will to work and the egalitarian nature of Japanese society." Then he asks, "Why does Japan feel secure in exchanging the sweat of its citizens' brows for U.S. Treasury bonds? Who can say that such bonds will not one day tumble in value and turn into worthless pieces of paper?"[87] Who indeed. The irony of Japan-America is not how the weight of the relationship has shifted over the past sixty years, but how closely the two are bound that they insist on defining, or blaming, each in terms of the other. Perhaps Eisenstadt has a point here when he describes the two countries "in many paradoxical ways" as the "mirror image" of one another.[88] At least it seems that each sees itself reflected in the mirror of the other, when it might be better to hold the mirror together to the world.

Fifth, it follows, is the paradox of Japan and the world. The mesmerism of the Japan-America looking glass is partly responsible for postwar Japan's having defined the world so much in terms of the United States. Now that both Japan and the world have changed, the definition must expand. Japan has the globe to deal with, and herein lies the greatest problem for Japan after Showa. Every essay in this book makes the point in one way or another.

Where is Asia in Japan's world? The legacy of the war is doubly negative. Not only does Japan have a dark prewar past of actions in Korea, China, and elsewhere, but it has a postwar history of preoccupation with the West and inattention, both moral and political, to Asia. The expansion of economic relations in the absence of the other dimensions only makes matters worse. I write about Asian criticism of Japan's public failure to confront its past, and Rimer comments that the same "vacuum of sympathy" for Asia exists among Japanese writers and artists. He adds, "The proponents of high culture in Japan may well have stressed the possibility of a Japanese culture able to function in a larger contemporary world, but not perhaps in the *whole* world."[89] Now the whole world is at issue, and Asia, for Japan, is an increasingly important part of it.

Tu admonishes Japan here, from an Asian point of view, "to reflect critically upon her more than a century-long Faustian drive to outsmart the West at its own game. The cost is high: the sensuality of her body, the sensitivity of her heart-and-mind, the purity of her soul, and the brilliance of her spirit are all at stake." He then asks whether the vision of Heisei, which is the name of the era that succeeded Showa, implies "a return to Asia, to home? One wonders."[90] Yes, one does. But if a cultural return to Asia seems unlikely, a responsive and responsible political relationship with the other countries in the region is essential. It will not be easy, either for Japan or for those countries, many of which do not wish to be dominated again by Japanese power, however peaceable.

Instead of emphasizing Japan's role in Asia, most writers here focus on the West and the global order, concentrating on the two subjects in the center of debate today. The first is the task of bringing Japanese practices in trade and domestic markets into line with international expectations—yet another "opening" of Japan. The bywords of the current phase are liberalization and deregulation, which the Japanese here claim are soon to come. The American essays suggest that what comes will again appear to be too little, too late to alleviate the growing pressure from Europe and North America. This, too, is a dilemma not readily solved, since it involves changes in domestic practices that cannot be achieved by fiat. "Internationalization" is easier to say than to do.

The second task concerns Japan's acceptance of its responsibilities as an economic superpower, another widely agreed upon goal. The means to achieve this end, however, are less clear. What kind of contribution should Japan make to the world? As the writers here suggest, and as the Japanese response to the Gulf War in 1991 attested, Japan does not see itself as a military power. Kitaoka gives the preservation of world peace as one of Japan's international tasks, but his example of Japan's contribution to this goal is the two civilian officials Japan dispatched to the United Nations in 1988. Something more will be needed, and it is likely to take the form of yen.

Kitaoka suggests ODA (Official Development Assistance), which would spread some of Japan's wealth to the Third World. Japan now proudly tallies itself as the world's largest aid donor, having recently passed the United States. But there is foreign criticism of the strings that attach the aid too tightly to Japanese interests. Some recommend that Japan discharge its international responsibilities by assuming large shares of the multilateral financial burdens of the UN, the IMF, the World Bank and the like. The established powers, and the United States in particular, have sometimes shown themselves more willing to accept increased yen donations than to surrender voting rights or decision-making authority to the Japanese, who in turn have not gained a reputation for burnished diplomatic finesse in multilateral contexts. Others propose the environment as a place for a meaningful international contribution by Japan, and at times it appears that the ozone layer, being more or less inert, might be easier for Japan to manage than the volatile arena of multilateral negotiations. But this initiative, too, remains largely for the future. The list of possible Japanese contributions continues, but it tends to be formulated in reaction to international pressure, which keeps shifting, and therefore so does the list.

There is no answer offered here to the dilemma posed by the world to Japan and Japan to the world. The paradox remains that modern Japan has proved itself more successful at domestic transformation than in international relations. Now that relative internal success has thrust the nation into the external world again, Japan seems at a loss, not for words, but for actions. Most of these essays end not with ringing declarations, but with daunting challenges and hovering uncertainties.

Much has changed in Japan, in America, and in the world. Nearly a half century has passed since the war that set Japan and America on their separate and intersecting postwar paths. Japanese and Americans both feel the extent of the difference between the present and the past. But old habits of interaction die hard, and it is easier to react reflexively than to adjust constructively to the new situation within and between the two countries. This is especially true now that the post-postwar age is upon us and the invoked new world order is as yet nowhere in sight. It may well be a world without superpowers, at least in the familiar sense of the preponderance of military, economic, political, and ideological might all concentrated within a single country. If so, then not only Japan and America but every one of the nearly two hundred nations in the world today faces adjustments of power, alignment, and responsibility.

The current Japanese-American experience demonstrates two common pitfalls that lie in the way of these adjustments. The first is the tendency to defend oneself by blaming others, as the transpacific bashers in both countries do so loudly and so well. This "advanced-country nationalism," as I think of it, is one of the most dangerous forms of national defensiveness, if only because the countries that exhibit it wield so much power. The second is the proclivity to assume that the past provides all the analogies, patterns, and precedents necessary to guide plans and actions in the future. The United States and Japan, like many other countries, are suffering from a retrogressive syndrome that impairs their ability to adapt to a world that has changed profoundly over the last several decades.

Perhaps the most important conclusion we may draw from Japan-American Showa is the need to accept the magnitude of that change and move forward from here. The twentieth century lies behind us, its particular configurations not to be repeated. Though there are lessons enough in history, the past is no guide to the future. It is a heartening thought.

NOTE: In the essays Japanese names are generally given in Japanese order, surname first, except in the chapters by Johnson, Royama, and Yamazaki. The authors' names at the top of the pages are in Western order, surname last. For the sake of simplicity, the introduction uses surnames only. Macrons in Japanese transliteration are omitted throughout.

ENDNOTES

[1] *Nichibei no Showa,* ed. Asuteion (Tokyo: TBS Buritanika, 1990).

[2] Kitaoka, p. 168.

[3] Dower, pp. 53–54.

[4] Nakamura Masanori, *Showa no kyoko, Shōwa no rekishi,* Vol. 2 (Tokyo: Shogakkan, 1988), p. 384.

[5] Barnhart, Michael. *Japan Prepares for Total War: The Search for Economic Security, 1919–1941* (Ithaca: Cornell University Press, 1986).

[6] Lincoln, p. 193.

[7] Kosaka, p. 32.

[8] Gluck, pp. 18–19.

[9] Maruyama Masao, "The Ideology and Dynamics of Japanese Fascism," in Ivan Morris, ed., *Thought and Behavior in Modern Japanese Politics* (New York: Oxford University Press, 1963), pp. 25–83; Yoshimi Yoshiaki, *Kusa no ne no fashizumu: Nihon minshu no senso taiken* (Tokyo: Tokyo daigaku shuppankai, 1987).

[10] Yamazaki, p. 258.

[11] Kosaka, p. 37.

[12] Maruyama Masao, "Thought and Behavior Patterns of Japan's Wartime Leaders," in Ivan Morris, ed., *Thought and Behavior in Modern Japanese Politics* (New York: Oxford University Press, 1969), p. 128, quoted below by Johnson.

[13] Johnson, p. 86.

[14] Kosaka, p. 28.

[15] Hans-Ulrich Wehler, *The German Empire, 1871–1918* (Leamington Spa: Berg Publishers, 1985), p. 62.

[16] See for example, Ienaga Saburo, *The Pacific War, 1931–1945: A Critical Perspective on Japan's Role in War II* (New York: Pantheon, 1968); Maruyama Masao, *Thought and Behavior in Modern Japanese Politics* (New York: Oxford University Press, 1969).

[17] Gluck, p. 16.

[18] Iokibe, p. 98.

[19] Kosaka, p. 37.

[20] Lincoln, p. 206, 193.

[21] Johnson, p. 74, 88.

[22] The Japanese book (in a pirated translation made in Washington and read into the Congressional Record) figured in the escalation of mutual Japan and America

bashing during 1989. For Ishihara's version, revised for an American audience and without Morita's contribution, see *The Japan that Can Say No* (New York: Simon and Schuster, 1991).

[23]Royama, p. 183.

[24]Lincoln, pp. 202–203.

[25]Dower, p. 59.

[26]Kelly, p. 222.

[27]Yamazaki, p. 261.

[28]Tessa Morris-Suzuki, *A History of Japanese Economic Thought* (New York: Routledge, 1989), pp. 103–196.

[29]Hidaka Rokuro, *The Price of Affluence: Dilemmas of Contemporary Japan* (Tokyo: Kodansha International, 1984), pp. 63–78.

[30]Iokibe, pp. 104–5.

[31]Kosaka, p. 44.

[32]Amaya Naohiro, cited in Kosaka, pp. 43–44.

[33]Iokibe, p. 105.

[34]Iokibe, p. 106.

[35]Seidensticker, pp. 294–95.

[36]Kitaoka, pp. 172–74.

[37]See Peter N. Dale, *The Myth of Japanese Uniqueness* (London: Croon Helm, 1986); Hiroshi Mannari and Harumi Befu, eds., *The Challenge of Japan's Internationalization* (Tokyo: Kodansha, 1984).

[38]Dower, pp. 61–65; Johnson, p. 74; Lincoln, p. 200; Kelly, p. 216.

[39]Johnson, p. 79, 81.

[40]"Conservative establishment line" in Muramatsu's "Bringing Politics Back into Japan," p. 146, the *hoshu honryū* appears elsewhere in English as the "conservative policy line," sometimes CPL. See Yamamura Kozo and Yasukichi Yakuba, eds., *The Political Economy of Japan,* Vol. 1, *The Domestic Transformation* (Stanford: Stanford University Press, 1987), pp. 25–27, 516–554.

[41]Ezra Vogel, *Japan as Number One* (Cambridge, Ma.: Harvard University Press, 1979).

[42]James Fallows, "Containing Japan," *Atlantic Monthly* (May 1989), pp. 40–54.

[43]Gerald L. Curtis, *The Japanese Way of Politics* (New York: Columbia University Press, 1988), p. 249.

[44]Richard J. Samuels, *The Business of the Japanese State: Energy Markets in Comparative and Historical Perspective* (Ithaca: Cornell University Press, 1987), p. 260, 289.

[45] Daniel I. Okimoto, "Japan, the Societal State," in Daniel I. Okimoto and Thomas P. Rohlen, eds. *Inside the Japanese System* (Stanford: Stanford University Press, 1988), p. 214.

[46] Kelly, p. 217.

[47] Dower, p. 65.

[48] For his definitions, see Royama, pp. 189–90.

[49] Royama, p. 183, 185.

[50] Royama, p. 188.

[51] Lincoln, p. 197. The remarks about the beckoning stock market in this book were written before the fall of the Tokyo markets in 1990, which, some say, may prompt Japanese households to save as much or more than ever.

[52] Sato Kazuo, "Savings and Investment," in Yamamura and Yasuba, eds., *The Political Economy of Japan,* Vol. 1, *The Domestic Transformation,* pp. 137–185.

[53] Ishinomori Shotaro, *Japan, Inc.: An Introduction to Japanese Economics (The Comic Book),* trans. Betsey Scheiner (Berkeley: University of California Press, 1988). *Japan, Inc.* was added as the English title, which speaks to its American readers, but the text is a translation of the Japanese.

[54] Kelly, p. 219.

[55] Plath, p. 236.

[56] Johnson, pp. 78–79, 84, 88.

[57] Dower, p. 67.

[58] Passin, pp. 124–25.

[59] Muramatsu, p. 142.

[60] Murakami Yasusuke, "The Age of New Middle Mass Politics: The Case of Japan," *Journal of Japanese Studies* 8, 1 (Winter 1982), pp. 29–72. In Japanese, *shinchūkan taishū.*

[61] T. J. Pempel, ed., *Uncommon Democracies: The One-Party Dominant Regimes* (Ithaca: Cornell University Press, 1990).

[62] Margaret A. McKean, "Equality," in Takeshi Ishida and Ellis S. Krauss, eds., *Democracy in Japan* (Pittsburgh: University of Pittsburgh Press, 1989), p. 202; Ikuo Kabashima quoted, p. 218.

[63] Yamazaki, p. 263. *Yawarakai kojinshugi no jidai* (Tokyo: Chuo koronsha, 1985); *Yawarakai kojinshugi no tanjo* (Tokyo: Chuo koronsha, 1984).

[64] Plath, p. 241.

[65] Dore, p. 48.

[66] Kitaoka, p. 173; Muramatsu, p. 150.

[67] Johnson, p. 80, 82; Dower, p. 66. Johnson cites the "headless chicken" of the prewar period and "the System" of the postwar from Karel van Wolferen,

The Enigma of Japanese Power (New York: Knopf, 1989), pp. 39–41. For the "truncated pyramid," see Hosoya Chihiro, one of Japan's leading scholars of international relations, in Hosoya and Watanabe Joji, eds., *Taigai seisaku kettei katei no Nichi-Bei hikaku* [A comparison of the foreign policy decision-making process in Japan and the United States], (Tokyo: Tokyo daigaku shuppankai, 1977), pp. 1–20.

[68] Iokibe, p. 92.

[69] Rimer, p. 276.

[70] Seidensticker, pp. 280–82.

[71] Plath, p. 229.

[72] *New York Times* (August 6, 1985), p. A8.

[73] Seidensticker, p. 294.

[74] Passin, pp. 118–19, quoting Theodore Cohen's account of the occupation as a participant saw it in *Remaking Japan: The American Occupation as New Deal* (New York: The Free Press, 1987), pp. 381–82.

[75] Passin, p. 114, 118–19.

[76] Carol Gluck, "Entangling Illusions: Japanese and American Views of the Occupation," in Warren Cohen, ed., *New Frontiers in American-East Asian Relations* (New York: Columbia University Press, 1983), pp. 169–236.

[77] Gluck, p. 9.

[78] Iokibe, p. 104.

[79] Kitaoka, pp. 168–69.

[80] Iokibe, p. 106.

[81] Lincoln, p. 198. See Nakamura Takafusa, *The Postwar Japanese Economy: Its Development and Structure* (Tokyo: University of Tokyo Press, 1981).

[82] Passin, p. 125.

[83] Gluck, pp. 15–18.

[84] Kosaka, p. 43.

[85] Iokibe, p. 106; Yamazaki, p. 255.

[86] Seidensticker, p. 283, 296.

[87] Royama, p. 189.

[88] Eisenstadt, p. 228.

[89] Rimer, p. 275.

[90] Tu, p. 130.

FURTHER READINGS

On the war, Iriye Akira, *The Origins of the Second World War in Asia and the Pacific* (New York: Longman, 1987); John W. Dower, *War Without Mercy: Race and Power in the Pacific War* (New York: Pantheon, 1986); Ienaga Saburo, *The Pacific War: World War II and the Japanese, 1931–1945* (New York: Pantheon, 1978).

On postwar Japan, Kosaka Masataka, *A History of Postwar Japan* (originally *100 Million Japanese*) (Tokyo: Kodansha International, 1972); Hidaka Rokuro, *The Price of Affluence: Dilemmas of Contemporary Japan* (Tokyo: Kodansha International, 1984); Andrew Gordon, ed., *Postwar Japan as History* (Berkeley: University of California Press, 1992).

On the occupation, Takemae Eiji, *GHQ Tokyo: The Occupation Headquarters and Its Influence on Postwar Japan* (London: Athlone Press, 1992).

On the political system, Ishida Takeshi and Ellis S. Krauss, eds., *Democracy in Japan* (Pittsburgh: University of Pittsburgh, 1989); Gerald L. Curtis, *The Japanese Way of Politics* (New York: Columbia University Press, 1988); Chalmers Johnson, *MITI and the Japanese Miracle: The Growth of Industrial Policy, 1925–1975* (Stanford: Stanford University Press, 1982).

On the economy, Daniel I. Okimoto and Thomas P. Rohlen, eds., *Inside the Japanese System: Readings on Contemporary Society and Political Economy* (Stanford: Stanford University Press, 1988); Yamamura Kozo and Yasuba Yasukichi, eds., *The Political Economy of Japan,* Vol. 1; *The Domestic Transformation* (Stanford: Stanford University Press, 1987); Inoguchi Takashi and Daniel I. Okimoto, eds., *The Political Economy of Japan,* Vol. 2; *The Changing International Context* (Stanford: Stanford University Press, 1988).

On society, Robert J. Smith, *Japanese Society: Tradition, Self and the Social Order* (New York: Cambridge University Press, 1983); Gail Lee Bernstein, *Haruko's World: A Japanese Farm Woman and Her Community* (Stanford: Stanford University Press, 1983).

Showa

The Japan of Hirohito

The Idea of Showa

Carol Gluck

The death of Emperor Hirohito was an occasion for remembrance, not of a day or a decade, but of more than half a century of unprecedented turbulence and change. It provided an occasion for review—of the unsettled prewar years, followed by the catastrophe of war and the years of foreign occupation, leading to a political and economic revival that many abroad saw as a Japanese miracle. For the Japanese, it created a moment that linked the past with the future.

With the death of Emperor Hirohito in January 1989, the Showa era came to an end. The two events were connected by national artifice, the modern reign-name system which officially carves Japanese history since 1868 into emperor-centered blocks of time. To the naked historical eye, "nothing happened" at that moment to suggest either the portentous end of an era or the advent of a new age. But artifice soon became real in the outpouring of retrospectives of Showa that followed the emperor's demise. As a result of a highly public exercise in the construction of national history and collective memory, the six decades of Showa, from 1926 to 1989, were recounted in their first complete redaction as a single historical "era."

These accounts of Showa are not the stuff of academic history. More potent, they are the stories that nations tell themselves and teach their children in the name less of the past than the present. Each country weaves of them a national "mythistory," in which the myths are as important as the history and both are continually reworked.[1] That these tales are now largely told by the mass media, the village

Carol Gluck is George Sansom Professor of History at Columbia University.

elders of the late twentieth century, only increases the effect. In this case the media bore electronic and printed witness to the artificial moment in national memory during which Japan paused to think out loud to itself about itself, arraying and arranging the past to explain the present in a way it could live with in the future.

It was not an easy past to arrange. The Showa period encompassed not only much of Japan's twentieth century and fully half its modern history, but also aggressive and catastrophic war, defeat and foreign occupation, domestic transformation and spectacular economic growth. Relating these events first one to another and then to today's Japan was difficult in personal, national—and international—remembrance. Imagine rendering Italian history from Mussolini to the present, German history from Hindenburg to Kohl, or Soviet history from Stalin to Gorbachev—with all that went between—as a national story suitable for prime-time television and worldwide exposure. No wonder that "turbulent Showa," the epithet immediately established as if in long Homeric usage, posed questions and aroused contention about the nature of contemporary Japan.

In the open debate over national history occasioned by the end of Showa, the past was itself a medium, in which fundamental political, social, and cultural issues were being expressed or contested on the terrain of public memory. It is a debate worth overhearing, not only for what it says about Japan but for its resonances with the stories those of us in other countries are weaving, more gradually perhaps but just as busily, about our own national selves.

IN THE HALF-LIGHT OF EARLY SHOWA

The idea of Showa, now so vivid, was actually quite late in developing. Much like the current reign name *Heisei* at its inception in 1989, *Showa* in 1926 amounted to a formulaic citation from the Chinese classics. Indeed, both names were chosen (without hint of irony) to invoke the same innocuous meaning of good government and peace. Looking to the past, Showa's first contemporaries spoke vaguely of continuing the "progress" achieved during Meiji, the imperial era from 1868 to 1912 which had "made our country modern." In the present they heralded the passage of universal manhood suffrage in 1925 as well as the need to reform the "hopelessly corrupt money politics" of the day. This coincidence of imperial ceremony with political scandal was to become practically perennial throughout the era, which ended as it had begun, with the by then "big money politics" of the Recruit scandal bringing down the government during the mourning rites for Hirohito in early 1989. Laments about the state of political affairs and imperial pomp were, however, generally regarded as separate, as if politics and the emperor had nothing to do with one another, when in fact one might argue that their connection was central to the story of Showa.

In world affairs early Showa commentators boasted of Japan's new role in the 1920s as "one of the Five Great Powers or even one of the Three, our status since the World War now advanced to being entirely par with the European powers." Some demurred, suggesting that if the West "needs a third-rate country, they already have Italy and Spain" and urged Japan to remain instead "forever Oriental." But few saw any "clear purpose or national policy" to guide the Showa future through the international and domestic uncertainties that threatened.[2] In the economically hard times of early Showa, *reform, reconstruction,* and *renovation* were already watchwords hailed by left, right, and center, sometimes with more conviction than precision of content. The "Showa Restoration" invoked in the 1930s had less to do with Showa than with what was seen as the unfulfilled promise of the original Meiji reforms some sixty years before. Linked to the terrorism of the radical right, the slogan eventually disappeared into the political miasma of the prewar years. And by 1940 when the wartime calendar celebrated the twenty-six-hundredth anniversary of the "beginning of Japan's world history," which dated Japan's imperial line back to the Sun Goddess, Showa time had been submerged, like so much local business, in the grandiose delusions of empire.

SEVERED HISTORY AND "THE LONG POSTWAR"

With the defeat in World War II, a different chronology immediately established itself. At noon, August 15, 1945, the emperor broadcast the announcement of surrender, seeming to end the war and the past in a single calendrical stroke. At that moment, recalled one writer, the year "Showa 20" suddenly turned into "1945."[3] And "the postwar" began. It was as if history itself had been severed and could start again from scratch, the Japanese equivalent of the German sense of

1945 as "the hour zero." The two prewar-war decades of Showa were considered a dark and damnable legacy which had fully to be eradicated so that postwar Japan could begin anew. Rarely in history has the scrutiny of a blighted past so systematically been made the basis for fundamental societal change. This, it is important to note, happened concurrently with, but did not depend upon, the potent presence of the Allied Occupation. The passion for "democracy," however differently the resurgent left, the recumbent conservatives, and General MacArthur chose to define it, was well and widely shared in the years following 1945.

So strong was the willed separation of past and present that it dominated subsequent historical ordering for over thirty years, displacing the idea of Showa with the founding myth of "the new Japan." The decades after 1945 were marked, as self-consciously as Meiji decades had once been commemorated, as "postwar 10" (1955), "postwar 20" (1965), and so on. Long after Germany and nearly every place else had closed out their domestic *après-guerre,* in the enduring as well as the immediate sense, the postwar retained its prominence in Japan's contemporary consciousness. Despite frequent pronouncements, the earliest in 1956, that the postwar period was over, the Japanese postwar went on and on and on—at least rhetorically. People spoke, and still speak, of the country at present as "postwar Japan," a mythistorical coupling of remarkable tenacity. This "long postwar" owed much of its durability to the premise of a clear break with the past which had underlain the immediate postwar commitment to peace and democracy. It was almost as if the insistence on a seemingly perpetual postwar served to reaffirm that Japan had indeed been born again. However imperfect the transformation, the origins of the present lay in the myth of a new beginning, and the severed prewar-postwar past remained, in the most visceral sense, contemporary history.

THE REEMERGENCE OF SHOWA

Then, in the midseventies, after long eclipse by the chronology of the postwar, the idea of Showa as a whole seemed suddenly to spring to life full-blown. Of course the coincidence of "postwar 30" and "Showa 50" in 1975 provided a commemorative opportunity that the media could not miss and did not shirk. Official ceremony contributed in the form of the emperor's trip to the United States in 1975 and the celebration of the fiftieth year of his reign in 1976, both with fanfare that would have been inconceivable in, say, the thirtieth year in 1955, which had been still too authentically "postwar" to permit Showa to reemerge as a historical whole. But now an "emperor boom" ensued in the middle of a larger "Showa history boom," which laid out "fifty years of light and dark" in every possible popular format.

People expressed surprise at such an idea of Showa. "They are using 'the fifty years of Showa' as one term, but the first twenty years and the last thirty years are utterly different in nature," wrote a person old enough to have experienced the difference.[4] Younger Japanese "did not talk in terms of 'Showa,' " wrote a singer born in 1943. "It was the sixties, the seventies. I graduated in '68 and got married in '72. We thought of such things in Western dates," the calendrical vernacular of postwar cosmopolitanism.[5] The reappearance of the idea of Showa in the mid-1970s, while it exploited the rich vein of personal memory in endless media reminiscences, did not seem to have originated because of it.

It had rather to do with a sense of change in the historical air. The new idea of Showa emerged during the years widely identified as a break with the earlier postwar decades. It became customary to identify at least three phases since the war: the first decade of occupation, democratic reform, and economic reconstruction; the period from the mid-1950s to the early 1970s, which saw political stability under conservative dominance, rapid economic expansion (identified by the standard phrase "high growth" *[kodo seicho]*), and international status within the American imperium; then, from the seventies, something called the "post-high-growth period," defined largely in terms of uncertainty, whether domestic or international. Although the nature of the third period remained in debate, it seemed to many that something important had ended. The common suggestion was the perennial one: with post-high-growth Japan, the postwar period was finally over.

Although reports of its rhetorical demise proved premature, it is true that by the mid-1970s the postwar period had itself become history. And it became history at a time during which Japan, like Britain, Germany, the United States, and elsewhere, was experiencing the phenomenon known as "conservatization." The earlier postwar ideas of change, reform, and growth seemed less important to many Japanese than the need to preserve what had been gained. Private livelihood took full precedence over social concerns; domestic achievements and international abrasions combined to raise the banner of national pride. It began to seem a different world.

The dominant "postwar consciousness" had emphasized the break at 1945 for the sake of creating an utterly different Japan. Progressive critics—including many who in Europe would be called left liberals—had long judged the postwar present in terms of its failing to be different enough from the prewar past. Their period of greatest ascendancy had been in the first decade after the war, when it seemed in Japan as elsewhere that the left might finally win the political day. But they had kept the faith, if not the optimism, through to the seventies, when "high growth" prevailed and in combination with the new conservative trends led to a waning of the progressive hegemony. At just this point, the outbreak of "reconsiderations of Showa" appeared in popular conservative journals.[6] The writers countered both the separateness and the sanctity of the idea of the postwar by examining the prewar parts of Showa and relating them to postwar developments in a direct and positive sense. They were more favorably disposed than their opponents both to the way things had turned out in post-high-growth Japan and to the parts of the past that they thought had contributed to it. Their assertion of Showa entire was part historical revisionism and part political attack on the progressives who had held the public floor for so long.

Thus the idea of Showa emerged as a conservative one in intellectual and political contention with the idea of the "postwar." The importance of this historical context is unmistakable. Had Showa ended in 1955 before the postwar had turned out the way it did, how very different the story of Showa would have been.

STORIES OF SHOWA

Showa did not end until 1989, by which time contemporary Japan looked different again than it had in the 1970s. The death of the emperor and the end of the era, however unbearably protracted, were not of course unexpected. As part of the vast media preparations for "X-day"—as the event was unceremoniously called before it occurred and became, with sudden reverence, the "imperial demise"—

the initial post-Showa stories of Showa, which presented the era for the first time from beginning to end, had in fact been written or produced over several years and reflected Japan of the mid- to late 1980s. This was accumulated rather than instant history, and like most such moments in public memory, was constructed so that all lines of the past were drawn—inevitably—toward the vanishing point of the present. How, then, did the story turn out?

First, the narrative remained a tale of two Showas. In its most public and visible form, the television documentaries shown (without commercial interruption) on every channel, the break in 1945 generally ended a segment, as if to say, the dark old Japan is behind us—tune in tomorrow for the bright new one.[7]

The prewar segment included some social history of early Showa, notably the popular mass culture of Tokyo with its dance halls, jazz, and sailor pants, and sometimes the Depression and the harsh suppression of the left. But overwhelmingly the period was recounted in terms of the war, the state, and the national events that marked the course of militarism abroad and terrorism at home. This meant the march of time through images from the Manchurian Incident of 1931, the assassination of the prime minister and other leaders in 1932, Japan's withdrawal from the League of Nations in 1933, the visit of Pu Yi (China's "Last Emperor" and Japan's puppet ruler of Manchuria), the attempted coup d'état of the army revolt of February 26, 1936, the beginning of the so-called China Incident (sometimes even called by its proper name, the China War) in 1937, the twenty-six-hundredth anniversary celebration of 1940, Pearl Harbor, Singapore, the Doolittle raids, Saipan, *kamikaze,* the fire bombings of Tokyo, the mushroom cloud over Hiroshima, the surrender broadcast. The half century of imperialist rule in Korea, the Rape of Nanking, the defeat at Midway, the brutality on Okinawa, and the like were visually missing, though occasionally mentioned; this was national television after all. But despite the pomp of imperial iconography—the enthronement, the troop reviews, the victory *banzais*—there was no mistaking the image of prewar Showa as a period of war and darkness, however incomplete the historical picture.

Then the postwar segment—told as a tale of occupation and recovery, democracy and prosperity, peace and world economic power. The state all but disappeared in the chronicle of social and economic betterment; ever-improving livelihood, not the march of national politics, provided the story line. With the exception of the graphic images of immediate postwar privation, postwar Japan appeared as a different world, unconnected to the horrors that preceded it. The War Crimes Trial completed the "unconnection" as the leaders responsible for those horrors were neatly indicted and sentenced. The main narrative ran rather from MacArthur's arrival, the emperor's "declaration of humanity" in 1946, the first postwar election, the 1947 constitution, the San Francisco Peace Treaty of 1951, the crown prince's marriage to a commoner in 1959, the anti–Security Treaty riots of 1960, the Olympics and the bullet train of 1964, the Osaka Expo of 1970, diplomatic rapprochements in Asia, Hirohito and Mickey Mouse photographed in tandem at Disneyland in 1975, a succession of visiting American presidents, and the oldest (and only) emperor anywhere feebly greeting the people of the second (and rising) most powerful economy in the world. There was no mistaking the lineaments of postwar Showa either, illuminated as they were in the bright light of economic well-being and national pride.

In a sense, one might argue that nothing had changed in contemporary historical consciousness at all, because dark and light had been there since 1945, with the difference that the light appeared brighter in the late 1980s than anyone could have imagined it would be four decades before. But there is more to this moment of national memory than immediately meets the eye, just as there is more wide-ranging and contentious debate about the past in Japan today than was broadcast on national television. And the issues contested, six of which I will mention here, arise very much from the present toward which all the lines of the past were drawn so neatly to converge.

SHOWA AND THE POSTWAR

The first is the still vexing relationship between Showa and the postwar, but with a twist that focused less on the origins of the postwar than on its outcome. The tale of two Showas continued to assert a radical discontinuity at 1945 and an unusually, even anachronistically, long postwar. But common sense attested to the contrary, since personally, socially, or nationally history does not begin again. Also, Japan's domestic postwar was surely comparable to that of other countries, and like theirs, long since over. The issue is rather the validation and authenticity of the present political system, which had its origin in the crucible of the postwar "new beginning." The postwar riddle ran: If the democratic system was directly continuous with its prewar antecedents, in what way was it new? And if it was new, but established under foreign occupation, in what way was it Japanese? These questions have long appeared as the leitmotif of constitutional debate.

The left, which once criticized the constitution as imposed by MacArthur and hence undemocratic in relation to the people whose sovereignty it declared, now defends it against the right, which would revise it and end the postwar once and for all. Ishihara Shintaro, a politician lately famous for urging Japan to say no, spoke of the constitution as "a diaper put on by the Occupation" which Japan would have to remove in order to get beyond the "democracy games" imposed by the Americans.[8] In the face of such strident conservative rhetoric, which also aimed at revising Article 9 and permitting rearmament, the customary anti-American tone of the progressives paled before the need to protect the institutional anchor of "postwar democracy." More than four decades of debate over "revision" versus "defense" of the constitution is further evidence of the long postwar. As one German scholar commented in surprise, Germany operated for forty years under a constitution established under similar conditions without this sort of debate over origins and outcomes.[9]

Meanwhile the polls in Japan showed ever-rising popular favor for the "peace constitution." On the occasion of its fortieth anniversary in 1987, 62 percent thought it a "good constitution," for reasons of its democracy, renunciation of war, and respect for individual rights and freedom. These were cardinal elements of the postwar system, given point by the anecdote that the character *ken,* which in prewar years was explained as the first part of the word for the secret police *(kenpei),* is now habitually defined as the first part of the word for the constitution *(kenpo).* And polls also showed that people thought the constitution "had an important relationship" to the improved standard of living, which they identified as the main characteristic of the postwar and with which they were "content." Things were better than in prewar days, said the older generations; things had always been good and could be better, said the younger.[10] The postwar constitutional system was thought to operate, in the English words of the Japanese television commercial, "for beautiful human life," which was defined in terms of peace, democracy, livelihood, and the social myth of 95 percent of the people identifying themselves as middle class.

Clinging to the "postwar" thus seems to be an overt expression of support for the status quo, as if to discard the name would throw the present system open to change or question. Since democracy is socially and economically (rather than politically) defined, politics as practiced by the government appears peripheral to the colloquial definition of this system. Indeed, criticism of the venality of politicians is standard, a part, it almost seems, of the support for the status quo. But politics is by no means irrelevant. The insistence on the postwar also reflects the deeper issue of the nature of the state. What is the character—to use the cool language of social science—of a "bureaucratic state" in a "one-party-dominant democracy," and what is the relation of this state to the prewar imperial state and to the postwar political reforms? Such questions surely lie at the heart of Showa history. But they remain polemical because they breach the postwar principle of discontinuity. While scholars of twentieth-century Europe have established the longer view of the development of the contemporary political economy across the gulf of politics and war, in Japan such a suggestion contravenes the rule of diametric difference between prewar and postwar politics.

Among the available perspectives on the conundrum of continuity are those which looked back beyond Showa to find democratic roots in the era of Taisho democracy in the 1920s and before that in the Popular Rights Movement of the 1870s and 1880s. The Americans during the Occupation, most official Japanese commentators since then, and progressives who are more populist than Marxist have often argued in this fashion. According to one eccentric interpretation, Japan was occupied twice—first by its own military after 1931 and then by America until 1952—both occupying powers having suppressed the democracy that existed in Taisho in the 1920s.[11] In contrast to these views, in which prewar Showa remains discontinuous, others have recently asserted a direct link between the prewar and wartime state and the postwar political system.[12] Although such assertions are common elsewhere, an argument like John Dower's here on the legacy of the war is innovative in the Japanese context. In

Japan it was primarily the conservative intellectuals who argued for continuity and phrased it in positive terms, for which they were labeled "reactionary" by the progressives and accused of "the affirmation of the prewar structures of authority" and "the denial of postwar democracy."[13] Again the issue is the old hope for a new postwar politics, which was not to be related, except by negative contrast, to its immediate prewar antecedents. In ideological contention as in public memory, the rupture of Showa runs deep.

SHOWA AND THE WAR

But what ruptured it, of course, was the war. And the war usurped the central place in the immediate post-Showa accounts of the era. While this centrality seemed perfectly natural to older Japanese and to foreigners around the world, it came as something of a surprise to younger people in Japan, the generations born since the war who now comprise some two-thirds of the population. Many of them saw the footage of the China War for the first time in television documentaries, their school textbooks having been visually as well as narratively "reticent" on the subject. So *this* was Showa:

> What shocked me the most in all the recent coverage and debate was that Showa was recounted above all as an era of war. And this includes all the people who argued over the war responsibility of the emperor. The discussion focused almost entirely on the relation of the Showa emperor to the beginning of the war and to August 15th; or people saying that "during the war I did such a thing"; or, "on August 15th my whole sense of values collapsed"; or "at that point there was nothing for it, so the emperor . . . ."
>
> I tried to think of what I could say about the emperor or Showa. . . . But there is no physiological connection between me and these things. I just felt overwhelmed by how terrible it all was. Remember that song, "The Children Who Don't Know the War"—that's it exactly.[14]

The writer, born in 1956, was a child of "high growth." The voices of media history, however, belonged overwhelmingly to the generation who not only knew the war but remembered Showa in terms of it. And because they dominated the discourse of public memory for over forty years, their views on the war have had effect beyond their time.

The issue, then, is not whether the Japanese remember the war, but how they do so, and to what contemporary effect. The received myth here, like that of the postwar new beginning, was established almost immediately upon the end of the war. And again, though for independent reasons, the Japanese and their American occupiers together produced the account of the war that became and remained authoritative.

Culpability was accepted from the first, in that "the reckless war" was confronted as unjust and catastrophic. Responsibility was sought and found in the military, who with the collusion of the bureaucracy, big business, and the landlords, laid a grid of domestic oppression and military aggression across Japan and much of Asia. In 1946 the first postwar history textbook stated that "the Japanese people suffered terribly from the long war. Military leaders suppressed the people, launched a stupid war, and caused this disaster." In 1975 a popular version read: "the Pacific War—a war of peculiar savagery which Japan could have avoided if only its armed forces had kept away from politics."[15] Had things truly been that simple, and inevitable, the burdens of Showa history would be light indeed.

Two points may be made about the view that has endured. First, it is history in the passive voice, or "victims' history," as the Japanese would call it. In textbooks, the copula abounds: the China Incident was caused, Pearl Harbor was bombed, the atomic bomb was dropped. The war appears as a natural catastrophe which "happened" to Japan, as if without the intervention of human agency. The people "were embroiled" in the war by their reckless leaders, twenty-eight of whom were tried and convicted by the Tokyo War Crimes Tribunal for conspiracy to wage aggressive war. Seven of the war criminals were hanged, in itself a persuasive demonstration of culpability. Without doubt, the trial was "victors' justice," as critics have often charged in regard to the Allies, but in a different sense it was also "victims' justice," in that it contributed to the emphasis on what the Japanese people suffered at the hands of the villains in the docket.

The American contribution to the so-called War Crimes Tribunal view of history was considerable. Not only did the Americans share the general Western notion that they could identify wartime leadership in Japan analogous to the more familiar European perpetrators, but then they proceeded to remove the leading Japanese candidate, Hirohito, from the lineup. The American decision not to try the emperor as a war criminal, which was made in the service of running a successful occupation—in a separate compartment, as it were, from the one in which war was being waged—set the official question of war responsibility further from the mark. So it turned out that in the court of national history neither the emperor nor the people were arraigned.

The contemporary issue here has to do with mastering the past. The victims' history repeated in the post-Showa retrospectives omitted a painful lesson of World War II since learned around the world: that it is not possible to wage a total war with 28, 280, or even 28,000 people and that the responsibility for war lies far more broadly in society than was earlier believed, or hoped. Just as in Europe, where it is no longer possible to explain such things solely in terms of Hitler, Mussolini, or Pétain, the ways in which vast numbers of ordinary people were entwined in the complex mesh of war must be counted. Even those who did not actively march or collaborate are now judged as participants. It takes both states and societies—which is to say the individuals who comprise them—to make a total war.

By their own critics and those abroad, the Japanese are chastised for their amnesiac history. Comparisons with Germany suggest that whereas the Germans remember Nazism, the Japanese remember the war, not the system that engendered it. The chronology of remembrance is also different. For years a quiet generation of Germans remained silent until a younger generation challenged public memory to confront the Nazi past in the 1960s. In Japan the confrontation was immediate in 1945, and the postwar reforms were deliberately constructed in the negative image of the prewar system. While this early mastery of the past had genuine institutional consequences, it also had disadvantages since it froze the condemnation of the war into orthodoxy at a stage when the division of villains and victims seemed starkly clear. Mastery remains an issue in both countries, as in others, and passivity and indifference erode the impulse to assume responsibility for history. Yet not to feel responsible for the past is not to feel responsible for the present, a pattern itself crucial to the story of Showa and the war.

The second point about the old, and still the main, view of the war is its concern with the Pacific War coupled with an avoidance of the war in China. This does not mean, as the Showa retrospectives showed, that there was no mention of Manchuria, Shanghai, or even Nanking (though there was virtually none of Korea). It means rather that the focus of historical explanation and moral attention did not lie on the continent, where Japan began its Showa aggression in Manchuria in 1931 and was engaged in total war against China from 1937 to 1945. Japanese historians who write insistently of "the Fifteen-Year War" do so to make precisely this point: that for Japan, World War II did not begin at Pearl Harbor. But the weight of national memory still falls heavily on the Pacific War.

Here again the Japanese had initial help from the Occupation, which in 1945 decreed a change in name from the imperialistic *Greater East Asian War* to the *Pacific War,* the war the Americans had experienced. This abbreviation of conflict has remained congenial for many reasons. The tidy moral equation of Pearl Harbor to Hiroshima acknowledged the attack at the same time that it gave Japan its *bona fides* as victim of nuclear war in a new postwar mission of preserving peace. There was no comfort, even as cold as a nuclear one, for the Rape of Nanking. The Japanese-American relationship was also the most important one in postwar Japanese foreign affairs, and the persistence of the emphasis on the Pacific War only replicated in national memory the focus of its international geopolitics. Asia, with which modern Japan had had a history of hostile, imperialist, paternalistic, and generally uncomfortable relations, was until the 1960s less a factor than a cipher in Japan's postwar foreign relations.

It is significant that in the 1980s, when Japanese officials began publicly to revise the standard view of the war, they chose the China War, not the Pacific War. In 1982 the Ministry of Education sought to substitute the benign term *advance* for the more accurate *invasion* of China in history textbooks. It is hard to imagine a similar suggestion to the effect that the Japanese navy did not *attack* but *engaged* the enemy at Pearl Harbor. In 1986 the education minister remarked that the Rape of Nanking was no worse than the atrocities committed by other nations. In 1988 another Cabinet official pronounced the Marco Polo Bridge Incident of 1937 (which started the China War and was deliberately provoked by the Japanese army) "an accident" and argued that Japan, far from being an aggressor nation, had waged war only to defend itself against the colonizing white races. Both these officials lost their jobs, and the revised textbooks were not accepted either.

The main cause of these failures of official revisionism was the outcry in Asia. Whether Japanese progressives could have managed it on their own, as they continued their decades-old battle against textbook revision, is not clear. That they did not have to was a sign of the change in international times. The signs continued in early post-Showa in the full glare of the global media gathered for the funeral of the former wartime emperor, when the prime minister mincingly deferred the question of whether Japan's had been "an aggressive war" to "later generations of historians." Asian officials again reacted with public outrage to his "distortions of history." Perhaps they thought that after fifty years, "later" could be said to have arrived.[16]

When it comes to the war, national history is clearly an international affair. Revising one's own history is one thing; revising another country's history is something else altogether. The Rape of Nanking, after all, belongs at least as much to China as to Japan. As Asia and Japan increase in mutual importance to one another, the demand for something more than routine diplomatic apology—for those rhetorical rituals do not suffice—will continue to prod the Japanese to confront the Asian parts of the war. The contemporary issue is whether Japan will meet the challenge with sober remembrance or resist with a forgetting born of arrogance and power.

SHOWA AND THE EMPEROR

Closely linked to the representations of the war is the relation between the emperor and the era, both of which bear the same name, *Showa*. Just as there were two Showas in mythistory, so there were two Hirohitos. In imperial iconography the first sat astride a white horse in uniform, the wartime commander-in-chief; the second (after a brief interlude in tails with a new commander, the shirt-sleeved MacArthur) walked among the people or along the seashore in a suit and hat, peaceable Mr. Hirohito. In the Showa retrospectives, the first had been borne helplessly toward the war: the second made a decision to end it. His was a transformation worthy of "the new Japan" that it so closely mirrored.

The cognitive dissonance that arises from contemplating the same imperial figure in such visible new clothes is considerable. How much easier it would have been for public memory, and for him, had the era name changed with the defeat, as it did in premodern times on the occasion of calamities far smaller than this one. It is appropriate, on the other hand, that contemporary remembrance be saddled with the problem of two Hirohitos in one. The reign name did not change precisely because, following the modern system instituted just two reigns earlier, the same emperor who reigned in dark prewar times continued to reign in bright postwar times, a continuity of no small institutional importance. Many older Japanese, having themselves experienced the alchemical change from empire to democracy, were able to credit both imperial roles. To foreigners—with the single exception of the Americans who alone gave credence to the postwar figure they had had a hand in creating—Hirohito remained to the end "the last of the wartime leaders," part of the Axis trinity of evil. The expressions of international hostility at the time of the funeral surprised many Japanese, who assumed perhaps that the world had accepted the imperial quick change in the same way they had.

Placing the Showa emperor in national history means dealing with the war. The post-Showa debates over the emperor's war responsibility were only the most recent in a long series of controversies over the question. Arguing in the press about moral versus legal responsibility, scholars addressed the claim that while Hirohito may indeed have fulfilled his role as constitutional monarch by approving the war making of his ministers, he nonetheless occupied a position of such supreme moral power that he need not have waited until the surrender deadlock to use that position in the name of peace.[17] Few Japanese could follow the string-him-up arguments in the West, which presented Hirohito in the unlikely role as mastermind in an institutional context known for its diffuseness. Yet 25 percent of the Japanese polled after his death said bluntly that they thought the emperor bore responsibility for the war.[18] At that point people said the "taboo" against mentioning such a thing had finally been broken in popular utterance. Mayor Hitoshi Motoshima of Nagasaki, whose open statements had done much to break it by the public support they engendered, was first threatened and, over a year later in 1990, shot by an emperorist of the small but fanatic right. The taboo perhaps was back in business, threatening to crowd out the issue of the Showa emperor as a historical figure in the war with the invocation of the imperial institution in its old, overblown, and reportedly long discarded, prewar incarnation.

Herein lies the larger issue of the nature of the imperial institution in the present. At the end of Showa a full 83 percent of the population declared themselves content with the so-called symbolic emperor system, by which the emperor is constitutionally defined as "the symbol of the state and of the unity of the people."[19] Young Japanese cared little for imperial doings, except to be "a part of history" and sign the mourning books for Hirohito or to wish for more crown princely pizazz of the British sort. One chronicler of the nonresponse among youth to the emperor's death called it a "voiding of the emperor and the postwar," and indeed the event did not evoke anything like the general expression of emotion that the earlier orgy of "self-restraint" at the time of his illness had suggested that it might.[20] Japan's emperor is the only one in the world today. What, then, is an imperial institution, especially one associated with the excesses of the recent past as well as with a mythistorical "time immemorial," doing in a late-twentieth-century democracy?

Two answers appear in the post-Showa discourse of public memory. The first treats the emperor system in constitutional terms. In his inaugural rhetoric the new emperor promised to protect the constitution together with his people—a "constitutionalized" utterance without imperial precedent and one which could make it difficult for the extreme right to crank up its loudspeakers to call for constitutional revision in the emperor's name. The controversy over the constitutionality of the imperial funeral ritual in 1989 and the upcoming enthronement ceremonies in 1990 made the constitution a central device for defining the post-Showa imperial institution. The constitutionalists argued that conducting these Shinto rites as state ceremony violated the constitutional separation of religion and the state. In their view the constitution should contain the institution.

In the second view, the imperial house is considered a cultural institution, a symbol of national identity, not containable by, because not relevant to, law or politics. Here the emperor system, past and present, becomes a benign cultural artifact that has embodied the distinctiveness of the Japanese through the ages. The supporters of this notion stress the value of the cultural continuity of the imperial tradition. They skip lightly over Showa and argue that since the emperor is now once again removed from politics, as he was for much of Japan's earlier history, the institution can serve as the center of what they see as an acceptable cultural nationalism. To them the imperial rituals belong to the cultural, not the constitutional, realm.

Both are old and recognizable arguments reflecting different politics and different versions of national self-definition. They are not mutually exclusive, and many Japanese are both constitutionalist and cultural nationalist at once, not only about the imperial institution but about the nation as a whole. As before in Japanese history, fundamental national issues are being played out on the contested public terrain of the emperor system, which ground is no less slippery for its being now symbolic.

SHOWA AND THE MODERN

Another long-contested area, both real and symbolic, is the nature of Japan's modernity and where Showa fits or does not fit in it. Recent signs suggest that the durable prewar-postwar chronology is gradually coming to share historical time with a second chronology that takes a longer view and sees Meiji-Taisho-Showa, 1868 to 1989, in terms of the full span of modern Japan.

This is precisely the way Showa had defined its task at the start, to complete the "progress begun in Meiji," but the war destroyed early Showa's association with a fulfilled modernization, and postwar Japan consciously set out to "get modernity right." Now the long view links the modernization begun in Meiji with the modernization completed in late Showa, or more precisely, by the end of the high-growth era in the 1970s.

Two scenarios explain the place of prewar Showa in this grand teleological scheme. In the first, the "root theory," which dominated in the early postwar years, the modernity wrought by Meiji appears deeply flawed, unmodern at its very roots, so that postwar Japan had to start from the ground up. According to the second, the "stumble theory," present since the early postwar but gaining currency in recent years, Japan moved with dispatch along the track toward modern times only to be derailed in the 1930s, imperialistically tripping, as it were, over China, but was soon back on track in the postwar years.

The current long view of modernization is rather more stumble than root. The historians who speak of the contributions of the wartime state suggest that when Japan rose up again, it brought something useful from the humbling experience. Others elide the prewar period to pick up in the postwar where Meiji-Taisho left off. In general, the further the distance from the 1930s and the surer the pride in the ultimate success of modern Japan, the easier it has become to see the Meiji Restoration as stage one and the postwar reforms as stage two of a process of modernization during which Japan scaled—not necessarily on the first attempt but eventually—most of the peaks of modernity.

But the completion of the modern by the 1970s (one critic offered a precise date: 1964) removed the mountain.[21] And the issue here reflected in public memory is an uncertainty about where to go next. Indeed, much of the ubiquitous loose talk of the postmodern in Japan refers not to the cultural but to the historical condition of being after the modern without a direction marked beyond.

Rhetoric and vision, so highly focused for most of Japan's modern history, now seem afflicted by scatter. Meiji pursued progress, Taisho and prewar Showa called for reform or reconstruction, and postwar Japan flung itself headlong toward democracy—all in the name of the modern and all now allegedly achieved. There are new descriptions enough—"economic great power," "new middle mass society," "post-high-growth Japan"—but no comparable prescriptive center to the social imagination. Seeking such a center is what the discourse on constitutionalism and cultural nationalism is about. And being without a focus, for a country whose modernization was nothing if not "directed," is a new experience for Japan.

There is also the problem of provenance. From early Meiji times modernity was associated with the West. Showa itself began with the *modan*—flappers, movies, Marx, and all—and ended with the high international *posuto-modan,* both words revealing their external origins. During seizures of nationalism, the West and its modernity were rejected in favor of a superior Japanese form presented in the guise of modernity's opposite, tradition, which had continually to be reinvented. The models, however, were Western and the axis of definition and critique, East-West.

Japan has now caught up, as they say, with the West. For the first time in modern Japanese history—and perhaps in Japanese history as a whole, which had long looked to China as a cultural source—there is no external model to catch up with. Indeed, others are talking of catching up with the model of Japan. For the Japanese this is satisfying but unsettling. Also, after more than a century, it is no longer possible to separate Western from Japanese in social, political, and cultural practices. A Western breakfast is still coffee and toast; a Japanese breakfast, fish and rice; but when it comes to thought and institutions, the naturalization is too complete to permit such clear distinctions. This is not satisfying—and is also unsettling.

Post-Showa, post-postwar, and postmodern at once, the current swelling of national pride and evocations of cultural distinctiveness are the latest metaphorical constructions of native tradition, this time against the loss of clarity once provided by the modern along the axis of East and West.

SHOWA AND HISTORY

The idea of Showa moved mythistorically in two realms. In the realm of "big history" in the documentaries, the state or the nation appeared as the protagonist of History with a capital H. From the Manchurian Incident to "high growth," Showa was recounted in much the way that Americans do in their "presidentist" history. The pageant of national events is standard national history in most countries. At the same time, however, there appeared a flood tide of "little history," the endless personal reminiscences entitled "My Showa," the recollections of "war experiences," the vignettes of the countless "people of Showa" who knew the war was over, for example, when they had to file the chrysanthemum off their rifles or black out sections of their schoolbooks on MacArthur's orders.[22] They did not themselves bear history but were borne along by it. This is far less standard fare in the domain of public memory elsewhere.

The contemporary issue here lies in the fact that the two planes of history, both extraordinarily well populated and recorded, seem to have absolutely no connection with one another. People seem to feel unconnected to their destiny in a way that is unusual in societies as advanced as Japan's. Not that such a feeling is universal in other places or that the feeling is borne out by a potency in historical reality, but that modern-day "history" is more often portrayed as occurring in the interactions between the two realms.

The separate worlds of big and little history in Showa Japan are reflected in the victims' history of the war, questions of war responsibility, the relation between the people and politics, the separation of political scandal and imperial ceremony, and the like. Polls show that while the predictable national events (the defeat, the atomic bombings, the constitution) are always listed when events are asked for, Showa is more widely recalled in the terms of daily life, whether wartime privation, postwar prosperity, or the ebb and flow of popular culture.[23] "They" make history; "we" suffer it: this is the condition of most of mankind, but public memory often makes it seem as if it were not always necessarily so.

The emphasis on personal recollection also affects the way in which views of the past are transmitted to future generations. For decades the Japanese have emphasized personal experience of the war *(senso taiken)* as the common coin of memory and the best insurance against forgetting the lessons of the past. As effective as this currency was, it is by definition difficult to transmit to generations who lack such personal experience. The long custodianship of Showa history by those who grew up in the belly of the war was so dutifully discharged that it seemed to belong to them alone. One younger Japanese compared the recounting of war experience to a *fumi-e,* the holy images early Japanese Christians were forced to tread to prove they had renounced their faith.[24] Just as anyone who was not a believer would find it easier to tramp upon an image of the Virgin, so recollections of the war have little meaning for those who have no war experience themselves.

In Germany the generation of 1968, most of them postwar born, condemned their parents for the war they had made. In so doing, the younger generation created a further chapter in the public memory of the war, not on the basis of experience but on that of historical judgment. In Japan the war and the earlier parts of Showa history cling to the older generation, who experienced them, while the later Showa of the younger generations is not linked except by hearsay to the earlier one. During the television flood of documentaries, young people found it easy to turn off the set; it was a question of how much of someone else's history one could be expected to endure.

SHOWA AND THE WORLD

From first to last Showa measured itself against the world. Ever since Meiji, the measurement had been conducted both domestically in terms of achievement in modernization and internationally in terms of status among the powers. In the latter respect the Showa story told of rejection by and of the world in the prewar years, symbolized by Matsuoka walking out of the League of Nations in 1933; then catastrophic failure in the war and defeat; followed by accommodation anew in the postwar period and the resultant regaining of international stature, epitomized by the Olympics of 1964. The world's attendance at the emperor's funeral—163 nations, 17 international organizations, 55 heads of state, repeatedly and proudly tallied (without mention that many of them were there with their hands out)—represented the international accounting at Showa's end.

The contemporary problem is clear, the solution not. Where in the world is Japan's place, now that Japan and the world have both changed so much? Long accustomed to seeing themselves as accommodative or reactive to the demands of what used to be called the world order, the Japanese feel doubly uneasy. Rather than the agenda being set for them, their economic power has placed them in the position of having to set their own agenda and even that of others. Their edgy reluctance is palpable. So is their inexperience, and history offers little help. No matter how successful a domestic modernization public memory may claim, Japan's international dealings were riven with travail before 1945—no successful precedent there. And for several decades afterward, Japan's peaceable growth took place largely in shelter from the world, with cues from the United States. Japan's economic emergence from that shelter over the last two decades has aroused criticism, friction, and hostility—no great encouragement there either. The partly arrogant, partly gun-shy stance of the present reflects the difficulty of dealing with the dual legacy of Showa: Japan as an economic and nonmilitary big power, about which no history anywhere has very much to say.

The related unease has to do with the changes in the world stage on which Japan must play its new as yet unscripted role. Modern Japan used to think of itself in terms of East and West, of both, sometimes of neither, but always juxtaposed between Asia and the Euro-American powers. Showa Japan began in diplomatic league with the West, then turned away to single-handed imperialistic domination of Asia, then joined with America in the Cold War context and avoided direct relations with Asia when it could. Now no longer the West-dominated world of the prewar years nor the bipolar world of the postwar order, the globalization of international relations only compounds Japan's old dilemma of "proper place." Japan has little historical experience in large parts of the distant Third World, Eastern Europe, and elsewhere, and its relations with its closest Asian neighbors need work as well. The emotional pathology that currently characterizes both sides of the Japanese-American relationship derives from similarly difficult mutual adjustments of international place and power. The earlier rhetoric of postwar Japanese foreign policy—low profile, equidistance, omnidirectionality—revealed a singular hesitation of geopolitical vision. And that was *before* the postwar order came unglued. Now it is all that much more complicated, and the uses of the oversimplified Showa past unfortunately lend themselves as easily to affront as to vision and conciliation.

BETWEEN THE PAST AND THE FUTURE

The idea of Showa as it first emerged complete did not render the national past with great amplitude, accuracy, or understanding. Public memory of this sort seldom does. But since people do not partake equally of the collective offering, there is no universal blanket of historical viewpoint either. More important perhaps is the tone of the exercise, which reveals an uncertainty about the future in the company of assertive national feeling.

The two go together in the rewriting of national history, which proceeds most energetically when national and international "verities" seem no longer to ring true. In this, Japan is not alone. Other advanced industrial countries are conservative, postmodern in the sense of lacking clear models or visions, vulnerable in their economies, unsettled by the globalizing world order, and apt to react to their situation with more nationalism than grace. They, too, revise their national histories without international sensitivity to the position of other countries or ethnic peoples. Third World nations, meanwhile, struggle to reclaim their past from a framework of domination and write their history on their own terms, sometimes for the first time, which can be a soul-wrenching task. Now other national histories, long frozen in a Cold War mold, are being kneaded and reshaped to serve promising but uncertain prospects. And in unsettled times, when the sense of security, stability, or certainty about the future is shakier than usual, nations tend to recast their history, not only in national but also in nationalistic terms.

This is fair neither to the past nor to the future. Imprisoning the story of Showa within national borders makes it seem as if the experiences from the 1920s through the 1980s were distinctive to Japan. In historical fact, the twentieth century produced a great deal of international history: world depression, world war, cold war, decolonization, oil crisis, and the like, which affected different countries in similar ways. The century also witnessed commonalities among national histories: patterns of political economy, ideology, technology, ecology, and social change, which are better understood when considered together than apart. There are elements of international remembrance, such as imperialism and the holocaust, which by now belong both within and across the narratives of a single country's past. Yet each nation is inclined to insist that its own circumstances are distinctive, if not unique. Japan habitually describes its culture in these terms; Germany argues over the incomparability of its recent history; and American exceptionalism places the United States in a historical class by itself.

National history, being by definition what it is, may remain everywhere inadequate to the task of presenting the international past. When it becomes nationalistic as well, it endangers the future. The world at the end of the century is too intertwined to allow much space for excesses of nationalism—grand or petty, state or ethnic—without consequences which the lessons of the past were supposed to teach us to avoid. That we are all in the same boat does not give any of us license to sink it. And the lessons drawn from watching Japan in a seizure of national history may also be a caution to ourselves.

ENDNOTES

[1]The term is William H. McNeill's, in *Mythistory and Other Essays* (Chicago: University of Chicago Press, 1986).

[2]"Shin gengo no shimesu Nihon no hofu," *Nihon oyobi Nihonjin* (27 January 1927): 11; "Taisho kara Showa e: Taisho kara Showa e utsuru ni atatte," *Kaizo* (February 1927): 30; "Showa Nihon no kokuze," *Nihon oyobi Nihonjin* (1 March 1927): 23.

[3]Ide Magoroku, "Showa hitoketa no ikon," *Sekai* (December 1975): 256.

[4]Sawachi Hisae, "Tabu no aru shakai ni ikiru fuko, *Asahi jaanaru* (5 November 1976): 88.

[5]Kato Tokiko, "Kikigaki: Watashi no Showa," *Asahi shinbun,* 21 January 1989.

[6]For example, "Showashi o minaosu," *Shokun!* (July 1976): 24–217.

[7] Visual sources here include "Gekido no Showa" (Turbulent Showa, produced by NHK), "Gekido 64nen" (Turbulent 64 years, produced by Fuji), and "Tenno Hirohito" (produced by TBS), and the like. All aired during the two days after the emperor's death, some have been rebroadcast since, and abbreviated forms are for sale in video. Countless magazine compilations showed most of the same photographs embedded in similar narrative. In the first days after the emperor's death, the viewer or the commuter had little choice of subject, since these retrospectives usurped the mass media entirely, causing vocal complaint and unprecedented business in video rentals.

[8]Ishihara Shintaro and Inoue Hisashi, "Nihonkoku kenpo o yomo," *Bungei shunju* (June 1982): 96–99.

[9]Wolfgang Mommsen in Hagihara Nobutoshi, Akira Iriye, Georges Nivat, and Philip Windsor, eds., *Experiencing the Twentieth Century* (Tokyo: University of Tokyo Press, 1985), 59.

[10]On the constitution, 20 percent "did not think so," and 18 percent had no response. Asahi shinbun yoron chosashitsu, ed., *Za Nipponjin: rittai chosa* (Tokyo: Asahi shinbunsha, 1988), 166–68. NHK hoso yoron chosajo, ed., *Zusetsu: sengo yoronshi* (Tokyo: NHK bukkusu, 1982), 122–24.

[11]Fujimura Michio, "Futatsu no senryo to Showashi: gunbu dokusai taisei to Amerika ni yoru senryo," *Sekai* (August 1981): 39–55.

[12]For example, Ito Takashi, "Showa seijishi kenkyu e no shikaku," *Shiso* (June 1976): 228; *Jugonen senso, Nihon no rekishi,* vol. 30 (Tokyo: Shogakkan, 1976), 16–21.

[13]Matsuo Shoichi, "Gendai handoteki rekishikan no ittenkei," *Rekishi hyoron* (August 1977): 2–25; Shibayama Toshio, "Hando ideorogu ni yoru rekishi no kakikae to sono hoho ni tsuite," *Rekishi hyoron* (September 1979): 25–34.

[14]Kisaragi Koharu, "Nippon cha! cha! cha!: kodo seicho to 'Showa' no owari," *Shiso no kagaku* (March 1989): 17.

[15]The text was the much disputed *Kuni no ayumi* (1946), in Ienaga Saburo, *The Pacific War, 1931–1945* (Tokyo: *Taiheiyo senso,* 1968), trans. Frank Baldwin (New York: Pantheon, 1978), 255; Mainichi Daily News, ed., *Fifty Years of Light and Dark: the Hirohito Era* (Tokyo: Mainichi Newspapers, 1975), 198.

[16]*Asahi shinbun,* 23 and 27 February 1989.

[17]"Tenno o meguru senso sekininron," *Asahi shinbun,* 9 January 1989.

[18]See *Asahi shinbun,* 8 February 1989: 31 percent said he was not responsible, and 38 percent said they did not know.

[19]*Asahi shinbun,* 8 February 1989.

[20]Nakamura Kenichi, "Shakai no kagami toshite no tenno," *Sekai* (March 1989): 49.

[21]Matsumoto Kenichi, "Fukei no henyo: 1964nen shakai tenkansetsu," *Shigo no tawamure* (Tokyo: Chikuma shobo, 1985), 4–54.

[22]Masuda Katsumi, "Tenno, soshite watashi," *Shiso no kagaku* (March 1989): 48; Ide Magoroku, "Showa hitoketa no ikon," *Sekai* (November 1975): 259; Yasuoka Shotaro, " 'Showa' wa itsumo atarashikatta," *Bungei shunju* (March 1989): 126.

[23]Harada Katsumasa, *Showa no seso, Showa no rekishi* (Tokyo: Shogakkan, 1983): 348–49.

[24]Kisaragi.

The Showa Era (1926–1989)

Masataka Kosaka

The prewar Japanese political structure, which plunged Japan into a disastrous war, was a relic of the Meiji period. The complex evolution of a peaceful people and a dedicated emperor into a militaristic juggernaut was partially the result of a flawed political order. The causes, both foreign and domestic, that led to Japanese imperialism and the reasons for Japan's success in the subsequent Pax Americana is the essential story of Showa.

The Showa era was comparable in duration to the Victorian age. Victoria ascended the throne at age eighteen in June 1837; her reign lasted sixty-three years and seven months until her death in January 1901. Emperor Hirohito, born about three months after Queen Victoria died, succeeded as emperor in December 1926, remaining Japan's monarch until his death in January 1989, slightly more than sixty-two years. Victoria's reign stands out in British history as a time of unparalleled change, but the Showa period was an even more turbulent time for Japan. Economic growth in both reigns exerted immense influence on the world economy; each witnessed fundamental changes in monarchy.

The Showa emperor was a constitutional monarch at his death, but the vicissitudes through which he passed were far greater than those of Victoria. When the Showa emperor died, the people grieved his loss, recalling the many trying experiences he had undergone. In many ways "trying" sums up Hirohito's life.

This essay will focus on the first twenty years of Showa, giving specific attention to the status of the emperor. I shall analyze the

Masataka Kosaka is Professor of International Politics in the Department of Law at Kyoto University.

challenges Japan faced during these years and how it came to be plunged into the tragedy of the Pacific War. Japan failed to modify and adapt a political order established during the Meiji period to hasten modernization. Since the emperor was at the center of that order, the key to the problems of the first two decades of Showa lies in the prewar emperor system. Though the emperor himself was not responsible for the failure to change the political order, it is undeniable that many of the acts that led to tragedy were carried out in his name, however painful they were to him. His anguish mirrored the distress of the whole country. If the second two-thirds of Showa was more successful, this must be attributed in great part to the postwar political-social order. It is important to look at how the status of the emperor and Japan's political system changed after 1945.

I

The early Showa period coincided with that most difficult and precarious phase in the course of a country's modernization, "take-off." Japan was shifting from agriculture and textile manufacture (chiefly of cotton and silk thread) to heavy and chemical industries. The numbers of white- and blue-collar workers were beginning to surpass those in agriculture.

This stage, which straddled the latter part of the Taisho period (1912–1926) and the early years of Showa—the 1920s and the early 1930s—is generally portrayed as gloomy, a sluggish phase of modern Japanese history, a time of economic stagnation brought on by rapid deceleration of business after the boom created by World War I came to an end. This stagnation did not end till the Great Depression.

During the five years beginning in 1914, industrial production grew five times; exports, more than three times. The deficit in international accounts, opened in the midnineteenth century, was replaced by a comfortable surplus. The industry that showed the most remarkable growth was shipbuilding; barely started in the latter part of the nineteenth century, in 1919 600,000 tons were built, putting Japan in third place after Great Britain and the United States.[1]

This sudden growth was not entirely natural; sustained by the exceptional situation created by the outbreak of World War I, the export and maritime capacities of the Western powers were greatly diminished. Into this vacuum, Japan quickly interposed itself. It was not a situation calculated to last. Shipbuilding fell from 600,000 to less than 50,000 tons when the war ended; in the following decade, it did not once exceed an annual output of 150,000 tons. As the European powers returned as serious rivals in the world economy, Japan found itself again struggling with current account deficits, a situation compounded by abnormally rapid growth which disproportionately bloated the economy. When that growth ran its course, remedial measures ought to have been taken.

Unfortunately, Japan's leaders failed to take resolute steps to put the economy back on a normal course; in the end, they chose the worst possible time—the end of 1929—to lift the gold embargo and return to the gold standard. As most scholars agree, the best time would have been immediately after World War I, but the government let the opportunity slip. The "return to normalcy," delayed in 1923 when the catastrophic Great Kanto Earthquake and Fire occurred, and again in 1927 in the financial crisis triggered by intraparty strife, left Japan as the only leading world power that had not returned to the gold standard after World War I.

Putting off the return to the gold standard until after the Wall Street crash brought the full force of the world economic crisis onto Japan in 1930. Plunged into severe depression, the reverberations were felt throughout society. Farming areas became impoverished, and some have argued that the military's adventures on the continent, beginning with the Manchurian Incident (1931), were prompted by rural dissatisfaction and social instability caused by the Depression. The government leadership failed to institute adequate measures to adjust the economy after World War I; disillusion with the liberal and democratic tendencies began to gain momentum during the Taisho period.

Recent studies by economic historians have demonstrated that the image of early Showa as an unexceptionally dark time characterized by stagnation and financial panic is not altogether accurate. In the economy, the growth of the heavy and chemical industries continued, though not at the same tempo as during the World War I period. The sluggishness of exports was serious, especially since Japan depended on exports as its engine for growth, but it was able to make use of the huge specie reserves it had accumulated during the war. Tuvia Blumenthal gives statistics showing that from 1920 to 1928 Japan's gross investment stood at 18.3 percent, more than twice that of

Britain (8.7 percent), topping not only that of Germany (13.8 percent), the fastest growing economy in Europe, but of the United States (17.3 percent). During the same period, per capita personal consumption rose 15 percent in terms of constant prices.[2]

It is possible to characterize early Showa as a time of consumerism, with the growth of large department stores in main cities.[3] Superficial as these phenomena may have been, being confined mostly to the Tokyo and Osaka areas, it is true that urban culture was both vigorous and lively. The period straddling the end of Taisho and the first decade of Showa (between the early 1920s and the mid-1930s) was one of slower growth; times were definitely hard, but that goes only part way in explaining Japan's submission to militarist rule. Because the economy grew in such a way as to fan popular dissatisfaction, partly because of extreme economic concentration, as economist Sato Kazuo has argued, the rate of profit of high capital-intensive enterprises was greater than that of low capital-intensive industries. Newer industries such as shipbuilding, silk spinning, gas, electricity, department stores, and finance enjoyed higher rates of profit than older industries, including merchant shipping, trade, cotton spinning, and coal mining. Industries at the forefront of modernization were growing, making the largest profits.[4] Dissatisfaction grew among those engaged in industries suffering from relative decline. Because the powerful industrial and financial combines (*zaibatsu*) dominated the high capital-intensive industries, the popular outcry tended to focus on the *zaibatsu*.

Perhaps even more important than the disparities in performance among different industries was the gap between farming and nonfarming, that is, between the rural and the urban areas. Japanese agriculture had developed steadily from the time of the Meiji Restoration (1868) to the Russo-Japanese war (1904–1905), providing the basic driving force behind economic development. From the beginning of the Taisho period (the early 1910s), however, arable land had been expanded to the limit and existing fields were subdivided into extremely small plots. The latter factor frustrated the development of technology to raise farm productivity further. Laws requiring land rents to be paid in cash rather than in kind caused absentee landlordism to spread; the leadership the landlord class had once provided in rural communities weakened. Statistics show clearly that during the 1920s, farmers became poorer in relative terms.

Between 1920 and 1929, while the proportion of the total work force in agriculture fell from 54.5 percent to 50.1 percent, the contribution of agriculture to the GDP dropped from 26.8 to 19.7 percent.[5]

It is easy to understand that this situation caused many to cry out against corruption. While it would be hard to demonstrate that corruption in Japan was worse during this period than before, the majority apparently thought it was. Political leaders were criticized for their foreign policy failures—their "weak-kneed diplomacy"—and polemics against government "corruption" became common. The mass-circulation newspapers persuaded their readers that political corruption was real; this helped ignite popular indignation.

As Samuel Huntington writes in his *Political Order in Changing Societies*,

> The initial exposure to modernism tends to give rise to unreasonable puritanical standards even as it did among the Puritans themselves. This escalation in values leads to a denial and rejection of the bargaining and compromise essential to politics and promotes the identification of politics with corruption. To the modernizing zealot a politician's promise to build irrigation ditches for farmers in a village if he is elected seems to be just as corrupt as an offer to pay each villager for his vote before the election. Modernizing elites are nationalistic and stress the overriding preeminence of the general welfare of society as a whole.[6]

In that sense Japanese party politics became blatantly "corrupt." Politicians promised to bring advantages to their constituencies, arranging for railway lines to be laid, high schools and colleges to be built locally. This, the key strategy adopted by parties to expand their influence, was joined to eager collection of political funds. Japanese had little confidence in parties known to be concerned with little other than partisan interests, with unabashed pork barreling.

The parties gave little attention to the welfare of society as a whole. Dealing with each issue as it came up, they formulated no long-term or even medium-term plans. Exploiting foreign affairs issues in their campaigns to topple the Cabinets of opposing parties, they were not above leaving false accusations, as, for example, at the time of the ratification of the Kellogg-Briand Pact (1930).

The armed forces, while undeniably engaged in their share of corruption and plotting, were disturbed by the gap between rural poverty and urban prosperity. The villages, the crucial source of men and supplies for the armed forces, desperately impoverished, filled military leaders with a sense of foreboding. As part of the modernizing elite, but at the same time basically agrarian, the military saw individualism fostered in the cities as a threat to nationalism. Their indignation grew even more vehement with the onset of the Great Depression.

Yet, to argue that the Depression created the conditions for the military's rise to power would be only partially correct. In 1931, thanks to the fiscal policies of Finance Minister Takahashi Korekiyo (1854–1936) and to Japanese adaptability in shifting to new export markets, Japan's economy recovered. By 1932, it had completely overcome the effects of the world depression. Japan had alternatives to military expansionism in the thirties. However, the scenario of militarism and military expansionism had been set long before the Manchurian Incident of 1931. In the spring of 1929, the expansionist elements were clearly dominant within the Imperial Army.[7] The rise of Japan's military during the 1920s was a social and political phenomenon that accompanied the modernization process.

II

The buildup of power that culminated in the military takeover of the government was the result of army and navy responses to changes in the international environment. International society in the early Showa period was at a difficult crossroad. The age of imperialism was coming to an end. While political forces opposing imperialism had been weak before World War I, after it was over, two great powers, the United States and the Soviet Union, took up the banner of anti-imperialism. Woodrow Wilson's Fourteen Points, calling for freedom of the seas, equal opportunity for trade, disarmament, self-determination of peoples, the establishment of a League of Nations, and an end to secret diplomacy, were qualitatively different from the purposes for which nations had waged wars until that time; the pronouncements of Lenin were even more revolutionary. While some were skeptical about the ideas of Wilson and Lenin, the death toll in World War I made it seem mandatory that disputes be settled by pacific means.

The impact of this new approach to international relations was greater in Asia than in Europe; the United States and the Soviet Union possessed greater influence there. Old-style power politics, still at work when the Versailles Peace Treaty was signed, seemed very remote from the Washington Conference that focused on disarmament and pledged the abolition of the unequal treaties between China and the imperialist powers. This was a decidedly new approach. The Soviet Union, meanwhile, declared its readiness to help China rise out of its semicolonial state.

These changes came quite suddenly; Japan found it difficult to cope with these new situations. Japan had entered international society when imperialism was at its zenith; it had proved that it could compete with the best of the imperial powers. The slogan of the nation since the Meiji Restoration (1868) was "Enrich the nation and strengthen its arms." Increasing the national wealth was in fact a means for building up military strength. Military expenditures, though smaller than those of the European powers until the time of the first Sino-Japanese war (1895), rose steadily thereafter. Japan was certainly militarized by the end of the Russo-Japanese War. Though inferior to others in per capita income, economic development, and amount of social overhead capital, it had become a first-class military power.

Another factor that made the new post–World War I international order difficult for Japan to accept was its tradition of pan-Asianism and its antipathy toward the white race. Konoe Fumimaro's denunciation of Anglo-American "pacifism" after World War I was the most open expression of those sentiments. He believed that the pacifism espoused by Great Britain and the United States was only a pretext for maintaining the global status quo. The two powers, with their control of capital and natural resources around the world, were able to dominate by "economic imperialism"; they did not require arms. Considering that imperialist expansion by the European powers dominated international politics in the nineteenth century, that Japan had sought to stave off the threat posed by that expansionist wave to the country's independence, it is not difficult to understand why Konoe's ideas had great appeal.

The Japanese quandary was compounded because imperialism had not come to an end; Britain and France continued their advances in the Middle East, creating mandated territories that were different from their colonies principally in name. In China, too, the age of imperialism was not over—the responsibility for which was partly Japan's—of course,[8] as indicated by the Western powers' unwillingness to give up their extraterritorial rights and return tariff autonomy to China. China was as much the arena of struggles among the world powers as it had been for almost a century.

It is not surprising that some Japanese were unwilling to go along with the new international order established at the Washington Conference, and the main target of their wrath was Shidehara's conciliatory diplomacy. Unfortunately, Shidehara lacked the toughness and realism of Hara Takashi and Kato Tomosaburo (1861–1923).[9] At the time of the second Fen-Zhi war (1924), which precipitated a crisis for Japanese protégé warlord Chang Tso-lin, Shidehara insisted on refraining from intervention. Shidehara was convinced that his nonintervention policy was correct; chroniclers like Ugaki Kazushige (1868–1956) dismissed him as "hopelessly naive."

Shidehara became foreign minister in June 1923, keying his foreign policy to four points: nonintervention in internal strife in China; coexistence and coprosperity with China through economic cooperation; tolerance and sympathy for China; reasonable defense of justifiable rights and interests. The contradiction between the first and fourth points is obvious. Fujimura Michio is correct when he says that the precondition for Shidehara's success was that the Chinese Nationalists' campaign to recover Chinese rights and interests not pose a threat to Japan's interests, as guaranteed by treaty.[10] But such a situation, even if it existed, could never last.

Shidehara's policy, vitiated by inconsistency, confronted Japan's imperialist elite in their all-too-consistent logic. Taking the lessons of World War I to heart, they were determined to be ready for the advent of an all-out war. Knowing that the struggle for hegemony was not over, they were persuaded that a war greater than any past war was bound to occur. Ishiwara Kanji (1896–1949) was the best known of their spokesmen. From their point of view, the resources and labor force of China would be indispensable in the final "war to end all wars," fought by Japan and Asia against the West. Simple and clear-cut, their arguments carried undeniable popular appeal.

From the standpoint of the military and their supporters, Shidehara's diplomacy denied Japan's true national interests and betrayed the nation. They set about building the political-economic system that would prepare the country for the war that was bound to come. The Manchurian Incident was not simply an external affair, as Harada Kumao (a baron, and secretary to elder statesman Saionji Kinmochi) notes, but the "prelude" to the army takeover of power.[11] That the army chose the Manchurian problem indicates their unusual tactical acumen.

Those who opposed the army's ideas were unable to offer a convincing and compelling alternative. While the Great Depression initially dealt a heavy blow to Japan, it worked to rally Japanese opinion behind the aggressive acts of the Kwantung army in Manchuria.[12] When the Great Depression came, as Charles Kindleberger states, the former world leader, Great Britain, had lost the strength to fulfill its global obligations; the United States, capable of taking world leadership, had no intention of doing so.[13]

The fact that the United States was unwilling to play the role of world leader is reflected also in the passage of the Immigration Law of 1924, which virtually excluded Japanese and had an immense impact on Japanese politics. The law outraged many Japanese; it became the spark that set into motion the movement opposing the world order set up under the Washington treaties. The shock this exclusionist, anti-Japanese law dealt to Japanese—and not just a few ultranationalists—can be measured by the decision of Nitobe Inazo (1862–1933), a man who had made bridging the gap between the two nations his mission in life, that he would never return to the United States until the law was repealed. Inasmuch as the Japanese were a proud people and not particularly well informed about conditions in other countries, the reaction was probably inevitable. The law greatly weakened the proponents of cooperation with the United States and Great Britain; the world depression and the movement toward bloc economies undermined the argument that economic interchange was the main pillar of world peace.

III

The Manchurian Incident of 1931, the first significant step toward the Pacific War, was not the sole determinant of the tragedy. The next ten years was a time of unsuccessful attempts to check a rising madness from leading the country headlong into a bloody clash in the

Pacific. Not long after the Manchurian Incident, a chain of assassinations began with the killing of former Finance Minister Inoue Junnosuke and of Dan Takuma, chairman of the board of the Mitsui Gomei Kaisha, and with the May Fifteenth Incident, in which Prime Minister Inukai Tsuyoshi was shot dead by military officers. These events thoroughly shook Japan's political world, encouraging further excesses. A vicious circle was created; adventures overseas isolated Japan, increased the sense of crisis among people, fanned the flames of extremism, encouraging further military expansion.

Resolute steps ought to have been taken to break this vicious circle. There was, I believe, some reasonableness in the argument that attributed the rise of extremism to rural hardships. The government tried to do something to remedy these conditions, but most of the action came only after the crisis had begun. The ¥830 million spent in the next three years for Takahashi's rural relief program was a major effort; compared with the military expenditure of ¥2.84 billion during the corresponding period, however, it seemed small. In fact, it was considerable; starting from almost nothing, it compared favorably with the new military expenditures, which increased by ¥1.16 billion from an already huge amount.[14]

As Maruyama Masao, citing a passage from the diary of Joseph Grew, U.S. ambassador at the time of the outbreak of the Pacific War, has pointed out, most Japanese did not think the aggression on the continent violated international law; those few who did deemed it necessary for Japan's survival.[15] They were mistaken. Tai Chi-t'ao, who served as interpreter to Sun Yat-sen and was a leading observer of Japan, wrote some years earlier: "Reading the many statements by them [the Japanese] that revere the West and insult China, I fundamentally doubt their sense of justice.[16]

To restrain the military by emphasizing the rule of law, citing the shortsightedness and recklessness of overseas activities, was what some attempted to do. Elder statesman Saionji Kinmochi (1849–1940), for example, after the May Fifteenth Incident, tried to steer the government back to constitutionalism. He compromised with the military by arranging for moderate navy admiral Saito Makoto (1858–1936) to succeed to a party-controlled Cabinet, and then for navy admiral Okada Keisuke (1868–1952) to follow Saito as prime minister. These efforts failed to achieve their intended objective.

The Machiavellian maneuvers common to the time, involving leading right-wing politicians like Hiranuma Kiichiro (1867–1952) and Navy General Staff Office member Admiral Suetsugu Nobumasa (1880–1944), were more successful. The selection of the basically irresponsible Konoe Fumimaro (1891–1945) to serve as prime minister, not once but twice, hastened the country toward self-destruction. These men were most to blame for what happened. Still, it is too simplistic to argue that a handful of men suppressed all opposition, dragging Japan to its tragedy. Many Japanese, including some who worried about the country's expansionist policy, cooperated with the government and the armed forces.[17]

When news of the outbreak of war with the United States came on December 8, 1941, many intellectuals felt that a weight had been lifted from their shoulders.[18] While most had been critical of the ongoing war against China, they welcomed—however brief was their elation—war with the United States and Great Britain. Lacking a grasp of world affairs, nursing grievances that made them wish for the United States and Great Britain to swallow the bitter medicine Asians had been compelled to endure, they felt something had to be done to destroy the status quo so disadvantageous to Asians. Japanese critics and opinion leaders engaged in an abstruse debate, redolent of the turgid and complex arguments used before the war. So preoccupied were they with abstractions that they rarely took time to consider simple facts.

Although there were Japanese leaders of ability and common sense, they failed to say no. Foreign Minister Hirota Koki (1878–1948), at the start of the Sino-Japanese war, and Navy Minister Oikawa Koshiro, just before the outbreak of the Pacific War, were conscientious men who failed to act responsibly.[19] The political system goes far to explain the failure.

Many of the leaders of the period were victims of characteristic Japanese illusions. Even conscientious and sensible leaders could not say no. The problem was not simply psychological. Latent in the whole political structure, it was epitomized in the person of the emperor. The emperor, consistently opposed to the dominance of the military and to policies of foreign aggression, was by custom prevented from expressing his personal opinion. Still he made his views known in his questioning of the leaders. He argued the cause of peace in a poem read at an imperial conference. All the same, his name was used to justify actions that went against his wishes; the war in the Pacific was started in his name.

How is all this to be explained? The prewar political system needs to be understood. The emperor was a constitutional monarch. Article 55 of the Meiji constitution stated that "the respective Ministers of State shall give their advice to the Emperor and be responsible for it," and that "all Laws, Imperial Ordinances, and Imperial Rescripts of whatever kind, that relate to the affairs of the State, require the countersignature of a Minister of State." The Cabinet was clearly in charge of state affairs. Ito Hirobumi (1841–1909), chief architect of the constitution, stressed the importance of rational administration, writing that "all the affairs of state should be administered according to organization and regulation."[20]

Though not explicitly stipulated in the Meiji constitution, a responsible Cabinet system based on the support of the Diet became a customary practice around the middle of the Taisho period (1912–1926). The dominant *genro* Saionji Kinmochi and others close to the emperor tried to implant this system, introducing a British type of constitutional monarchy to Japan. Approval from the emperor came when a unanimous decision was made by the Cabinet.

Not all Japanese, however, interpreted the emperor system in this way. The Meiji constitution stipulated in Article 1 that the empire of Japan would be reigned over and governed by a line of emperors "unbroken for ages eternal." From this point of view, the political system from the early Meiji through the end of the Pacific War acknowledged direct imperial rule. Before the Meiji Restoration of 1868, Japan was governed by two rulers—the emperor, essentially a spiritual authority, and the shogun, holding political power. In the Meiji period, power was concentrated in the emperor; a sovereign state was created. This was a necessity when nation building had to be achieved rapidly.

Yanagita Kunio's observation that it was "surprisingly recent that Japanese began to think of their nation as a single entity,"[21] is borne out by historical records. When Japan opened its doors and established relations with other countries, it had to be a unified nation. To solidify the nation, the new government probably had no alternative but to rely on traditional imperial authority, organizing institutions around the emperor.

The architects of the Meiji constitution must have been aware of the inherent contradictions in the emperor system they had created. They wanted a strong monarch unifying and leading the nation; they knew that the emperor's sovereign power had to be exercised constitutionally. Studies of the drafting process reveal the contradictions.[22] Great pains were taken to cover up the contradictions, as reflected in such subtly worded expressions as "The Emperor . . . combining in Himself the rights of sovereignity . . . . " (Article 4).[23] The constitution stated that the emperor would govern the nation, that such rule was impossible without the apparatus of government. According to the constitution, the emperor entrusted the handling of state affairs to the Cabinet. However, the prime minister was merely the head of the Cabinet and had no right to dismiss any of the ministers under him.[24] His rights and responsibilities were limited. To make matters worse, the military was accorded independent status. The powers of government in prewar Japan were fragmented; the prime minister was weak; the military was independent.

To make the system work, it had the *genro*, the veteran statesmen who played the key roles in the restoration of imperial rule in their youth, united to make the government organization operate effectively. As long as the *genro* worked in unison, maintaining firm authority, government was their responsibility. This, the "informal" part of the Meiji constitution, weakened as the elder statesmen advanced in age and passed from the scene. The death in 1922 of Yamagata Aritomo, the last of the leaders who had built the Meiji state, marked the end of an epoch in Japanese history.

After that, the power of the remaining elder statesmen weakened; substantive execution of direct imperial rule was up for grabs. Individuals and parties vied for the right to decide how the emperor's rule should be executed. Out of this came the ultranationalists' campaign to rid Japan of the "corrupt elements of the court." Their argument was that the emperor, who should be the embodiment of the will of the whole Japanese people, was in fact the prisoner of the elder statesmen, military leaders, the bureaucrats, and the powerful financial houses,[25] all of whom conspired to obscure "the sacred will." The ultranationalists resorted to repeated assassinations and to coup attempts, hoping to eliminate what they considered corrupt elements, returning the government to the emperor. Brandishing abstract slogans that defied clear definition, they took upon themselves the task of rebuilding Japan in the name of the emperor.

The military—with the emperor as supreme commander of the armed forces—was independent of both the Diet and the Cabinet. By the General Staff Office ordinance instituted ten years before the establishment of the Meiji constitution, the head of the General Staff Office, a direct subordinate of the emperor, was empowered to organize and lead the armed forces with imperial approval, that is, without government restrictions. Yamagata, who set up the system, was the first head of the General Staff Office; he had made it established practice for military leaders to appeal directly to the throne.[26] These systems and practices were recognized by the Cabinet Act set up along with the the Meiji constitution. The military became a "sanctuary" outside Diet and Cabinet control; military leaders later expanded the interpretation of the imperial prerogative of supreme command to increase their influence in political affairs. A good example is their well-known attack on the government's acceptance of the London Naval Treaty as a "violation of the prerogative of the supreme command."[27]

In 1900 it had been stipulated that the war minister should be a general in active service; this allowed the military to bring down a Cabinet that did not serve their purposes by having the war minister resign; alternatively, they could obstruct the formation of a new Cabinet by simply refusing to supply a war minister. This system was changed by a later party Cabinet to extend the qualification of war minister to persons in the first or second category of reserve. After the February 26 Rising (1936), however, the old system was reintroduced. Lee Hyoung Cheol writes that during the period from 1892 to 1940 the military used the system eight times directly to influence Cabinet politics.[28] The military also used indirect influence; it could have its desires reflected in national government policy simply by implying that it would break up a Cabinet. The military was clearly "a state within a state."

The emperor himself was probably aware that he was not being treated like a typical constitutional monarch. While he tried to exert political influence, usually by posing questions during imperial conferences, and sometimes, more explicitly, by expressing his distrust of specific persons, there were limits to what he could do. When the decision to declare war on the United States was made, the emperor expressed his opposition to war by reading a poem by his grandfather, Emperor Meiji, calling for world peace.

The Meiji constitution did not provide for direct decision making by the emperor. After World War II, Emperor Hirohito remarked to former Grand Chamberlain Fujita Hisanori that "each cabinet minister's jurisdiction as stipulated by the [Meiji] Constitution should not be interfered with or restricted at the emperor's discretion . . . . That would be tantamount to abrogation of the constitution by the emperor."[29] If the government and the supreme command (army and navy general staffs) disagreed, there was some room for imperial decision. When a policy was agreed upon by the government and the military in a joint conference, the emperor had no choice but to approve it.

Only once in the course of the events leading to the Pacific War did the emperor act decisively. At the time of the February 26 Rising, when the top military authorities were hesitating about punishing the young army officers who were responsible for the coup attempts, the emperor called the mutineers rebels and said he was himself ready to lead the Imperial Guard Division to put them down. Only then did the military authorities set about to quell the mutiny. Saionji, displeased with the emperor's intervention, is thought to have remonstrated with him later. Saionji believed that such involvement of the emperor in actual political affairs was bound to have a negative effect in the long run on the emperor system, on Japan's future. Still, he no doubt realized that what Hirohito had done was probably the only way to settle a difficult situation.

IV

The Pacific War, however foolish and even criminal, was intended to secure the survival of the nation. The Japanese people accepted its necessity. The war was made all the more tragic because certain of Japan's aims, formulated both before and during the war, were indeed legitimate.

The war effort of the 1930s and the 1940s led to laying the foundations of Japan's heavy machinery and chemical industries. Norman Macrae, the first to recognize Japan's miraculous recovery and to predict its economic success, wrote in the *Economist* that the reasons for that success were "pretty clear" and "at first sight, more than a little unmoral." He went on to say:

> The common base for most of these "second stage" [heavy and chemical] breakthrough industries was laid in the long period in the 1930s to the early 1940s, when virtually the whole of Japan's industrial effort (and thus a very large part of its very low national income) was devoted to building up or serving its capacity for war.[30]

It should also be emphasized that the rural areas became relatively well off, especially in the first two decades after the war. Their increased productivity was made possible by advances in chemical fertilizers and insecticides, and the dissemination of agricultural equipment suited to use in small fields. It was also encouraged by the policy, established through successive conservative administrations, of supporting agricultural prices, particularly of rice. The most important factor contributing to increased productivity was agricultural land reform, which transformed tenant farmers into owner-cultivators, thereby heightening their incentives.

At the risk of oversimplification, the postwar reforms promoted equality and broke down some of the forms of traditional discrimination, brought farmers closer to workers in real income, creating a society that was in many ways more just. The Cabinet system was made solid in the new constitution; the Diet became the supreme organ of sovereign power; it was given the authority to designate the prime minister, who enjoyed broad powers. The fragmentation of government, leading to abuses in the prewar period, was ended. The emperor's status was clarified. He had been an absolute sovereign and a constitutional monarch under the old system. The new constitution eliminated ambiguity and clearly defined the emperor as the symbol of the nation, though without sovereign powers. It was no longer possible for anyone to defy the Cabinet in the name of the emperor.

This change, far from violating traditional institutions, brought the Japanese system into a more faithful conformity with tradition. The U.S. Occupation may have "forced" the new constitution on Japan, but ultimately it brought the status of the emperor into line with traditions that went back to the thirteenth century and earlier. Emperors were rarely political; their purposes were more subtle. In ceremony, they gave meaning to the nation.

Japanese leaders, willing to end the war, insisted on the single condition that the emperor be retained. They were not fanatical; their insistence on protecting the person of the emperor simply indicates how important they believed the emperor to be to the nation. The Americans accepted this, viewing it as a practical solution. Hoping that the surrender would come quickly, that an assault on the Japanese mainland, with its huge casualties could be avoided, they saw it as a way to facilitate the implementation of Occupation reforms.

Since that most basic historic continuity—the emperor system—was maintained after the war, other institutional continuities also remained, though dramatically reformed. Some criticize and lament this lack of fundamental change; they believe the basic reason the reforms were not more thorough was the acceptance of the emperor system, though in a modified form. For those for whom the identity of the nation is important—this author included—the success of the postwar reforms stems from the historical continuity maintained.

The international milieu, the cause of grave concern for the Japanese in the first decade and a half of Showa, changed radically, to Japan's great advantage. The United States, partly in the interests of power politics—to counter the Soviet threat—but mostly out of idealism, created a system of free trade and saw to it that Japan would be included on an equal basis in that system, making its own market free, the most open market of all.

Amaya Naohiro, former vice-minister of the Ministry of International Trade and Industry and architect of Japan's industrial policy, wrote:

> Japan benefitted most from the IMF-GATT system . . . . For Japan before the war, the world seemed very small, almost claustrophobic. Determined to secure its survival and a place for itself in that world, Japan proclaimed the "Greater East Asia Co-prosperity Sphere," but its vision ended in miserable failure. The great irony was that through defeat, Japan gained admission to the IMF-GATT system, which allowed it to export its products everywhere in the world, in principle without discrimination. And it could import as much as its money could buy. Japan saw a world freer than it had ever been since the Meiji period, and realized that at last there was room to flex the muscles of rapid economic growth that had long awaited that moment. The unprecedented rapid economic growth of the postwar world and

especially of Japan, became possible by virtue of the stability provided by Pax Americana.[31]

Bipolarity and the Cold War were blessings for Japan. Due in part to the efforts of Prime Minister Yoshida Shigeru, to the fact that Japan was a minor power, that many countries demanded that it be kept so, Japan depended entirely on the United States in matters of national security. Japan was required to keep a low profile—indeed, to be completely passive—in foreign policy. This kept expenditures for security low, so low that Japan was sometimes criticized as "taking a free ride in defense." All this worked to the advantage of economic growth.

Japan's passive posture in diplomatic and security affairs was important; it left the government free to concentrate on the fundamental task of unifying the nation. Alexis de Tocqueville, in his *Democracy in America,* suggested that the unique political system of the United States was successful in part because it did not have to worry about foreign relations. The same may be said about Japan, at least in the first thirty years after 1945. At least until the 1980s, Japan was probably the most unified country in the world, but this was not so much because of the much vaunted "uniqueness" of Japanese character as the fact that the nation was not distracted by diplomacy. Once a country becomes involved in international relations, and has to take the management of those relations into account, centrifugal tendencies develop. Only when a country is relieved of such considerations can it concentrate its efforts on internal affairs alone.

Postwar Japan is radically different from prewar Japan; the difference is symbolized in the changed status of the emperor. The prewar emperor system, with its origins in the Meiji Restoration of 1868, was the product of careful thought by Meiji leaders, determined to unify the people, to speed up modernization. The difficulty of the task of modernization was revealed in the early Showa period.

The first twenty years of the Showa era was an exceptional period, but the later forty years may be called exceptional in another sense. Japan, in the late Showa era, entered a normal period in which it had to face up to many difficult problems. For one thing, it was no longer free to avoid the weighty concerns of foreign and security policy; it had to play an active role. Japanese foreign policy skills are not yet demonstrated; they remained in doubt. Also, the necessity to be more responsible in external affairs complicates the tasks of national integration; this is exemplified in the intricacies of formulating satisfactory agricultural policy.

Despite the many reforms carried out after the war, Japan's political structure still suffers from a lack of identifiable focus. This may be part of the legacy of a people living in the microcosmos of an island nation. They can manage the integration required to get on with one another without being able to agree on policies necessary for survival in international society. The Japanese may still prefer their own peculiar brand of logic to the universal principles and values of others. The dependable, clear-as-day system of Pax Americana is showing signs of wear and tear, of possible decline. Although it would be an overstatement to say that the world is in a crisis comparable to that of the early Showa era, Japan, after Showa, faces daunting challenges.

ENDNOTES

[1]Shipbuilding volume had only topped 10,000 tons in 1897. See *Nihon sangyo hyakunenshi* (A Hundred-Year History of Japanese Industry), (Tokyo: Kodansha International, 1972).

[2]Nakamura Takafusa, ed., *Senkanki no Nihon keizai bunseki* (An Analysis of Japan's Economy in the Interwar Period), (Tokyo: Yamakawa Shuppansha, 1981), 35–36.

[3]In the 1920s, construction of modern cities began in several parts of the country, first in Tokyo and Yokohama, which had been largely destroyed in the Great Kanto Earthquake and Fire of 1923. Osaka, Kyoto, Nagoya, Fukuoka, and Sapporo followed suit. The endeavor to modernize the cities is reflected in conspicuous increases in local spending at that time, especially what was directed to the cities. Ibid., 120–22.

[4]Ibid., 18–23.

[5]Ibid., 36–37.

[6]Samuel Huntington, *Political Order in Changing Societies* (New Haven: Yale University Press, 1968), 62.

[7]It was also in 1929 when reformist army officials organized the Isseki-kai and the Sakura-kai.

[8]Generally speaking, European countries took a negative stance toward abolition of extraterritoriality, and Japan took a hard line on tariff to protect its economic interests. See Akira Iriye, *After Imperialism* (Cambridge: Harvard University Press, 1965).

[9]Ikei Masaru, *Nihon gaikoshi gaisetsu* (An Outline of the History of Japanese Foreign Policy), (Tokyo: Keio Tsushin, 1982), 154.

[10]Fujimura Michio, *Nihon gendaishi* (Modern History of Japan), (Tokyo: Yamakawa Shuppansha, 1981), 105–6.

[11]Harada Kumao, *Saionji-ku to seikyoku* (Prince Saionji and the Political Situation), (Tokyo: Iwanami Shoten, 1950–1956), vol. 2, 81.

[12]Japan returned to the gold standard at the old par, that is, by revaluating the yen (November 1929). This revaluation naturally had a deflationary effect. Because Japan adopted such a policy at a time when world depression was just beginning, the damage to the nation was all the heavier. It is questionable, however, whether anyone could have predicted with certainty at the end of 1929 that the stock market crash in New York in October 1929 would develop into the worldwide and prolonged depression that was to follow. The stock market recovered somewhat for a while but began falling again in the spring of the following year, not turning upward again for a long time.

[13]Charles Kindleberger, *The World in Depression* (Berkeley: University of California Press, 1973).

[14]Nakamura, 112–33.

[15]Maruyama Masao, *Gendai seiji no shiso to kodo* (Tokyo: Miraisha, 1964); English edition: Ivan Morris, ed., *Thought and Behavior in Modern Japanese Politics* (New York: Oxford University Press, 1963).

[16]Tai T'ien-ch'ou (Tai Chi-t'ao), *Nihon-ron* (Discussion of Japan, Japanese translation of *Jih-pen-lun*, Shanghai, 1928), (Tokyo: Shakai Shisosha, 1972), 31.

[17]Ito Takashi, *Showa 10-nendai-shi dansho* (A Glimpse of the Second Decade of the Showa Period), (Tokyo: Tokyo Daigaku Shuppankai, 1981), chap. 2.

[18]Among the best-known examples are the sculptor and poet Takamura Kotaro (1883–1956), the psychiatrist and poet Saito Mokichi (1882–1953), and the poet Miyoshi Tatsuji (1900–1964). The reaction of Iwanami Shigeo (1881–1946), founder of Iwanami Shoten Publishers, is also interesting. He was opposed to the war with China but said, "I'd support a war if it were fought to strike down the United States and Britain." See Takeuchi Yoshimi, *Ajia shugi* (Asianism), (Tokyo: Chikuma Shobo, 1963), 49–50; Hayashi Fusao, *Zoku Daitoa senso kotei ron* (An Affirmation of Japan's Greater East-Asian War, Part II), (Tokyo: Bancho Shobo, 1965), chap. 17.

[19]Hirota Koki gave in to the unreasonable demands of the military when he formed a Cabinet in 1936. When the military initiated the second Sino-Japanese war in July 1937, there was strong opposition within the Ministry of Foreign Affairs to sending army divisions to China, but Hirota did not express this clearly. See Ishii Itaro, *Gaikokan no issho* (The Life of a Diplomat), (Tokyo: Taihei Shuppansha, 1972). On the weak posture of Navy Minister Oikawa, see, for example, Nomura Minoru, *Tenno Fushimi-no-miya to Nihon kaigun* (The Emperor and Prince Fushimi and the Japanese Navy), (Tokyo: Bungei Shunjusha, 1986).

[20]Matsuzawa Hiroaki, "Ito Hirobumi," in *Kenryoku no shiso* (The Ideology of Power), (Tokyo: Chikuma Shobo, 1965), 85–86.

[21]Yanagita Kunio, *Meiji Taisho shi* (History of the Meiji and Taisho Periods), (Tokyo: Heibonsha, 1967), 308.

[22]Toriumi Yasushi, *Nihon kindaishi kogi* (Lectures on the Modern History of Japan), (Tokyo: Todai Shuppankai, 1988).

[23]The literal translation would be "The Emperor *oversees* the national government," but *soran* (oversee, or watch over) is almost untranslatable.

[24]There were discussions about Article 55, which stipulated the power of the ministers. It was argued in the drafting process that the Cabinet would become similar to the British system once the prime minister acquired the power to dismiss ministers. The Meiji oligarchs did not aim at an absolute monarchy or a British system either. The result was a halfway house.

[25]The phraseology is by Nishida Chikara (1901–1937), who played an important role in promoting the nationalist ideas of Kita Ikki among young army and navy officers.

[26]Yamagata Aritomo believed a strong government was necessary. His distrust of the freedom and popular rights movement in political parties was so great that he did his best to make the military independent of party government.

[27]In the original draft of the Meiji constitution, it was stipulated that "the Emperor command the Army and Navy. The Emperor decides the organization of them by Imperial decree." Since an imperial decree must be countersigned by ministers, it was clear that the organization of the army and the navy was exercised through the Cabinet. But some opposed to the draft argued that not all of the organizing acts of the emperor needed the assistance of the Cabinet, and in the end the term *by decree* was deleted. Consequently, it was a little unclear who was to assist the emperor in organizing the military. See Toriumi, 233.

[28]Lee Hyoung Cheol, *Gunbu no Showa-shi* (A Showa History of the Military), (Tokyo: Nihon Hoso Shuppan Kyokai, 1987), vol. 1, 28.

[29]Fujita Hisanori, *Jijucho no kaiso* (Recollections of a Grand Chamberlain), (Tokyo: Chuko bunko series, Chuo Koronsha, 1987), 207–8.

[30]Norman Macrae, "The Front Runners," *The Economist* (September 8, 1962): 918–21.

[31]Amaya Naohiro, *Hyoryu suru Nihon keizai* (Tokyo: Mainichi Shimbun, 1975), 189–90.

The alternation of excitement and apprehension is for me the hallmark of the Showa period. The initial excitement of the opening to democracy was followed by mounting external tension and domestic repression; the excitement of victory in 1942, by the dread-filled years of nemesis. The exhilaration of spectacular growth rates in the 1960s evaporated in the oil shock, leaving a lasting sense of vulnerability. The excitement, in the early 1980s, of becoming the world's largest creditor nation was spoiled by growing anxiety, as that new wealth and power seemed to arouse hostility, not respect, in the outside world, most worryingly in conqueror-turned-benign-elder-brother, the U.S.A.

There are intellectual excitement cycles too. In the mid-twenties George Allen wrote, before the shades of the Japanist prison house began to close in, of the questing intellectual enthusiasms of his ever-debating students. The next peak, pivot of the era, was the great postwar renaissance—like the 1870s all over again except that in some form it touched everyone, not just a tiny intellectual elite. Thereafter, the spirit of naively earnest inquiry, of passionate advocacy, has slowly waned—or migrated to Beijing. Today's Japan is much more sophisticated—and duller.

Ronald Dore
Adjunct Professor of Political Science
Massachusetts Institute of Technology

The Useful War

John W. Dower

Nearly 3 million dead and the loss of a quarter of the national wealth were the costs of the Pacific War for Japan; most analysts in 1945 predicted a dismal future as a second- or third-rate power. To understand "the Japanese miracle," we must examine the war years, for modern Japanese capitalism was created in the crucible of conflict.

Of the many descriptive phrases associated with Showa Japan, three are especially popular and evocative. The first, well-known in Japan, is "the dark valley" *(kurai tanima),* referring to the decade and a half of militarism and repression that preceded Japan's surrender in 1945. The other two phrases refer to the postwar years. One, closely associated with early Occupation-period (1945–1952) policies of demilitarization and democratization, is "the new Japan." The other, popularized when Japan attained high growth rates in the 1960s and emerged as an economic superpower in the early 1970s, is "the Japanese miracle."

It is easy to see where all three phrases come from, but they are not equally accurate. For the peoples of Asia who suffered from Japanese aggression, and for most Japanese themselves, the period from 1931 to 1945 was indeed dark and tragic. While far-reaching reforms were carried out in the years that followed, however, it is misleading to speak of a "new Japan" risen out of the ruins of the old. And the notion of a postwar "miracle" belongs to mythology rather than serious history. In fact, many of the characteristics and accomplishments of postwar Japan are deeply rooted not merely in the prewar period, but more precisely in the dark valley of early Showa. In ways

John Dower is Henry R. Luce Professor of International Cooperation and Global Stability at the Massachusetts Institute of Technology.

we only now are beginning to understand, developments which took place in conjunction with Japan's fifteen-year war proved to be extremely useful to the postwar Japanese state.

This is not a popular argument, and can be easily misunderstood. That the policies and practices of the early Showa state brought misery to countless millions of people is beyond dispute, just as it is beyond dispute that postwar Japan has been a more democratic and obviously less militaristic nation. That the early, militaristic decades of the Showa era also were a period of immense complexity and diversity that influenced the nature and dynamics of postwar Japanese society in positive as well as negative ways is more difficult to comprehend. In many ways, however, the dark valley of early Showa resembles a tumultuous earlier period that preceded an epoch of dramatic renovation and change in Japan: the Bakumatsu era of 1853–1868 that began with the forced opening of feudal Japan to the West, and ended with the Meiji Restoration and overthrow of the ancien régime.

In both Bakumatsu and early Showa, we see not merely the "deep" legacies of the past, but also the accelerated processes of change that occur in periods of acute crisis. The wide-ranging reforms and accomplishments of the Meiji period (1868–1912) are inexplicable without an understanding of Bakumatsu dynamics—and much the same argument holds for the relationship between postwar Japan and the dynamics of the decade and a half before Japan's surrender, when the entire country was mobilized for total war in a comparable crisis atmosphere. In the twentieth-century case, as in the nineteenth, the linkages and influences are apparent almost everywhere one looks: in continuities of personnel and institutions, in technological and economic linkages, in bureaucratic and technocratic activities, and in the permutations and transformations of consciousness and ideology at both elite and popular levels. The Japanese of the postwar era, like their Meiji predecessors, may have undertaken to reinvent themselves; but they necessarily did so with the materials at hand.[1]

Some of these linkages, such as continuities in personnel and institutions, are fairly obvious. In retrospect, apart from the military officer corps, the purge of alleged militarists and ultranationalists that was conducted under the Occupation had relatively small impact on the long-term composition of men of influence in the public and private sectors. The purge initially brought new blood into the political parties, but this was offset by the return of huge numbers of formerly purged conservative politicians to national as well as local politics in the early 1950s. In the bureaucracy, the purge was negligible from the outset, apart from the temporary removal from public office of hundreds of former Home Ministry officials who had been intimately involved in running the apparatus of the police state. In the economic sector, the purge similarly was only mildly disruptive, affecting less than 1,600 individuals spread among some 400 companies. Everywhere one looks, the corridors of power in postwar Japan are crowded with men whose talents already had been recognized during the war years, and who found the same talents highly prized in the "new" Japan.[2]

Such continuity of influential personnel was facilitated by the fact that, at almost every level, the postwar state rested on organizational pillars that were firmly planted in the past. Much of this institutional continuity was readily apparent, as seen in the preservation of the imperial throne, the revival of prewar political party lineages across the ideological spectrum, and the straightforward carryover of powerful public institutions such as the Ministry of Finance and Bank of Japan. More often, however, the institutional genealogies are more complex than is apparent at first glance. The powerful Economic Planning Agency established in 1955, for example, traces back to the Economic Stabilization Board that was created in 1946 in the midst of the rampant inflation that followed Japan's surrender; and this in turn was the successor to the major bureaucratic superagency of the war years, the Cabinet Planning Board established in 1937. Similarly, the Ministry of International Trade and Industry (MITI), established in 1949, is not merely the successor of the former Ministry of Commerce and Industry (1922–1943, 1945–1949), which functioned as the Munitions Ministry between 1943 and the end of the war. It also absorbed trade functions of the Occupation-period Board of Trade, which was the successor to the semiautonomous Trade Bureau established for war purposes in 1937—thus combining authority over industrial and trade policy to a degree not even attained under the militarists.[3]

In the private sector, institutional continuities are similarly more complicated than they usually appear to be at first glance. Keidanren, the immensely influential Federation of Economic Organizations, for example, was established in 1946 but actually traces its genealogy not merely to the prewar Japan Economic Federation (Nihon Keizai Renmei, founded in 1922), but also and more suggestively to some of the "control associations" *(toseikai)* established by the government in the final stages of the war in a desperate last attempt to bring state and private economic interests in line. In analogous ways, the contemporary Japanese business world includes not only major corporations that had their origins in the war economy, but also older concerns that predated the Showa era but increased their scale and market share enormously in the 1930s and early 1940s. Even the mass media, often ignored in such analyses, reflects this phenomenon. Of the five great national newspapers in contemporary Japan, two *(Nihon Keizai*—often referred to as "Japan's *Wall Street Journal*"—and *Sankei)* are by and large offspring of wartime mergers, while the other three (the *Yomiuri, Asahi,* and *Mainichi*) date from the nineteenth century but greatly increased their circulation and influence during the war.[4]

More important than examples of individual organizations, however, is the dynamic legacy to the postwar economy of war mobilization in general. The picture of ruined Japanese cities and a run-down productive system that became etched in popular consciousness at war's end is not wrong. Rather, it is misleading. Sixty-six major urban centers including Hiroshima and Nagasaki were heavily bombed in the last year of the war, and the Japanese government later calculated that the war in its entirety destroyed one-quarter of the nation's wealth. This was equivalent to wiping out the tangible assets created during the whole decade prior to surrender—and this estimate did not include some $20 billion in overseas assets that also were lost through defeat. As John Stuart Mill noted long ago, however, from the perspective of economic production it does not matter greatly if a country is laid to waste "by fire and sword," for in a few years one can expect wealth to be reproduced. What matters is not the physical goods destroyed, but rather the population that remains—or, more precisely, the skills of the population and the resources available to them. The Japanese economy was collapsing even before the U.S. air raids began, but what the rubble and exhaustion of 1945 obscured was the rapid growth that had taken place throughout the 1930s and for several years after Pearl Harbor.[5]

In the 1930s, when much of the world was struggling to recover from the Depression, for example, Japan's annual growth rate averaged 5 percent of GNP (the United States, by contrast, was still attempting to regain the level of 1929 in the late 1930s). Growth was particularly rapid in metals, chemicals, and engineering: the index for consumption goods rose from 100 to 154 between 1930 and 1937, while that for investment goods rose from 100 to 264. By 1937, Japan was constructing most of its own plants, including many kinds of machine tools and scientific instruments, and was largely self-sufficient in basic chemical products. The British economic historian G. C. Allen estimated that Japan's industrial production at this time was twice as great as the rest of Asia's combined (excluding the Soviet Union). As a trading nation, Japan had become a major exporter of manufactured products (although still over half textiles) and a major importer of raw materials. Its merchant marine was the third largest in the world, and it was surpassed as an exporter only by the United States, the United Kingdom, and Germany. These accomplishments, moreover, reflected developments within Japan proper—that is, not including growth in the Formosa and Korea colonies, or in the rapidly industrializing puppet state of Manchukuo.[6]

On the eve of Pearl Harbor, Japan was thus one of the most rapidly growing economies in the world. As the government intensified its controls following the initiation of open war with China in July 1937 and then the Allied powers in December 1941, moreover, many of the newly emerging industrial sectors continued to experience accelerated growth. Between 1937 and 1944, for example, production indices showed increases of 24 percent in manufacturing, 46 percent in steel, 70 percent in nonferrous metals, and 252 percent in machinery. By another calculation, paid-in capital invested in machinery (including shipbuilding and machine tools) rose from 7 percent of total investment in 1937 to 24 percent in 1945. In metals, the comparable figures were 5 percent in 1937 and 12 percent in 1945. The labor force in manufacturing and construction increased from 5.8 million in 1930 to 8.1 million in 1940 and 9.5 million in 1944, and this was accompanied by a dramatic alteration in the percentage of workers employed in light and heavy industry. In 1930, only 27 percent of the industrial work force was in heavy industry; this rose to 47 percent in 1937 and 68 percent by 1942.[7]

Japan was still a late developer in comparison with the United States, and by war's end—after the colossal war boom experienced by the United States—the gap was greater than ever. Nonetheless, between the Depression and 1945, Japan underwent a "second Industrial Revolution" that carried with it profound changes in the basic structures of both capital and labor. After the war, the Japanese were called upon to play catch-up economics in a very different milieu, but they had a strong base of experience and know-how from which to do so. In the long view, the Japanese even may be said to have benefited by losing. In the Cold War context, they quickly became a favored client of the United States, rewarded for acquiescence in the "containment" of communism with access to advanced U.S. technology (much of which also represented breakthroughs of the war years). In certain instances, moreover, the destruction of physical plant in the air raids actually hastened the construction of more up-to-date factories after the war. And the dismemberment of the old empire that was one of the prices of defeat forced the Japanese to devote concerted effort to planning new market strategies in a world that was, in its own way, about to move slowly and painfully into an era of decolonization. One of these strategies, it soon became clear, was to promote the export of manufactured goods other than textiles—that is, to convert the new wartime technologies into peacetime trade advantages. This began to be emphasized in Japanese planning papers within a few years after surrender, and became a reality in the 1950s.

From the perspective of postwar development, then, what is important about the increasingly militarized economy in this critical decade and a half is not that it was militarized, but that it was diverse and sophisticated in ways that facilitated conversion to peacetime activity. The automobile industry illustrates this. Of the eleven major auto manufacturers in postwar Japan, ten came out of the war years; only Honda is a pure product of the postsurrender period. Three of these ten firms—Toyota, Nissan, and Isuzu—prospered as the primary producers of trucks for the military after legislation passed in 1936 had driven Ford and General Motors out of the Japanese market. For the seven other manufacturers, postwar auto production in most instances was a spin-off from wartime activity in such fields as aircraft, tank, and warship manufacture, precision machinery, et cetera. Even the major postwar lobby for the automakers (the Japan Automobile Manufacturers Association), which was founded in 1948 and played a major role in persuading the government to support protectionist policies and low-cost loans in the 1950s and 1960s, was obliquely connected to wartime organizations. Its precedents were to be found in two "control associations" established in 1941 and 1942 to coordinate the production and distribution of vehicles; both wartime associations were headed by company executives who worked closely with the government.[8]

Other corporate giants on the postwar scene gained comparable competitive advantage during the war years. Nomura Securities, for example, which is now the second wealthiest corporation in Japan after Toyota, was founded in 1925 as a firm specializing in bonds. Its great breakthrough as a securities firm, however, came through expansion into stocks in 1938 and investment trust operations in 1941. Hitachi, Japan's largest manufacturer of electrical equipment, was established in 1910 but emerged as a comprehensive vertically integrated producer of electric machinery in the 1930s as part of the Ayukawa conglomerate that also included Nissan. Similarly, Toshiba, which ranks second after Hitachi in electric products, dates back to 1904 but only became a comprehensive manufacturer of electric goods following a merger carried out in 1939 under the military campaign to consolidate and rationalize production. Dentsu, described as the world's largest advertising agency in the 1970s, took its present name only in 1955. Yoshida Hideo, the leading figure in its postwar success, however, had been intimately involved in the wartime consolidation that reduced the number of Japanese advertising companies from 186 to 12. In a good example of personnel continuity, moreover, Dentsu recruited so many ex-military officers and former Manchukuo bureaucrats after the war and Occupation that its corporate headquarters became known as the "Second Manchurian Railway Building."[9]

Whole sectors were able to take off in the postwar period by building on advances made during the war. Japan's emergence as the world's leading builder of merchant shipping by 1956, for example, is directly related to the almost frantic development of a capacity to turn out warships (and superbattleships such as the *Yamato* and *Musashi*) in the previous decades. Other manufacturing sectors which Japan relied on during the early stages of its postwar recovery—such as cameras, binoculars, watches, and the like—were similarly grounded in technologies given priority during the war. In some instances, the swords-to-plowshares transformation was so thoroughgoing as to border on the maudlin: in one instance, for example, sewing machines were produced by factories converted from making machine guns.[10]

Examples such as these give substance to John Stuart Mill's sensible observation that it is the capabilities of the population that matter most. It is well known that manpower policy under the Japanese militarists was often inefficient, and that by the final two years of the war the labor market was near chaos. Nonetheless, the nonagricultural work force was not merely larger but also conspicuously more skilled in 1945 than it had been fifteen years earlier. Almost 4 million new workers were brought into the industrial labor force between 1930 and 1945—while millions of males who had been exposed to military discipline survived to be reintegrated into the postwar economy. The number of technical schools increased from 11 to over 400 between 1935 and 1945, while at the same time in-firm technical training designed to create a highly skilled cadre of blue-collar workers became a widespread practice.

Science and engineering also were stimulated by war. University students in these fields became exempted from the draft, and the number of graduates between 1941 and 1945 was triple what it had been a decade earlier. While isolation from interaction with Western scientists was a grievous blow to first-rate researchers, moreover, the other side of the coin was the expansion of indigenous research facilities in both basic and applied science, centering on such institutions as the prestigious "Riken" laboratory. At the same time, the military's need for mass-produced goods of reliable quality led to the establishment of uniform standards. Although the "QC" (quality control) ideals that have become so famous in contemporary Japan were decisively influenced by postwar American technical consultants such as W. Edwards Deming, even in the mid-1980s the formal guideline for quality maintenance used by the Ministry of International Trade and Industry remained the Industrial Standardization Law introduced by the military government in 1940.[11]

As Nakamura Takafusa and other economic historians have demonstrated, the expansionary pressures of the wartime economy also brought about fundamental changes in the interweave of industrial and financial capital, as well as in labor-management relations. Mobilization for war stimulated a spectacular concentration of capital. As military orders came to play an increasing role in the economy, the hegemony of the four "old *zaibatsu*"—Mitsui, Mitsubishi, Sumitomo, and Yasuda—was challenged by the emergence of a group of so-called "new *zaibatsu*" *(shin zaibatsu)* more exclusively dependent on military contracting. Six conglomerates dominated the new *zaibatsu*: Asano, Furukawa, Ayukawa, Okura, Nomura, and Nakajima. In 1937, these ten largest *zaibatsu* controlled 15 percent of total paid-in capital in Japan; by the end of the war, this had risen to over 35 percent.[12]

These big capitalists did not evaporate after Japan surrendered. Although the *zaibatsu* concentrations were weakened by the dissolution of holding companies and diversification of shareholding in the early Occupation period, many of the key enterprises have remained close through a variety of formal and semiformal relationships. The vaunted "big six" enterprise groups *(kigyo shudan)* and related "financial enterprise groups" *(kinyu keiretsu)* of postwar Japan, for example, consist of three old-*zaibatsu* groupings (Mitsui, Mitsubishi, and Sumitomo) and three groups headed by giant banks (Fuji, Dai-ichi Kangyo, and Sanwa). The Fuji Bank is in fact the former central bank of the old Yasuda *zaibatsu*, and its so-called Fuyo group includes many former Yasuda enterprises. Corporations affiliated with the "big six" accounted for 23 percent of the assets of large corporations in 1955, and almost 30 percent in 1970. In the early 1980s, more than 17 percent of all corporate assets were associated with these six enterprise groups.[13]

The central role played by a highly concentrated banking structure in the postwar economy is itself a conspicuous legacy of the war years. Prior to a severe banking panic in 1927, there were approximately 1,400 ordinary commercial banks in Japan. By the end of 1931, the number had declined to 683. At the end of 1936, it stood at 418. Between then and the end of the war, the number of banks was drastically reduced by mergers and absorptions to 61—and there has been little change since. Moreover, the powerful "city banks" (really national banks) that stand at the hub of the postwar enterprise groups were in most instances greatly strengthened by critical legislation introduced between 1942 and 1944, which designated a small number of "authorized financial institutions" to receive special support from the government and Bank of Japan in providing the great bulk of loans to over 600 major producers of strategic war materials. Even the famous "overloan" or "leveraging" policy that has characterized postwar Japanese lending practices had its genesis in the war economy. As Sakakibara Eisuke and Noguchi Yukio have shown, the figures here are quite striking. Thus, in 1931 the ratio of direct (equity) to indirect (bank loan) financing of industry was roughly 9:1. By 1935, the ratio had become 7:3, by 1940 it was 5:5, and in 1945 it was exactly the opposite of what it had been in 1931—and almost exactly the same as what it would be during the high-growth 1960s—that is, 1:9.[14]

In the nonconcentrated sector of the economy, the war years witnessed the emergence of tens of thousands of small and medium-sized enterprises which also greatly influenced the dynamics of postwar growth. The negative side of this industrial "dual structure" became widely criticized in the 1950s and 1960s, for it was associated with gross wage and income differentials and recognized as being a primary facilitator of dumping abroad. Such legitimate criticism, however, should not obscure the dynamism of the nonconcentrated sector. Many small enterprises flourished as subcontractors as well as independent entities under the war economy, and continued to do so after the war. In the late 1960s, for example, over 40 percent of the ancillary firms supplying parts to Toyota traced their subcontracting relationship back to the war years. And in certain critical sectors such as the machinery industry, small-scale firms frequently were responsible for a major portion of relatively high-skill output. During the war, small entrepreneurs developed effective networks of political and bureaucratic patronage, and generally responded with strong support for the militarist government. In the postsurrender period, their support was successfully cultivated by the conservative politicians who eventually merged to form the Liberal Democratic Party in 1955. Much of the genuinely innovative entrepreneurial energy that lies behind Japan's postwar economic takeoff, moreover, has come from such smaller enterprises.[15]

Inevitably, the war-stimulated "second Industrial Revolution" altered not merely the size, composition, and competence of the labor force, but also the basic nature of industrial relations. In recent decades, a great deal of attention has been given to the existence of a purportedly unique "Japanese employment system," and commentators both in and outside Japan delight in finding deep, peculiar cultural explanations for this. Japanese industrial relations, this thesis goes, reflect old Confucian values of harmony and hierarchy, or the master-apprentice relationships and lifelong loyalties of feudal merchant houses, or "familial" values that transcend Confucianism and reflect some quintessentially Japanese consciousness of the *ie*, or "household." In fact, the three distinct features associated with labor-management relations in contemporary Japan—lifetime employment, seniority-based wages, and company or enterprise unions—do not apply to the majority of industrial workers, but rather primarily to workers in large enterprises. They reflect the peculiarities of a dualistic labor force, rather than some old cultural legacy. And they did not become fixed in their present form until the 1950s. Like the dual structure itself, however, all three distinctive features of labor relations in large enterprises have strong roots in the war years.

At no time prior to the postwar period is it possible to speak of a stable labor market in Japan. Surveys conducted by the government between the 1937 China Incident and the attack on Pearl Harbor four years later disclosed alarmingly high rates of employee turnover in critical industries, and job jumping actually continued till the very end of the war. It was in response to this instability that the military government intervened to try to bring the industrial labor force under greater discipline and control. Thus, between 1939 and 1942, the authorities sponsored a series of ordinances prohibiting unauthorized changes in places of employment. Between 1939 and 1943, an equally dense and detailed series of laws and regulations was introduced aimed at stabilizing the wage structure in a manner that would likewise hold workers to their jobs; this included fixed starting salaries and clearly defined raises at regular intervals. As a result of these government actions, two of the three pillars of "the Japanese employment system"—permanent employment and wages pegged to seniority for skilled and semiskilled employees—came into general practice. With them came other practices that also characterize postwar labor relations in large firms, such as greater reliance on on-the-job training, as well as certain supplemental in-company benefits such as family allowances.

The genesis of the third feature of the postwar employment system in large firms—enterprise unionism—is more controversial among Japanese industrial-relations specialists, some of whom stress the decisive influence of early postwar developments. Here, however, it is in any case impossible to ignore the organizational and ideological influence of the wartime mobilization of labor under the notorious "Sampo" organization (Sangyo Hokokukai, or Industrial Patriotic Association). Established under government auspices in 1938, Sampo brought some 6 million employees in 87,000 companies under a nationwide umbrella distinguished by corporatist ideals, a company-focused modus operandi, and "enterprise family" *(jigyo ikka)* rhetoric. Such ideological fixations had much more of a future in Japan than they did a past.[16]

While accelerating trends in the modern sector, mobilization for war simultaneously undermined one of the most basic and retrogressive features of the prewar economy: the extensive prevalence of landlordism in the countryside, where over 40 percent of the total national work force was engaged in agricultural production. At the time of Pearl Harbor, only 36 percent of Japanese peasants owned all the land they farmed, and 46 percent of all cultivated land was worked by tenants. Rents for riceland commonly were paid in kind, at a rate of slightly more than half the average crop, thus perpetuating a large "semifeudal" sector within the developing economy. Although some landlords may have been paternalistic, poverty and unrest were widespread in rural Japan. The militarists came to power after the Depression promising, among other things, to rectify the rural crisis; and, wittingly and unwittingly, their policies rang the death knell for the landlord class.

The land reform carried out between 1946 and 1948 dispossessed the landlords and virtually eliminated tenancy. This was a critical step in achieving an expanded domestic market and mature bourgeois capitalism in Japan, and that it was accomplished so swiftly and smoothly is due almost entirely to the exceptional circumstances of war and defeat. The land reform was a central part of the "demilitarization and democratization" agenda introduced by the victorious Americans, and it is indisputable that the authority wielded by the victors was essential to ensuring that the reform was implemented thoroughly. As the Americans themselves acknowledged, however, success ultimately depended on circumstances beyond their control. That the vast majority of the rural population welcomed such a drastic transformation of relations was of course essential, but the reform also was facilitated by two additional circumstances. First, there existed a cadre of Japanese academics and former wartime bureaucrats who were themselves committed to land reform, and possessed the technical and administrative expertise to carry it out. And second, it quickly became apparent that wartime developments, especially after 1940, had severely eroded the traditional power of the landlords.

The second point is frequently overlooked. The precipitous decline in landlord authority can be dated from 1941, when the government introduced a "food administration system" designed to increase agricultural production and expedite delivery. By paying tenants directly for their produce, the government essentially undercut the landlords economically and destroyed their direct relationship with their tenants. Andrew Grad, who was involved in planning the postwar Japanese land reform, acknowledged the profound ramifications of this in an early résumé of what had been accomplished. "The separation of the landlord from the land was far-reaching in its consequences," Grad wrote concerning the war years. "As the produce of his land was not permitted to reach him, as the price paid him for rice was considerably lower than the price paid to the tenant, and as he was not permitted during the war to evict his tenants, the bond between the landlord and his land was all but severed. In the eyes of the government he became little more than a good-for-nothing rentier—a view that paved the way for the postwar land reform. It became much easier to take land from the landlords when they could not claim it, its produce, or even its rent." Grad concluded that "it is doubtful that, even with the support of the Occupation authorities, land reform could have been carried out by a conservative government as successfully as it was, if the way had not been smoothed during the war."[17]

In most of these developments, there was a visible hand. More accurately, there were many visible hands, and the most blatantly manipulative of them came from the military and civilian bureaucracy. These were years of extraordinary intervention and experimentation on the part of the Japanese state, and the practice and ideology of technocratic control which emerges so vividly here is certainly among the most conspicuous and controversial of the wartime legacies to contemporary Japan.

War strengthened the bureaucracy, and the seven-year Occupation that followed strengthened it further. Each in its own way, both war and peace fostered an overwhelming sense of crisis and an intense preoccupation with national security. Both stimulated renovationist thinking among the bureaucrats—a deep commitment to the necessity of guided change—and in this sense there was no real break between the presurrender and postsurrender periods. Immediate tasks changed drastically, of course, from "war" to "peace." What remained was a deep dissatisfaction with the status quo, and an abiding commitment to top-down, long-range planning to create a strong state in a new world order.

Nor was there any break in the elite status and intellectual élan of the civilian bureaucracy. Before as well as after 1945, huge numbers of the brightest university graduates gravitated to careers in the bureaucracy. This was the elite course, and during the war it attracted thousands of ambitious young planners who drew eclectically and voraciously on intellectual and ideological thinking outside Japan—meaning Nazi and fascist and national-socialist thought, to be sure, but also Marxism, Leninism, and Stalinism, and also Fordism and scientific management and New Deal interventionism where these seemed to offer solutions to the crisis of economic depression and war. These "new bureaucrats" *(shin kanryo)* or "renovationist bureaucrats" *(kakushin kanryo)* had allies among the intelligentsia and even in certain corporate circles, as well as within the military. In contrast to the United States, wartime government service was not a temporary diversion from normal career paths for most of these flexible young technocrats. Sharp and agile, they stepped lightly across the surrender and continued to administer the postwar state.

One of the less abstract, and more neglected, legacies of the presurrender renovationist bureaucrats lay in the area of social-security and social-welfare legislation. For some bureaucrats, a genuine populist idealism may have lain behind this. More often, social reform was rationalized as being essential to the creation of a strong defense state, for the Depression and war crisis exposed how physically unfit and psychologically demoralized the Japanese populace as a whole really was. A nationwide survey of draft-age men conducted by the army in 1936, for example, revealed a shockingly high percentage of males who were unfit for military service because of malnutrition, communicable diseases, or job-caused disabilities. The Japanese were in much poorer physical condition than their American or European counterparts, and the army attributed this to conditions such as low income, poor nutrition, excessive working hours, and hazardous job conditions. Such exploitation was not new, but its scale and implications were greater than ever before. Military conscription was hampered. The civilian work force was enfeebled. The morale of parents and elders, as well as young servicemen and workers themselves, was undermined. The possibility of communist upheaval—always a fear of the ruling groups after 1917—was strengthened. Because for decades the private sector had failed to ameliorate such conditions, the task devolved on the bureaucracy.

Such reports merely confirmed what had been apparent earlier, and the bureaucratic response to this social crisis was intense. A new Ministry of Health and Welfare was created in 1938. That same year, in the wake of the invasion of China, medical-insurance coverage was expanded. By war's end, over half of all Japanese were covered by these entitlements, which became the basis of the postwar medical-insurance system. Similarly, the postwar pension system was built upon a series of laws enacted between 1939 and 1944, which originally were designed to hold workers to their jobs while simultaneously creating a capital fund which the government could tap to help finance the war.[18]

After Japan's surrender, the "social bureaucrats" who had been involved in formulating such reformist wartime legislation played a complex role. On the one hand, they helped draft such progressive legislation of the early Occupation period as the fundamental labor laws (the Trade Union Law of 1945 and the Labor Standards Law of 1947), revision of the civil code, and reform of the educational system. They also played an important role in implementing the land reform. On the other hand, former wartime social bureaucrats also were able to temper some of the early drafts of reformist legislation introduced by the U.S. Occupation authorities—without, however, ever attempting to gut them entirely. This occurred in such basic reforms as the new constitution and legislation aimed at promoting greater local autonomy. Once the Cold War intensified and U.S. Occupation priorities turned from reform to economic reconstruction, the Japanese technocrats and their American counterparts found common cause in antileftist activities such as the McCarthyist "Red purges" of 1949 and 1950, which resulted in the firing of over 20,000 employees in the public and private sectors. Many of the former Home Ministry officials who were depurged near the end of the Occupation quickly rose to important and conspicuously reactionary "social control" positions under the conservative Liberal Democratic Party, America's new ally in Asia. All along the line, "convergence" made for unexpected bedfellows.[19]

Even more far-reaching than the influence of the social bureaucrats, however, was the postwar impact of their colleagues who had been directly engaged in managing the war economy. The postsurrender dissolution of the military and Home Ministry removed two of the strongest institutional rivals to the economic bureaucrats. At the same time, the early Occupation policy of dissolving *zaibatsu* holding companies and introducing antimonopoly legislation placed the private sector at a temporary disadvantage. In the chaos of the early postsurrender transition, the United States even transferred to the bureaucracy some of the economic regulatory functions which the private sector had struggled to maintain all the way through the war. The rule-from-above style of the U.S. Occupation staff reinforced the acceptability of bureaucratic direction; the policy of running the Occupation "indirectly" through the Japanese government enhanced the real power of the career bureaucrats; and the truly stupendous economic disorder and confusion which prevailed until almost the very end of the Occupation in 1952 placed economic and technocratic expertise at a premium. It is generally acknowledged that the economic bureaucrats had even more influence under the Americans than they did under their own military leaders during the war.

Even after 1952, the rigidly Cold War nature of the peace settlement with Japan helped perpetuate the preeminence of the economic bureaucracy. Because the country was so thoroughly subordinated to the United States militarily and diplomatically, it really had no foreign policy of its own. As a consequence, even the proud Ministry of Foreign Affairs found itself overshadowed by MITI, which is the most conspicuous example of the long ride of the economic bureaucrats. Until the mid-1970s, all top officials in MITI came out of the presurrender bureaucracy; and their memories, clearly, were excellent. As Chalmers Johnson has shown, for example, the controls over trade and foreign exchange that enabled MITI to orchestrate a successful industrial policy from the 1950s to the 1970s were first codified in the 1930s and then perpetuated, almost willy-nilly, in the 1949 Foreign Exchange and Foreign Control Law enacted while Japan was still under U.S. direction. Another feature of the MITI modus operandi, its ability to target specific industries for official guidance and support, can be traced back not merely to organizational arrangements introduced in the late 1930s, but also to a panoply of industry-specific laws introduced between 1934 and 1941—many of which were "resurrected" during the 1950s and 1960s, when MITI power was at its zenith.[20]

The economic bureaucrats, whether managing war through such organs as the Munitions Ministry and Cabinet Planning Board, or peace through MITI and the Economic Planning Agency, pose a challenging question for political analysts: what sort of capitalism have the Japanese been practicing since the 1930s? Clearly, it is not laissez-faire in the manner associated with Adam Smith. On the other hand, state ownership is not the issue, for in fact this is minimal in Japan. The question is really one of laissez-faire in a box—that is, how (and how much) control is imposed on the market—and in recent years numerous phrases have emerged which all suggest that the box is very intricately constructed indeed. Japan is said to be a plan-rational as opposed to a market-rational nation, a mixed capitalist state, a capitalist development state, a technocratic state, a neomercantilist state, a "smart" state, a network state, a corporatist (or corporatist-without-labor) state. It practices industrial policy, administrative guidance, "window" guidance, patterned pluralism, canalized pluralism, bureaucracy-led mass-inclusionary pluralism, administered competition, compartmentalized competition, guided free enterprise, managed capitalism, quasi-capitalism, state-directed capitalism. In Chalmers Johnson's phrase, since the 1930s Japanese development has been powerfully guided by an "economic general staff"—a most effective metaphor for conveying both the historical and the ideological mesh of war and peace that lies behind the so-called Japanese miracle.

These catchphrases are lively and useful, but they can be misleading if taken to mean that Japan is first and foremost a bureaucratic state. More pertinent is the fact that it is a strong capitalist state, and its version of capitalism is brokered by conservative interests in a manner that retains the market while controlling "excessive" competition and promoting nationalistic goals. The economic bureaucrats are indeed influential actors in this grand enterprise, but so also are big business and the conservative politicians. This brokered capitalism is neither very new nor very old. It is not simply a postwar phenomenon—a "Japan, Inc." or "new Japanese capitalism" that emerged out of the ashes in the 1950s. On the other hand, neither is it a traditionally "closed" system rooted in the economic nationalism of the Meiji period, or in the insular and consensual values of an even earlier time. Japan's brokered capitalism is fundamentally a transwar phenomenon. The conservative elites that work the system now are no longer militaristic. As we have seen, however, a great many of their institutions, ideas, practices—and leaders—were formed in the crucible of war.

In peace as in war, this brokering of power has been fierce and costly. Even in the most desperate years of World War II, Japan's leaders never succeeded in establishing a totalitarian state, or a consensual polity, or a harmonious body politic. Contrary to the popular image of a fanatically loyal populace resolutely united behind the war effort, intense competition and conflict took place within as well as among different constituencies—the military, the civilian bureaucracy, old *zaibatsu* and new *zaibatsu,* political parties, small and medium-sized enterprises, rural versus urban interests, et cetera. Like the myth of the "enterprise family," the wartime slogan "one-hundred-million hearts beating as one" was an illusive goal rather than a description of reality, and this internal tension and competitiveness is as important as any other legacy to the postwar years. It helps explain both high levels of achievement and what often appears to be indecisive and even two-faced behavior, especially in the international arena in recent years. The curious image that Japan has acquired in the 1980s of being a powerful but seemingly decapitated state, especially when it comes to assuming the responsibilities that should accompany economic eminence, can be partly explained by this internal conflict.

Many observers would agree that nationalism and a paternalistic elitism have held this brokered capitalism together ideologically since the war. If this is so, then what can we say about postwar Japanese democracy? We can say that this too has been brokered, in ways that respect the form but frequently kill the spirit of democracy. The intellectual and ideological legacy of the war is blatantly contradictory in Japan. Without question, there is a radical legacy in the form of antimilitarist sentiments and cynicism toward authority at the popular level. That much of the "democratization" agenda of the early postsurrender years has survived to the present day, as exemplified in the liberal "peace constitution," is testimony to popular support for democratic ideals. Had the conservative elites had their way, the early postwar reforms would have been jettisoned more extensively. Yet, at the same time, regimentation and susceptibility to rather crass indoctrination are also conspicuous legacies of the war. "Loyalty" to the firm and "sacrifice" for the country remain effective appeals. In some instances, acquiescence to these ideals may reflect a real sense of reciprocal obligation; in many instances, it reflects plain weariness and existential resignation on the part of the average citizen. Whatever the case, the ethic of self-denial has depended on the maintenance—even the reinvention—of immense pressures ranging from carefully nurtured social taboos to overtly paramilitary rituals such as company drills and "boot-camp training." As international tensions arise in response to Japan's new economic eminence and economic nationalism, moreover, more strident ideological legacies of the war years have emerged in the form of disturbing neonationalist appeals to the homogeneity and superiority of the "Yamato race."

The nature of Japan's brokered postwar democracy is a subject that still awaits its historian. In suggestive ways, however, it returns us to an observation made at the outset of this essay, namely, the resonance between Japan's mid-nineteenth-century transition from feudalism to industrialization and "Westernization," and its mid-twentieth-century transition from war to peace. In both cases, far-reaching and even revolutionary transformations took place. And in both cases, these were revolutions "from above." Where democratic ideals are not defined by and won by the general populace, they are relatively weak. From the perspective of Japan's civil elites, this too was a useful legacy of the war.

ENDNOTES

[1]If one defines "postwar" Japan as equivalent to the latter part of the Showa period (1945–1989), a popular and reasonable equation, the comparison between Bakumatsu-Meiji (1853–1868, 1868–1912) and wartime-postwar (1931–1945, 1945–1989) is remarkably close in terms of years. There is a danger of falling into numerology here, but the parallels should not be dismissed out of hand. That the period of crisis lasted a decade and a half, or roughly half a generation, in both cases helps explain the intensity as well as the incompleteness of the processes put in train. The longer duration of the renovationist aftermath (four-plus decades in both cases) permits a clearer picture of how these processes unfolded in the long run—but is still short enough to retain the visibility of personal, institutional, and behavioral linkages.

[2]For basic coverage of the purge, see Hans H. Baerwald, *The Purge of Japanese Leaders under the Occupation*, vol. 12 of University of California Publications in Political Science (Berkeley: University of California Press, 1959), esp. 78–98. On the negligible effect of the purge in bureaucratic and business circles, see T. J. Pempel, "The Tar Baby Target: 'Reform' of the Japanese Bureaucracy," in Robert E. Ward and Yoshikazu Sakamoto, eds., *Democratizing Japan: The Allied Occupation* (Honolulu: University of Hawaii Press, 1987), 160; Eleanor M. Hadley, *Antitrust in Japan* (Princeton: Princeton University Press, 1970), 87–99.

[3]Cf. Chalmers Johnson, *MITI and the Japanese Miracle: The Growth of Industrial Policy, 1925–1975* (Stanford: Stanford University Press), chap. 4.

[4]Ishikawa Ichiro, one of the founders of the postwar Keidanren, actually was nicknamed "god of the control associations"; see Karel van Wolferen, *The Enigma of Japanese Power* (New York: Knopf, 1989), 354. On the press, see Gregory J. Kasza, *The State and the Mass Media in Japan, 1918–1945* (Berkeley: University of California Press, 1988), 281.

[5]For the basic 1949 government assessment of war damage, see Arisawa Hiromi and Inaba Hidezo, eds., *Shiryo: Sengo Nijunen Shi,* vol. 2 *(Keizai)*, (Tokyo: Nihon Hyoronaha, 1966), 2–5. Cf. Takafusa Nakamura, *The Postwar Japanese Economy: Its Development and Structure,* trans. Jacqueline Kaminski (Tokyo: University of Tokyo Press, 1981), 15; T. F. M. Adams and Iwao Hoshii, *A Financial History of the New Japan* (Tokyo: Kodansha International, 1972), 17 (for overseas assets). Paul Sweezy called attention to Mill's observation (from *Principles of Political Economy,* bk. 1, chap. 5, sec. 7) in a review article on Japan in *Monthly Review* (February 1980): 6.

[6]The best concise summary of the economic legacies of the war mobilization appears in Nakamura, chap. 1, esp. 14–20. For an earlier general overview, see G. C. Allen, *Japan's Economic Recovery* (London: Oxford University Press, 1958), chap. 1, esp. 4–6. Hugh Patrick and Henry Rosovsky estimate the 1930s growth rate at 5 percent in "Japan's Economic Performance: An Overview," in Patrick and Rosovsky, eds., *Asia's New Giant: How the Japanese Economy Works* (Washington, D.C.: Brookings Institution, 1976), 8–9. The paucity of close analysis of the war years in basic economic overviews of modern Japan borders on the scandalous and is reflected in the slight attention to this period in the

standard "Long-Term Economic Statistics" (LTES) of Japan on which most recent scholarship is based.

[7]Nakamura, 12; Michael A. Cusumano, *The Japanese Automobile Industry: Technology and Management at Nissan and Toyota* (Cambridge: Council on East Asian Studies, Harvard University, 1985), 14; Jerome B. Cohen, *Japan's Economy in War and Reconstruction* (Minneapolis: University of Minnesota Press, 1949), 296–97. It should be kept in mind that productivity in many sectors began to decline conspicuously by 1944, and economic data which singles out 1945 as a key point for comparison or generalization can be extremely misleading.

[8]Cusumano, 1–72; Konosuke Odaka, Keinosuke Ono, and Fumihiko Adachi, *The Automobile Industry in Japan: A Study of Ancillary Firm Development* (Tokyo: Kinokuniya Company and Oxford University Press, 1988), esp. 1–39, 89–100, 107–119, 251–55.

[9]Company and institutional information is generally available in standard reference works such as the nine-volume *Kodansha Encyclopedia of Japan (KEOJ)*, (Tokyo: Kodansha, 1983). On Dentsu, see also van Wolferen, 386–87.

[10]Masataka Kosaka, *A History of Postwar Japan* (Tokyo: Kodansha International, 1982), 220; Nakamura, 15. For an effusive comment on the technological legacies of "the *Yamato* and the Zeros," see *U.S. Naval Institute Proceedings* 105 (September 1979): 86.

[11]On manpower mobilization (and chaos), cf. Cohen, chap. 5, and Andrew Gordon, *The Evolution of Labor Relations in Japan: Heavy Industry, 1853–1955* (Cambridge: Council on East Asian Studies, Harvard University, 1985), 314–17. On science and engineering, cf. Christopher Thorne, *The Issue of War: States, Societies, and the Far Eastern Conflict, 1941–1945* (London: Hamish Hamilton, 1985), 309; Thomas R. H. Havens, *Valley of Darkness: The Japanese People and World War Two* (New York: Norton, 1978), 30, 139, 213. The basic 1940 standardization law is noted in David A. Garvin, "Japanese Quality Management," *Columbia Journal of World Business* 19 (3) (Fall 1984): 9.

[12]In critical sectors of the modern economy, the influence of "the big ten" *zaibatsu* had become truly awesome by 1945: 49 percent of paid-in capital in mining and heavy and chemical industries, 50 percent in banking, 85 percent in trust funds, 60 percent in insurance, 61 percent in shipping, 30 percent in real estate and warehousing. The "big four" old *zaibatsu* alone controlled 10.4 percent of paid-in capital in 1937 and 24.5 percent at the end of the war. See Mitsubishi Economic Research Institute, ed., *Mitsui-Mitsubishi-Sumitomo: Present Status of the Former Zaibatsu Enterprises* (Tokyo: Mitsubishi Economic Research Institute, 1955), 6.

[13]Patrick and Rosovsky, 499, for 1955 and 1970 percentages; *KEOJ* 2:221 for early 1980s.

[14]*KEOJ* 1:137–41; Eisuke Sakakibara and Yukio Noguchi, "Dissecting the Finance Ministry–Bank of Japan Dynasty," excerpted in Daniel I. Okimoto and Thomas P. Roheln, eds., *Inside the Japanese System: Readings on Contemporary Society and Political Economy* (Stanford: Stanford University Press, 1988), 43, 61.

[15]Odaka, Ono, and Adachi. David Friedman, *The Misunderstood Miracle: Industrial Development and Political Change in Japan* (Ithaca: Cornell University Press, 1988), presents the argument for the viability of small and medium-sized enterprise in detail through analysis of the prewar and postwar machine-tool industry.

[16]For general overviews of the industrial relations system, see Gordon, esp. chap. 7 and 8; Solomon Levine's essays "Labor" and "Labor Laws" in *KEOJ* 4:343–49, 351–53; Taishiro Shirai, "A Theory of Enterprise Unionism," in Shirai, ed., *Contemporary Industrial Relations in Japan* (Madison: University of Wisconsin Press, 1983), 117–43; Ernest J. Notar, "Japan's Wartime Labor Policy: A Search for Method," *Journal of Asian Studies* 44 (2) (February 1985): 311–28; Sheldon Garon, *The State and Labor in Modern Japan* (Berkeley: University of California Press, 1987), 187–227.

[17]Andrew J. Grad, *Land and Peasant in Japan: An Introductory Survey* (New York: Institute of Pacific Relations, 1952), 34, 39–40. See also Ronald P. Dore, *Land Reform in Japan* (London: Oxford University Press); and Tsutomu Takizawa, "Historical Background of Agricultural Land Reform in Japan," *The Developing Economies* 10 (3) (1972).

[18]See Notar, 314–15, for the 1936 survey. For welfare problems and projects in general, see Yoshida Kyuichi, *Gendai Shakai Jigyoshi Kenkyu* (Tokyo: Keiso Shobo, 1979), 271–401; *KEOJ* 5:144–45, 6:172–73, 7:209–11; Havens, 46–49; Garon, *The State and Labor,* 203–5, 236; Koseisho Nijunen Shi Henshu Iinkai, ed., *Koseisho Nijunen Shi* (Tokyo: Kosei Mondai Kenkyukai, 1960), and Koseisho Gojunen Shi Henshu Iinkai, ed., *Koseisho Gojunen Shi* (Tokyo: Kosei Mondai Kenkyukai, 1988), esp. 339–572.

[19]On labor, see Takemae Eiji, *Sengo Rodo Kaikaku: GHQ Rodo Seisaku Shi* (Tokyo: Tokyo Daigaku Shuppankai, 1982), 102–11; Sheldon M. Garon, "The Imperial Bureaucracy and Labor Policy in Postwar Japan," *Journal of Asian Studies* 43 (3) (May 1984): 446–48; Garon, *The State and Labor,* 235–37. For the Japanese role in revision of the civil code, see Kurt Steiner, "Reform of the Japanese Civil Code," in Ward and Sakamoto, 188–220. On educational reforms, cf. *Senryoki Nihon Kyoiku ni kansuru Zai-Bei Shiryo no Chosa Kenkyu* (Tokyo: Sengo Kyoiku Kaikaku Shiryo 6, Kokuritsu Kyoiku Kenkyujo, March 1988). For the U.S.-Japan interplay in reforms involving local autonomy and the national charter, see Ward and Sakamoto and Kenzo Takayanagi, "Some Reminiscences of Japan's Commission on the Constitution," *Washington Law Review* 43 (5) (June 1968): 961–78. On the role of the former Home Ministry officials in "reverse course" policies, see Garon, "The Imperial Bureaucracy," 448–53. The "Red purges" are covered in J. W. Dower, *Empire and Aftermath: Yoshida Shigeru and the Japanese Experience, 1878–1954* (Cambridge: Council on East Asian Studies, Harvard University, 1979).

[20]See Johnson on these various aspects of MITI. Another recent historical study that identifies transwar influences as central to understanding postwar and contemporary Japan is Richard J. Samuels, *The Business of the Japanese State: Energy Markets in Comparative and Historical Perspective* (Ithaca: Cornell University Press, 1987), see esp. chap. 5.

The People Who Invented the Mechanical Nightingale

Chalmers Johnson

In Japan, the politicians reign, but the bureaucrats rule. The bureaucrats have brought Japan unparalleled economic success, accompanied by political underdevelopment. Japan, striving to catch up with Western powers, developed a unique system to achieve imitative results. The move toward democracy, stagnant since the early 1960s, has shown a recent resurgence, as Japan moves toward an effective multiparty system.

It is uncanny that in 1843, a decade before Perry's ships steamed into Edo Bay and more than a century before the Japanese began to inundate the world with Walkmen, Hondas, and FAX machines, Hans Christian Andersen supplied the most persistent metaphor of their civilization. In *The Nightingale,* Andersen invented the story of a Chinese emperor who banished his wonderfully singing nightingale in preference for a jeweled mechanical imitation sent to him by the emperor of Japan. The fake bird sang almost as well as the real thing and was much more consistent. But it finally broke a spring and fell silent, causing the emperor almost to die of despair. Then, on his deathbed, the emperor once again heard the song of the real nightingale and was miraculously revived.

This charming "children's" story is not either intentionally or inadvertently anti-Japanese. Stravinsky, who in 1916 set Andersen's tale to music as *Le Chant du Rossignol,* was not an early "Japan basher," as every foreigner who today dares to address Japan in a

Chalmers Johnson is Rohr Professor of Pacific International Relations at the University of California in San Diego.

philosophically critical manner is called. *The Nightingale* is simply declarative: if anyone was going to invent a really excellent mechanical bird, it would of course be the Japanese. That is to say, imitation lies at the heart of modern Japan's achievements and contributes to the persistent identity crisis that is the subject of endless treatises in its serious monthly magazines. The situation is well known to Japanese intellectuals, and they have invented many concepts and distinctions that allow them to discuss it—*tatemae* (aspirations) and *honne* (realities) are perhaps the best examples.[1] The people who do not understand this, who are in fact intellectually alarmed by it, are the English-speaking foreigners who must deal with Japan. They do not even begin to devote a fraction of the resources they should to the serious study of Japan (virtually nothing compared with the resources expended by the Japanese to study *them*), and they therefore try to comprehend Japan by projecting onto it their own norms, expectations, and theories about how the Japanese should behave.

Japan is not, of course, inherently imitative; and its indigenous culture is a distinctive amalgam of native feudal institutions and Chinese literary, religious, and philosophical influences. But the most important thing about contemporary Japan is that it was, like Germany, a late developer. It was not one of the original beneficiaries of the Industrial Revolution, and industrialism in Japan owes nothing to the "invisible hand" of Adam Smith. Industrialization in Japan was introduced from above, for political and not economic reasons, in order to counter the threat of Western imperialism, and with genuine foreign models as the only true measures of success or failure. Japan's modern achievements are imitative in their results but not in their methods.

Japan is part of the Sinitic cultural area. Although its heritage of feudalism and rule by a military aristocracy distinguish it from traditional Chinese society, Japan and China today share three things in common. The ethics of both countries derive from Confucianism even though Confucianism as a formal institution no longer exists in either society; both countries were more or less closed to contacts with the outside world from the seventeenth to the nineteenth centuries; and both countries came under the direct, military impact of Western imperialism in the space of fifteen years—the Opium War of 1839–1842 for the Chinese and the arrival of the U.S. Navy in

1853–1854 for the Japanese. After that their histories diverge completely.

China and Japan adopted diametrically opposite strategies for dealing with the challenges of the West, and each nation is today the embodiment of the strengths and weaknesses of its respective strategy. Japan pursued a course of domestic reform and emulation of the West; China pursued a course of domestic revolution and resistance to the West. Both carried these strategies to such extremes that by the midtwentieth century they could be considered as archetypes of reform and revolution. Japan has become by a very wide margin the most advanced industrial nation that set out to catch up with and surpass the countries whose modern wealth is based on the theories of English economists, and contemporary China is the product of the longest ongoing process of revolution among all known historical examples.

There were unintended consequences of each strategy, however. For Japan successful emulation has meant that it is very rich but also concerned that its process of modernization was one of Westernization; the Japanese remain deeply insecure about their achievements and what these may have cost them. For China successful resistance has meant that it remains very poor but also deeply satisfied by its unimpaired cultural uniqueness. The fact that the Japanese have institutes, magazines, and even a pseudoscience *(Nihonjinron)* devoted to studying what it means to be Japanese suggests that many of them suspect that it no longer means much at all.[2] The Chinese do not feel the need for such navel gazing.

In the Meiji era (1868–1912) the Japanese emulated the West in two ways. First, they adopted the West's scientific and technological culture and made it the foundation of their military machine, a machine that ensured that Japan, unlike China, would not be colonized or otherwise victimized by the West. Instead Japan joined the imperialists, tried to colonize China, and ended up as the only Asian nation to be included in the annual summit meeting of the world's seven leading industrialized democracies. Second, the Japanese emulated the West by creating a governmental structure of laws, institutions, and practices that were modeled on those of some Western nations but that operated differently and for different purposes. The Japanese did this not because they necessarily admired these Western institutions (as they did admire Western science and technology) but because it was prerequisite to ending the "unequal treaties" imposed on Japan by Perry and his successors. Foreigners did not give up exempting themselves from Japanese criminal laws and return to Japan the ability to set its own customs duties until they were convinced that Japan had become more or less their clone. It was always important, therefore, that foreigners not know how Japan really was governed. The Japanese became accustomed to and had an interest in living with a very broad difference between principle *(tatemae)* and actual practice *(honne)*.[3]

The *tatemae* of prewar Japan was that it was a constitutional monarchy operating under the rule of law, such laws being enacted by the representatives of the people who, since 1925, were elected by universal manhood suffrage. The *honne* of prewar Japan was that it was a capitalist developmental state, one that had creatively merged the effectiveness of bureaucratic absolutism with the efficiency of the bourgeois market but that was fundamentally unstable because of what Masao Maruyama has called the "system of irresponsibilities" built into it.[4]

Although it is a product of historical evolution and undoctrinaire experimentation rather than a single person's creative genius, the capitalist developmental state is probably Japan's most important invention. It combines private ownership of property with state goal setting. The state operates not by displacing the market, as under socialism, but by becoming a player in the market—creating incentives, supplying capital and information, lowering risks for approved activities, providing protection from foreign competitors, encouraging competition in strategic industries, and facilitating changes of industrial structure in order to keep as many high-value-added jobs in Japan as possible. The Japanese system was (and is) somewhat comparable to what in the United States is called "the military-industrial complex." It is based in part on an intentional blurring of the public and the private.[5] Achievements of privately owned and managed enterprises are regarded as national achievements, but any profit that results is treated as private property.

During the Allied Occupation following World War II, American reformers set out to dismantle this system. As we know today, they actually succeeded only in modernizing and rationalizing it. Many of the Occupation's reforms were long overdue in Japanese society, and many Japanese leaders not only welcomed them but helped the

Occupation to achieve them. These included such policies as land reform, extending the vote to women, eliminating the military from political life, and insisting that the emperor was only a symbol of the state, as he had normally been in the centuries before Meiji. But in one area, reform of industry, the Americans proved to be fundamentally misinformed about Japanese economic realities, blinded by their own ideology, and vacillating in terms of their goals for the economy.

They began by defining the wartime Japanese military-industrial complex as a threat to peace that arose from the misuse of *private* economic power. They therefore decided to break up the *zaibatsu*—that is, the big conglomerates such as Mitsubishi, Hitachi, Toshiba, Nissan, and Toyota that had been the government's chosen instruments for economic development. In their focus on the "private" sector, the Americans ignored the official economic bureaucracy that had actually guided the private sector. They did so for two reasons; the first was ideological—they could not imagine that the owners of the means of production might not also be responsible for what they produced—and the second was practical—they were using the economic bureaucracy to control Japan's war-ravaged economy and did not want to disturb it. As a result, the economic ministries, particularly the Ministry of Finance and the Ministry of International Trade and Industry (MITI, the postwar name for the wartime Ministry of Munitions), emerged from the Occupation not only unscathed but with their powers enhanced. They were also strengthened by the elimination or weakening of their major prewar competitors, the military and the *zaibatsu*.

The attempt to break up the *zaibatsu* took the form primarily of separating the descendants of the founding families from their ownership rights. Reform thus eliminated the families' tendency to become a rentier class and made the conglomerates leaner and more competitive with each other than they ever had been before the war. Moreover, by 1949, with the arrival in Tokyo of Ambassador Joseph Dodge and the isolation of General MacArthur from economic policy making, the priorities of the Americans shifted from economic democratization to economic rehabilitation. The Japanese call this shift in priorities the "reverse course." It reflected the failure of wartime American policy toward China and the United States' belated recognition of Japan's strategic importance in the developing Cold War.

The Americans did not think seriously about the powers and performance of the Japanese economic bureaucracy partly because they did not think it was necessary to do so. Never having experienced a government that performed developmental rather than regulatory functions in the economic area—or, more accurately, not focusing on the developmental functions performed by their own government because these were regarded as exceptional from the point of view of American economic ideology—they believed that any temporary excesses of state power displayed by Japanese officials could be checked by strengthening the bureaucracy's political overseers.

It was a plausible approach but it did not work. For more than half a century state officials in Japan, both military and civilian, had guided the country's development. These officials were an elite of talent, education, and access through family status to the centers of power in the society. By contrast, the political parties had come onto the scene after the ministries had already been created, and they had been seriously compromised in the 1930s by their inability to check the moves toward militarism and war. The Occupation tried to deal with the last problem by purging all older politicians, but this only made the contrast in talent between the bureaucrats and politicians more obvious. It should of course also be recalled that this was an indirect occupation: all American orders to the Japanese were funneled through and executed by the bureaucrats themselves. It did not require too much acumen on their part to protect and even enhance their own positions. Moreover, as a result of the "reverse course," by the time of the Korean War the Americans began to depurge most of the old politicians, a development that was in marked contrast to Allied policy in Germany.

With the return of sovereignty to Japan in 1952, the *tatemae* of politics looked something like an upgraded version of the 1920s. Japan was still a constitutional monarchy, operating under the rule of law, but the whole system had been formally strengthened. According to the American-inspired constitution of 1947, the Diet was now "the highest organ of state power" and the "sole law-making organ of the state" (Article 41). The Supreme Court, which has proved to be the most disappointing of all the institutions strengthened by the Occupation, was made "the court of last resort with power to determine the constitutionality of any law, order, regulation or official act" (Article 81). War had been renounced as a sovereign right of the nation, and land, sea, and air forces, "as well as other war potential," were never to be maintained (Article 9). "All of the people are equal under the law and there shall be no discrimination in political, economic or social relations, because of race, creed, sex, social status, or family origins" (Article 14), a set of stipulations that goes well beyond the unratified Equal Rights Amendment to the U.S. Constitution. Labor was given the right to organize and to bargain collectively (Article 28). "No person shall be convicted or punished in cases where the only proof against him is his own confession" (Article 38). And the right of the people to "life, liberty, and the pursuit of happiness" was declared to "be the supreme consideration in legislation and in other governmental affairs" (Article 13). No American could have said it better, but over time this constitution has proved to be more than a wishful document forced on a captive people by a conqueror. It inspired, and still inspires, a great deal of Japanese idealism; and it helped fuel the greatest period of democracy in Japan's history, from the coming into force of the constitution of 1947 until the Security Treaty riots of 1960.

The *honne* of the 1950s, however, unleashed forces that were to produce a very different political system after 1960. To begin with, the party system of the 1950s never measured up to the potentiality bequeathed it by the Occupation. Partly this was the Americans' fault. Their militarism and Cold War preoccupations caused them to tolerate all sorts of unsavory Japanese politicians who had conveniently become rabid anticommunists, and the Americans never looked with favor on the Japanese left's coming to power.

As for the left, Japan's labor parties split, as in Europe, into pro-democratic and pro-class-struggle factions, except that in Japan the class-struggle types were the majority. As a result the business community, not unreasonably, refused to countenance any political role for labor. Management and labor reached an implicit compromise after the bloody Mitsui Miike coal mine strike of 1960. In the future, business in the upper tier of Japanese industry would contribute to labor peace by providing all regular employees (male heads of households who joined an enterprise directly from school) with career job security. In return, labor was to transform its federations and industrial unions into company unions—usually just employees' associations run by foremen—which meant that labor would be restricted to the problems of a factory or an office and not have any influence on public policy. This was a development that was unimaginable from the point of view of the Occupation's mid-1940s labor reformers.[6] Generally speaking, labor is not exploited in Japan, even though wage increases are not commensurate with increases in productivity. But organized labor has never taken seriously the possibility that it might make a political contribution to society. This is one of the reasons that the government has been able to formulate and execute its industrial policy with such comparative ease.

The reactionary and conservative parties ran scared throughout the 1950s. In 1955, fearing growing electoral strength of the socialists, the conservatives amalgamated into a big coalition party, the Liberal Democratic Party (LDP), that held majorities in both houses of the Diet until July 1989. Almost as soon as the LDP was created, it began to display its most distinctive characteristic—it divided internally into four or five nonideological factions formed to reelect their members and advance the careers of their leaders. The roots of the LDP's factions are multiple. The most basic is the continuing ethos of patrimonial relations from Japan's feudal past and the tendency of all large Japanese organizations to structure themselves internally not into horizontal classes of members but into vertically divided competitive groups.[7]

More concretely, the factions reflect (1) differences between pure politicians and former bureaucrats who have entered politics upon retirement from officialdom; (2) the fact that the party president, who automatically becomes prime minister of Japan so long as the LDP retains its majority in the lower house, is not chosen by the people or in a convention but by negotiations among party leaders; (3) the fact that Japan has multimember constituencies in which each voter has only one vote but each district may return as many as five contestants, thus pitting members of the LDP against each other; and (4) the need for some system to reinvigorate a party that is normally always in power.

Over time the factions have become fixed features of the party, and the largest of them, such as that of former Prime Minister Kakuei Tanaka, developed into political machines.[8] As a result, since the 1950s all politics (although not necessarily all policy making) tended to go on within the LDP, the opposition parties having allowed themselves to be turned into ornaments to give citizens and the outside world the impression that Japan was a multiparty democracy. This situation only began to change in 1986 when the Socialist Party gave its chairmanship to Takako Doi, a woman and former professor of constitutional law. Although she was initially dismissed as a mere symbol, she led the party to its first victory over the LDP in the upper-house election of 1989. Part of her appeal was that she was not part of the old Socialist ideological disputes and, even more important, in an election that turned on the issue of corruption, none of the main interest groups had thought her important enough to bribe.

From the time of the Occupation and at least until Tanaka's prime ministership (1972–1974), the official bureaucracy made all the policies and actually supervised the government. This role reflected a continuity with the past—the emperor's officials *(tenno no kanri)* had always claimed and been granted greater legitimacy than the politicians—as well as the fact that at least a quarter of the LDP members in the Diet actually were ex-officials. In the 1950s and 1960s, the bureaucrats knew more about public policy than the politicians; and the constraints on a nation short on capital, forced to import all its raw materials, and unwilling to trust its key investment decisions to the market, meant that economic management had to be put in the hands of impartial, technical experts. They became famous for the results they achieved, further legitimizing their policy role. As a result the tradition developed that the politicians reign but the bureaucrats rule. This is still largely true today, but the relationship has gotten more complex; and it is no longer clear who is responsible for formulating public policy.[9]

Generally speaking, the postwar system worked well so long as the only people participating in it were Japanese and the economy was growing at a double-digit rate. But whenever the bureaucrats were divided among themselves or the unintended consequences of their own policies started to mobilize the people, as was the case with pollution, the machinery slowed down. It fell apart completely whenever the Japanese were forced to deal with international problems or when they had to conform to standards not of their own making—as, for example, in ratifying the Japanese-American Security Treaty in 1960, in normalizing relations with South Korea in 1965, in normalizing relations with China in 1972 and 1978, and in attempting to deliver on Japan's innumerable promises to the rest of the world to open its domestic markets to international trade. Each of these issues produced major internal political instability, sometimes resulting in the resignation of the prime minister, or else there was only a pretense of a policy for external consumption while internal patterns continued unchanged.

Given its structural contradictions, Japan currently lacks the capacity for true political leadership. Its most experienced leaders acknowledge that public opinion, as distinct from the influence of special-interest groups, has almost no effect on the political system except in a crisis and that the equivalent of public opinion in other systems is pressure from abroad *(gaiatsu)*.[10] This impasse, and the strenuous efforts of Japan's professional intermediaries with the outside world to disguise it, derives from the continuing separation between reigning and ruling, which tends to recreate Masao Maruyama's system of irresponsibilities in new forms. Maruyama identified the prewar personae of Japanese politics as *mikoshi* ("portable shrines," those with authority but no real power, the emperor being the ultimate example); officials (meaning the actually ruling bureaucrats, although neither the prewar nor the postwar constitutions authorized them to do so); and *ronin* ("masterless samurai," or "outlaws," those whose acts force the *mikoshi* and officials to attempt to legitimate them after the fact). In this system the *mikoshi* were responsible, but since they could not do anything it was a meaningless responsibility—which is why the Japanese people have held the Showa emperor largely blameless for the disasters that befell them during his reign.

The situation today is different from that prevailing before the war, but the influence of the old system is still discernible. The portable shrines are now the leaders of LDP factions—that is, the formal, extrinsic political leaders of the nation. The officials are still the officials, except that economic officials have now replaced military officials as the makers of national strategy. And the *ronin* have proliferated mightily. They now include leaders of the major interest groups (farmers, physicians, small retailers, and so forth), covert financial backers of the LDP (for example, the construction industry), the demimonde (reformed gangsters, *sokaiya, jiageya,* ultranationalists, and the unscrupulous generally), and anybody with a lot of money (for example, Hiromasa Ezoe, the former chairman of an up-and-coming publishing, telecommunications, real estate, and financial services conglomerate named Recruit Company, which during 1986 managed to bribe almost the entire Japanese ruling establishment).*

During the 1950s and 1960s the LDP reigned over the political process, spending most of its time raising money for its own reelection and fighting off charges of corruption; the bureaucrats initiated all major policies; and the electorally significant interest groups whose votes the LDP needed, primarily farmers in thinly populated but never reapportioned districts, were paid off. Big business is not a separate interest group in Japan; it is the prime beneficiary and virtual *raison d'être* of the Japanese system, as the theory of the capitalist developmental state stipulates. For that reason it is meaningless to speak of the role of big business in Japanese politics; the two are indistinguishable. The Japanese system of political economy as it was formulated in the 1950s and particularly after the Security Treaty crisis of 1960, intentionally favored manufacturing over all other activities, exporters over importers, producers over consumers, and industrial needs over environmental needs. The intent of the system was to rebuild Japan economically and free it from dependence on U.S. foreign aid and offshore procurements. Over time vested interests developed around these priorities, including vested interests in the continuing reign of the LDP and the groups the party relied on to ensure its reelection. Tension began to build within the system during the late 1960s as the need to alter the priorities of the high-growth system (by, for example, ending protectionism and servicing domestic demand) increasingly clashed with the old arrangements to keep the LDP in power.

During the 1970s the relationship between the LDP and the bureaucracy also began to change. Long-serving LDP politicians began to rival and challenge the bureaucrats in terms of policy expertise. Some politicians became known as *zoku giin,* literally "tribal Diet members" as in the "postal tribe" or the "welfare tribe" but actually meaning sectoral policy specialists and deal makers. This had the effect of politicizing policy making much more than it had been in the past, since politicians were more susceptible to the favors

---

**Sokaiya* (general meeting specialists) are extortionists who intimidate large companies by threatening to disrupt their annual stockholders' meetings; *jiageya* (land-price-rise specialists) are thugs who force small landowners to sell their property so that it can be traded on Tokyo's speculative real estate market. Both groups have long been tolerated by Japanese police and politicians.

of special-interest groups than the bureaucrats. The end of high-speed growth and the appearance of large government deficits also meant that the bureaucracy could no longer dominate the system by giving everybody something. Interministerial conflicts over jurisdiction grew as the issues facing Japanese society changed but the ministries did not; the politicians were often called on to resolve these disputes. New interest groups tended to cultivate politicians because rival older interest groups had already developed symbiotic relationships with the ministries (for example, securities trading companies favored politicians because banks were already close to the Ministry of Finance). And smart bureaucrats, thinking of their own soon-to-come *amakudari* (descent from heaven) into the private sector, avoided highly controversial subjects, such as defense or school textbooks, that might embroil them in political conflict.[11]

The result was the appearance of what Karel van Wolferen has called the "headless chicken" or the "truncated pyramid"—the "headless monster" for short—meaning a Japanese system in which no one was ultimately in charge.[12] The economy ran on unchecked, and no one could cause it to change course: prime ministers went to Washington or to summit meetings and made promises, but with their only authority coming from their fellow faction leaders in the LDP, they lacked the power to force the bureaucracy to act; the bureaucrats spent more and more time servicing *zoku giin* as a way of fighting their own turf battles; and the old vested interests dug in their heels against the promises made to foreigners and consumers.

As the last months of Showa unfolded, the anomalies of the Japanese political process began to pile up. Japan emerged as the world's richest nation in terms of per capita income, even though its per capita consumption changed hardly at all (indicating that it was not the Japanese "people" who were getting rich). The figures for 1988 were $23,765 as Japan's per capita gross national product, compared with $19,050 for the United States, even though per capita consumption in Japan was only 63 percent of the U.S. level.[13] On a different front, the Japan Civil Liberties Union celebrated its fortieth anniversary by chronicling a record during the most recent decade of a steady retreat in defending, much less advancing, the civil and human rights listed in Japan's constitution, particularly as they concern discrimination against the Korean, Chinese, and other minority people who permanently reside in Japan but who are not protected by the Japanese government.[14] The Supreme Court managed to make a shambles of the separation of church and state (Article 20 of the constitution) by upholding the right of the state to give a Self-Defense Force officer who had died in an automobile accident a Shinto ceremony for the dead over the objections of the widow. Japan continued to achieve monumental trade surpluses, even though its prominent economists and bankers, such as the late Haruo Maekawa, former governor of the Bank of Japan, warned that the excess of exports over imports was untenable and advised the government to enact a new land-use law in order to serve the huge unmet demand for better housing and an improved quality of life.[15]

All of this was capped, on December 9, 1988, by the resignation of Kiichi Miyazawa, the minister of finance, because his secretary admitted making $181,130 on an insider stock trading deal. Prime Minister Takeshita himself temporarily assumed the post of minister of finance because there were no other senior members of the party who had not been equally involved in the stock scam, even though associates of the prime minister had also received stock from the Recruit Company before it was officially listed on the stock exchange and for sale to the general public. Typical of experienced *mikoshi,* the LDP faction leaders received their bribes—actually advance payments for future favors, a form of *nemawashi* (preparing the groundwork)—in the form of payments to their secretaries, whereas the senior bureaucrats and businessmen involved, new to the game, accepted theirs in their own names.[16]

Before it was all over, Takeshita resigned as prime minister when the LDP's popularity in the public opinion polls fell to under 2 percent. Sosuke Uno replaced him but promptly made the situation worse by seeming to insult Japanese women through his extramarital liaisons. The prosecutors eventually indicted some thirteen people on charges of bribery, but only two were politicians even though some sixteen politicians admitted publicly that they had received payoffs from the Recruit Company. The long-suffering Japanese public had finally had enough. In the upper-house election of July 23, 1989, they for the first time failed to give the LDP its customary majority.

The election turned on many issues other than the Recruit scandal. Probably the most important was the phenomenon known as "rich Japan, poor Japanese," meaning that the upward revaluation of the yen against the value of the U.S. dollar by some 60 percent since 1985 had made the Japanese the world's richest people on paper but not in their lives.[17] They still commuted to work for an average hour and a half each way in incredibly overcrowded trains, lived in minuscule apartments that they could never afford to buy, and spent more than a third of their household income on food. To add insult to injury, the Ministry of Finance forced the LDP to enact a poorly constructed and inequitably administered sales tax at precisely the same moment the Recruit scandal revealed that LDP members and other insiders were being paid millions of yen by people trying to buy access to the government.

The Socialist Party was the net gainer in the July 1989 election, but its victory was based on a patently unstable coalition. Takako Doi had temporarily put together urban labor union members; women voters outraged over prices, taxes, and gender discrimination; and farmers in revolt against the LDP because the party had slightly breached the protection against all forms of international competition they had enjoyed for more than thirty years. This contradictory coalition is obviously fragile, and if the Socialists stick to their position on agricultural protection they will doom the so-called Uruguay round of GATT negotiations and guarantee retaliation against Japan's exports. The real significance of the July 1989 election was that, for the first time, it broke the grip of vested interests on the Japanese political system and opened up the possibility that Japan might resume its development toward democracy, a process that has been more or less on hold since the 1960s.

The fundamental problem of Japanese politics since the Meiji era has been to contain the social tensions generated by extremely high-speed economic growth. Writers in English-speaking countries commonly believe that economic growth, particularly if it is achieved under capitalist auspices, facilitates political stability and even democratization.[18] The opposite is actually the case. As Hans-Ulrich Wehler has argued concerning Bismarckian Germany:

> One of the dangerous legends of contemporary development-politics is the belief that rapid economic growth promotes social and political stability, and inhibits radical and irresponsible policies. Historical experience has shown however that rapid growth produces extremely acute economic, social and political problems. Germany is a particularly illuminating case. Here, after the breakthrough of the industrial revolution 1834/50–1873, industrialization was necessarily associated

> with a large number of profound difficulties in Germany's internal development. More than half a century ago, Thorstein Veblen stated the basic problem: the absorption of the most advanced technology by a largely traditional society within a then unprecedentedly short time. And one of the most important contemporary experts on the problems of economic growth, Alexander Gerschenkron, had the German experience in mind when he propounded his general theory that the faster and the more abrupt a country's industrial revolution, the more intractable and complex will be the problems associated with industrialization.[19]

Japan is an excellent illustration of these relationships.

As we have seen, Japan's industrialization occurred from above for political reasons in accordance with the goals of small, self-appointed elites. In the Meiji era these elites were the oligarchs who had engineered the Restoration; in the 1930s these elites were militarists and their bureaucratic and industrial collaborators who came to power essentially through coup d'état; and in the 1950s and 1960s these elites were economic bureaucrats of the central government who were attempting to rebuild Japan and restore self-respect to its people. The economic interventions of these elites have produced three clear cycles in which bureaucratism displaced underlying trends of democratization. Rokuro Hidaka periodizes them as follows:

Cycle One: (a) Meiji Restoration, 1869 to c. 1890, a period of "enlightenment" with movements toward liberty, people's rights, and democracy; (b) 1890 to c. 1912, a period of nationalism and imperialism, in which democracy waned.

Cycle Two: (a) 1912 to 1931, a period in which attempts were made to bring the absolutist system under democratic constraints, known as the era of Taisho Democracy; (b) 1931 to 1945, a period of militarism, ultranationalism, and the suppression of all democratic tendencies.

Cycle Three: (a) 1945 to 1960, a period of intense democratization in the wake of Japan's defeat and the reforms of the Allied Occupation; (b) 1960 to 1989, a period of high-speed economic growth based in part on single-party government and the avoidance of political problems.

Concerning the main postwar cycle, Hidaka argues:

> In the prewar period, the state unified the Japanese people by fostering loyalty to the Emperor. Today, the state coopts the people by elaborately redistributing profits to meet the people's expectations. . . . The high-growth economy made the ability to redistribute profits possible. The postwar period can be divided into two phases: the phase of postwar democracy and the phase of high-economic growth. . . . The high-growth economy of Japan which began in the 1960s created a new state completely different in quality from the Japanese state during or immediately after the war.[20]

During the bureaucratic phases of these cycles, comparable to the Bismarckian era in German development, Japanese elites had to devise systems of government that reconciled their goals with the mass politics inherent in modernized, mobilized, nontraditional societies with highly developed markets, private ownership of property, and large cities—i.e., sectors and locales in which self-government and autonomy was the only feasible form of social organization. Except tentatively during World War II, Japan has not resorted to the despotism inherent in Leninism and Stalinism, which is one of the reasons why it is more developed than either Russia or China.

The political solutions that Japanese elites have come up with are variations on the following four-part model. First, at the center is an establishment that perpetuates itself through a conservative alliance among the minimally necessary interest groups. Second, the elite takes preemptive measures to forestall formation of a mass alliance that could interfere with its goals; above all it prevents the emergence of a unified labor movement. Third, the elite develops and propagates ideologies to try to convince the public that the social conditions in their country are the result of anything—culture, history, language, national character, climate, and so forth—other than politics. Fourth, the elite undertakes diversionary activities that promote national pride but that also deflect attention from constitutional development. The most common such diversion, learned from Bismarck, has been imperialism—but export promotion and competition for market share may be even more engrossing.

At the heart of this model is the conservative alliance that keeps the elite establishment in power. In the late Meiji era, after the promulgation of the Meiji constitution, the conservative allies were the imperial household, the Meiji oligarchs, landowners, and the original *zaibatsu*.[21] In the militarist era, after the seizure of Manchuria, the conservative allies were the imperial household, military leaders, the economic bureaucracy, and the new *zaibatsu*. In the era of high-speed growth, the conservative allies were the economic bureaucracy, the LDP, and the leaders of big business. Since elections were now unavoidable, this elite made the narrow interests of farmers and small retailers sacrosanct so long as they voted for the LDP.

The other elements of the model can be only briefly touched on here. The great contribution of Karel van Wolferen's *The Enigma of Japanese Power* is to show in great detail that the ideology of Japanese uniqueness that accompanied postwar high-speed growth was, in fact, an ideology. It was perhaps not as dangerous as the ideology of personal sacrifice for the emperor, but it had the same effect: to convince Japanese that *gaman* (austerity and perseverance) was in their genes. The postwar implementation of the model also differed in other important ways from the prewar precedents. The difference between export promotion and imperialism is only too obvious and much to the credit of Japan's postwar elites. The essence of the model is the elite's recognition that high-speed economic growth for political rather than economic reasons generates social problems that may render the country ungovernable. The elite distrusts democracy because it expects that any attempt at broad-based democracy will cause the society to spiral out of control. This was the lesson learned by Japanese elites during the Security Treaty crisis of 1960: the combination of economic growth guided by MITI plus mass democracy threatened to turn Japan toward revolution. It was thought necessary to divert attention from constitutional issues in order to avoid serious instability. Prime Minister Ikeda did precisely this with his "income doubling plan."

A Bismarckian, late-economic-development perspective on Japanese politics is useful in attempting to understand the central paradox of Japanese politics. Japan is extraordinarily powerful and adept when engaged in routine matters of production and marketing but extraordinarily vacillating and inept when confronted with critical issues requiring vision and choice. It is not that Japan cannot make cardinal decisions or respond to changes in its environment, as its performance in the wake of the 1970s oil price hikes demonstrated. Japan is not a "headless monster" when the need for action is obvious and unavoidable. But Japan's elites must have overwhelmingly powerful incentives to undertake basic changes of policy, since these involve disturbing or even breaking the conservative political alliance. Basic shifts of policy in Japan require social changes of an almost revolutionary magnitude, and the elites are always fearful that they will lose control of the process.

For foreign nations attempting to influence Japanese policy making, it is essential to remember that the obstacles to basic change in Japan are almost never what Japanese spokesmen say they are. What stands in the way is not the need for consensus, or an island mentality, or racial and cultural differences. The obstacles to change are invariably political vested interests, but these may be harder to address and to alter than in other political systems. This is so because although the *tatemae* of Japan is a constitutional monarchy operating under the rule of law, the *honne* is a developmental state based on a covert conservative alliance to keep the people docile and preoccupied with nonessential matters. Such a system can change, but only when the status quo has clearly become untenable.

It is possible that the social forces mobilized and set in motion by the political crisis of 1989 will lead to renewed and sustained democratic development in Japan. The strongest reason for optimism is that some of the people who voted against the LDP were motivated by personal frustrations. Too often in the past Japan's attempts at democracy were based on foreign examples or pressures and lacked indigenous roots. In order to thrive, democracy in Japan must be something that the Japanese people themselves create. It is also possible that Japan's persistent configuration of great economic development, significant social development, and serious political underdevelopment will generate such instability that a new repressive conservative alliance will come into being. Friends of Japanese democracy can affect this outcome only if they understand clearly the origins and nature of Japan's political development and are responsive to both its strengths and weaknesses.

ENDNOTES

[1]For other examples, see Chalmers Johnson, "*Omote* (Explicit) and *Ura* (Implicit): Translating Japanese Political Terms," *Journal of Japanese Studies* 6 (1) (1980): 89–115.

[2]On *Nihonjinron,* see, *inter alia,* Takeshi Umehara, "Watakushi wa Yamatoisuto de wa nai" (I Am Not a Yamatoist), *Chuo koron* (August 1987): 242–57; Ian

Buruma, "Umehara Takeshi-shi wa yahari Yamatoisuto" (Takeshi Umehara is Too a Yamatoist), *Chuo koron* (October 1987): 236–43; brochure of the International Research Center for Japanese Studies, Takeshi Umehara, director general, Kyoto, October 1988; Harumi Befu, "Internationalization of Japan and Nihon Bunkaron," in Hiroshi Mannari and Harumi Befu, eds., *The Challenge of Japan's Internationalization* (Tokyo: Kodansha International, 1986); Peter N. Dale, *The Myth of Japanese Uniqueness* (London: Croom Helm, 1986); and James Fallows, "The Japanese Are Different from You and Me," *The Atlantic* (September 1986): 35–41. For an example of *Nihonjinron* in English, see Shoichi Watanabe, *The Peasant Soul of Japan* (New York: St. Martin's Press, 1989).

[3]The best study of Japan's emulation of the West is D. Eleanor Westney, *Imitation and Innovation: The Transfer of Western Organizational Patterns to Meiji Japan* (Cambridge: Harvard University Press, 1987).

[4]Masao Maruyama, "Thought and Behavior Patterns of Japan's Wartime Leaders," in Ivan Morris, ed., *Thought and Behavior in Modern Japanese Politics* (New York: Oxford University Press, 1969), 128. On the capitalist development state, see Chalmers Johnson, *MITI and the Japanese Miracle* (Stanford: Stanford University Press, 1982), and "Political Institutions and Economic Performance: The Government-Business Relationship in Japan, South Korea, and Taiwan," in Frederic C. Deyo, ed., *The Political Economy of the New Asian Industrialism* (Ithaca: Cornell University Press, 1987).

[5]See Patricia Boling, "Public and Private in Japan," *The Pacific Review* (forthcoming).

[6]See Theodore Cohen, *Remaking Japan: The American Occupation as New Deal* (New York: Free Press, 1987). During 1946 and 1947, Cohen was chief of the Labor Division in General MacArthur's headquarters.

[7]The locus classicus on Japanese-type vertical organization is Chie Nakane, *Japanese Society* (Berkeley: University of California Press, 1970).

[8]Chalmers Johnson, "Tanaka Kakuei, Structural Corruption, and the Advent of Machine Politics in Japan," *Journal of Japanese Studies* 12 (1) (Winter 1986): 1–28.

[9]See Clyde V. Prestowitz, Jr., *Trading Places: How We Allowed Japan to Take the Lead* (New York: Basic Books, 1988).

[10]See the dialogue between Masao Kamei, chairman of Sumitomo Electric, and Nihachiro Hanamura, adviser to Keidanren, in *Seiron* (September 1988): 110–21.

[11]See H. Fukui, "The Policy Research Council of Japan's Liberal Democratic Party: Policy-making Role and Practice," *Asian Thought and Society* 12 (March 1987): 3–30; and Chalmers Johnson, "MITI, MPT, and the Telecom Wars: How Japan Makes Policy for High Technology," in Chalmers Johnson, Laura Tyson, and John Zysman, eds., *Politics and Productivity: The Real Story of Why Japan Works* (New York: Ballinger, 1989).

[12]K. van Wolferen, *The Enigma of Japanese Power* (New York: Knopf, 1989), 39, 41.

[13]U.S. Congress, Joint Economic Committee, *Restoring International Balance: Japan's Trade and Investment Patterns* (Washington, D.C.: Joint Economic Committee Staff Study, 1988), 47. These figures are calculated on an exchange rate of U.S.$1=¥125.

[14]See "Celebrating the Fortieth Anniversary of the Japan Civil Liberties Union," *Law in Japan* 20 (1987): 1–73.

[15]See Kenneth B. Pyle, ed., *The Trade Crisis: How Will Japan Respond?* (Seattle: Society for Japanese Studies, 1987); and Chalmers Johnson, "Understanding the Japanese Economy: Barriers to Increasing Trade," *Economic Development Quarterly* 2 (3) (August 1988): 211–16.

[16]For details, see Asahi Shimbun, Yokohama Shikyoku, *Tsuiseki rikuruto giwaku* (Pursuing the Recruit Scandal), (Tokyo: Asahi Shimbun Sha, 1988).

[17]For an evaluation of just how rich Japan has become, see R. Taggart Murphy, "Power without Purpose: The Crisis of Japan's Global Financial Dominance," *Harvard Business Review* (March-April 1989): 71–83.

[18]Cf. Chalmers Johnson, "South Korean Democratization: The Role of Economic Development," *The Pacific Review* 2 (1) (1989): 1–10.

[19]Hans-Ulrich Wehler, "Bismarck's Imperialism 1862–1890," *Past and Present* 48 (1970): 119–53. My thanks to Peter Gourevitch for drawing this important study to my attention.

[20]Rokuro Hidaka, "Personal Retrospective," in Gavan McCormack and Yoshio Sugimoto, eds., *Democracy in Contemporary Japan* (Armonk, N.Y.: M. E. Sharpe, 1986): 228–46.

[21]The exact nature and forms of the conservative alliances in prewar Japan were the focus of one of the most important Marxist debates in this century. See Germaine A. Hoston, *Marxism and the Crisis of Development in Prewar Japan* (Princeton: Princeton University Press, 1986).

Japan Meets the United States for the Second Time

Makoto Iokibe

B*e "good losers" was the message of Japan's first postwar foreign minister to the defeated populace. During the seven years of the Occupation, the Americans achieved their goals of democratization and demilitarization. As the Japanese saw the "advantages of doing the inevitable," the nation took the first steps toward its current position of world power.*

In the summer of 1853, Commodore Matthew C. Perry led a fleet of U.S. ships into Tokyo Bay and demanded that Japan establish diplomatic relations with the United States and other nations. The appearance of the "black ships" immediately divided Japan's ruling class into two camps: those for and those against opening the country's doors. Those in favor viewed the military superiority of Western civilization (and most conspicuously, of its warships) as an incontrovertible reality and saw no reasonable alternative to opening the country and learning from the West. Those against demanded that "the barbarians" be expelled; opposed to capitulation from a position of weakness, they advocated resistance and defense of Japan's cultural identity and ethnic pride.

United States–Japan relations before World War II passed through three stages: (1) fifty years of initial, albeit superficial, friendship; (2) twenty-five years of see-sawing between cooperation and conflict; and (3) ten years of hostility that culminated in the attack on Pearl Harbor of December 7, 1941.

Makoto Iokibe is Professor of History in the Department of Law at Kobe University.

In a sense, the United States determined the destiny of modern Japan: America's existence and influence were decisive factors in the opening of Japan to the outside world, in the establishment of its empire, and in the path that its leaders took. By misjudging its most important bilateral tie and attacking the United States, Japan committed an error that imperiled the Meiji empire, and it was the United States that delivered the coup de grace.

Restricting our examination to the period following 1931, we can say that in almost every respect, this outcome resulted from a series of aggressive and thoughtless blunders by Japan. But if we trace events further back to the era of mixed cooperation and conflict, America undeniably shares responsibility because of its insensitive handling of the immigration question, which injured Japanese ethnic pride and made it difficult for Japan's leaders to promote cooperation. Nor did the U.S. government's attempts to restrain Japan after the Manchurian Incident demonstrate much foresight. The United States might more effectively have shocked Japan by applying economic sanctions immediately.

But, citing the risk of war, President Hoover restrained Secretary of State H. L. Stimson from applying economic sanctions. Only after 1939, when Japan had racked up so many military and diplomatic coups, did the U.S. government resort to economic sanctions "to avoid war"—with the result not of checking but of provoking Japan.

In retrospect, the more appropriate course for preserving peace would probably have been to take strong action from the start. But during the 1930s, domestic constraints made it difficult for both Japan and the United States to adopt rational external policies.

Three factors are generally held to be important in determining whether a defeated nation later seeks revenge on its conqueror: the way a war is ended, the conditions of peace, and the style of postwar international relations. Peace treaties, above all, define the way a defeated nation reacts.

In postwar Japan, however, Occupation policy was much more important than the Peace Treaty of San Francisco. What would normally have been required under the terms of a peace treaty was accomplished through Occupation reforms.

THE TWO SIDES OF OCCUPATION POLICY

The U.S. Occupation of Japan was simultaneously severe and lenient, both to an unprecedentedly high degree.

Severity

The severity of the Occupation resided first in its scope and duration. Usually victors do not occupy more territory than what they hold at the time hostilities end. When Japan accepted the terms of the Potsdam Declaration on August 15, 1945, only Okinawa was occupied by the Allies and the main central islands of Japan had yet to be subdued, but the Allied powers began to move into every part of Japan. Such total occupation of a country that has surrendered before being invaded is rare.

Article 43 of the Hague Regulations Concerning the Laws and Customs of War on Land (1907) stipulates that changes in the laws and institutions of a conquered nation are not to be made "except in cases of absolute necessity." The customary interpretation of *absolute necessity* is military security. After the war, Allied troops were stationed throughout Japan, not out of military necessity but with the intent of totally reforming Japan's domestic institutions. Since by accepting the Potsdam Declaration, Japan had agreed to this situation, it did not constitute a violation of international law.

Nonetheless, the occupation of all territories, in concept and practice, undeniably contradicts the spirit of international law and historical precedent. The international law against belligerency is premised on the wisdom of nations limiting how they wage war and occupy other nations. The two world wars that took place in this century were conducted on an unparalleled scale, however, making it possible to argue for the universal benefit of destroying a country's capacity to wage a war of aggression. It became justifiable for the winner to impose domestic reforms on a defeated nation that had waged an aggressive war in fulfillment of the duty to preserve peace, a value transcending the principle of noninterference in nations' internal affairs. Following this logic, the United States occupied Japan for many years after its defeat and subjected it to compulsory reforms affecting every aspect of its society, although it had laid down its arms before its home soil was attacked. In short, the Occupation of Japan by the United States was, by historical standards, extraordinarily invasive.

Leniency

If the Occupation of Japan by the United States had been severe in every respect, however, the Japanese would not respond to questionnaires as most do today by citing the United States as the foreign country they trust most or like best. Why have U.S.-Japan relations remained stable and friendly since the Occupation, despite its rigor? The reason lies in the unexpected leniency and constructive nature of the U.S. Occupation policies.

Many Japanese believed that men would be enslaved and women raped *en masse* if the "Anglo-Saxon beasts" invaded Japan. Some even prophesied the annihilation of the Japanese race. This propaganda fanned racial prejudice and was aimed at preparing the masses for final resistance against the foe. Some Japanese soldiers with field experience took the warnings literally, for they remembered comparable mayhem during the Japanese army's Asian campaigns.

Taking the possibility of retribution into account, Japan had every reason to anticipate a catastrophic defeat. The vanquished Japanese expected to meet their nemesis but found instead that American troops were good-natured and kind, often doing such things as giving chewing gum to children. At first the Japanese authorities isolated the Occupation troops to prevent unpleasantness but later began to let down their guard and came to feel quite at ease with the occupiers.

On the other side, arriving American troops expected to meet guerrilla-style resistance and terrorism—or at the very least, open verbal hostility. Nervously disembarking from their ships, troop carriers, and aircraft with their guns at the ready, they found the Japanese to be instead quiet and cooperative. The Americans were as relieved as the Japanese.

Even more important was the nature of Occupation policies. The ultimate objective of the United States was to ensure that Japan would never again threaten U.S. security. It regarded two measures as necessary to accomplish this goal: demilitarization and democratization. Both were exhaustively enforced. Not only were all Japanese soldiers disarmed and demobilized, but the Japanese military organization was completely dismantled. All militaristic and ultranationalistic organizations were abolished, military leaders were tried for war crimes or at the very least purged from public office, and the imperial colonies were freed. Believing that strongly authoritarian and centralized political power had facilitated Japanese aggression, the United States decentralized Japan's national government organs, established individual human rights, gave voters (notably women) a greater voice in politics, and reinforced local autonomy. Democracy was regarded as crucial to preserving peace.

On the economic side, the United States completely disassembled the arms industry, but also dissolved *zaibatsu* (large industrial and financial combinations) and abolished monopolies; the United States promoted workers' rights through the fostering of union membership, and it confiscated large landholdings and helped tenant farmers acquire acreage through land reform policies. All this was done in the belief that an economic structure concentrating the rewards of industry in the hands of a privileged few and not benefiting the common people had left domestic markets underdeveloped, aggravated the need for overseas markets, and goaded the military to aggression.

Many Japanese in positions of responsibility viewed demilitarization and democracy with obvious displeasure. But if they voiced their discontent, they did it in a whisper. With surprisingly little resistance, most Japanese accepted, indeed welcomed, demilitarization and democratization.

One reason was the shock of defeat. Japan had made an unwise gamble, had lost, and was resigned to the inevitable. Another reason was that the Japanese people desired peace and democracy.

Japan's modern history thus far had been a pursuit of two long-term goals: liberalization and reform on the one hand and military power on the other. Depending on the period, emphasis was always being shifted between the two poles. For example, Japan's best experience with political parties had been after World War I, a time when the movement for peace and democracy made great strides. After it gained political control during the 1930s, the military proceeded to force the country to grow through military expansion. It was therefore entirely consistent with the internal logic of Japanese history for the pendulum to swing again toward democracy. People were sick of war and wanted nothing to do with either militarism or nationalism.

Also important was that the victor presented these policies not vindictively as punishment but idealistically as reforms based on values shared by the postwar international community.

JAPANESE ACCEPTANCE OF THE OCCUPATION

Between May and June 1945, the political leaders of the United States and Japan formulated the desire to avoid a continuation of the war. America showed itself prepared to step down from an insistence on unconditional surrender, if by doing so it could bring about an early end to the war. The rational course for the Japanese government would have been to announce Japan's capitulation to the United States in the middle of June 1945. Suzuki Kantaro's Cabinet had been informed in early June that Japan could resist only until August or September at the latest, for most of its military and commercial fleets had already been sunk or incapacitated and its railroads severed. Although the terms of surrender would not have differed substantially, a mid-June surrender would have prevented two months of tragedy and destruction at home and abroad, including the atom bombing of Hiroshima and Nagasaki and the Soviet Union's entry into the Pacific War and the consequent loss of Japan's northern territories.

However, at the time, the Japanese government did not have sufficient information to detect the crucial change that had taken place at the top levels of government in Washington. It had to wait until July 26 for the Potsdam Declaration. Although Minister of Foreign Affairs Togo Shigenori, Prime Minister Suzuki, and Emperor Hirohito recognized the declaration's significance as a step toward ending the war, the Japanese army exerted strong pressure on the prime minister to reject it. He was thus forced to make his famous *mokusatsu* statement to the press, which was inevitably interpreted overseas as the Japanese decision to ignore the Potsdam Declaration.

Article 6 of the Potsdam Declaration announced that militarists in Japan would be deprived of their authority and power forever. It is naive to believe that a military organization in the midst of a "sacred war" will meekly accept conditions that signify its annihilation. Japanese soldiers would continue to fight given the slightest hope of winning. As proclaimed by the minister of the army, Anami Korechika, it was a matter of "ethnic pride." Mindful of the heroes who had died before them, they found it easier in their psychology to ask for a glorious death than a dishonorable surrender.

Bearing the Unbearable

Why was it impossible for Japan to back off from such a colossal impending catastrophe?

First, the Meiji system was not up to the task. The Cabinet was required to reach decisions not by a majority, but unanimously. A single dissenting member sufficed to postpone any decision; the only alternative was for the entire Cabinet to resign *en bloc* over the discrepancy. The prime minister was merely *primus inter pares,* with no power to dismiss a fellow Cabinet member. He therefore could not modify a policy until he had every member's consent. In July 1945, a change in Japan's war policy could not be made, however reasonable and necessary, simply because the military had exercised its political privilege to block surrender.

Even after two cities had been destroyed by atom bombs and a new foe, the Soviet Union, had entered the war, the system was still unable to overcome the military's official opposition. However, a subtle but discernible change did occur in the way the military opposed capitulation.

Although the minister of the army continued to espouse last-ditch resistance, deep down he could not help thinking that his country's cause was lost. Anami did not modify his official position, but he no longer resisted the opposing faction's efforts to make peace as tenaciously as before.

The Supreme War Council meeting, held in the emperor's presence the night of August 9, ended up split into two equal camps (three versus three) as a result of Minister of the Navy Yonai Mitsumasa and Privy Council Chairman Hiranuma Kiichiro's support of Foreign Minister Togo. The fact that Prime Minister Suzuki, presiding over the meeting, could have broken the tie if the majority had had the power to make a decision was irrelevant. Suzuki stated that the situation was so grave as not to allow a single moment's delay, and because of the exceptional circumstances, turned to the emperor and asked him to decide the question—a step that had never before been taken in modern Japanese history.

Today, the decision in such cases would be made by the prime minister. But under the Meiji constitution, a crisis affecting the nation's destiny could be submitted to the emperor for his "sacred decision." Unable to reach a unanimous decision, with the Cabinet neither postponing the decision nor resigning *en bloc*, Suzuki took the exceptional measure of returning decision-making power to the sovereign. It was a momentary, but momentous, restoration of imperial rule.

The Japanese race was in danger of extinction if the war continued; preserving even part of the nation left a glimmer of hope that it could rise again in the future. Emperor Hirohito was unexpectedly masterful at making the decision that it was best to "bear the unbearable, endure the unendurable, and seek peace."

Still, it was not enough just to hand down a rational decision. In a country where the emperor's subjects customarily prostrated themselves, obeyed in fear and trembled whenever the emperor made an announcement, there was an insurmountable psychological hurdle to opposing his pronouncements. Whether the "sacred decision" was a departure from customary practice under constitutional government or not, opposition to his sacred will was treason.

This notwithstanding, the emperor's words were invalid without the signatures of each of his Cabinet ministers, according to Article 55 of the Meiji constitution. Had the minister of the army refused to sign on the pretext that the organization he represented would not modify its stand, the imperial decision would have remained without effect. Something was needed to make the minister of war go against the will of his organization.

Unpretentiously, the emperor, then only forty-four, lamented having to order "you, my loyal subjects, to lay down your arms and deliver yourselves up as war criminals." It was "unbearable," he continued," to think of those who have lost their lives in battle or in performing their duties and of their families, to think of the wounded and those suffering because of the war, those who have lost their homes . . . . " He expressed his identity with his people and described the anguish his nation had undergone: "Whatever happens to my person, I wish to save the lives of my people."

To those weeping as they listened to the emperor seeking to save his people from their fate, it was impossible to object or to fall back on factional loyalties. Military representatives knew that the army might be doomed to destruction, but were willing to stand with the emperor and share his fate. Thus, out of consideration for the emperor, Army Minister Anami signed the Cabinet decision, and killed himself on the eve of the surrender.

The emperor mentioned that one could not, of course, place full confidence in the actions of the Allies, but, he continued, "I judge that the Americans are quite well disposed toward us."

What evidence could the emperor possibly have had to indicate that the United States was favorably disposed toward Japan? Telegrams from Sato Naotake (ambassador to the Soviet Union), Kase Shunichi (Japanese minister in Switzerland), and Okamoto Norimasa (Japanese minister in Sweden), for example, did state that the Potsdam Declaration granted Japan terms far more generous than those granted to Germany and that rapid acceptance was in Japan's national interest. Some of the emperor's closest associates also drew assurance from the fact that former U.S. ambassador to Japan, Joseph Grew, was in Washington and occupied an important post. The emperor was himself a patron of good relations with the Anglo-Saxons and expressed his confidence, though he could not have had any firm assurances. In sum, he probably felt that, compared with Japan's disappearance from the face of the earth, this course was the lesser evil.

The first official document drafted in Washington about the emperor was dated May 25, 1943, and titled the "Status of the Japanese Emperor." It contained the following passage:

> Recent U.S. Ambassadors to Japan have enjoyed the warm friendship of many of the important people close to the Emperor—including Count Makino, Viscount Saito, Mr. Matsudaira, and Prince Konoye—and on many occasions have been entrusted with some of their most confidential thoughts.*

Grew, and others like him who knew and loved Japan, held the emperor in respect and did not doubt his friendly feelings toward the United States and his sincere advocacy of international cooperation. They stressed the emperor's pacifistic tendencies and argued strongly within the U.S. government that the imperial institution would be a useful "asset" in ending the war and furthering Japan's recovery.

In this sense, the emperor's optimistic trust in the United States was not betrayed, but the Japan experts in the U.S. State Department were

*T315: Territorial Subcommittee Documents, 315, Notter File, National Archives.

but a minuscule group with opinions far removed from those of the vast majority of Americans. The experts' lack of political influence, however, was compensated for by the ability of such diplomatic strategists as Secretary of War Stimson, who effected wise and considerate decisions in the last phase of the war, through extensive powers spanning both political and military affairs. The Japanese, including the emperor, had no way of knowing about these internal circumstances in America, but the emperor decided nonetheless to grasp the outstretched hand. It was another victory of the Open Door faction, and it came in the nick of time.

The Abrupt Turnabout

At the time of his decision, the emperor was the object of a reverence that is difficult to imagine today. By announcing the end of the war to the people himself, he left no doubt about the imperial purpose to win over opponents to capitulation.

After the surrender, the press switched from propaganda intended to heighten the nation's will to fight, to a tone that encouraged people to approach the Occupation calmly, though some anxiety could not be concealed. In an interview with the *Asahi Shimbun* on August 19, for instance, Foreign Minister Shigemitsu Mamoru called on the Japanese to "carry out their commitments manfully, face reality squarely, and rebuild the nation."

When Yoshida Shigeru became foreign minister on September 17, he exhorted the assembled Foreign Ministry staff to accept Japan's defeat and be good losers, to speak out when something had to be said but otherwise to cooperate with the occupier.

Some Japanese felt that even the vanquished could resist an occupier by adhering to what they believed was right and by standing up for their independence. The Japanese military, heir in 1945 to the party that had sought roughly a century earlier to "expel the barbarians," was humiliated and naturally opposed to the occupation and demilitarization of Japan and to the trial of its leaders for war crimes. Others, including the above-mentioned diplomatic leaders, stressed that the vanquished had yielded supreme authority to the victors through the act of surrender and that the occupier could be encouraged to be a good ruler through the cultivation of friendly relations and willing cooperation with Occupation policies.

From the Meiji period on, Japan's career bureaucrats had successively served the *genro hanbatsu* (founding fathers of the Meiji state and their factions), then the first political parties, and finally the Japanese military. The supreme commander for the Allied powers was but the fourth in line of the higher authorities who issued directives, and deciding to help was a quick and easy step to take for bureaucrats of this school. Their service to the Occupation forces while waiting for their withdrawal was little different than their relationship to others in power had been.

In the context of Japan's history of responses to outside civilizations, the Occupation was again an opening of the country to outside influence. Through the Occupation, Japan was able to achieve yet greater reforms and growth than through the Meiji Restoration.

As early as November 1945, the Ministry of Foreign Affairs set up a study committee in preparation for a peace treaty. The Foreign Ministry naturally suspected the victor of seeking to sanction through a peace treaty whatever it had set in place as *faits accomplis* through the Occupation, since demilitarization and democratization were also intended to debilitate Japan. But scarcely two months later, in January 1946, a memo from the Foreign Ministry's policy bureau stated that the hasty conclusion of a peace treaty was not in Japan's best interest: it was more advisable to continue to cooperate with the occupiers. The committee feared that to sign a peace treaty while the United States still regarded Japan with deep hostility would only lead to a punitive treaty with long-lasting ill effects and unpopularity. A year and a half later, on June 5, 1947, there appeared an even more surprising memo declaring that demilitarization itself was the key to Japan's reconstruction.

What had taken place in the Foreign Ministry? It was effectively saying that Japan's occupation and demilitarization—which, in anticipation, had been "unbearable"—were in Japan's own best interest. Japan began to advance toward a glimmer of hope for recovery when it saw the advantages of doing the inevitable instead of protesting with force.

COMMON TASKS OF JAPAN AND THE UNITED STATES

As victor, the United States was able to achieve authority as supreme Occupation power in Japan. The power of occupation was stipulated in the Potsdam Declaration and was accepted by the Japanese government. The Japanese government made it a fundamental policy to cooperate.

According to the legal principles incorporated in the Potsdam Declaration, not only the defeated country, but the victor as well, was subject to the written pledge. There was no reason that Japan might have been forced to deviate from the conditions of the Potsdam Declaration. However, the Potsdam Declaration did not specify the actual content of the reforms. It was no more than an extremely abstract guide to suggested directions. Let us consider, for example, the provisions of Article 10: "The Japanese government shall remove all obstacles to the revival and strengthening of democratic tendencies." This could be seen as a basic justification for constitutional revision and all democratic reforms. However, it was not possible to judge from this article which reforms should be carried out and which should not. It was likewise not possible to decide from such a general provision the extent to which these reforms should be implemented. Matters like this were left entirely to the discretion of the enforcer. Consequently, the supreme commander held extremely wide-ranging authority. The purging of leading figures in the Japanese government like Ishibashi Tanzan, who were too proud to obey the conquerer, and the dissolution of stubborn Japanese government institutions, such as the Ministry of Home Affairs, were examples of the unfortunate use of that authority.

Nevertheless, indiscriminate reform by the victor, taking no account of the historical and prevailing circumstances of Japanese society, was also unacceptable. Even if the victor was capable of deciding on reforms and forcing their acceptance, Japan was not only the provider of the knowledge and information on which they were based but also the final executor. What degree of progress could the military officers of GHQ have achieved, given their inability to read Japanese, without the cooperation of the Japanese government and people? That there was a certain degree of willingness and eagerness on the Japanese side to implement each of these reforms is of great significance. We could divide the Occupation reforms into three categories based on nature of initiative.

Three Types of Reform

First, there were GHQ-directed reforms (we shall call them type A), which forced compliance with reforms Japan did not want to put into practice. For example, had coercion not been employed, Japan would not have wanted to introduce the following: the initial demilitarization measures such as war crime trials and purges, the decentralization of police authority, and the dissolution of the *zaibatsu*.

Even after the Ministry of Home Affairs agreed to the election of local governors from among ordinary citizens, it insisted on retaining the right of the central government to make the appointments. Also, the Ministry of Home Affairs opposed the establishment of an independent police force among the smallest autonomous bodies. GHQ enforced the reforms in both cases and, following the completion of the reform measures by the Ministry of Home Affairs, abolished this ministry. Such conspicuous cases of GHQ-directed reforms could easily lead one to the conclusion that forces from abroad did change Japanese society completely and that no continuity could be found between pre- and postwar Japan.

Second, there were reforms that were preempted by Japan (we shall call them type B). In such cases, the Japanese government instigated a reform, passed a bill, and effected the reform before GHQ issued a directive. These reforms included revision of the electoral law and of the labor union law.

Preparations for these revisions had been initiated toward the end of the war by enlightened areas of the bureaucracy, and following defeat, these reforms received Cabinet decisions and were passed by the Imperial Diet in late 1945. Although the GHQ's Government Section subsequently examined the new bills, they were eventually approved.

It is most important to remember that in Japan's prewar experience, the necessity for reform was already recognized in the ranks of the Japanese government. If one focuses on this method of preemptive reform implementation, then the notion of continuity between Japanese prewar and postwar history begins to emerge.

The third kind of reform, type C, was a combination of types A and B. This category covered situations in which Japan had attempted reform and made some progress; GHQ subsequently intervened, judging the scope of the reforms to be insufficient, and introduced more thorough reforms by directive. Agricultural reform and revision of the constitution are cases in point.

Japanese politicians and bureaucrats were fully aware of the necessity for land reform given the country's history of impoverishment on farms and peasant uprisings. The example of agricultural reform clearly falls into type B in its initial stages. However, if one considers the opposition of the landholding classes to their execution, it becomes clear that the capacity of the Japanese government to introduce such preemptive reforms was somewhat limited. The absolute power held by GHQ enabled it to enforce these reforms to an extent which would not have been possible in peacetime.

Thus, had the determination of the victor not existed, such reforms would probably not have eventuated. On the other hand, whatever shape a reform took, the formation of the bill and the execution were all processes carried out exclusively by the Japanese government. In the final analysis, then, Occupation reform overall was a joint task carried out by both the United States and Japan.

The revisions to the constitution received broad support from the Japanese people. The local autonomy law created new beneficiaries centering on publicly elected regional governors and members of local assemblies. If reforms were welcomed by the people, especially if they created a new class of beneficiaries, it was impossible for anyone to undo them even after the occupying powers had returned home. To establish an independent government, Japanese political parties had to gather supporters from among the beneficiaries of Occupation reforms.

Pro-Americanism, Light Rearmament, and the Commercial State

Following the introduction of Occupation policies, such dramatic measures as the dissolution of the empire and the military structure progressed rapidly. The second stage of the democratic reforms was implemented at the beginning of 1946 with the setting up of the Government Section. Announcing in March of 1947 that the first objective of achieving demilitarization had been accomplished and that the movement toward achieving the second objective of political reform was under way, MacArthur advocated early settlement of peace.

There was a feeling that economic regeneration should be entrusted to the Japanese side rather than being left to the directives of the Occupation army. The Initial Post-Surrender Policy for Japan supported this viewpoint. Consequently, it became a main trend in the Department of State to set up the framework for Japan's independence between 1947 and 1948 and then to leave the work of economic revival to the Japanese government itself. The State Department's Far East Office drew up a Japanese peace treaty during the spring and summer of 1947. This draft formed part of the American commitment to weaken its former enemy.

In the summer of 1947, however, as part of America's global Cold War strategy, George Kennan opposed the early signing of a punitive peace treaty with Japan and advocated the promotion of Japan's economic recovery and amity toward the United States. This approach was ratified by Washington in October 1948 when President Truman approved NSC13/2, a policy document prepared by the National Security Council. Joseph Dodge, a Detroit banker, was sent to Japan to implement it.

The start of the Cold War in 1947 did not lead to the rapid conclusion of the Occupation but instead effectively prolonged it. The result was that Japan's postwar economic recovery began under the Occupation.

When the Korean War broke out in June 1950, Washington lost interest in enforcing Japan's demilitarization and began to hope that Japan would become a military ally in the fight against communism. John Foster Dulles visited Japan in January 1951 with the object of negotiating a peace treaty. Yoshida, back in power, stalled, promising only to lightly arm Japan under strict civilian control. This enabled his country to spend little on defense and the remainder on economic reconstruction. In the world of atomic ages, arms had become so well developed that they were almost unusable. Furthermore, Japan's reestablishment of friendly relations with the United States, together with America's commitment to defend South Korea, left Japan situated comfortably behind the superpower's shield.

Not only did the United States provide security by military might; it sustained the free-trade system by providing an international currency. Even when the prohibition on its rearmament was lifted, Japan chose not to modify its pacifistic way of life and became a commercial state busy carrying on industrial production and international trade under U.S. protection.

CONCLUSION

The seven Occupation years brought bitter change to some Japanese who lost their privileges but new opportunities to the majority. Those benefited by the change formed the basis for the postwar Japanese political system.

Encouragement of labor unions under the Occupation created a political base for the Socialist Party, which embraced pacifism and democracy and enthusiastically supported the initial Occupation reforms. This group later became dissatisfied and openly critical of Occupation policies. Although remaining hostile to the United States, the Socialist Party continued to support the constitution, seen as the main achievement of the early Occupation.

Conservative forces coalesced in 1955 into the Liberal Democratic Party. Their initial political support came mainly from independent farmers (beneficiaries of Occupation land reforms) and from independent small merchants and manufacturers, the only group not affected by Occupation reforms. The LDP found political allies in big business and finance and the upper echelons of the bureaucracy. Its leaders included people like Yoshida, who believed economic matters to be of prime importance, as well as a considerable number of traditional party politicians like Hatoyama Ichiro, who viewed reconstruction of Japan's military capability as urgent for affirming Japan's independence. Both schools, however, shared a liking for the United States.

Had the Japanese monarchy been abolished by the Occupation authority, postwar history would have witnessed traditional nationalists joining the ranks of America's enemies and both extremes of the political spectrum forming anti-American movements. Conservatives who did not benefit from the Occupation's initial reforms did at least profit from its economic recovery policies. Hence, the majority of the Japanese supported the Occupation policies and regarded the United States as a friend.

The heritage of the Occupation is responsible for a considerable part of Japan's postwar growth and for the long-term stability of the United States–Japan relationship. The American Occupation of Japan as well as the Marshall Plan will always be regarded as America's highest achievements. The Japanese economy's tremendous strength is the result not of the Occupation's failings but of its unconditional success. The United States has no cause to regret such commendable behavior. On the contrary, Japan should model its behavior on America's good example.

The Occupation—Some Reflections

Herbert Passin

The Americans began the Occupation assuming that democratic tendencies existed in Japan, that the United States could unleash them by changing the domestic balance of power. In any assessment of those seven years, several factors are crucial: the political biases of individual occupiers, the failure to reform the bureaucracy, and the American emphasis on decentralization. A subtle question remains: did America merely accelerate reforms long in gestation?

Forty-four years have passed since the end of the Pacific War, thirty-seven since the end of the American Occupation of Japan. The majority of the population of both countries was not even born at the time the war ended. In Japan, not surprisingly, the memory remains strong, although even there it is fading fast. Most Americans, however, seem to remember little, if anything, about it. Last year I had occasion to lecture a group of American university students visiting Japan: the majority did not even know that the United States had occupied Japan.

I propose to offer some reflections on the Occupation with regard to two broad questions: what were some of the assumptions, implicit or explicit, that Americans brought to the Occupation; and did the Occupation make a difference in Japan's history?[1]

The position from which I look at these issues is that of a kind of insider-observer. I was an insider in the sense that I was an officer of the Occupation. But I was an outsider because I was not directly involved in any of its major programs. The closest I came to real Occupation-

Herbert Passin is Professor Emeritus, Sociology, at Columbia University.

eering was working with the Cabinet Secretariat, which was in charge of attitude research within the government. My unit's task was to monitor the secretariat's members closely, one hand offering training, advice, and ideas, the other reining them in to be sure they would not fall back into the bad old ways of thought control. This reached its apogee when we finally got a law through the Diet establishing the National Public Opinion Research Center[2] inside the Cabinet Secretariat that we considered provided the necessary guarantees of autonomy and freedom from political control.

These, however, were minor, compared with the enormous responsibilities of the staff section of which we were a part, Civil Information and Education (CIE), which was in charge of, among other matters, the educational reforms,[3] the media,[4] women's rights,[5] and religion.[6] Our main connection with the other Occupation programs—such as the land reform, the economic reforms, and the political reforms (all of which were, incidentally, outside the jurisdiction of CIE)—was to do research on them when requested by the appropriate authority, and from this outside position, to come up with (what we hoped would be) useful information, insights, and suggestions, presumably to improve their operations. (I doubt that we had much effect).[7]

THE OCCUPATION

The Occupation started formally on September 2, 1945, with the signing of the documents of surrender aboard the USS *Missouri*. It ended at 11 A.M., April 28, 1952, just short of six years and eight months later. Until his removal by President Truman on April 11, 1951, General Douglas MacArthur was supreme commander for the Allied powers (SCAP).

Despite the term *Allied* in the title, the Occupation was an American show. The Allied powers were represented in essentially powerless advisory commissions: the Far Eastern Commission in Washington, consisting of twelve nations, and the Allied Council for Japan in Tokyo, made up of the four main powers.

Although the occupations of Germany and Japan shared many features in common (apart from the quadripartite division of Germany and the heavy Soviet presence, which General MacArthur managed adroitly to avoid), there was one important difference: in

Germany, the occupying powers abolished the existing government and governed the country directly. It was not until 1949, by which time the division of Germany into East and West was complete, that full sovereignty was restored by the Allies to a German government in their part of the country.

In Japan, however, the decision was made not to resort to military government but to leave the existing government in place and operate through it. There was, in fact, something called military government, but it consisted of small teams, largely of young soldiers, under Eighth Army command (not directly under SCAP headquarters) in each of Japan's forty-six prefectures[8] (Okinawa was then under separate command). They had no direct authority, their only function being to monitor compliance and report to headquarters. As part of the indirect-rule arrangement, the emperor system was allowed to remain, although the new constitution reduced his role from "Head of the Empire . . .[in whom] the rights of sovereignty are invested[9] . . . sacred and inviolable"[10] to "symbol of the nation and of the unity of the people . . . whose position is derived from the will of the people with whom resides sovereign power."[11]

Occupation measures therefore had to go through a more circuitous course than in the case of Germany. Instead of direct order, directives were issued to the Japanese government. These were then "urged" (with varying degrees of forcefulness) upon the government. The lengthy process of negotiation that this entailed opened the way, whether for good or for bad, to much more Japanese influence in shaping Occupation measures than had originally been expected.

The possibility of Japanese influence was enhanced by several other factors. First was the internal political change going on in the United States. When the war ended, the Democrats were firmly in power; in 1944 they lost the Congress to the Republicans. With this loss came a decisive shift in the relative power of the constituencies for various Occupation measures. "New Dealers" were increasingly pushed aside by technocrats and by probusiness advisers and staffs. Many reform programs began to slow down or grind to a halt, the emphasis shifting to making Japan economically self-supporting and politically part of the Free World.

A second factor was the ongoing battle within the Occupation between the reform-minded elements in various SCAP sections and the military-minded, led by General Charles Willoughby and his G-2, which had a completely different agenda of its own. The third factor was the American staff members' low level of knowledge about Japan, which made them heavily dependent upon Japanese interpreters, English-speaking Japanese, and official informational sources. All of this provided a rich field for maneuvering by different Japanese interest groups.

By the time the Occupation ended, the Korean War had been on for almost two years, and MacArthur's replacement, General Matthew B. Ridgeway, was in office. Ridgeway was primarily concerned with Korea and knew and cared little about the American reforms in Japan. The world that Ridgeway looked out upon in 1952 was very different from MacArthur's world of 1945. The Soviet Union and the Western allies had split, the Communists had taken power in China and driven out our allies (the Nationalists), a major war was being fought in Korea, the United States had changed, and Japan had changed massively.

In this new atmosphere, a bare six and a half years after the start of the Occupation, Prime Minister Yoshida Shigeru reported that he had no difficulty persuading Ridgeway to allow the Japanese government to "consider the revision of the laws framed in accordance with the Potsdam Declaration."[12]

The purpose of the Occupation, as phrased in the United States Initial Post-Surrender Policy for Japan (USIPPJ)[13] was "to insure that Japan will not again become a menace to the peace and security of the world." This was to be achieved, however, not by "destroy[ing Japan] as a nation" but rather by turning it into a "peace-loving nation."[14]

This required, in effect, a two-pronged approach: demilitarization and democratization.

Demilitarization

The Occupation did the usual things one expects of any conquering army: it disarmed and demobilized Japan's armed forces; it destroyed and impounded war materiel, and it punished the perpetrators of battlefield crimes.

It was at the next step, the dismantling of the "infrastructure" of the military system that ambiguities began to appear. Many industrial facilities that had served military needs during the war could as easily be turned to civilian use. Aircraft plants could produce trucks and automobiles, military uniform factories could make civilian clothing, and even "munitions" plants after a little restructuring might serve civilian needs. Therefore, the destruction, dismantling, or shipment of these facilities as reparations to countries that had suffered from Japan's aggression raised serious issues.

Not all of them were self-evident at first, but when the time came to implement the reparations directive, which had been mandated early in the Occupation, MacArthur and his top advisers had begun to regard the policies requiring Japan to pay "just reparations in kind" as misguided. Japan's capacity to achieve economic self-sufficiency would be seriously harmed, and it was the American taxpayer who would have to foot the bill. Nor was there any compensating advantage for the receiving countries: their economies were just too undeveloped to make use of sophisticated equipment. Rumors made the rounds about steel plants rusting away in Philippine ports and cement left exposed on the Rangoon docks in the rainy season. In the end, very little did go out because of resistance at the very top of the Occupation.

Many silly things also were done in the early stages. For example, Kyoto University's atomic reactor, which was no more than a very primitive experimental research tool, was impounded and sunk in the Pacific Ocean.

And many things that should have been done were not done or were done badly. During the last year or so of the war, the Japanese military had stored away several years' supply of food, clothing, raw materials, equipment, and funds in its arsenals, caves, and other hiding places. As the surrender and the arrival of the American forces loomed near, the military, through a variety of means, distributed vast amounts to favored individuals and groups and continued to do so right through the early stages of the Occupation.

The Occupation failed completely to prevent this traffic and indeed only became fully aware of it when it surfaced as a scandal early in the Socialist administration of 1947. At that very time, the Occupation was trying to wring a $75 million appropriation out of the United States Congress for the import of industrial raw materials for Japan's use, several of which were on the list of vanished military inventories.[15]

Programs of this kind (including purges of civilians considered to have responsibility for bringing on the war)[16] constituted the "negative" phase of the Occupation.

Reform

But the underlying American concept that Japan was to be turned into a peace-loving nation required something more than just dismantling its militarism. The basic political and social institutions that were responsible for or that had contributed significantly to the war were to be eliminated or reformed.

The Occupation therefore embarked upon a massive reform program which in the course of unfolding came to affect virtually every part of Japanese life. The centerpiece consisted of the political reforms,[17] which MacArthur rated as "probably the single most important accomplishment of the occupation, for it brought to the Japanese people freedoms and privileges which they had never known."[18] A new constitution intended to entrench the basic principles of democracy replaced the Meiji constitution, which had been in effect since 1889 without amendment. The new constitution remains a source of contention in Japanese politics today. Ironically, it is the somewhat anti-American left, in particular the Socialist Party, the trade unions, intellectuals, and a good part of the media, that "defend" the "American-imposed" constitution against the conservatives, who favor its revision.

In addition, the Occupation instituted, or attempted to institute, reforms at almost every level of Japanese life: landlord-tenant relations,[19] labor rights,[20] the civil code[21] the penal code, the electoral system, local autonomy,[22] the cartel structure of Japanese business,[23] the school system,[24] the separation of church and state,[25] the family system,[26] the organization of science, the legal status of women.[27] Except for the communization of the countries the Soviet Union occupied after World War II, modern history has probably never seen so drastic a reform program imposed by an outside power.

AMERICAN ASSUMPTIONS

Two concepts were particularly important during the early Occupation period. First, latent forces formerly held down by the military-dominated regime or by the general ideological atmosphere of the times were to be released. The Potsdam Declaration had specified that "the Japanese Government shall remove all obstacles to the revival and strengthening of democratic tendencies among the Japanese people."[28] The implication, of course, was that these "democratic tendencies" existed, and they were to be encouraged in "labor, industry, and agriculture." Where they did not exist, they were to be fostered.

The second key concept was that the Occupation was to provide conditions favorable to the emergence of democratic tendencies. This meant that the balance of forces within Japanese society had to be altered long enough for these tendencies to arise.

A good example was the Occupation's land reform program, generally regarded as one of its most successful. It was not, however, a purely American invention. There had already been plans before the war to increase farm ownership by reducing tenancy, and there had even been a law drafted (although not put into effect because the outbreak of the Pacific War put it on the back burner). What the Occupation did, guided by the skillful hand of special adviser Wolf Ladejinsky, the guardian angel of the land reform, was to press it toward a more radical solution than originally intended.

The land reform also illustrates the concept of altering the balance of forces. Even though some kind of land reform had been advocated since before the war—by peasant organizations, by friendly bureaucrats, and even by some young right-wing army officers—it had been powerfully opposed by landlords and their political supporters. Would the reform have taken place without the massive intervention of the Occupation? Very likely not. "Without Occupation backing," as Wada Hiroo, the then agriculture minister, was to reminisce some twenty years later, "agricultural land reform might not have been realized."[29] Or in the drier formulation of sociologist Tadashi Fukutake, "It was a drastic reform, the like of which could hardly have been contemplated in prewar Japan."[30]

The same might be said of the labor reforms. The constituency was there: modern trade unions already had a history of some fifty years by the time the war ended. They had, to be sure, never exceeded 420,000 members at their peak (1936), just 7 percent of the labor force. Yet in spite of the harassment and suppression in the 1937 elections, the last before the forced dissolution of political parties into the Imperial Rule Assistance Association (and of the trade unions into the Nazi-like "patriotic labor fronts"), the Social Masses Party, which the unions supported, won over 1 million votes (9.1 percent of the total) and 36 out of the Diet's 466 seats (just under 8 percent). When the unions were released from constraints at the end of the war, they startled even their most loyal advocates by their speed of growth. Within one year of the passage of the Occupation-sponsored Trade Union Law on December 21, 1945, union membership reached some 5 million. By 1949, trade union membership had grown to 7 million (out of an industrial labor force of 15 million).

So labor reform obviously had its natural constituency. It also had its powerful and determined opponents from before the war who were not ready to lay down their arms. Clearly, stalemate or possibly even civil war was in the offing. In this situation, it was the fact that the Occupation, at the early stages, threw its weight on the side of labor that made the difference. The final outcome was shaped by many different factors in the course of time, and it was disappointing to many on both sides, but the starting point was probably decisive.

Even the enfranchisement of women in Confucian, male-dominated Japan was not simply an American idea. Granted that without the effort of several extraordinary American women operating skillfully in the special atmosphere that prevailed in the early part of the Occupation this would not have come about, nevertheless there were antecedents. In prewar Japan women suffragists and their supporters—Christians, liberals, socialists, and some intellectuals—together with their organizations, journals, and literature already added up to a substantial force. Had they not been severely repressed by the regime, they might very well have come forward as a much stronger force than they appeared to be immediately after the war.

The American Model

Many assumptions underlay the reforms. Some were embedded in the very formulation of policy directives; others were idiosyncratic to particular Occupation officials. In toto, they reflected the full range of the then American political spectrum: left, liberal, New Deal, mainstream American, conservative, military.

Most of the Occupation forces believed that the American model, or more accurately, a generalized or transmogrified American model, was, on the whole, the best one. Since, for example, states rights were fundamental to the structure of government in America, it seemed self-evident that that was "the democratic way" to go. Hence the Occupation's decentralization and local autonomy reforms. A new system of elected local officials was instituted, replacing the previous system of appointive prefectural governors and mayors, which had been modeled largely on the French system.

In education, which had been under the tight control of the Ministry of Education—again on the French model—strenuous efforts were made to reduce central authority. Local governments were to take charge, and an American-style system of elected local boards of education was instituted. In place of the traditional "parents association,"[31] the American-style PTA system was encouraged.

The restructuring of the educational system came to be epitomized in the term "6–3–3 system" (referring to the new sequence of six years of elementary school, three years of junior high school, and three years of senior high school to replace the older system) and then somehow enshrined on both sides as *the* American system.

In spite of this disposition, however, the American model was not always followed to the letter. The more sophisticated constitutional, political, and legal reformers often resorted to European models, experiences, and ideas. The constitution, which MacArthur characterized as "undoubtedly the most liberal constitution in history,"[32] borrowed from what the American framers of its draft regarded as the most advanced constitutional ideas they could find anywhere in the democratic world. The Japanese constitution contains many provisions, however we may ultimately regard them, that are not found in the American constitution.[33]

Sociopolitical Theories

Some of these assumptions had a curiously sociological flavor to them—for example, that aggression was the inevitable outcome of certain aspects of Japanese social and political structure. It was easy enough (it was thought) to identify the systems that allowed the warmongers to lead Japan into war. But to understand why the Japanese people themselves had been so willing to allow themselves to be led, one had to look deeper. It was, in fact, their domestic institutions—schools, state religion, feudal structures (as in landlord-tenant relations), business structure, and civic organizations—that were to blame. They drilled obedience into the people, suppressed individuality, and preached the subordination of the self to the collective goals set by higher authority.

The Occupation's approach to agrarian reform emerged in part from some such implicit theory of the sociocultural origins of aggression. There were, of course, many reasons for the Occupation to favor agrarian reform: the existing system was inherently unjust, a violation of democratic and egalitarian principles; it kept the peasants under the control of ultranationalist landlords and political leaders; it entrained the danger of a Communist-led agrarian revolution, as was occurring in other parts of Asia at that time. Occupation authorities were not unaware that the Chinese Communists, then advancing to power on the mainland, were presenting themselves to the world as agrarian reformers. But the high rate of rural support for the military in recent times suggested something more: a unique relation between the agrarian situation and militarism.

The army had a special appeal to rural areas.[34] Most of the soldiers were themselves from the countryside, and many of the younger officers came from these same villages (although usually from higher social strata). The army provided one of the few channels of upward mobility for many farm boys who would otherwise not have been able to rise in Japanese society. In addition, the army's expansionist goals had a deep appeal, at least in the abstract, to a land-starved peasantry: the vast open spaces of Manchukuo beckoned to skilled farmers cramped in their meager one or two acres in the homeland and especially to noninheriting second and third sons, who had no land at all to look forward to.

Peasants gave their support to the military, and the reservist organization found in every village became a key local institution for control and mobilization. Because of this relation, the army was especially attentive to the problems of the peasantry. Officers were immediately aware of the effects of rural distress on the morale of their peasant soldiers.

The young officers and ultrarightists indicted for terrorist acts in the 1930s often cited rural distress as one of the factors that moved them to direct action. "The impoverishment of the agricultural villages," said Lieutenant Goto Akinori in defense of his involvement in the May 15, 1932, attempt by a small group of young officers and farmers to overthrow the government,

> is the cause of grave concern for thoughtful persons. It is extremely dangerous that while soldiers from the villages expose themselves to death at the front they should have to worry about their starving families . . . . In utter disregard of the poverty-stricken farmers, the fabulously rich continue their pursuit of private gain. Meanwhile the children of the farmers are so poor that they must go to school in the morning without breakfast . . . . To let a day go by without doing something is to endanger the army one day longer, was my thought- . . . .[35]

The Occupation's penetration into even the most intimate of Japanese institutions—the family, parental authority, parent-child relations, marriage and relations between men and women—was no mere exercise of missionary impulse. "Familism," as many Japanese social scientists and liberals had themselves pointed out to their American associates, was a comprehensive ideology[36] that embraced all the undesirable ideas that led to or, at the very least, lent themselves to imperialistic expansion: Confucian hierarchy, subordination of the self to collective goals, suppression of individuality, absolute obedience to higher authority, the idea of Japan as a unique family-state under a father-emperor. Furthermore, once the concept of individual rights was installed as the centerpiece of the new constitution, many traditional Japanese family practices and the civil code became automatically, almost deductively, unconstitutional.

Political Economy

The dissolution of the *zaibatsu* remains one of the most controversial of the Occupation measures, with respect to both its desirability and its effectiveness. The intent was to dissolve the "large industrial and banking combinations which have exercised control of a great part of Japan's trade and industry."[37] It is worth looking at the assumptions that underlay this objective.

For some, it was the "merchants of death" theory: wars came about because some people profited from them. The "malefactors of great wealth" had to be brought under control. For others, it was the more sophisticated Marxist view: capitalism led, through its own inner dynamic, to the stage of monopoly capitalism and thence to imperialism and war. As long as Japan's monopoly capitalistic structure existed, the menace of militarism would never be laid to rest. Much less would a true democracy come into existence. Still others saw the issue as one of monopoly and trust busting in the American sense. The Far Eastern Commission's FEC 230 statement of May 1947 contained the new concept that "absolute size . . . is to be considered grounds for defining a specified concentration as excessive."[38]

What emerged from this complex of views, all of them possible interpretations of the vague phrasing of the USIPPJ, was a series of measures: the dismantling of the *zaibatsu* structure, the liquidation of the holding companies, the public sale of *zaibatsu* securities, the Anti-Monopoly Law of 1947, the Shoup Mission's tax democratization program, and the economic purge. All of these underwent, in varying degree, changes from the original conception and the original form of the programs.

Views of Occupation Officials

The views held by the Occupation officials in strategic positions were often very important in the outcomes of programs. Very few Americans in the Occupation knew much about Japan when they first arrived in Japan. Therefore, many important things were missed or misunderstood. A case in point was the problem of the Japanese bureaucracy. The bureaucracy had been one of the principal powers in political life, along with the military, the politicians, and the big business community. From a democratic point of view, the bureaucracy had a dangerous degree of independent power in relation to the elected political sector and was dominated by graduates of the elite imperial universities, principally Tokyo University.

Yet while the Occupation had plans for the other leadership sectors, it never had a clear concept of what to do about the bureaucracy, and indeed whether anything needed doing at all. When a mission was finally sent, under the leadership of Blaine Hoover, president of the Civil Service Assembly of the United States and Canada, it failed completely to deal with the central problems: "Because . . . [it] saw everything through American eyes, it ignored perhaps the most striking feature of the tightly knit Japanese bureaucracy, the 'old school tie.' "[39] Its proposals were based on American concepts: "a compound of merit examinations, 'scientific' job descriptions, wage classification, efficiency ratings, plus an independent civil service authority. What had all this to do with feudalism? An American arrangement designed historically to eliminate the spoils system was to be applied to a country that had none."[40]

The Hoover mission is best remembered not for the defeudalization of the bureaucracy, which should have been its primary task, but for its restrictions on the right of government workers to organize, to bargain collectively, and to strike, controversial policies that still prevail today. At the time, many elements of the Occupation, including the Labor Division, opposed the Hoover recommendations, but there were also many Japanese bureaucrats, politicians, and businessmen who welcomed them and were delighted to take advantage of the disagreements they saw dividing the Occupation.

Prime Minister Yoshida in his memoirs describes how he tried, often successfully, to manipulate these divisions, which he saw as the "idealists" versus the "practical men"[41] (most of whom, it turns out, were professional military men).

But idiosyncratic interpretations of "democratization" were not always so consequential. I do not know who was responsible for introducing square dancing to Japan, but I remember meeting young military-government officers in the provinces who were absolutely convinced that square dancing was the magic key to transforming Japan into a democratic society.

THE EFFECTS OF THE OCCUPATION

Before we can begin to answer, or even to approach, the question of whether the Occupation made a difference, we have to decide exactly what question it is that we are asking. Did the Occupation make any difference in the totality of Japan's history; or only in its modern history; or in the history of the Showa period? A case can be—and has been—made that the Occupation was one of the main turning points in Japan's history, comparable to the introduction of Chinese civilization in the seventh and eighth century and to the Meiji Restoration of 1868.[42] There are few who would disagree that the Occupation had some effect, so the question becomes: did it just make *some* difference, or did it make a big difference?

Too Much or Too Little

Those who think the Occupation did too much usually regard its effects as major and, for the most part, undesirable. Writer Eto Jun, for example, argues that the Occupation period censorship was not only bad at the time but that its effects continue right up to the present. Its "censorship and propaganda plan," he writes,[43] "became entrenched in our media and educational systems, so that even when the CCD [Civil Censorship Detachment] was disbanded and the Occupation itself had ended, the internal destruction of the identity of Japanese people and trust in our history continues, making us permanently exposed to threats of foreign censorship."[44]

I agree that many foolish things were done in the censorship operation. (I myself happened to be assigned for three or four months to CCD down in Fukuoka.) There was, after all, a basic contradiction between the Occupation's (negative) mission of "suppression of ultranationalistic ideology" and its (positive) mission of promoting democracy.

"Actually," as Kazuo Kawai, editor of the *Japan Times* the first few years after the war, wrote,

> it [censorship] left few serious ill effects. Practically all Japanese recognized that censorship was unavoidable in any military occupation; and . . . the censorship probably was continued longer than was really necessary . . . . Before any serious harm could be done, as the Occupation neared its end the censorship was sharply curtailed and then abolished altogether.[45]

Similar objections are heard about one or another of the reforms. Whether the new constitution (particularly Article 9), the rights of labor, the education reforms, economic deconcentration, or the decentralization of government, they all went too far.

Those who wanted the Occupation to do more, however, tend to belittle its effects: it did not go far enough, it reversed its course, it abandoned Japan prematurely to the control of the old elites. For many, doing more meant creating, or paving the way for, a "socialist" Japan, and anything short of that was a failure. In John Dower's view, "The result [of the Occupation] was a new stage of bourgeois society under the emperor, rather than a radically new Japan."[46]

Deferred Change

An alternative formulation of our original question might be: would Japan be different today had there been no Occupation? The question assumes that we are able to distinguish the effects of Occupation actions from other changes going on in Japanese society. It may be useful here to consider the concept of "deferred change."

Japan's postwar economic growth was spectacular. Was it the result, if only in part, of the economic policies and actions of the Occupation, or would it have happened anyway? "These gains," wrote William Lockwood, "are not so spectacular . . . when compared with what might have occurred had Japan remained at peace from 1937 to 1945. Per capita income in 1965 was actually not far above the level it could have reached had growth continued uninterrupted at its prewar rate."[47]

In other words, as I have argued earlier,[48] from one point of view the war and its immediate aftermath may be regarded as an interruption in a normal, secular development and the miraculous growth rates that started in the 1950s as deferred growth. The Occupation might have impeded or helped this recovery to "normal" rates. But over the course of time, many other factors went into the process. The early phase of the Occupation emphasized economic democracy, that is, land reform, labor rights, and *zaibatsu* dissolution. Some argue that the continuation of this phase would have prevented, or delayed, such a development and that it was the post-1947 phase, the so-called reverse course, with its emphasis on economic rehabilitation and self-support, that gave the economy the fillip it needed.

Theodore Cohen, however, argues the contrary: that it was economic democratization itself, by creating a "domestic mass market for consumer goods for the first time in Japan's history,"[49] that laid the basis for the high-growth mass-consumption society that Japan has since become.

The enfranchisement of women is another example of a change that might have come about anyway. Since the historical trend in the world from the middle nineteenth century on was toward female suffrage and there was already a significant women's movement in Japan before the war, it seems likely that eventually Japanese women would have obtained the vote. The Occupation did make a difference, but probably only of one generation.

Was the rise in the general level of educational attainment, and particularly of university-level enrollment, a result of the Occupation's reforms? To some extent, yes: the reforms opened up access to higher levels of education to far larger numbers than could have been imagined earlier. Before the war, only 10 percent of the young adults (overwhelmingly boys) went through higher secondary school and only about 1 percent (all males) through the university. After the war, the numbers rose rapidly to their present 95 percent or so through senior high school and almost 40 percent through college and university.

But would this not have happened anyway? In 1945 Japan did lag far behind the United States in school enrollment at the higher levels; but this was not very different from the levels prevailing in Europe at that stage. The Occupation pushed the process faster and farther than might otherwise have occurred, but educational growth would have come inevitably in the natural course of events.

The Fate of the Reforms

Some Occupation programs remain virtually unchanged. The constitution has never been amended. Even the controversial Article 9[50] still remains unamended despite (largely conservative) opposition. The civil code reforms have, on the whole, survived with little change. Japanese agriculture has undergone major changes, just like the other advanced industrial countries, but there has been no return to the semifeudal prewar landlord-tenant system. The complex of women's rights legislation has not been reversed; if anything, it has been expanding slowly, and now Japan appears close to the takeoff point we saw in the United States of the 1960s. The Hoover mission's restraints on the rights of government workers' unions still remain, despite strong opposition. And the basic tax structure initiated by the 1949 Shoup mission, with the exception of the local tax provisions which were rejected by the Japanese government in 1950, remained in place until the explosive tax reforms of 1989. Many of the educational reforms[51] too remain relatively intact, in spite of the constant reshaping that continues to the present time.

Ironies abound: some American ideas, whether introduced by the Occupation or in some other manner, took deeper root in Japan than in the United States. W. Edwards Deming, then a visiting consultant from the U.S. Bureau of the Budget, introduced the Japanese to quality-control circles. The Japanese took up "the American Q-C" ideas with enthusiasm. The Americans, alas, did not, until the 1980s, when in shock about declining productivity, they began to pay attention to what had now become "the *Japanese* Q-C system." (In Japan a "Deming Award" is still given every year.) Perhaps we should now be studying "the Japanese PTA system" for ideas on how to improve our own schools.[52]

Most Occupation programs, however, have continued to evolve in response to the changing values of the Japanese people and the changing balance of political forces. The dissolution of the *zaibatsu* and the antitrust legislation, for instance, have been substantially modified, but not entirely eliminated. From the very start the politics of the economic reforms were complex. The American side itself was not fully united. Although the Occupation generally favored some kind of action, and indeed this had been mandated, there was opposition back at home from business and others who felt that the Occupation had gone too far. And there was strong opposition within Japan.[53]

The decentralization of government must be rated only a qualified success. Local autonomy has increased, but not as much as the reformers had hoped. Nor was the hope of major decentralization of the educational system ever realized. The Ministry of Education still retains predominant authority over the national school system. Given the fact that the American reformers' implicit model was the American system, the most decentralized in the world, this outcome is not surprising. They seem never to have realized that there are many good alternatives that lie between the two extremes—total centralization, as in prewar Japan or modern France, and American-style anarchic decentralization.

Still other programs have disappeared entirely, never having taken root in Japanese society or too much in conflict with one or another vested interest. The system of elected local school boards, modeled after our own, was tried out for a while, but in 1955, three years after the Occupation ended, it was repealed. The same fate overtook the Occupation purges of political, business, educational, and other public leaders: some purges were terminated before the formal end of the Occupation, others just as soon as the Occupation was over. In some cases the purges shifted the balance of forces long enough to retire older leaders and give new ones a chance to rise and entrench themselves.

The Objectives of the Occupation

Did the Occupation reforms achieve what they were intended to? There were, of course, clear failures, such as the handling of the bureaucracy. The education reform did not diminish the elitism of the university system and the brutal competitiveness of the "examination hell." The Shoup mission's local tax reforms were a nonstarter from the very beginning because they conflicted with the political needs of the government party, which was just then facing elections.

And some major issues were never dealt with at all: for example, the *burakumin,* descendants of the "untouchables" of the pre-Meiji era. It is estimated that there were between 1 million and 3 million of them living in about 6,000 ghettoes, by and large excluded from the mainstream of Japanese life and discriminated against. This difficult social issue fell between all stools.[54]

Nevertheless, in a large sense, the Occupation did accomplish its broad objectives. The Initial Post-Surrender Policy was to transform Japan from a militaristic, ultranationalist, fascist, imperial state into a peacefully inclined, democratic, and economically healthy nation that would never again be a threat to the peace and security of the world. While each of these terms contains many ambiguities, by and large, modern Japan falls comfortably within the limits we can accept as satisfying these criteria. The empire is gone, its military force is politically weak and little respected, and its polity is a parliamentary democracy.

Thought control is an ancient memory. Dissenters walk the streets freely (with but occasional harassment from a small minority of right-wing thugs). Dissenters are free to publish their views widely in all of the media without censorship. They hold secure positions in the universities. Opposition parties regularly take about one-half the vote. The labor movement has declined, as have labor movements in all of the advanced countries, but nevertheless it continues to take part in the political process, mainly through its support—and sometimes control—of opposition candidates.

As for USIPPJ's wish list, Japan is more than economically viable, if anything all too peacefully inclined, and certainly stable as a democracy. In another of history's little ironies, the Occupation appears to have succeeded too well, to have given us too much of a good thing. Economic viability has turned into economic rivalry, and for some, into economic menace. And "peacefully inclined" translates into refusal to carry a "fair share" of the Free World defense burden.

For all of its failings the Occupation did make a difference, and a major one, in the transformation of Japanese society. Specific reforms can be faulted in various ways, but the reform program as a whole did succeed in bringing the common people of Japan into the mainstream of citizenship, both politically and economically, in a way they had never been before.

The Legacy

During the Occupation, Americans often wondered: "Will the reforms last, or will they disappear as soon as we leave?" This is, and was at that time, a fair question. But it is unanswerable: despite all the fanfare of futurology, we cannot really predict the future in any degree of complexity.

It seems to me that the social history of any great people may be visualized as a majestic flowing stream. Outside influences, great or small, enter this stream at various points. At the point of entry, the influences are clearest. As the stream moves on, the new forces may move forward more or less intact, swerve off into small eddies and side pools, form new currents through interaction with older ones, or be overwhelmed by newer currents entering farther down the stream. By the time it reaches the delta, just before emptying into the sea, it is very different from the river just shaping up at the mountain freshets and streams.

Many elements set in motion by the Occupation may still be seen in relatively undiluted form. Others have entered varying degrees of interrelation with older Japanese currents. Some have been transformed beyond recognition. Some have been sidetracked or dispersed so completely as to be unidentifiable. Some have been left behind, stuck in the gravelly riverbed as it were; still others have been overwhelmed by the new currents or simply by the aggregate flow of Japanese historical development. It is in some such way that we must view the fate of the reforms.

ENDNOTES

[1]More than twenty years ago, I wrote a long piece on the Occupation (*The Legacy of the Occupation—Japan* [New York: Columbia University, East Asian Institute, Occasional Papers, 1968]). The rare reader who may have chanced to see that piece is herewith warned that he may pick up occasional echoes from it here.

The reason is that I find myself still in substantial agreement with much of what I had to say at that time. I have therefore taken the liberty of occasionally quoting from myself directly or in slightly modified form.

The references offered in these footnotes are directed toward English-speaking readers, not toward Japanese readers; therefore, with the exception of three items, which as of this moment exist only in Japanese, they are all in English. It should be understood that the literature on the Occupation available in Japanese is a hundredfold more extensive than in English. For general accounts, the following books will be useful:

Theodore Cohen, ed. by Herbert Passin, *Remaking Japan—the American Occupation as New Deal* (New York: The Free Press, 1987).

J. W. Dower, *Empire and Aftermath—Yoshida Shigeru and the Japanese Experience, 1878–1954* (Cambridge and London: Council on East Asian Studies, Harvard University, 1979), particularly chap. 8–9.

Meirion and Susie Harries, *Sheathing the Sword—The Demilitarisation of Japan* (London: Hamish Hamilton, 1987).

D. Clayton James, *The Years of MacArthur,* vol. 3, *Triumph and Disaster, 1945–1964* (Boston: Houghton Mifflin, 1985).

Kazuo Kawai, *Japan's American Interlude* (Chicago: University of Chicago Press, 1960).

Robert E. Ward and Sakamoto Yoshikazu, eds., *Democratizing Japan: The Allied Occupation* (Honolulu: University of Hawaii Press, 1987).

There is also a number of accounts of specific programs or aspects of the Occupation. These will be cited where appropriate.

[2]Law No. 128, 1949, "Law for the Establishment of the National Public Opinion Research Institute," effective June 1, 1949.

[3]See writings by two direct participants: Mark T. Orr, "Education Reform Policy in Occupied Japan," University of North Carolina doctoral dissertation, 1954–1955 (Orr was one of the top officers in the Civil Information and Education Section of the Occupation); and Ronald S. Anderson, *Japan: Three Epochs of Modern Education*, Bulletin No. 11 (Washington, D.C.: Department of Health, Eduction and Welfare, 1959) (Anderson was the leading education expert in the "military-government" teams). Also, Herbert Passin, *Society and Education in Japan* (New York: Columbia University Teachers College Press, 1965), Part II.

[4]For an early account of the media reforms by one of the actors, see John Wilson Gaddis, *Public Information in Japan under the American Occupation—A Study of Democratization Efforts through Agencies of Public Expression* (Geneva: Imprimeries Populaires, 1950).

[5]See Susan J. Pharr, "A Radical U.S. Experiment: Women's Rights Laws and the Occupation of Japan," in L. H. Redford, ed., *The Occupation of Japan: Impact of Legal Reform* (Norfolk, Va.: The MacArthur Memorial, 1978).

[6]See William Woodard, *The Allied Occupation of Japan, 1945–52, and Japanese Religions* (Leyden: Brill, 1972). Woodard, along with William T. Bunce, was in charge of the reforms affecting state-religion relations in CIE.

[7]See "Social Research in a Military Occupation," chap. 1 in *Paternalism in the Japanese Economy* (Minneapolis: University of Minnesota Press, 1963), by two of my colleagues of the period, John W. Bennett and Iwao Ishino.

[8]See Robert B. Textor, *Failure in Japan* (New York: John Day, 1951). Textor was a member of the Kyoto military-government team.

[9]Chap. 1, Article 4, Meiji constitution of 1889.

[10]Chap. 1, Article 2, postwar constitution.

[11]Chap. 1, Article 1, postwar constitution.

[12]Shigeru Yoshida, *The Yoshida Memoirs* (Boston: Houghton Mifflin, 1962), 46.

[13]For this and other relevant documents, see U.S. Department of State, *Occupation of Japan, Policy and Progress,* Department of State Publication 2671 (Washington, D.C.: U.S. Government Printing Office, 1946).

[14]Potsdam Declaration, Article 10. See Hugh Borton, *Japan's Modern Century* (New York: The Ronald Press, 1955), Appendix I.

[15]Cohen, 348.

[16]See Hans H. Baerwald, *The Purge of Japanese Leaders under the Occupation*, vol. 8, University of California Publications in Political Science (Berkeley and Los Angeles: University of California Press, 1959).

[17]Justin Williams, Sr., *Japan's Political Revolution under MacArthur—A Participant's Account* (Tokyo: University of Tokyo Press, 1979).

[18]Douglas MacArthur, *Reminiscences* (New York: Fawcett World Library, Crest Books, 1965), 346.

[19]See Ronald P. Dore: *Land Reform in Japan* (London: Oxford University Press, 1959).

[20]For a full account of the Occupation's labor policy, see Cohen, chap. 4.

[21]On the legal reforms, see Alfred C. Oppler, *Legal Reform in Occupied Japan—A Participant Looks Back* (Princeton: Princeton University Press, 1976); and Kurt Steiner, "Postwar Changes in the Japanese Civil Code," *Washington Law Review*, 25 (3) (August 1950). (Steiner was also a participant.) Also see Redford.

[22]See Kurt Steiner, *Local Government in Japan* (Stanford: Stanford University Press, 1965).

[23]See Eleanor M. Hadley, *Antitrust in Japan* (Princeton: Princeton University Press, 1970).

[24]See Orr, Anderson, and Passin.

[25]See Woodard. Also, William K. Bunce, *Religions in Japan—Buddhism, Shinto, Christianity* (Rutland, Vt. and Tokyo: Charles E. Tuttle, 1955). This is a report prepared by the Religions Division of CIE in 1948, when Bunce was its chief.

[26]See Kurt Steiner, "The Revision of the Civil Code of Japan: Provisions Affecting the Family," *The Far Eastern Quarterly* 9 (2) (February 1950).

[27]See Pharr.

[28]Article 10.

[29]Hiroo Wada, "Japan's Decisive Century," in *Britannica Book of the Year, 1967* (Chicago: Encyclopaedia Britannica Co., 1967).

[30]Tadashi Fukutake, *Japanese Rural Society* (Ithaca and London: Cornell University Press, 1972), 18.

[31]The *fukei-kai,* literally "fathers and older brothers association."

[32]MacArthur, 345.

[33]Especially in chap. 3, "Rights and Duties of the People;" for example:

Article 22: "Every person shall have freedom to choose and change his residence and to choose his occupation . . . ."

Article 23: "Academic freedom is guaranteed."

Article 24: "Marriage shall be based only on the mutual consent of both sexes and it shall be maintained through mutual cooperation with the equal rights of husband and wife as a basis . . . ."

Article 25: "All people shall have the right to maintain the minimum standards of wholesome and cultured living . . . ."

Article 26: "All people shall have the right to receive an equal education correspondent to their ability . . . ."

Article 27: "All people shall have the right and the obligation to work . . . ."

Article 28: "The rights of workers to organize and to bargain and act collectively is guaranteed."

[34]For a good account of this period see Richard J. Smethurst, *A Social Basis for Prewar Japanese Militarism—The Army and the Rural Community* (Berkeley: University of California Press, 1974); Thomas R. H. Havens, *Farm and Nation in Modern Japan—Agrarian Nationalism, 1870–1940* (Princeton: Princeton University Press, 1974), particularly chap. 13; and Ronald P. Dore and Tsutomu Ouchi, "Rural Origins of Japanese Fascism," in James W. Morley, ed., *Dilemmas of Growth in Prewar Japan* (Princeton: Princeton University Press, 1971).

[35]Cited in Passin, *Legacy,* 6–7.

[36]The title of a collection of articles by the distinguished sociologist of law Kawashima Takeyoshi, which translates as *The Family System as Ideology,* suggests the flavor of this thinking. Kawashima and his ideas had a considerable influence on the family-law reforms of the Occupation.

[37]USIPPJ, item b.

[38]Far Eastern Commission Statement of Broad Policy, 230, para. 2, subpara. 3.

[39]Cohen, 381.

[40]Cohen, 382.

[41]Yoshida, 49.

[42]See Cohen, 1.

[43]Eto Jun, *Tozasareta Gengo Kukan—Senryogun no Kenetsu to Sengo Nippon* (The Blockaded Speech Space, The Occupation Army's Censorship and Postwar Japan), (Tokyo: Bungei Shunju, 1989), 298.

[44]Referring to protests from China, Korea, and other Asian countries about the treatment of the history of the Pacific War in Japanese school textbooks. In his recent book *Nichibei Sensowa Owatte Inai* (The U.S.-Japan War Is Not Yet

Over), (Tokyo: Nihon Eizo Shuppan, 1987), Professor Jun Eto also holds that the United States–Japan war is still going on.

[45]Kawai, 215.

[46]Dower, 306–7.

[47]William Lockwood, "Political Economy," in Herbert Passin, ed., *The United States and Japan* (Englewood Cliffs: Prentice-Hall, 1966), 101–2.

[48]Passin, *Legacy.*

[49]Cohen, 457.

[50]" . . . the Japanese people forever renounce war as a sovereign right of the nation and the threat or use of force as a means for settling international disputes [to which end] land, sea, and air forces, as well as other war potential, will never be maintained."

[51]See Ben C. Duke, "American Educational Reforms in Japan Twelve Years Later," *Harvard Educational Review* 34 (4) (Fall 1964): 525–36, and "The Irony of Japanese Postwar Education," *Comparative Education Review* (February 1963): 212–17.

[52]See Merry White, *The Japanese Educational Challenge—A Commitment to Children* (New York: The Free Press, 1987).

[53]See Martin Bronfenbrenner, "The American Occupation of Japan: Economic Retrospect," in Grant K. Goodman, compiler, *The American Occupation of Japan: A Retrospective View* (Center for Asian Studies, The University of Kansas, 1968), 20.

[54]In the end, nothing was done, in the hope that Article 14 of the constitution (whereby "all of the people are equal under the law and there shall be no discrimination in political, economic or social relations because of race, creed, sex, social status or family origin . . .") and the normal evolution of Japan as a democratic society would automatically take care of the matter. This polyannishness seems to involve either forgetting about our own race problems or perhaps assuming that they too would be resolved in the normal course of events.

Deeply rooted in her ethnic purity, attachment to the fatherland, obsession with mother tongue, powerful creation myth, carefully constructed collective memory and elaborate ritual, Japan is embedded in the lived concreteness of being the place where the sun rises and Mount Fuji resides. Despite her responsiveness to Buddhism and Confucianism, Japan, until the Western impact, steadfastly maintained her bearings as a well-protected island. The sense of crisis with which Fukuzawa Yukichi (1835–1901) urged his countrymen to "leave Asia," as dictated by a perceived Social Darwinian imperative to survive as a race, culture, and form of life, was echoed in Natsume Soseki's (1867–1916) poignant warning. Japan, by her physical and mental exertions, might indeed achieve "precipitous advance" in her competition with the West, but the danger of a "nervous collapse" was imminent. Now that the Japanese phoenix has risen from the ashes and the "economic miracle" has prompted Nakasone to proudly announce that Japan is already part of the West, it is time for her to reflect critically upon her more than a century-long Faustian drive to outsmart the West at its own game. The cost is high: the sensuality of her body, the sensitivity of her heart-and-mind, the purity of her soul, and the brilliance of her spirit are all at stake. Does the vision of Heisei (bringing peace to fruition) imply a return to Asia, to home? One wonders.

Tu Wei-ming
Professor of Chinese History and Philosophy
Harvard University

Rice and Melons—Japanese Agriculture in the Showa Era

Chikashi Moriguchi

In 1945, Japan was on the verge of starvation; the postwar lean years created a desire for self-sufficiency in rice production. The system of subsidies in Japan led to high prices and surpluses, but had support even in urban areas. Throughout Showa, farming was always a political question, complicated by the role of rice as a cultural symbol.

Rice is thought to have been introduced into the Japanese archipelago from southern China sometime during the Jomon era, between 5000 and 3000 B.C. In the millennia since, rice has been the primary staple of the Japanese diet and, until recently, the foundation of the national economy.

Compared with other grains, rice is extremely high in protein content (450 grams daily will supply one's complete physiological carbohydrate and protein requirements) and simpler to store or process.

The rice-growing culture took firm root in Japanese society during the Yayoi period, from 250 B.C. to 250 A.D. The Imperial Court, which dominated the country's economy at the time, upheld the land system and presided over Shinto rituals to divine the extent of the rice harvest. During the harvest festival the emperor would make an offering of rice harvested that year to the gods and then dine on it himself. Though now confined to the realm of the Imperial Court, these ceremonies are still performed today. At the rice paddy main-

Chikashi Moriguchi is Professor of Econometrics and Quantitative Economic Policy and Director of the Institute of Social and Economic Research at Osaka University.

tained within the Imperial Palace grounds, Emperor Showa himself would conduct a rice-planting ceremony in early summer and a harvest ceremony in the autumn. The sight of the emperor so engaged seemed a fitting symbol of the people's unity.

DEVELOPMENTS CENTERING ON RICE

The turbulent times of the Showa era were closely tied to the society's shifting attitudes concerning rice. During the early years (1925–1945), for instance, widely fluctuating rice prices often made the grain an investment target for speculators. (Indeed, it had long been traded—since the Edo period—primarily on the Osaka futures market.) In the years after World War II, the rice supply began to stabilize; however, the market soon began to suffer the effects of an excess. Of late, these conditions of oversupply have been punctuated by growing cries from abroad urging the deregulation of agricultural imports. Indeed, agriculture is set to become a major focus of structural readjustments in the Japanese economy. It is also true that many Japanese feel liberalization will all but destroy the nation's rice economy. The end of Showa in 1989 came at a time when deregulation of the rice market seemed imminent.

Developments centering on rice transpired at a bewildering pace during the Showa era. Predated by the rice riots of 1918, they include the destitution suffered by farming communities during the Great Depression years after the stock-market crash (1930–1935); the rapid population growth and food shortages of the immediate postwar years (1945–1948); the stabilization of agricultural harvests coupled with dramatic improvements in agricultural productivity during the nation's high-growth years (1959–1970); and a decrease in rice consumption due to Westernized diets in parallel with a worsening oversupply (1970 to present). Such events have contributed to a uniform reduction in rice acreage nationwide.

During the Showa era, Japan grew into a major industrial power. The agricultural population that had, at the outset, constituted nearly half of the economy gradually diminished in macroeconomic significance. The agricultural contribution to the net national product dropped to a minuscule 2 percent. Currently, the number of full-time and Class I nonexclusive farming households has declined to within 600,000 to 700,000 each. Taken together, they still fall short of even

5 percent of all the nation's households. Agricultural issues no longer possess the importance they once did: rice continues to lose its status as a major staple as diets steadily diversify. Yet the same cannot be said about agricultural issues at the political level, where a policy of ensuring self-sufficiency in rice supply remains predominant. The rice issue has, without question, simply been overemphasized in the political arena.

Counter to these statistical trends, however, most Japanese still possess a farmer's mind-set typified by abiding affection for the land and for nature, tentatively labeled here "agrarian idealism."*

This attitude has become all the more apparent in association with a desire for safe food and guaranteed food supplies in times of emergency, the popularity of organic farming, and environmental and farmers' protection movements. Consumer-protection activities are rather low-key in Japan at present; while consumer interest groups zealously check the safety of domestic food produce, they remain quite cool to the idea of purchasing cheaper foodstuffs from abroad. Moreover, agrarian idealism has found a place in the rationale of the nation's intelligentsia, many of whom came from farming communities.

Modern agricultural problems are influenced by a veritable Achilles heel afflicting Japanese society today: the price of land. Several explanations exist as to why, despite this problem, there has arisen no pressing class struggle between landowners and the "landless proletariat." For one, landowners are not confined to any single social stratum. Most Japanese possess some opportunity to inherit land, because they can trace their ancestry back to a farming family in the countryside. The vast majority of the nation's urban population has not descended from some dispossessed, penniless peasant class from the countryside; rather, most are essentially farmers at heart, since they still have relatives in the countryside.

At the end of the Taisho era the proportion of income expended for food was nearly 50 percent, with rice accounting for more than half. Even then, the rice consumed by low-income households usually consisted of crushed grains into which they mixed barley, chestnuts, or millet.

---

*Unlike the theoretical terms *physiocratism* and *mercantilism,* which define economic concepts, *agrarian idealism* is intended to convey aspirations steeped in rediscovered agrarian values, which see industrial capitalism as a retrogression of human culture.

Rice consumption in farming villages was much lower than that in urban districts. As much as half the rice crop produced by tenant farmers was paid to the landowner as rent. Virtually all of the remainder was sold for cash, with only enough left over to be consumed by the farming family on special occasions like the Bon Festival or New Year's Day. Whereas the relatively well-off farmers of western Japan usually enjoyed a rich rice diet, their comparatively needy counterparts to the east viewed rice as a cash crop, not something for their own personal consumption. In fact, records indicate that some farming families first began to eat rice regularly only upon receiving supplies under food-rationing programs in effect during World War II. Military recruits from the nation's northern districts reportedly found the soldier's life bearable because military chow included a satisfactory amount of rice.

DIFFICULTIES DURING AND AFTER THE WAR

The antecedents of the current debate over agricultural import liberalization go back to the food shortage Japan experienced immediately after World War II. In 1945 and 1946, the food crisis was further exacerbated by poor agricultural production conditions (only half the level attained before the war) and a massive influx of Japanese settlers returning from overseas areas no longer under imperial control. In 1942, the Staple Food Control Act was enacted to ensure the availability of food and to stabilize the national economy. It became the basis for controlling the grain market. Nevertheless, the general public was unable to produce enough food by its own efforts. To feed their hungry children, most urban mothers eventually had to go out and buy rice on the black market. Many city housewives bartered their cherished kimonos for rice and potatoes. No one who raised children at the height of the food shortage or who spent his childhood years during that period on an empty stomach (as I did) can ever forget the misery of starvation.

In the conviction that Japan's prewar agricultural system had been the principal factor behind its transformation into an expansionist, imperialist power, the Occupation forces undertook land reform. The Occupation authorities had no particular blueprint for reform, but worked with the Japanese on this legislation.

The postwar reform laws compelled absentee landlords to sell all of their tenant farmland to the government, and each resident landlord all but one hectare. Implemented from 1946 through 1948, the reform program succeeded in freeing up 81 percent of the nation's tenant acreage.

This proved to be one of the most far-reaching social reforms ever carried out anywhere, and it should go down in history as one of the most peaceful, regardless of the fact that it took place under the eye of foreign occupation forces. Behind its implementation were the enthusiastic officials in the Ministry of Agriculture and Forestry and the farm councils set up at the community level. While keeping in mind the unique conditions of each agricultural region, these groups performed a variety of tasks, including the rezoning and exchange of resident landlords' tenant farmland and the classification of absentee landlords and independent and tenant farming operations. The landowners' associations were unable to launch any means of effective resistance, since the vast majority of their leaders had been officially run out of public office.

Under these measures, highly productive tenant farmers were free to start new, independent operations and encouraged to actively invest in them, thus further expanding their agricultural productivity. The overriding emphasis on developing a system of small-scale operations, however, resulted in new types of households that were not exclusively engaged in farming but that preferred to hold onto their property, thus leading to one of the major problems facing Japanese agriculture today.

Not only did Japan's agricultural system suffer a severe drop in productivity after the war; it also faced the prospect of finding or developing new farmland to accommodate the vast numbers of Japanese settlers returning from former overseas colonies. Several programs expanded production by developing new farmland, either through the utilization of forested regions or through land reclamation projects. Vast sums of capital were poured into them.

THE HIGH-GROWTH YEARS

Demand for rice increased together with the burgeoning population during Japan's era of rapid economic growth in the 1960s. Chemical fertilizer, mechanization, and seed improvements contributed to major advances in agricultural productivity. Rice cultivation intensified even in Hokkaido. Levels of production not only stabilized; they went up. Moreover, periodic crop failures, common before World War II, became a thing of the past. With the help of industrialization and farmland reform, Japan had at last succeeded in realizing the objectives agricultural administrative officials had only dreamed of before World War II: self-sufficiency in rice production under a system of independent farmers.

Though Japan's export market improved during the high-growth years, it was domestic demand that led the economy forward. The increasing popularity of electric appliances and other durable goods sustained a growth in consumption which larger incomes made possible. The life-style of the typical American housewife had lost much of its drudgery with the help of labor-saving appliances. And as such, it became a model for Japanese housewives to emulate. The closing gap between incomes in the urban and agricultural communities not only allowed farming housewives to join in the rush to acquire new durable items; more importantly, it helped free them from much of the dual burden they traditionally bore at home and in the fields. The era of dramatic economic growth brought astonishing improvements in the living standards of the farming household when compared with conditions before World War II.

Unfortunately, Japanese agriculture was not to enjoy a happy ending. True, its development had been largely supported by the nation's high degree of industrialization. Yet, at the same time, a price had been paid. Industrial sector growth ensured greater tax revenues, revenues which the government used to heavily subsidize the agricultural sector. But the rising living standards that accompanied economic growth began to alter Japanese dietary habits. The Japanese diet began to shift from eating one's fill of white rice to enrichment with a variety of side dishes typical of Western diets. The consumption of bread, dairy products, and meat surged. In short, rice consumption began to decline in the mid-1960s, just when Japanese agriculture had at long last attained the capacity to produce a good rice crop every year.

The transformation Japanese agriculture underwent from 1960 to 1980 is without historical precedent. Over this period, the per capita share of real GNP expanded some 3.3 times, while the agricultural component of the net national product dropped from 9.8 to 2.5 percent.

In addition, the farming population dropped from 35.7 to 6 percent of the national total as many formerly full-time farming households began supplementing their operations with other business activities.

In the early 1980s, for example, the author had the opportunity to visit a new farming community named Ohgatamura, in Akita Prefecture. The outgrowth of a large-scale government land-reclamation project from 1957 to 1966, this community had transformed 221 square kilometers of Lake Hachirogata, the nation's second-largest lake, into dry, arable land. In 1968, full-scale rice-growing operations got under way, and by 1970, some 1,600 settlers had moved in. Each household was allotted a large, rectangular, fifteen-hectare strip of land. Considering that the average full-time Japanese farming household managed at most but one to two hectares, the Ohgatamura tracts were expected to be efficient large-scale models for rice cultivation.

The government's rice-acreage reduction measure has prevented these Ohgatamura "pioneers" from cultivating rice on more than half their available acreage. Under such restraints, their farmland has begun to take on a changed appearance: the once-expansive tracts of rice paddy are either being replaced by or interspersed with vinyl-sheet-covered structures for greenhouse cultivation or dry-land fields for other crops.

Climbing a fire tower in the middle of Ohgatamura to have a broader view of the perimeter, the author spotted several traditionally styled black-shingle estates among the settlers' homes. As the guide explained, they were the homes of wealthy melon growers. Several households had taken advantage of crop-conversion subsidies and quickly devoted rice-paddy acreage to Ams melon cultivation.

The era of high growth raised both productivity and wages in the nation's major manufacturing industries. As industrial workers' wages climbed, that of farming households fell further behind. Nevertheless, the benefits of economic growth became more evenly spread: comparatively higher prices became the rule in comparatively less productive industries like the farming and distribution trades. Calculations of the producer's price for rice eventually took into account both the labor costs associated with rice cultivation and the average wage of urban workers. Since it could prove politically suicidal to directly pass on the burden of high producer prices to urban dwellers, the government instead held consumer rice prices down. The difference is paid out through a special food-control budget in the general account, but with the resulting deficit covered by national tax revenues.

The Basic Agriculture Act prohibits individuals or corporations from entering agricultural activities. In addition, it guarantees the government purchase of rice at producer's prices. By the mid-1970s, such favorable treatment enabled the average farm household to enjoy an annual income surpassing that of wage-earner households (calculated per household member). In spite of this policy, higher producer prices have done more to enable nonexclusive farming households to bolster their farm income with a minimum of effort than they have to spur greater production by full-time farmers. Improvements in agricultural chemicals and mechanization have made tilling, planting, cutting, threshing, and drying operations much easier. The head of a nonexclusive farm household eventually needed only about ten days of his paid vacation from other employment to raise a successful rice crop each year.

Besides enabling many rice-producing households to enter into other nonexclusive operations, the real absurdity of the method used to set the producer's price for rice manifested itself in other ways. For instance, though full-time farm households were made the model in calculations of the costs associated with rice cultivation, the results were also applied to the rice the government purchased from nonexclusive households. This signified none other than an endorsement of the status quo, in that it offered supplementary income to small-time operations, be they the suburban agribusinessman who utilized his paid vacation time to cultivate rice, or the exclusively rice-oriented farm household that, nonetheless, had offered no gains in efficiency. This state of affairs only encouraged the nonexclusive households to cling to their landholdings, thus hindering the development of large-scale farming operations or the more effective utilization of farmland in urban districts.

Through the high-growth years, central government policies sought primarily to raise the efficiency of Japan's domestic industries by deregulating the import of raw materials. On the other hand, by protecting the manufacturing sector from foreign competition, these policies were also intended to improve domestic productivity and employment opportunities as well as to continue the viability of small, independent businesses. The same can be said of agricultural policy: dairy and livestock farming were also treated like manufacturing industries that imported coarse grains as raw materials to produce animal-protein products. Imports of meat, processed meat products, canned vegetables or fruit, and other agricultural goods had long been subject to strict regulation. Import quotas remain in effect on some of these items even today.

Do Japanese consumers prefer the deregulation of agricultural imports? The government conducted an opinion poll at the end of 1987 to find out. The results revealed surprisingly deep concerns regarding food supplies. In effect, the majority of urban respondents expressed anxiety about the extent to which the nation had already become dependent on imports for food, and answered that they would not like to see that dependence increase even further. The same reasoning made them pessimistic about opening the agricultural market to imports.

Since 1987, the disparities between Japan's high domestic food prices with those abroad have widened as the yen has continued to strengthen and food prices have generally sagged worldwide. Such developments only mean a greater burden for the Japanese consumer. Yet, one thing is now clear: as long as the strong yen persists, rice—the bulwark of Japanese agriculture—will be subjected to phased market deregulation. This should by no means result in the destruction of Japanese agriculture. First of all, it does not matter whether nonexclusive farm households lose their benefits from rice cultivation because their earnings from other activities surpass their income from farming. And in any event, the Japanese farming population will now decline substantially over the interim because most farm households have been unable to find heirs or successors to take over anything other than the land.

Deregulation of agricultural imports would eventually lead to the liberalization of the heretofore untouchable domestic rice market, be that a phased-in reality or not. This development would undoubtedly strengthen the government's rice-acreage reduction policy. Here, however, commentators agree that the shortage of suitable residential space could also be overcome if the government were to adopt a more discriminating approach favoring full-time farming households yet prohibiting rice cultivation by nonexclusive farming operations in suburban areas. This would encourage the latter to leave agricultural pursuits behind and thereby help open up farmland for more efficient utilization.

It is simply wishful thinking, however, to expect that farm deregulation alone is going to spontaneously initiate the above process. Though more and more multistoried apartment complexes are under construction in Tokyo, within the perimeter of the city's main Yamanote commuter-train artery, residential structures still average no more than three stories high. Hence, not only agricultural land in the suburbs but even expensive urban residential areas are being used inefficiently. In addition, exceptionally strong private property rights put yet another damper on the adequate provision of residential land.

Efforts have long been under way to develop a tax structure that would encourage more effective land use. Also, agricultural imports could replace farming operations that tie up inordinately large tracts. Relocating government functions to other regions could slow the concentration of the nation's population in urban regions, such as Tokyo. And "farm factories," which draw on hydroponic techniques to efficiently cultivate vegetables and fruit indoors, have also become commercially feasible. These new high-tech farm industries are likely to prosper even without any increase in farmland.

Though the agricultural issues that spawned so much turbulence in early Showa have been settled, the successes enjoyed in late Showa have failed to result in a happy conclusion. Deregulation and greater efficiency remain as problematic legacies of this era.

REFERENCES

Yujiro Hayami, *Nogyo Keizairon* (Agricultural Economics), (Tokyo: Iwanami Press, 1986).

Ronald Dore, *Nihon no Nochi Kaikaku* (Japan's Agrarian Revolution), (Tokyo: Iwanami Press, 1959), a translation of *Land Reform* (London: Oxford University Press, 1959).

Ryo Matsuoka, *Nosei Muyoron* (Farm Administration Unneeded), (Tokyo: Marunouchi Press, 1985).

Taro Oyama, *Kome Jiyuuka-kakumei* (The Rice Liberalization Movement), (Tokyo: Shinchosha, 1989).

Bringing Politics Back into Japan

Michio Muramatsu

Because Japan's Diet has been dominated by one party for so long, many Western observers have missed the legislature's mode of operations, its effectiveness in responding to public opinion, in negotiating differences. The prewar Diet, so limited in its powers, bore only the slightest resemblance to what now exists.

In Europe it is common to refer to a "postwar settlement" in which the major social forces of each country reached an accommodation of interests that enabled all to participate in a stable political framework.[1] By contrast, postwar Japan is often portrayed as a country governed by relatively exclusive political and social elites who have been able to ignore or direct a basically passive population. In reality, however, Japan has experienced its own version of postwar settlement, and in this article I should like to outline its evolution.

The prewar legacy left Japan without a coherent political leadership and without the institutional means to accommodate the country's major social forces in a stable political system. The Meiji constitution of the late nineteenth century, while incorporating many progressive elements from Western models, failed to establish a stable pattern of interaction among state institutions, resulting in instability and a lack of effective national leadership. Moreover, mass social forces had only begun to be organized in the prewar period, and their accommodation in a democratic context was aborted by the military-dominated politics of the wartime era.

The American Occupation provided a basic institutional design for postwar Japanese politics, but its reforms also introduced many new groups to the national political scene: a new class of independent

Michio Muramatsu is Professor of Government in the Department of Law at Kyoto University.

farmers, a highly organized and vocal labor movement, leftist parties enjoying unprecedented success, and a less integrated business community. Once the controlling hand of the Occupation army was lifted, it was by no means a foregone conclusion that these new social forces would be able to reach a stable accommodation of interests within the new parliamentary democracy. Economic success, when it came, facilitated the accommodation of diverse social interests in many ways, but it also distributed the political resources of money, time, and political skills more widely than ever before, perpetually heightening the conflict between groups.

I would like to argue that Japan's success at achieving political integration and stability has been able to overcome political crises and nurture public trust in government. This is not an argument for state dominance, as is often made in analyses of Japan's postwar economic growth.[2] Rather, it is an argument for the centrality of politics in Japan's own postwar settlement.

After a brief review of the prewar heritage, I will demonstrate how each major phase of postwar political development has witnessed the accommodation of more social forces in the political system. In the 1950s, the conservatives consolidated their leadership on a foundation of agriculture and business, largely excluding opposition social and political elements from state decision making. The 1960s, however, saw a new politics of inclusion pursued in relation to opposition parties, and by the 1980s the conservative political establishment had begun to increase its urban support by addressing more and more of its programs to the interests of the new middle class. This process of expanding accommodation has involved constant pushing and pulling between diverse social groups, and it has acquired continuous policy innovation. The success of this process so far should not blind us to the pluralistic political dynamics that have made that success possible.

PREWAR POLITICS

At the core of the prewar political system was the Meiji constitution, which left lawmaking, the administration of justice, and all major governmental powers legally in the hands of the emperor. If the true exercise of authority was in the Imperial Diet, the Cabinet, the bureaucracy, the Privy Council, and the army and navy, then forging a consensus satisfying the separate demands and interests of all these institutions was next to impossible. Until the Imperial Diet started functioning in 1890, a small group of founding fathers managed to integrate the political system. After 1890, however, growing opposition between elected and unelected officials precluded the easy emergence of a solid political leadership.[3] Those elected included members of the House of Representatives and, except for prefectural governors, the chief executives and assemblymen of local governments.

Political authority shifted gradually into the hands of the elected elite in the Imperial Diet and especially the House of Representatives. But there were still deep-rooted constraints on the Diet's ability to form a strong national leadership. For one, the Cabinet was appointed by the emperor on the instructions of his advisers; its composition was beyond the control of the Diet. Moreover, though he was head of the Cabinet, the prime minister did not have ultimate authority over the ministers of the army and the navy. They had implicit veto powers and reported directly to the emperor.[4]

The power of elected officials evolved in three phases. In the first, the appointed elite successfully prevented elected officials from gaining authority; it also tried to wield total control over the Cabinet. In this period, from 1889 to the Sino-Japanese War of 1894–1895, "the clan bureaucrats made their greatest bid to exclude opponents and to consolidate their own power under the Meiji constitution that they had themselves engineered."[5] Although the clan bureaucrats were by no means unified, they did enjoy a certain degree of solidarity as founders of the Meiji state, and they shared a common enemy, the emerging people's parties.

In the second phase, the founding "oligarchs" attempted to facilitate the workings of the Diet through an alliance with elected legislators. This avenue, chosen because the people's parties in the Diet had ultimate authority over approval of the national budget and had thus become a force to be accommodated, led to the great alliance which spanned the so-called Katsura-Saionji period (1901–1912). In the 1920s, however, the influential power of the elected legislators eclipsed that of the founders and their nonelected disciples. In 1918 Takashi Hara organized the first Japanese Cabinet consisting mainly of elected officials. The subsequent establishment of universal suffrage in 1925 symbolized the new political order.

In 1926, the first year of the Showa emperor's reign, the elected political figures in both the upper and the lower house of the Diet consolidated their power and embarked on a competitive quest to satisfy the electorate's new political demands. Among the Diet's most pressing challenges were public cries for reform from the masses. Both the Diet and the political parties were faced with successive public demands, including a tax-reduction movement carried on by the Chamber of Commerce and an anti-rice-dumping movement led by the Keitonokai Party.

From the late 1920s on, the demands of the army and the navy became more pronounced. Both military branches, determined to upgrade their level of preparedness, sought a larger slice of the national budget. As a result, the military was politicized, becoming involved in debate and compromise with the Diet and various societal groups. The military, in conflict with various political parties, imagined that the latter were putting their interests first.

In the third phase, which begins with the Manchurian Incident of 1931 and extends to the end of World War II, the political system became inured to demands from below, and elected officials gradually lost influence. The "new order" founded by Prime Minister Konoe in the late 1930s sought to organize all social groups into a single body of national support. Konoe failed, however, to unite the political elites around a coherent set of objectives. In the end the military took charge of the government to oversee the conduct of war operations. In the face of this raw exercise of authority, the Diet was essentially powerless. Neither the elected Diet nor the nonelected civilian political elite could control the military.

THE ESTABLISHMENT OF A DIET-CENTERED GOVERNMENT

The postwar political system resolved the issue of national leadership by giving the Diet highest authority in policy-making decisions. This is not to imply that Diet members and their staff were solely responsible for the preparatory work involved in performing that duty. Some assert that the official bureaucracy made a larger contribution to policy formulation. Others point to the growing influence of the political parties and the importance that the policy-making process assumed within the ruling party itself, with certain Diet functions falling under control of the Liberal Democratic Party (LDP) alone. The Diet was charged with the responsibility of making decisions and aligning policies to help resolve conflicts between differing societal interests and ideologies. More than that, it had also to develop a national consensus for its solutions. Postwar political practice demanded that such a consensus be derived through the bargaining process, in Diet deliberations attended by the opposition.

According to some observers, the Japanese Diet subjects bills to far more revision than the British Parliament.[6] Diet members typically wield considerable influence over the legislative process by exercising their authority to question or submit motions on bills.[7] About 60 percent of the Diet's members answer that they have major influence in deliberations on national policy. Critics who downplay the role of the Diet say that it is dependent on bureaucrats who serve as administration representatives. Some say that bureaucrats have literally invaded the Diet. A more accurate assessment would be that while the system may have initially fostered dependence on the bureaucracy, it underwent a transformation that has changed all this.[8]

The Diet-centered policy-making process eventually split into two separate stages, primarily because the conservative party held the reins of power for so long. The first involves submission of policy proposals to the Diet. As the key political actors in this process, LDP Diet members, concerned interest groups, and bureaucrats negotiate, and bills are drafted within the administrative branches. It is at this stage that agreement is forged among all parties concerned. The LDP has developed the most powerful policy-making system of any political party in a modern Western democracy.

The second stage involves Diet debate and compromise between "the government"—that is, the ruling party—and the opposition parties. Most LDP-drafted bills obtain national approval because Diet deliberations permit opposition parties and their supporters to revise and criticize. This second process offers the LDP the opportunity to obtain a bare minimum of assent from individuals and groups who oppose its bills in draft form. On many occasions, the LDP has withdrawn bills in the face of strong opposition though it possessed a majority in both houses.

THE FIRST TURNING POINT: YOSHIDA'S LEADERSHIP

Postwar Japanese politics have undergone three major turning points since the nation formally regained its independence. The first, from

1951 to 1954, allowed Japan to establish its own postwar political system. At the reins of the government during this period was Shigeru Yoshida (1946–1947, 1948–1954). He introduced a political strategy, the "conservative establishment line," that became the fundamental framework for the Japanese political system. It rested on two pillars: Japanese dependence on the United States for its military security; strong emphasis on economic development while downplaying constitutional reform.[9] During this first period, the government redirected the Occupation's reforms to the task of consolidating its own authority. In effect, these actions came to be known as "reverse-course"; they amounted to revisions of the democratic policies promulgated by the Occupation forces. The reverse-course strategy was strongly opposed by the Japan Socialist Party (JSP) on the Diet floor. Indeed, when revisions to the Police Act were sought, the Diet became a place of chaos. The explosive Japanese Diet has often been presented as an example of political immaturity. In fact, it has served as a viable platform for even the smallest opposition parties to articulate their ideologies.

The major conflict of postwar Japanese politics, the growing standoff between conservatives and reformists, came to a head during this period. There were the intense disputes over the "one-sided" peace treaty signed as a condition for Japan's regaining its independence, and also over the security treaty formed with the United States. The reformists sought to atone for Japan's complicity in World War II through a pacifistic stance. They feared that the plans of their conservative opponents to "revise" the Occupation's reforms were part of a provocative strategy to restore the prewar political system. On the political battlefield, the LDP represented the conservatives, and the JSP the opposition. This antagonism between leftists and conservatives would define the character of Japanese politics for years to come.

Conservative Japanese politicians struggled to develop the political system set out under the new constitution. In essence, they sought to have their influential powers in the policy-making process translate into greater support from their constituents back home.[10] If final decisions were to be made within the Diet, then the Diet had to be reinforced as a forum for compromise. Unlike their leftist counterparts, who tried to influence the public with avant-garde doctrines that held little appeal to a still predominantly agrarian population, more traditional conservative political parties rooted their appeal in culture and pragmatic policies.[11]

During the same period, the Japanese administration clearly displayed its will to rule the country, to reemerge as an independent state. Yoshida's refusal to capitulate to John Foster Dulles's demand that Japan rearm itself is already well known. The same resistance to outside influence may be seen in the establishment of national policies dealing with matters other than national defense or security.[12]

Conservative parties utilized the Diet-centered system to their own advantage. It allowed for the expression and absorption of public opinion, enabling conservatives to test the limits of opposition cooperation or compromise. Still, it left little room for compromise on issues of principle. On such matters, opponents were effectively ignored. We could say, then, that the Yoshida leadership employed "exclusionary strategies." The political base upon which conservatives had once stood had been severely eroded. The emperor's ideological importance had been destroyed; agrarian reforms had weakened the traditional conservative order in farming communities. For these reasons, it became all the more important to mobilize voters in legislators' home districts. The Yoshida administration employed the policy-making abilities of the bureaucracy; national policy preparation became a function of the bureaucratic organs of government.

THE SECOND TURNING POINT (1960–1980)

Hayato Ikeda's administration marked the beginning of the second turning point in postwar Japanese politics.

Ichiro Hatoyama and Nobusuke Kishi, who led the government after Yoshida, presided at a time when the forces of conservatism and socialism clashed over major political issues, including revision of the constitution, remilitarization, and the introduction of single-member electoral districts. The political environment was unstable. The climax came in 1960 with the violent collision over the Japan-U.S. Security Treaty, the greatest challenge the government experienced in the postwar era. Some 100,000 citizens were said to have been actively drawn into the fracas as national opinion divided over the issue. To the government, the challenge lay in proving that it could successfully overcome this crisis and set out on a new political course.

What, then, was Ikeda's choice? An apolitical pact, to foster economic growth and enhance industrial productivity.[13] It eased dissent with material surpluses generated through the economic growth in the 1960s and restrained the extreme political activism of the Socialists and the labor unions. Ikeda's settling of the violent coal miners' strikes at the Mitsui and Miike mines symbolized a new era of reconciliation.

Within the political framework of postwar Japan, it was easy enough to do. Since the days of Meiji, Japan had sought relentlessly to catch up with the West; no military defeat would cool that interest. It was easy to accept the persuasive imagery of the political elite, who suggested that the pie be made bigger so that each would have a larger slice. In the Ikeda government, such economic concerns took on importance as major political priorities. The Cabinet decided to implement an industrial growth policy based on Ikeda's "income doubling plan." This official stress on the potential of the Japanese economy stimulated economic development by convincing businessmen that they would have a favorable political environment; it also drew public attention away from political and diplomatic issues, focusing it instead on the economy and internal affairs.[14]

The second goal of Ikeda's apolitical pact also met success through his "low profile" in the Diet. Measures were introduced to foster reconciliation with the opposition parties and to win over labor. Success in this area called for new efforts in diplomacy. Japan's sovereignty over Okinawa had been lost during the Occupation. For the Japanese government, regaining control over Okinawa was an important, unresolved issue. The Kishi administration had demanded that Okinawa be placed back in Japanese hands, but Ikeda stopped short of directly mentioning the issue by name, opting instead to stress that Japan would strive to improve Okinawa's social and economic status. By handling the Okinawa question through quiet diplomacy, Ikeda prevented it from becoming a topic of open contention with opposition parties.[15]

The opposition, exhausted by its battles against the Japan-U.S. Security Treaty, went along relatively quietly with Ikeda's emphasis on internal affairs rather than international relations. The same may be said for the labor unions. The key features of Ikeda's leadership success may be summed up as the application of Yoshida's conservative strategy toward expressly economic goals. This assured Ikeda's growing base of national support. In short, he succeeded in achieving the goals of his apolitical pact on a national scale.[16]

In principle, the Ikeda government adopted a strategy of inclusion to deal with the opposition, just the reverse of the exclusionary policies practiced by the four previous Cabinets: those of Yoshida, Hatoyama, Ishibashi, and Kishi. Subsequent administrations, headed by Tanaka, Miki, and Fukuda, adopted political policies similar to those of Ikeda. It was the record-breaking eight years (1964–1972) of Sato's leadership that achieved complete public approval of the pact Ikeda had introduced.

The inclusive strategy of the LDP government thus continued into the 1970s. Environmental regulation laws were passed in the Diet in response to citizens' movements and an increase in the number of leftists' local governments in major metropolitan areas such as Tokyo and Osaka. Furthermore, the LDP's support among the voters continued to decline in this period, leaving the party with only the slimmest majority in the Diet in the mid-1970s. To overcome these "crises," the LDP government had to create new welfare programs such as pension plans and health insurance.

THE THIRD TURNING POINT: THE NEW CONSERVATISM

The third turning point in postwar Japanese politics began during the Fukuda administration (1976–1978) when the nation's budget deficit grew to immense proportions. Political strategies of inclusion were no longer feasible in the face of a monstrous ¥200 trillion deficit. Whereas Japan in the late 1970s survived several international crises (currency revaluation and the oil crises), another danger was developing internally. It was at this point that trade friction with the United States finally boiled over. U.S. demands were at first limited to the textile, communications equipment, and automobile industries. By the mid-1980s, however, they had extended to calls for liberalizing Japan's agricultural production, for participation in bidding for construction projects, and for the removal of "cultural barriers" to trade in Japan's distribution system. This was a direct attack on the LDP's primary base of political support. As it turned out, though, the extent of the dual shock from the internal deficit and the outside trade pressures would not be adequately recognized during the Fukuda and Ohira administrations. Concrete steps to deal with these issues would have to wait until the 1980s, when they were implemented by the Suzuki and Nakasone Cabinets. In that undertaking, Nakasone's leadership qualities were displayed.

First, both the Suzuki and the Nakasone Cabinets targeted financial reconstruction through measures forged by the Second Ad Hoc Commission on Administrative Reform. The commission, asserting that it would achieve that goal without raising taxes, set out to cut national expenditures, keeping a tight budget while imposing certain selected cuts in public-project and farm subsidies. These actions showed that the ruling party had second thoughts about the policy of accommodation it had heretofore followed. The commission called for the reform of the Administrative Organization Act and the privatization of the nation's railway (JR) and telephone system (NTT); both recommendations were accepted. The railway system's privatization alone created immense change. In addition to his efforts to rebuild the national finances, Nakasone, near the end of his tenure, proposed a sales tax to reduce the rate of income tax. Meanwhile, trade dissension between Japan and the United States grew all the more intense.

The secret to Nakasone's strong leadership was the successful formation of a network of government administration, with him at the center.[17] From this pivotal position, Nakasone was able to display leadership of presidential proportions. To get a supporting base for his influence, he went beyond the LDP and the bureaucracy to seek the support of public opinion. However, most LDP politicians, together with the government bureaucracy and the "alliance of policy beneficiaries" grew increasingly antagonistic toward Nakasone's comprehensive strategy, for it threatened their own vested interests. This opposition would have important repercussions in the course of time.

Nakasone's authority rested on two bases: central structure and public opinion. Public opinion, in fact, was middle-class opinion as reflected in public opinion surveys. Urban dwellers, and particularly the salaried class, had become fed up with the government's heavy dependence on income taxes for its financial base, which extracted more and more of their hard-earned income and reallotted it to rural communities. This dissatisfaction fueled their support for the efforts of the Nakasone government and the Second Ad Hoc Commission on Administrative Reform to make government smaller.

The alliance between corporate labor and management in large enterprises deserves attention; it was the basis for Nakasone's political support in public opinion.[18] Managers and workers, largely urban dwellers, share interests. Rather than expect help from government, they much prefer that it stay out of the private sector's business affairs. What they do expect are the basic functions of government—promoting diplomacy, law and order, and macroeconomic policies. While conflicts exist between labor and management on minimum wage and employee welfare standards, neither side feels the need to politicize such issues. In fact, workers agree that these are matters best resolved by companies themselves. Such a labor-management alliance constitutes a frontal assault on the vested interests of groups that have benefited under the government policy of inclusion. The third turning point was reached when these opposing forces assumed central political roles in expressing their preferences for less government influence and involvement.

In the midst of this growing political turmoil, Nakasone decided to link the urban middle class's preferences for "small government" and greater internationalism to his own policies for administrative reform and diplomacy. In doing so, he conceived of a means to rebuild the structure of public support for the LDP. Behind the effort to cut income taxes and compensate for that with an indirect tax was one explicit goal: to shift away from the LDP's traditional base of support in a rural and urban periphery coalition of farmers and small businesses and better accommodate the interests of an urban middle-class coalition. But this aim was easily defeated when Nakasone's proposal for a flat-rate sales tax to be paid by manufacturers ran into opposition. He won the 1986 election only when he promised not to introduce the large-scale sales tax he was considering.

Obviously, the LDP could not shift to complete reliance on an urban coalition if it wanted to remain the ruling party. To translate its failures of 1986 and 1987 into its successfully implemented reforms of 1988 and 1989, the party realized it had to make major concessions to groups with vested interests. Even if the LDP recognized the desires of urban dwellers, it would not be able to win a majority of seats in the Diet on their votes alone. It was politically dangerous for the LDP to adopt policies shifting its accommodation toward urbanites and workers. Such circumstances meant that for every two innovative steps forward, it had to take one traditionalist step back.

SUMMARY

Unlike the prewar years, the postwar era brought Japan stable political leadership, though in the form of single-party dominance. With the first turning point of the early 1950s, the principles of postwar Japanese politics were sought in a climate of ideological warfare; the conservative government held its right wing in check and set up a conservative establishment line in opposition to left-wing socialist parties. More than merely an ideological platform for economic development, however, the conservative establishment line was a sound basis for moderate Japanese nationalist and pacifist expression. The second turning point came in 1960. Ikeda's Cabinet reapplied Yoshida's conservative establishment track with a distinct new emphasis on economic development. Japanese politics finally began to reach its own postwar settlement. As such, the period saw a conservative-progressive reconciliation of sorts. Under its new inclusive strategy, the LDP government expanded public programs in order to respond to broadly based popular demands in the 1970s.

The primary issues of the third postwar political period, the budget deficit and international trade friction, have been addressed by successive prime ministers. A ruling coalition centered around Nakasone was responsible for inaugurating the Second Ad Hoc Commission on Administrative Reform. Its bold policies—subsidy cuts, deregulation, and privatization—were seen as a direct menace to a host of vested interests. Evidently this gave rise to a new form of political contention far different from the conservative leftist rivalry of bygone eras. Specifically, it is symbolized by the opposition between two alliances: one, the interest groups that have benefited most from the development of large government; the other, an anti-large-government group of urban middle-class elements. In Japan, the growing political conflict defies traditional definition as a standoff pitting conservative against leftist.

ACKNOWLEDGMENTS

I am indebted to Professors Gregory Kasza and Toshiya Kitayama for their valuable comments on the draft of this paper.

ENDNOTES

[1]For a useful argument on the case of postwar settlements in European countries, see Mark Kesselman et al., *European Politics in Transition* (Lexington, Mass.: D.C. Heath, 1987).

[2]For scholarly treatments of the Japanese state, see James C. Abegglen, "The Economic Growth of Japan," *Scientific American* 222 (March 1970): 31–37; Chalmers Johnson, *MITI and the Japanese Miracle* (Stanford: Stanford University Press, 1982); Karel Van Wolferen, *The Enigma of Japanese Power: People and Politics in a Stateless Society* (New York: Macmillan, 1989); and T.J. Pempel, "Japan Inc. Unbundled," *Journal of Japanese Studies* 13 (2) (Summer 1987): 271–306.

[3]The concepts of the "elected" and the "unelected" are borrowed from the following article: Ryuji Miyazaki, "Sengonihon no seijihatten to rengoseiji" (Political Development and Coalition Politics in Postwar Japan), in Hajime Shinohara, ed., *Rengoseiji* (Coalition Politics), vol. 1 (Tokyo: Iwanami, 1985).

[4]Ibid., 202–3.

[5]Ibid., 203.

[6]Michael Mochizuki, "Managing and Influencing the Japanese Legislative Process: the Role of Parties and the National Diet," Ph.D. dissertation, Harvard University, 102.

[7]Michio Muramatsu, "Parties, Pressure Groups and Bureaucrats in the Japanese Legislative Process," *Law Journal of Hokkaido University* 34 (1) (1983): 139–66.

[8]Koji Kakizawa, "Kasumigaseki sanchome no Okurakanryo wa megane o kaketa dobunezumi to iwareru zasetsukan ni nayamu sugoi eriitotachi" (Discouragement and Frustration for Japan's Super-Elite: Kasumigaseki's Bespectacled, Drab-suited Finance Bureaucrats), *Finance* 12 (4) (1976): 36–37.

[9]Shigeru Hori, *Sengoseiji no oboegaki* (Postwar Political Memorandum), (Tokyo: The Mainichi Newspaper, 1975); Michio Muramatsu and Ellis Krauss, "The Conservative Policy Line and the Development of Patterned Pluralism," in Kozo Yamamura and Yasukichi Yasuda, eds., *The Political Economy of Japan*, vol. 1 (Stanford: Stanford University Press, 1987).

[10]Takashi Mikuriya, "Mizushigenkaihatsu to sengo seisakuketteikatei: Showa 20 nendai–30 nendai" (Development of Water Resources and the Postwar Policy Decision-making Process: 1945–1965), in *Nihon Kindai Seijishi Kenkyukai: Kanryosei no seisei to tenkai* (The Modern Japan Political History Research Institute: The Formation and Development of the Japanese Bureaucracy), (Tokyo: Yamakawa, 1986).

[11]Ibid., 186–87.

[12]Ibid., 257.

[13]Masaru Mabuchi uses this term in a different context. See "Financial Deregulation in Japan: Limits of Bureaucratic Dominance," paper presented at the SSRC Workshop in Washington, D.C., Public-Private Exchange, June 3–4, 1989.

[14]Yutaka Kozai, "The Politics of Economic Development," in Yamamura and Yasuda.

[15]Yasuko Kono, "Okinawa-henkan o meguru Nichibeikosho 1965–1969, Kakunuki, Hondonami" (U.S.-Japan Negotiations on the Return of Okinawa 1965–1969: Nuclear Restrictions as Severe as on the Main Islands), in *Nenpo Kindai Nihan Kenkyu: Nihongaiko no kikiishiki* (Modern Japan Research—Annual Report: Sense of Crisis in Japanese Diplomacy), vol. 7 (Tokyo: Yamakawa Publishing Co., 1985), 245–80.

[16]Charles Maier, "The Politics of Productivity: Foundations of American International Economic Policy after World War II," in Peter Katzenstein, *Between Plenty and Power* (Madison: University of Wisconsin Press, 1978).

[17]Michio Muramatsu, "In Search of National Identity: Politics and Policies of the Nakasone Administration," *Journal of Japanese Studies* (2) (Summer 1987): 307–42.

[18]Mitsutoshi Itoh, "Daikigyoroshirengo no keisei" (The Formation of the Large Enterprise Labor-Management Coalition), *Leviathan* (2) (Spring 1988): 53–70.

Diplomacy and the Military in Showa Japan

Shinichi Kitaoka

When Showa began in the twenties, Japan saw itself as a vulnerable, resource-barren nation surrounded by rapacious empires. The greatest of these was the United States, the heir, in Japan's mind, to earlier European dominations. The events that led Japan into the Pacific War need to be recalled if its postwar economic victory under Pax Americana is to be understood.

The Showa period began officially on December 25, 1926, but Crown Prince Hirohito had become regent five years earlier, on November 25, 1921, when he took up imperial duties on behalf of his ailing father, Emperor Taisho. This date is significant because it followed so closely on the beginning of the Washington Conference and the assassination of Prime Minister Hara Takashi, who was the first Japanese leader to become concerned about the rise of the United States as a world power and who arranged for Japan's participation in the Washington Conference to strengthen the ties with the United States.

During this time the United States was not only a major power; it was an empire. The American empire was not so much based on the drive to acquire colonies as to impose the U.S. conception of justice and right upon other countries. Japan's other large neighbors were also empires with ideologies of their own—the Soviet Union, carrying the banner of Marxism-Leninism, and China, building on

Shinichi Kitaoka is Professor of Japanese Political History in the Department of Law and Politics at Rikkyo University.

its Middle Kingdom heritage toward national liberation and eventually Maoism. The major problem for Japanese diplomacy in the Showa period was how to cope with these neighboring empires, particularly the strongest and richest in the modern era—that of the United States.

In the pre–World War II period Japan felt far from self-sufficient in comparison with these giant neighbors. Consequently, her prewar foreign affairs pivoted around a sense of the country's vulnerability. Her postwar relations must be considered from this vantage point as well. The history of Showa diplomacy, then, centers on the issue of security.

THE COLLAPSE OF INTERNATIONAL COOPERATION

Following World War I, the central principles of international relations, especially in East Asia, were those espoused by the United States, though it had been a maverick in world affairs before the war. The termination of the Anglo-Japanese Alliance through the Washington Conference symbolized the demise of the old order: the tie between two nations, sealed by an alliance, the most orthodox and powerful instrument of foreign policy in classical diplomacy, was abrogated for the sake of preserving Anglo-American relations, which were not bound by any such formal document.

With the declaration of its Open Door policy in 1899, the United States extended its policy beyond the North and South American continents and became a contender for power in East Asia. It was only natural for the United States, having arrived in East Asia after the European powers had established their spheres of interest, to seek an equal place for itself in trade.

Hoping that a Japanese victory would open up Manchuria, the United States favored Japan in the Russo-Japanese War (1904–1905). After this war, however, U.S. exports to Manchuria decreased rather than increased. Far East experts in the U.S. State Department were convinced that Japan was not playing fair, that the only way to prevent Japan from taking over all of Manchuria was to challenge its monopolistic South Manchurian Railway, the lifeline of Japan's control over the region, by building another railway paralleling the Japanese-operated line.

Revolutionary U.S. Foreign Policy

With this shift in U.S. Far Eastern policy, the meaning of the Open Door policy began to change. The original Open Door policy had been premised on de facto recognition of spheres of influence. Demanding equality of opportunity for the construction of a project with the immense strategic implications of a railway was tantamount to repudiating existing spheres of influence. It also contradicted the agreement that had been concluded between Japan and China prohibiting the building of a line in the vicinity paralleling the South Manchurian Railway.

Initially, the United States did not know that such an agreement existed, but even after being informed, did not respect it. There are many indications that U.S. State Department officials of the time did not think it necessary to respect agreements and treaties thrust upon weaker nations by the strong.

Another example of the heretical nature of American diplomacy occurred in 1915, when, through its Twenty-one Demands to China, Japan sought the right for Japanese temples and shrines to purchase and own land in China. Fearing that large Japanese temples would become fronts for spies, the Chinese were reluctant to give in on this point. The Western powers, on the other hand, found denying land ownership for Japanese shrines and temples difficult since land ownership for churches was allowed. President Woodrow Wilson, however, stood firmly on the Chinese side, rejecting the advice of his secretary of state, William J. Bryan.

Soon after the controversy over the Twenty-one Demands, the United States declared that it would not tolerate any violation of its treaty rights or of the principle of the open door and equal opportunity, a pronouncement reflecting its disdain for international treaties and agreements imposed by force. Needless to say, America's own beginnings as a nation that had risen from colonial status to independence lay behind this view of affairs. The anti-imperialist stance of the United States was indeed admirable, but at that time, it represented a deviation from the norms of big-power international politics.

The Post–World War I International Environment

When World War I came to an end, it was this once-revolutionary diplomacy of the United States that became preponderant in the world. Japan had contrived to keep the United States at bay by forming alliances with other imperialist powers—Russia, France, and England. The United States emerged from World War I the most powerful nation in the world, however, and Great Britain, which had fallen to second place, found itself far more dependent on relations with the United States than before. The empires of Russia and Germany had collapsed; France had been severely weakened. Japan had no strong ally to turn to.

Japan also used persuasion to cope with its rivalry with the United States. Under the Ishii-Lansing Agreement of 1917, America had declared its acceptance of the idea that "territorial propinquity creates special relations between countries and . . . that Japan has special interests in China, especially the part to which her possessions are contiguous." In the notes signed at that time, the United States essentially recognized Japan's interests in Manchuria but later became critical of the agreement and began to deny any concession with regard to China policy.

Another method Japan used to resist the United States was to bring China over to its side. Typical of this effort were the Nishihara loans for the support of the Duan Qirui government negotiated in 1917–1918. After the war, as American influence spread and the strength of pro-American Chinese Nationalists rose, it became impossible to sever China's ties with the United States and make it pro-Japanese. Nor did Japan succeed in establishing itself as an independent defense zone or an economic bloc.

To make matters more difficult, a global movement repudiating imperialist foreign policy had begun. The May Fourth Movement (1919) in China, the March First Movement (1919), and the Karakhan Declaration of 1919, in which Russia in the throes of revolution declared the return of colonial interests in China, were part of that movement. This represented not only a threat to the colonial interests Japan had painstakingly carved out for itself but the advent of an age in which imperialism faced a moral challenge. When the United

States called the world powers to the Washington Conference in July 1921 to discuss disarmament and problems in Asia and the Pacific, not a few Japanese—fearing that their country was sure to become the target of world criticism regarding its special interests in China—were convinced that Japan was facing its worst crisis since the Mongol invasions of the thirteenth century.

The Emergence of the Washington System

Japan's greatest concern was the Manchurian issue. The United States had refused to recognize sphere-of-influence politics since before World War I. Japan believed its special interests in Manchuria were vital to survival and development. It seemed these two viewpoints could never be reconciled. That they finally were and that the Washington system did go into effect is testimony to the exercise of judicious and forceful statesmanship.

Japan's role in Manchuria became an issue during the year before the Washington Conference, when the Quadruple Loan Consortium (Japan, Great Britain, the United States, and France) was organized to supply funds to China in May 1920. Wishing to protect its special interests in Manchuria, Japan sought exclusion of Manchuria from the scope of the consortium's investment.

It was Hara Takashi who settled the controversy. While giving in on the issue of exclusion of the Manchurian region, he managed instead to exclude projects in which Japan had established interests such as the South Manchurian Railway, and he persuaded the army and other forces to compromise with the United States. Hara's vision and leadership were indispensable, but the role of Wall Street leaders such as Thomas W. Lamont of J. P. Morgan also contributed greatly to the settlement. Lamont understood the nature of the commitment that the Japanese had made in Manchuria and felt it only realistic to respect its psychological and material investment there.

Although Hara was assassinated before the Washington Conference began, the compromise between the United States and Japan went according to the Hara line. The Nine-Power Treaty was clearly based on Open Door policy, but America compromised by agreeing that it would not deal with the previously established special interests of the powers in China and would call only for the gradual and conditional liquidation of those interests and China's fulfillment of its promises. Japan was unable to persuade the other powers to recognize its sphere of influence in Manchuria and was forced to concede on some points but in actuality did not forfeit all that much.

Another issue in which a wise compromise was reached was that regarding naval forces. The Imperial Navy pressed for acceptance of a 7-to-10 ratio vis-à-vis U.S. capital ships for technical reasons, and the United States was determined to keep it at 6-to-10 for that very reason.

The United States had already launched the most ambitious shipbuilding program in the world. Because of the pacifist trend that had arisen after World War I, it was unlikely that the United States could go ahead immediately with this plan, but if it came to an arms buildup race, Japan would never have been able to build 70 percent or even 60 percent of what the United States was capable of producing.

The Imperial Navy held out stubbornly for a 10–10–7 ratio of ships vis-à-vis the United States and Great Britain. The man who managed to break the deadlock was Admiral Kato Tomosaburo (1861–1923), who had been convinced that Japan had no other alternative but to cooperate with the United States. It was Hara who had chosen Kato as one of the delegates with plenipotentiary powers, and who as prime minister had taken the unprecedented step of assuming control of Navy Ministry affairs and securing the navy's support for Kato's discretion at the conference.

The United States accepted a measure prohibiting the strengthening of military bases in the western Pacific, which prevented the United States from building up its naval depots in the Philippines and Guam and made the western Pacific a safer place for Japan. If the United States had decided to engage in a shipbuilding race, Japan would have had either to give up or go bankrupt in the attempt to keep up the rivalry. Considering that a few leaders on the American side called for just such a policy, it does appear that the United States was practicing the self-constraint befitting its power status.

The End of the Post–Washington Conference Order

Many factors made the international arrangement hammered out at the Washington Conference work, but even more brought about its demise. There was the decline in the influence of pro-American forces in Japan as a result of the passage of the U.S. Immigration Act of 1924 barring Japanese from obtaining immigrant status; there was the start of the Great Depression in 1929 and the protectionist tariff policy adopted by the United States soon after; there was the controversy over the London Naval Conference.[1]

The main reason that compromise on the Manchurian problem at the Washington Conference had been possible is that China's resistance was so slight. The Kuomintang government in southern China was virtually powerless at the time of the conference but rapidly increased in strength after infusion of Soviet assistance in the wake of the first national unification campaign in 1924. In 1926, the Northern Expeditionary Campaign began. The supreme propaganda tool in the campaign was the rallying call to expel the imperialists, and bitter antiforeign incidents broke out throughout the country. In order not to lose out to the Nationalists, the Peking government, too, responded with an anti-imperialist stand, and this prompted internal forces to compete with each other in the anti-imperialist movement.

In the face of these developments in China, the three leading nations at the Washington Conference (the United States, Great Britain, and Japan) did nothing to demand that China fulfill its responsibilities as agreed upon by treaty; rather, each made moves to placate China and hoped to avoid the brunt of the antiforeign movement. The Western powers recognized the revolutionary government of China and competed to show it favors. The erosion of cooperative spirit in 1925 as the United States, Britain, and Japan scrambled to shower the Chinese Nationalists with goodwill may have brought about the collapse of the Washington system.[2]

It was Japan that set in motion the sequence of events leading to this collapse. When Great Britain called for a joint response to China's antiforeign movement from Japan, the United States, and the United Kingdom, Japan's reaction was indifference. This allowed traditional pro-Chinese sentiment to rise in the United States and encouraged Britain's unilateral overtures to the southern-based government. Under circumstances such as these, Japan could hardly expect support from either nation should its interests in Manchuria be threatened.

At the time Japan's interests in Manchuria did indeed come under attack by Nationalist forces advancing from the south, another threat was forming in the north. In 1929, when a dispute broke out between China and the Soviet Union over the Eastern Chinese Railway, China responded with force, only to be met by firm retaliation from the Soviet Union demonstrating its overwhelming military superiority. This thoroughly shook the confidence of the Japanese army.

Japan's attachment to its interests in Manchuria was essentially less a matter of economic necessity than of military policy. Judging from the traditional army line, the presence of strong Russian forces in northern Manchuria and Siberia would have incited the army to seek an even stronger hold over Manchuria. This would have made compromise all the more difficult on the Quadruple Loan Consortium in 1920 and the Washington treaties in 1921–1922. It was not surprising, then, that the rise in Soviet military strength brought about the swift rise of the faction within the army dissatisfied with the Japanese government's Manchurian policy.

After the Manchurian Incident, in the summer of 1932, Foreign Minister Uchida Kosai, formerly president of the South Manchurian Railway, declared to the Diet that Japan should not concede an inch of what had been gained in the Manchurian Incident even "should the country be burnt to the ground." This was the beginning of the nonconciliatory "scorched earth diplomacy" for which Uchida became known.

Uchida, however, was no hot-blooded youth; he had first served as foreign minister more than twenty years earlier in the second Saionji Kinmochi Cabinet, and was among a handful of foreign affairs veterans when he became foreign minister for the fifth time in 1932. As foreign minister he had contributed to the launching of the international system set up at Versailles in 1919 and at Washington in 1921–1922. What caused this drastic about-face in Uchida's views was above all the change in the situation revolving around Japan's Manchurian interests. He had supported the Washington treaties in the belief that they would sustain the status quo in Manchuria; when he realized that the treaty system would not after all guarantee Japan's interests, he moved to assure Japan's firm grip over the region following the Manchurian Incident. The belief that Japan's security and future was at stake in the issue of its control over the special interests in Manchuria was the most important factor that led to the Manchurian Incident, and it was a belief not limited to army leaders alone.

THE PATH TO WAR

The Manchurian Incident and Japan's subsequent withdrawal from the League of Nations had far greater impact upon Japanese foreign relations than many expected. It ushered in, for example, the rise of pan-Asianism. In his rescript issued at the time of Japan's withdrawal from the League of Nations in March 1933, the emperor stated that the empire:

> has now parted company with the League of Nations, and will follow its own policy, but this, of course, does not mean we should confine our attention only to the Far East, breaking friendly ties with other countries. I pray each night that we shall gain the greater confidence of international society and enhance the cause of justice throughout the world.

The rescript reflected the fears of the court that the Manchurian Incident might cause Japanese diplomacy to depart from the policy of cooperation traditionally maintained with the Western powers.

The Manchurian Incident, Pan-Asianism, and the Military

The fear was well founded. In 1933 Japan held a conference of its ministers to make new foreign policy decisions, including the idea that:

> Under the leadership of the Japanese Empire, a relationship of alliance and cooperation should be formed among Japan, Manchukuo, and China, so as to secure permanent peace in the Far East and contribute to promotion of world peace.

Proposals had been advanced for establishing a Japan-Manchukuo bloc since the Manchurian Incident, but this newly adopted policy was even more drastic. It represented an epoch-making departure in Japanese foreign policy from its former position of recognizing the universal framework of international order and treating Manchuria as an exception.

Hirota Koki (1878–1948), who was then foreign minister, devoted himself to improving relations with other countries, particularly the United States, after the establishment of Manchukuo (1932) and the withdrawal of Japan from the League of Nations. Pan-Asianism was fundamental to Hirota's foreign policy, however, and he sought to improve relations with the United States only within that framework. In a January 1934 speech to the Diet, he stated that Japan would shoulder the entire responsibility for preserving peace in East Asia. In April, Amo Eiji, chief of the Information Bureau of the Foreign Ministry, stressed Japan's responsibility in the Far East, and declared that the Western powers should be prohibited from playing any politically significant role in China. Hirota's January speech did not draw much attention, but Amo's statement provoked considerable response around the world. Such Pan-Asianism was ultimately incompatible with the Open Door policy.

For some time after the Manchurian Incident, the army's plan of operation vis-à-vis Soviet forces was formulated on the assumption that the Soviet army was not much superior to the Russian army under the czar. The men most responsible for the plan were Obata Toshishiro and Suzuki Yorimichi, both serving as operations section chiefs on the General Staff, and both members of the Imperial Way faction, which believed war with the Soviet Union to be inevitable. To combat communism, the faction, led by Araki Sadao, hoped to form an anticommunist alliance with Britain and the United States and therefore supported Hirota's foreign policy.

After the Manchurian Incident, however, Araki and his group delayed implementation of the plan to improve national defense capabilities vis-à-vis the Soviet Union. While the Soviet Union was building up its forces in the Far East at that time, Japanese military preparedness, especially air force capability, began to lag behind. This situation aroused a sense of crisis that was to lead to the decline of the Imperial Way faction and the rise of the rival Control faction (Toseiha). The Control faction did not believe an anti-Soviet alliance among Japan, Britain, and the United States was possible. Its members thought that the only way to defend the nation was to raise Japan's own defense capability. In that endeavor, they reasoned, stable relations with the Soviet Union were crucial. Some of them urged that Japan conclude a nonaggression treaty with Moscow when the Soviet Union made such a proposal in 1932–1933. This attempt was frustrated by Army Minister Araki. The Control faction also thought the innermost parts of Manchukuo should be more strongly fortified. This was the origin of the Japanese maneuvering that began in 1935 to separate five northern provinces from the rest of China under the pretext of self-rule.[3]

The maneuvering caused the rift in relations with China to widen. Even the Chinese Nationalist government, while it was ready tacitly to recognize Manchukuo, never approved of self-government in North China, and the United States and Britain were unwilling to accept it, for they believed self-rule in the north would bring about the political and economic disintegration of China. It was not until after the Sian Incident in December 1936 that Chiang Kai-shek finally gave up fighting with the Communists and united with them to resist Japanese aggression. But the Japanese maneuvering in North China had already pushed Chiang to the verge of this shift.

In this way, Japan's efforts to defend its interests against the Soviet Union ended up aggravating its relations with the United States and Britain. And still Japan felt insecure. In 1936, it signed the Anti-Comintern Pact with Germany, which was not only a potential ally against the Soviet Union but also one of the nations most advanced in military technology. Outdated technology was the Japanese military's weak point at that time. Japan's cultivation of close ties with Germany made the United States and Britain suspicious that Japan was trying to obtain military technology from Germany under the guise of anti-Comintern policy.

The controlled economy was another inherently contradictory feature of the Japanese defense endeavor. The program to build a powerful military force required enormous quantities of imports, which inevitably meant curtailing imports for civilian industry. Distribution of domestic resources, too, was controlled, oppressing civilian demands. As long as the country operated under a free economy, it was impossible to monopolize material for military use. Therefore, those who were pro-American or pro-British or who sought to maintain the capitalist system had to be gotten rid of. Japanese army leaders made sure that pro-Westerners did not get important government posts, so improving relations with the United States and Great Britain became all the harder.

Outbreak of War with China

When the Marco Polo Bridge Incident occurred in July 1937, the already complex relationship between Japan's foreign policy and the activities of the military became even more entwined. Prime Minister Konoe Fumimaro and Foreign Minister Hirota Koki did little to prevent the clash between Japanese and Chinese troops from developing into war. Neither did they cooperate five months later with the efforts of the General Staff to reach a settlement to prevent Japan from being drawn into a quagmire of protracted war. Konoe and Hirota, however, seemed unimpressed by such a danger and in January 1938 issued a statement that Japan would not deal with the Nationalist government. Although the General Staff, which carried the greatest responsibility for the fighting, insisted that it would be impossible to bring an end to the war if the capital of China fell and the core of the Chinese government with which they were fighting was damaged, and although a liaison conference, composed of members of the Cabinet and the Supreme Command, which was a decision-making body, was available, Konoe and Hirota did not move to put an early end to the war. The men in charge of Japan's foreign policy were even more belligerent than the Imperial Army.

The United States responded to the Sino-Japanese war relatively calmly. President Roosevelt did make his "quarantine speech" at Chicago in October 1937, and the Japanese sinking of the American gunboat *Panay* on the Yangtze River in December did cause a sensation among Americans, but then the United States remained quiet for a while. In September the following year, the American government sent a long letter of protest declaring that Japanese policy violated the Open Door principle. In November Foreign Minister Arita Hachiro finally sent a reply to Washington to the effect that the principles applied prior to the outbreak of the war were no longer workable. It was just about that time that Prime Minister Konoe announced Japan's plan for a "new order in East Asia."

Attacking Arita's reply to Washington, Kiyosawa Kiyoshi decried it as the decision bound to have the gravest consequences since the Manchurian Incident. For one thing, it did not make clear what Japan meant by a new order in the Far East, and second, it made it obvious that such an order was a rejection of the Open Door policy. Kiyosawa argued that a foreign policy so openly and blatantly at cross-purposes with the interests and principles of the United States, a country that tended to be moved by public opinion, was extremely dangerous.[4]

Not surprisingly, in December the United States sent Tokyo the reply that no country was qualified to direct the building of a so-called new order in any area outside the territory of that nation's sovereignty. About that time, the United States decided to extend loans to China. As Kiyosawa had feared, Konoe's Far Eastern new-order statement and Arita's reply marked the beginning of a Japan-United States war on the ideological level.

The Pacific War

Half a year after this exchange, in July 1939, the United States announced abrogation of the 1911 Treaty of Commerce and Navigation with Japan. The proportion of Japan's trade with the United States was not what it had been before the Depression, but it was bringing in many vital materials, including strategically important petroleum and scrap iron. This rupture in bilateral relations indicated clearly the need for drastic compromise; if a breakthrough could not be found, Japan would have to build up its defenses. While seeking resolution of the tensions with the United States on the one hand (abrogation of the treaty was to be effective in January 1940), the Cabinet leaned toward strengthening the Tokyo-Berlin Anti-Comintern Pact. That naturally made it all the more difficult to find a way to ease tensions with Washington.

The desire for better relations with the United States yet the need to prepare for the worst continued. In August 1939, Germany and the Soviet Union signed a nonaggression treaty, and in the next month German troops invaded Poland and the Second World War began. Japan calmly watched the development of the war at first and devoted its efforts to settlement of the dispute with China. When Germany blitzed the Western front in April 1940, however, Japan's foreign policy was set in motion. After the Netherlands and France surrendered, and when Britain seemed about to give in, voices calling for closer ties with Germany and for southward advance grew very loud in Japan. If Japan could not expect to restore good relations with the United States, it should seize French Indochina, rich in strategically vital resources, and take steps to cultivate the Tokyo-Berlin alliance in terms of strategy and military technology. In September 1940, the Tripartite Alliance was formed and Japanese troops advanced into the northern part of French Indochina.

In July 1941, the danger from the north having been settled by a neutrality pact concluded with the Soviet Union (in April), the Japanese troops advanced into the southern part of French Indochina. While trying to avert war with the United States through diplomatic negotiations in Washington, the second Konoe Cabinet nevertheless made this decision—a very provocative move in the eyes of the United States.

Japan's fantasies of the period need to be understood. In order to buttress an independent defense zone, Japan believed it was absolutely necessary to have a prosperous Manchukuo and a cooperative China. Japan also thought it vital to form an alliance with Germany in order to obtain advanced military technology and restrain the

Soviet Union. Since there was no assurance of sufficient supply of raw materials from the United States, Japan turned to the possibility of acquiring them in Southeast Asia. To justify these measures for national defense and enlist further cooperation from the people, the Japanese government adopted the pan-Asianist line and the idea of a new order in the Far East.

Surrounded by great powers, Japan became nervously aware that it was not self-sufficient. During the ten years preceding the Pearl Harbor attack, the Japanese leaders tried to create a self-supporting zone of a size comparable to other world powers'. Had military technology been at a less developed stage in which the bulk of required fuel was coal rather than oil, for example, then Japan might have been able to build such a self-defense zone. With the technological level the powers had reached in the 1930s, however, the creation of such a zone was completely out of the question. Various symbols of pan-Asianism were used to make that impossible task seem possible. Japan tried to become an empire that could uphold its own values vis-à-vis the United States, the Soviet Union, and China but failed in the attempt.

COEXISTENCE WITH THE UNITED STATES

The most important change in Japan's foreign and defense policy after the 1945 surrender was the disappearance of its program of self-defense. Faced with the overwhelming power of the United States and the development of nuclear weapons, the Japanese gave up the idea of defending their country on their own. Pan-Asianism evaporated, and the Japanese people did not resist the necessity for coexistence with the United States.

Pax Americana

Ultimately, that choice turned out to be very much to Japan's advantage. The American Occupation of Japan was probably the most magnanimous occupation in human history from the economic and humanitarian point of view. Developments in the Cold War between East and West, moreover, served to accelerate Japan's economic recovery. Despite the frequent objections of European countries to seeing Japan restored to full membership in international society, the United States actively supported it. Great Britain, which had tended toward appeasement vis-à-vis Japan before World War II, took a tough stance toward it after the war; the United States, which had been very harsh before the war, made a complete about-face in its policy toward Japan after 1945.

The main feature of America's prewar legalistic-moralistic approach was the unwillingness to take responsibility for the consequences of its policy in other parts of the world. The United States decided the rules it expected other countries to follow but refused to take any action to ensure their implementation. After World War II, the United States not only decided the rules but also bore the cost required for seeing that they were followed.

It is not pleasant, however, to be continually on one's knees before the overwhelmingly dominant power of other countries. Having suffered greatly through the war, the Japanese developed an abhorrence for conflict that led to the emergence of strong pacifist sentiments. People dedicated to peace attacked the country's policy of following the lead of the United States and claimed that the alliance could draw Japan into war. The protest movement that erupted against ratification of the revised U.S.-Japan Security Treaty in 1960 reflected both pacifism and anti-American sentiment.

Around 1970 Japanese foreign relations changed rapidly. The first sign of the new climate in bilateral relations came with the textile issue of 1969–1971. At a 1969 summit meeting with President Nixon, Prime Minister Sato discussed Japanese voluntary restraints on exports of textile products to the United States. The United States apparently believed that Sato had pledged himself to implement restraints; the Japanese did not believe such a promise to have been made. When Japan did not introduce such restraints after many months, the Americans grew increasingly distrustful. Tensions continued, and the United States exerted pressure until voluntary restraints on Japanese textile exports finally came into effect in early 1971.

The textile issue was not economically significant, but it was symbolic in three respects. First, although the Japanese government was ultimately forced to comply with U.S. demands, it said no to Washington for the first time since the end of the war. Second, the textile feud marked the beginning of a shift in U.S.-Japanese relations from protection and obedience to competition and confrontation. Third, low-level policy issues of specific industries became a major part of the agenda for discussion between the top leaders of the two nations. Japan compromised on the textile issue in exchange for facilitating the reversion of Okinawa.

Toward Greater Autonomy

The deteriorating diplomatic relations between the two countries in the wake of the textile war were exacerbated by the United States making sudden policy changes in 1971 without first notifying the Japanese government. The first shock came in July when President Nixon announced that American relations with the People's Republic of China had resumed and that he himself would be visiting Beijing the following year. One month later came the second shock: a new economic policy was to be launched, detaching gold from the dollar. The first shock had the greater political impact on Japan, which had been treating Taiwan as the only legitimate Chinese government since 1951. Many Japanese had long felt that nonrecognition of Beijing was unnatural, but as long as the United States remained unfriendly toward the People's Republic, Japan could not very well adopt an independent policy. The Japanese were taken aback when they learned that the United States had been approaching Beijing without first consulting them. Remembering the prewar history of U.S.-China amity, many Japanese feared that the United Sates was seeking to cultivate close ties with Beijing to the exclusion of Japan.

As they witnessed America's unilateral actions in these cases, the Japanese became critical of their country's heavy reliance on the United States and began to call on their government to take a more autonomous stand in foreign policy. Arguing that consistency would serve Japanese national interests most, the Sato Cabinet did not significantly alter previous China policy and failed to get support at the time of the U.N. decision as to which was the legitimate government of China.

The succeeding Tanaka Kakuei Cabinet (July 1972) tended to be more sensitive to public opinion and sought to attain considerable distance from the United States. Tanaka went to Europe in 1973, the first visit to Europe by a Japanese prime minister in nine years.

In the fall of 1973, Japan faced a real dilemma in foreign policy. With the outbreak of the fourth Middle East war, the Organization of Petroleum-Exporting countries (OPEC) announced a new oil strategy, treating Japan, with West Germany, Italy, and others, as unfriendly nations. Concerned that it might not be able to maintain a secure supply of oil from Arab nations, Japan made a quick diplomatic shift. It assumed a pro-Arab stance despite the conflict with America's pro-Israeli position. The preconditions for Japan's rapid economic growth in the 1960s had been cooperation with the United States and availability of large quantities of inexpensive oil. After the oil crisis, the two conditions became mutually incompatible.

The first half of the 1970s was a period of conspicuous efforts among conservative forces in Japan to forge a more autonomous foreign policy. Some conservative leaders went so far as to call for Japan to acquire its own nuclear weapons. Business circles, too, asserted the need for a foreign policy independent of the United States on the oil issue, and many expressed interest in resources in Siberia. In retrospect, however, we see that the first half of the 1970s was the only period since 1960 when the U.S.-Japanese security system was shaky.

The Economic Summits

Although Japanese foreign policy during the 1970–1973 period was unstable, with the beginning of annual summit meetings of the leaders of the major industrial democracies in 1975, it began to move in a new direction. Japan's participation was rather nominal at the beginning, but its presence turned out to have far greater significance than expected.

Because the summits focused on economic problems, Japan with its new economic status became more significant. These world summits gave the prime ministers a good opportunity to win political points.

Fukuda Takeo was a case in point. Apparently promising to step down after serving one two-year term in deference to Ohira Masayoshi, Fukuda became president of the ruling Liberal Democratic Party and prime minister with the help of Ohira. When the time came to concede the prime ministership, however, Fukuda sought reelection as LDP president. He cited his responsibility to carry out the international commitment made at the 1978 Bonn summit; he declared that trust in Japan was at stake. At this summit, Fukuda actively supported the portrayal of Japan, the United States, and West Germany as the principal "engines," whose role it was to pull the world out of the post-oil-crisis recession. To foster international solidarity was critical. In the end, Fukuda was defeated, but it was abundantly clear that foreign affairs had become a powerful weapon in domestic politics.

The economic summits also ushered in important changes in Japan's diplomatic style. In bilateral diplomacy, Japan had always made decisions in response to what the other side demanded. At a multilateral summit, however, that posture became awkward, making it necessary for Japan to express its own opinion from the outset.

The Japanese people also greatly changed their attitudes toward foreign policy in the wake of these summit meetings. They accepted the formula that took the European situation into account; they showed a willingness to make sacrifices. This was probably the first time Japan had taken such initiatives in international affairs since it sent naval forces to the Mediterranean during the First World War. After the oil crisis of 1973, the task of building the international economic order became the responsibility of individual countries. In the mid-1970s, the Japanese began to accept the fact that a country must shoulder a burden in world affairs commensurate with its national strength.

The Maturing of Consciousness as a Western Power (1978–1985)

The sense of shared destiny among Western nations was enhanced in 1979 by the Iranian revolution and the Soviet invasion of Afghanistan. When Iranian terrorists seized fifty Americans as hostages in the U.S. embassy in Teheran in November, the United States imposed sanctions against Iran, including the prohibition of imports. When a Japanese trading firm bought large volumes of Iranian oil at an exorbitant spot price, U.S. Secretary of State Cyrus Vance criticized Japanese conduct as insensitive. The Japanese government immediately restricted the purchases of oil from Iran; American criticism abated.

At the end of that year, the Soviet Union invaded Afghanistan. The Jimmy Carter administration announced sanctions against Moscow, and Japan followed suit, boycotting the Moscow Olympics. This was a bold decision; the Japanese are enthusiastic Olympic Games fans; joining the boycott was a big risk for the Ohira Cabinet. It did provoke a good deal of criticism from the opposition parties and the media, but at the time, Japan was more cooperative toward the United States than some European countries, and the government's decision to support the U.S. sanctions against the Soviet Union was accepted with relative calm.

Thus, under the Ohira Cabinet, Japan assumed a clear posture among the nations of the West in the realm of security, and the people firmly supported that stand. As prime minister after the Soviet invasion of Afghanistan, he took the initiative in furthering pro-Washington policy.

Ohira passed away suddenly during the election campaign in 1980, and Suzuki Zenko became prime minister. Under the Suzuki Cabinet, Ohira's foreign policy of situating Japan among the Western powers was pushed back. When Nakasone Yasuhiro took office, however, he set Ohira's policy in motion again. At the 1983 Williamsburg summit, in discussing the issue of weapons deployment, Nakasone stressed the necessity of concerted action from the nations of the West, not only in Europe but also in Asia. This caught the other leaders at the summit by surprise, so accustomed had they become to the passivity of Japanese prime ministers. The Nakasone Cabinet adhered consistently to that line throughout the following five years. Through increasing cooperation in security and economic affairs, Japan began to gain a stronger awareness of itself as a full-fledged member of the Western alliance.

Responsibilities as an Economic Superpower

Enormous changes began taking place in Japan's foreign policy around the time Nakasone became prime minister. In overcoming the second oil crisis, Japanese companies rationalized and streamlined their operations, thus contributing to a growing trade surplus, which in turn touched off fierce criticism overseas. The value of the yen soared and forced Japanese industry to make structural adjustments. As a result, the tasks for Japan's foreign policy have been unmistakably transformed. Those tasks require drastic changes in the existing politico-economic line; indeed, they are such that they cannot be fulfilled without a certain degree of adjustment in traditional institutions and culture.

The first task is to open the market. To ensure its survival, inasmuch as it relies heavily on trade and commercial intercourse, Japan must liberalize its market. A second task is to assist developing countries. To stabilize the world order, remedies must be found for dire poverty and human suffering. The third task is to contribute to the preservation of world peace. The Takeshita Noboru Cabinet made this one of the three main pillars of Japanese foreign policy, and in 1988 Japan did send two civilian officials to join a United Nations military surveillance team. The importance of such tasks is widely recognized in Japan.

The last full year of the Showa era, 1988, was a time of political instability resulting from the dilemmas of internationalization. It was dominated by the agricultural issue (the opening up of the beef and citrus markets), the Recruit scandal, and the controversy over the consumption tax. The tax issue, more than any other, exposed the weaknesses of Japan's political system. While vaguely aware that such a tax was necessary, people resisted what they considered the too hasty decision to introduce it and stubbornly clutched to their vested interests. The government and the Liberal Democratic Party (LDP) lacked the courage and the ability to meet the criticisms head on and settled for one unprincipled compromise after another in an attempt to reduce the opposition, considerably damaging the effectiveness of the original plan. Since the opposition parties proved incapable of coming up with a persuasive or practical countermeasure, the weaknesses of the LDP bill came under even closer scrutiny.

In 1985–1987, the appreciation of the yen led to some expectations for the amelioration of the trade imbalance. When exchange rates finally began to level off, it was time for Japan to undertake structural reform on its own initiative; it was, in fact, the last task for Showa foreign policy. But structural reform proved too much for the political system; politics ran aground on this issue, and the result was instability as the era came to an end in the early days of 1989.

CONCLUSION

The international situation surrounding Japan has been growing increasingly difficult since the end of the Showa era. Following improved relations between the United States and the Soviet Union, public opinion polls in the United States have begun to show that more Americans consider Japan a threat to their nation than the U.S.S.R. And in their arguments regarding Japan, criticisms of Japan's politics and economy as well as the structure of its very culture have grown more pointed than disagreement with its government policies. This situation thus closely resembles the time when Hirohito first took up imperial duties.

But it would be a mistake to say that U.S.-Japan relations have changed little since the prewar period. In Nakae Chomin's famous book *San suijin keirin mondo* (Political Discussions of Three Inebriates), written in 1887, the realist character Nankai Sensei (Professor South Seas) charges the other two characters, Shinshi (the advocate of demilitarization and neutrality) and Gokatsu (the apologist for further military adventures on the Chinese continent), with being "extreme." Their arguments make no sense; they consider only the most extreme cases, presuming ill will on the other side. In fact, that was the most fundamental problem in Japan's foreign policy in the prewar Showa period.

The U.S.-Japan relationship has changed greatly since then. No longer do the two sides pose a military threat to each other. And while each may feel economically threatened by the other, both benefit fundamentally from their relationship. We must not be blinded by confrontation on issues that are in the final analysis superficial. The problems, moreover, are not narrowly bilateral; if we consider Japan's relationship with the United States in a global context, we see that the world's major economic powers all have problems for which common solutions are required.

As for the nationalist assertiveness of Japan and the United States, neither has reached the extreme levels that prevailed in the prewar period, when there were virulent anti-Japanese spokesmen in the U.S. State Department and anti-American diplomats in the Japanese Ministry of Foreign Affairs. Today, by comparison, both American diplomats and defense officials as well as Japanese foreign affairs specialists are more professional and objective, capable of recognizing the pressures under which their counterparts labor. In short, there is a much firmer foundation for constructive bilateral relations than ever existed before the Pacific War. The Showa period is literally and psychologically over.

ENDNOTES

[1]See my article "Nichi-bei kankei no juyosha kara sozosha e" (From Recipient to Creator of U.S.-Japan Relations), *Asteion* (Autumn 1988).

[2]See my essay "Washinton taisei to kokusai 'kyocho' no seishin" (The Washington Conference and the Spirit of "International Cooperation"), *Rikkyo Hogaku* (December 1984).

[3]See my "Rikugun habatsu tairitsu (1931–35) no sai-kento" (A Reexamination of the Factional Strife within the Army, 1931–35) in Kindai Nihon Kenkyukai, ed., *Showa-ki no gunbu* (The Japanese Military in the Showa Period), (Tokyo: Yamakawa Shuppansha, 1979).

[4]See my *Kiyosawa Kiyoshi* (Tokyo: Chuo Koronsha, 1987).

Money and the Japanese

Shoichi Royama

Showa began with massive bank failures and ended with Japan as the world's largest repository of capital. Whether Japan's macroeconomic policies are unique among advanced democracies is an open question; it is indisputable that its role as world banker has had large and unexpected repercussions. Whether the financial system must be changed so that the average Japanese acquires wealth commensurate with his labors is one of many questions raised.

Money is generally translated as *kahei* or *tsuka* in written Japanese. In the spoken language, however, *money* most frequently becomes *okane*, something that banks supply. This important function of banks stopped working at the start of the Showa era. By the end of the era, however, Japan and banks that once had no money to give depositors had become wealthy.

The world of money underwent dramatic changes during the sixty-two years of Showa. Particularly from 1983 to 1989, Japan and the world experienced unprecedented economic expansion. Current account imbalances rose. Global money and capital markets grew. The United States became a net debtor nation, and Japan and West Germany net creditors. The ten largest banks in the world were Japanese, and the Dai Ichi Kangyo Bank was the largest in the world, with assets totaling $380 billion at the end of September 1988. Among all banks of the United States, the European Community (twelve countries), and Japan, Japanese banks accounted for 33 percent of the total assets at the end of 1987.

Shoichi Royama is Professor of Monetary Theory and Policy in the Department of Economics at Osaka University.

What brought about Japan's transformation into a financial power during the Showa era? Were there special factors at work? Does this important historical development signify a shift in the position of the world's dominant nation? Investigating the monetary phenomena during the Showa period in Japan will provide the foundation for addressing these questions. In examining these issues, I will concentrate on how money and finance have been regulated in Japan.

TOWARD HIGH ECONOMIC GROWTH

The Showa period opened with financial panic. The stage for the panic was set by a slowdown in the growth of effective demand following the end of World War I and drastic supply bottlenecks caused by the Great Kanto Earthquake of 1923. This blow to both the supply and the demand side of the economy created severe deflationary conditions. It was a shock that the financial system, particularly banks, could not completely absorb. The resulting run on financially troubled banks was overcome by transferring a portion of their deposits to the major commercial banks. The share of ordinary bank deposits held by Japan's five largest banks at the time (Mitsui, Mitsubishi, Sumitomo, Yasuda, and Daiichi) amounted to 19 percent at the end of 1922. This figure swelled to 41 percent at the end of 1932. The March 1928 implementation of the Banking Act, whose purpose was to ensure the sound management of Japanese banks, forced smaller banks that could not meet its conditions to merge. As a result, commercial banks, numbering 1,420 at the end of 1925, shrank by two-thirds, to 466, by the end of 1935.

The mainstream of response to this severe deflation was to restrict government and consumer spending and return the yen to the gold standard.

Robust debate accompanied the proposal to revive the gold standard. A group of four then leading economists including Tanzan Ishibashi, who became the prime minister after World War II, argued for the establishment of a new parity for the yen. In the spring of 1929, one of the four economists, Kamekichi Takahashi, who was the most popular economist in those days, even after the war and until his death proposed pegging ¥100 at $45. He believed that Japanese industry would not be internationally competitive at the pre–World War I parity of ¥100 = $49.845. Industry and the banking community, in contrast, maintained the appropriateness of the prewar parity. The major commercial banks were particularly eager to invest abroad, since they believed investment opportunities were lacking in Japan at the time. They therefore preferred the advantage of a stronger yen.

Finance Minister Inoue chose the old parity for the yen. On November 21, 1929, he ordered the lifting of the gold embargo and the yen's return to the gold standard on January 11, 1930. His directive came less than a month after the collapse of the New York Stock Exchange on October 24, 1929. None of the Japanese policy-makers at the time realized that this signaled the start of a global depression. In fact, traders at Kabuto-cho, the site of the Tokyo Stock Exchange, considered the market crash good news. They believed that lower U.S. interest rates would create a positive environment for the removal of Japan's gold embargo. The world economic situation, however, drifted downward. Lifting the gold embargo returned the Japanese economy to the international arena just in time to receive a blow from the spreading reach of global depression. This was a serious setback, particularly for the silk and cotton textile industries, the principal Japanese export industries of the time. Exports retreated significantly both in volume and in amount, marking the beginning of the Showa economic crisis. The Japanese economy declined by a large margin between 1929 and 1931. The GNP shrank 18 percent, exports 47 percent, personal consumption 17 percent, and capital spending 31 percent. Private-sector factory employment declined 18 percent and real wages 13 percent. Labor strife became rampant, college graduates were unable to find jobs, and farmers suffered extreme hardship.

In macroeconomic terms, the Showa depression led to aggressive deficit spending by Prime Minister Korekiyo Takahashi. Government expenditures accelerated significantly beginning in 1932. The resulting debt was covered by the flotation of government bonds which were directly purchased by the Bank of Japan. The flood of money which ensued kept interest rates low. This was a classical case of Keynesian intervention in the economy, though the concept of Keynesian policy had never been formulated.

The stimulative Takahashi fiscal policy nevertheless turned out to be a double-edged sword. Even though the economy returned to nearly full employment in 1935, the government was unwilling to restrain its expansionary policy. This erroneous application of fiscal stimulus caused an inflationary spiral, fueled by military expenditures and the building of a wartime economy.

The microeconomic effect of the Showa depression was the streamlining of Japanese industry—a development that was actively promoted by the government. Many industrial cartels, mergers, and trusts came into being. The government also lent its authority to a "buy Japanese" movement. These developments acted in concert to militarize the economy and resulted in the Japanese government taking direct control of industry.

Command over industry began with the passage of three economic control acts in 1937. One of these, the Provisional Fund Control Act, established government control over capital. Government approval was then needed to establish a company, increase its capital, merge it with another, change its business goals, and issue new stock or to expand, renovate, or newly invest in plant and equipment. Corporate borrowing from financial institutions and the solicitation of investment in stocks or bonds also required prior government consent. In addition, autonomous controlling entities were established for each category of financial institution. Guidelines for granting government approval were established by categorizing industries according to their role in meeting military demand, their contribution to Japan's international balance of payments, and their productive capacity. This procedure was then used to elaborate priorities for the distribution of capital, formalized in the Standards for Procuring Business Capital. The success of the Provisional Fund Control Act is evident in the fact that, of the more than ¥30 billion available for capital outlays between September 1937 and June 1940, 64.5 percent went to industry and 12.8 percent to mining.

The three economic control acts were further strengthened by the National Mobilization Act of March 1938. Banks were once again forced into mergers under the act. The number of commercial banks diminished from 186 in 1931 to 61 by the end of 1945.

In 1942, the Bank of Japan Act became law. (Until then there were only bylaws regulating the Bank of Japan.) The first article of the law stated that the Bank of Japan would act to encourage the appropriate development of the Japanese economy. The central bank was to carry out its activities with reference to the policies of the government. The relationship between the printing of yen and specie reserves was severed, marking the start of a managed currency system.

Rebuilding the devastated nation and reestablishing lost employment opportunities became the economic priorities of postwar Japan. Indeed, with the memory of the inflation that preceded and continued during the war still fresh in people's minds, eliminating its causes was also a major goal. However, it would be difficult to argue that Japan's financial system was retuned to encourage economic recovery and control inflation. Its principal structure was inherited from the system existing before the war. The framework created by the National Mobilization Act was preserved and strengthened. The need to promote economic recovery was addressed by establishing long-term credit banks, trust banks, and banks specializing in foreign exchange. The allocation of scarce long-term capital and foreign exchange that did exist was turned over to these specialist banks. Government-run financial institutions, such as the Japan Development Bank and the Export-Import Bank of Japan were also founded to support private-sector financing needs. The creation of employment opportunities was promoted by reorganizing the smaller financial institutions into mutual banks (*Sogo Banks*) and credit associations (*Shinkin Banks*). This reorganization ensured the smooth flow of capital to small and medium-size businesses. The establishment of financial institutions specifically for agriculture and forestry can be viewed as another manifestation of this type of intent. Other government-run financial institutions were set up, such as the Small Business Finance Corporation and the Agriculture, Forestry, and Fisheries Finance Corporation. These institutions were also expected to lend their support to the private sector's credit needs.

Specialized financial institutions have had a prominent place in the history of Japan's financial system. The only difference after the war was how the system was employed, which is evident in the laws based on the principle of financial specialization that were passed. They include the Securities and Exchange Law (particularly Article 65), which was modeled on the U.S. Glass-Steagall Act, and the Foreign Exchange Control Law, which separated domestic from international finance.

The issue of inflation was tackled by enacting the Public Finance law and by setting up the Policy Board of the Bank of Japan. This law banned the issuance of government bonds, and the board ensured the democratic administration of monetary policy. In this way government officials sought to learn from their bitter prewar experience, but postwar inflation was not finally tamed until 1949, when the recommendation of Detroit banker Joseph Dodge committed the government to a balanced budget and an exchange rate of 360 yen to the dollar.

These various postwar financial measures promoted Japan's recovery, propelled the nation through a period of high economic growth, and enabled it to supersede Europe and the United States. While the measures proved effective, they did exact a price. One outcome was a high rate of saving despite low interest rates, a development assisted by measures encouraging saving. The tax system favored saving over spending, of which the tax exemption of interest on small savings deposits (the *maruyu* rule) was a prime example.

WAS THE JAPANESE FINANCIAL SYSTEM UNIQUE?

Determining what was unusual about the flow of funds in Japan's high-growth period is both an old and a new problem. Financial experts and others who stress the uniqueness of Japanese finance generally refer to the primary role of indirect finance, the overborrowing of business corporations, the overloaning of banks, and the uneven endowment of funds availability among banks.[1]

One must be careful, however, when studying the particularities of Japanese finance not to deduce that the Japanese finance system itself was unique. Even though surface characteristics such as indirect finance, overborrowing, overloaning, and uneven endowment are financial phenomena observed in Japan but not in other nations, their cause could be the distinctiveness of the activities of corporations and financial institutions, or the uniqueness of the Japanese financial system, or a combination of both. Determining which case applies to Japan will require further analysis. Japanese financial phenomena have yet to be adequately investigated from a comparative standpoint to distinguish what is distinctive and what is shared with other nations.

If we accept the argument of Yoshio Suzuki, author of *Money and Banking in Contemporary Japan,* that these four financial phenomena are natural outcomes of holding interest rates artificially low and restricting the cross-border flow of capital, then low interest rates and restricting capital flows were the real characteristics of the Japanese financial system during high growth. This is a position widely held in Japan today.[2]

Nevertheless, numerous questions still surround these issues. To this day, the Japanese financial system has significant areas that analysis has not touched. Whether a policy of maintaining artificially low interest rates was a characteristic of Japan's postwar financial system and whether cross-border restrictions were unique to Japan are open to debate. One must therefore not limit one's examination of Japan's financial system, particularly the system during the period of high economic growth, to the question of its uniqueness.

Two approaches are inseparable in considering the distinctiveness of Japanese finance: structural questions, represented by the issue of artificially low interest rates, and questions concerning financial behavior, represented by the issue of distinctiveness in the activities of Japanese financial institutions, corporations, and even households.

The conclusion of a widely read essay by Henry and Mabel Wallich is that Japanese finance cannot be explained as profit-maximizing behavior.[3] Expanding on this understanding, one could reason that the financial activities of Japanese people and companies cannot be reduced to a theory of rational behavior based on a formula of optimizing goals subject to some restrictive conditions. This point of view was widespread during the decade that followed 1955.

That such a conclusion is not appropriate has now become quite clear. Numerous research papers that have followed Wallich and Wallich's essay have shed new light on the subject. A methodology based on the analysis of the rational behavior of various economic entities has become the accepted point of departure for understanding Japanese financial phenomena.

The issue remaining is how to understand the structural conditions that restrict and regulate the behavior of various Japanese economic entities.

FROM SCARCITY TO ABUNDANCE

A controlled financial system which avoided the guiding hand of free markets left Japanese families and corporations under the constant sway of insecurity. While high economic growth made the Japanese wealthy, they could not shake off the feeling of being short of money.

I do not mean that the economy lacked sufficient funds. Rather, it was their limited access to funds that left individuals feeling low in money. It is worth inquiring how the Japanese raise the money they need and how their methods have changed over time. Articulating an answer is not as simple as stating that change resulted from financial deregulation and internationalization. One frequently seen position seeks to explain recent financial change in terms of the disappearance of the four characteristics of Japanese finance—indirect finance, overborrowing, overloaning, and uneven endowment of funds availability among banks. Such a conclusion, however, stands on weak ground.

Let us take a closer look at the dominance of indirect finance. One measure of indirect finance is the indirect finance ratio, which refers to the degree to which final borrowers procure funds on financial markets through the intermediation of financial institutions. This ratio has been steadily declining since 1975, despite some small upturns.[4] Nevertheless, it would be hasty to conclude that the structural dominance of indirect financing is weakening. First of all, the indirect finance ratio previously demonstrated a downward trend between 1966 and 1971, falling from 96.0 to 87.4 percent. Second, the average of the indirect finance ratio's annual values for the years following 1952 (the earliest that relevant statistics are available) comes to 87.4 percent. Therefore, while a coincidence, the average of annual indirect finance ratios preceding and following 1975 registers 87.4 percent. These two facts suggest that the indirect finance ratio has a strong cyclical tendency and that it is still too early to conclude that the ratio's recent decline indicates a structural shift or a long-term tendency.

Even though it continues to hold its own against direct finance, indirect finance has altered significantly. The growth in the flotation of government bonds and the internationalization of Japanese finance are the principal causes of this change.[5] Through what process have these factors affected the makeup of indirect finance? And what precisely is the nature of the change these factors have brought to Japanese finance?

To state only my conclusions, the growth in markets where participants pay primary attention to market prices has had a significant effect on all Japanese financial transactions. This was facilitated by the development of a secondary market for government bonds, following their issuance in large numbers. The price mechanism therefore began to work throughout the Japanese financial system. This change that took place within the entire financial system may be called a form of securitization since the major places where market prices dominate are markets for securities. This securitization strongly affected the financial behavior of such economic entities as families, corporations, the government, public organizations, and financial institutions. Securitization can therefore be labeled the foremost factor behind the recent changes in Japanese finance.

Financial systems carry out multiple economic functions. In being part of a financial system, securities markets fulfill functions other than administering the flow of funds. The recent transformation of the Japanese financial system is perhaps best grasped as a growing dependence on securities markets in areas other than the flow of funds.

What are these functions that the Japanese financial system expects securities markets to provide? Principally, the supply of liquidity. People dispose of their assets in order to acquire liquidity. One way of doing this is to negotiate the terms of the transaction (price, collateral) with a particular buyer. This method, known as bilateral transaction, is commonly employed when the asset in question is strong in individual and not in general use (for example, the discounting of a bill at a bank window). It should be readily understandable that this method of acquiring liquidity often becomes the basis for establishing a long-term business relationship between banks and asset suppliers.

A second method employed to exchange assets for liquidity is to use an open market composed of an indefinite number of participants. While this method requires a mediator (a broker or an exchange), the potential sellers and buyers of assets are many. In this setting there is little interest in or need to know who the two parties to a particular transaction are. Rather, the participants' concern is the price and/or the rate of return. The quality of the asset in question must be commonly agreed upon for this method of acquiring liquidity to become possible. This becomes practical only with the appearance of rated and standardized financial assets. The flotation of vast amounts of government bonds such as those in Japan after 1975, therefore, swelled the number of financial assets that could be exchanged for liquidity on open markets, particularly because the ratings of such bonds were widely accepted. Thus, the securitization of Japanese finance should be understood as the process by which participants in the Japanese financial system attained new and widespread methods for exchanging their assets for liquidity in open and fair markets.

The securitization of Japanese finance also meant the transformation of the market for bilateral transactions, the formerly dominant financial transaction that relied on close customer relationships between banks and their customers. The process by which various new transactions and products came into being accelerated the evolution of the entire financial system. The basis for such financial innovations were found in the general trend toward securitization. This is the perfect word for describing the present state of Japan's financial system. Such phenomena as the easing and abolishment of financial regulations and the growth of international financial transactions can therefore be viewed as arising out of securitization.

THE MEANING OF SECURITIZATION

It is often said that finance has entered the age of deregulation and internationalization. The transformation of Japanese finance, however, is better understood as securitization. What will be the effect of securitization on the efficiency, impartiality, and soundness of finance? These are the present-day issues that must be elucidated through corroborative financial analysis.

Financial institutions are pioneers of financial change and the economic entities that are directly affected by such change. *Financial institutions* refers not only to what John Gurley and Edward Shaw describe in *Money in the Theory of Finance*[6] but to all specialist institutions coordinating the opposing interests of those on both sides of financial transactions. Securities houses therefore are also included in this definition. This is why the term *financial service industry* has come into frequent use to characterize specialist financial institutions in their entirety.

Most prominent in the financial service industry are banks. In the decade following 1955, interest in the stock market mounted. The structural changes that have occurred since then have been remarkable. The market-making activities of securities houses are expanding at a rapid pace. In such a period of flux, what are the changes that are engulfing banks, the leading actors during high economic growth? What will be the outcome of the reapportionment of banking and securities activities? How should the various barriers that exist between the banking and the securities business as well as between different categories of banking be understood? The securitization of finance is not only a theoretical problem; it also has a direct and profound effect on the formation of financial policies.

Financial institutions participate as specialists in various financial transactions. That they do not clearly separate distribution activities from intermediation activities is a fundamental problem. Two factors have caused the merging of these activities. First, the securitization of the financial system following the flotation of large amounts of government bonds spurred the development of distribution techniques. The process enlarged the secondary market for government bonds and expanded the open money market, thus promoting the blending of distribution and intermediation techniques. While the know-how for managing and procuring funds on open markets is not proprietary to any financial institution, proprietary know-how does make a difference in making loans. Second, the integration of financial techniques was accelerated by the improvement of telecommunications and data-processing technology. Nevertheless, it is doubtful whether the merging of distribution and intermediation techniques would have occurred because of the information revolution alone.

The internationalization of finance (the expanded availability of overseas markets) can also be understood as a form of securitization. This is because distribution and intermediation techniques tend toward integration when they concern certain kinds of open market securities. If such securities account for the predominant share of primary securities, distribution and intermediation techniques will begin to converge as each tries to adapt to the characteristics of open- market securities. Such changes in financial techniques create a mismatch between the division of financial activities based on regulations and division based on technical capabilities, thereby powering a movement to reapportion the activities of financial institutions.

Japanese financial institutions up till now have operated in separate business environments as prescribed by the government. This was an inheritance of a prewar system of specialist financial institutions that prospered during the Japanese economy's postwar recovery and growth. Such institutions tended to coordinate or harmonize their activities on a regular basis. This situation continued for as long as it did thanks to the regulations and directives of financial authorities. Even more important, however, was that financial techniques were still quite distinct and that differences prevailed among financial institutions of unlike categories. As a result, no mismatch existed between the division of financial activities based on regulations and that which was based on technical capabilities, making the system of financial specialization resistant to change. This situation, of course, no longer holds. With the financial system in flux, the regulatory division of financial activities calls for reevaluation. The development of open markets has made it increasingly possible for financial institutions to stake out new business territories, either directly or indirectly. The result has been heightened competition among financial institutions of differing categories. This has also made it feasible to foresee financial institutions operating independently in a deregulated environment.

IN LIEU OF A CONCLUSION

To the Japanese, money has usually been something with which to acquire material goods. Until recent years, acquiring money for money's sake has never been a Japanese preoccupation. This attitude gave shape to Japan's financial system, which is now in the throes of change. Since the choices regarding money have expanded, techniques to take advantage of the new freedom of choice have become necessary, techniques whose other name is financial speculation. The appearance and spread of new technology is always accompanied by excessively enthusiastic application. Will this enthusiasm finally quiet down, just as the pendulum always makes a return stroke? Or will Japan turn into a nation of coupon clippers and degenerate?

Imagine the following scenario: Upon waking, a Japanese hastily glances at a computer terminal. Over breakfast, he pokes at the keyboard to check on the New York market and to anticipate the performance of today's Tokyo market. He issues buy-or-sell instructions to appropriate financial institutions and begins to relax. Then he commutes to the office on an overcrowded train.

If such a scenario becomes necessary to ensure the safety and effective management of one's precious savings, this is certain to change the Japanese will to work and the egalitarian nature of Japanese society. Certainly the continuing rise of Japanese stocks since 1983 will be enough to bring about a transformation.

On the macroeconomic level, Japan is mishandling the economic product harvested by the nation's work ethic and its period of high economic growth. Why does Japan feel secure in exchanging the sweat of its citizens' brows for U.S. Treasury bonds? Who can say that such bonds will not one day tumble in value and turn into worthless pieces of paper? The Japanese are said to have become wealthy. That may be true in terms of per capita national wealth, but few Japanese individuals believe that they are the richest people in the world. High prices for land and houses relative to personal income earned and expensive imported goods relative to their original prices are typical examples of why the Japanese do not feel that their wealth is sufficient to give their life the quality they deserve. Should the Japanese therefore stop saving? I would not argue so, nor do I know of a way of compelling them to stop. They will continue to set aside their earnings and dream of becoming rich.

The time for merely deregulating and internationalizing Japanese finance has passed. We have reached the stage where we must reconstruct a systemic framework based on deregulation and internationalization of a type that will ensure that the Japanese people acquire amounts of money commensurate with their efforts.

ENDNOTES

[1] *Indirect Financing:* A borrower wanting to procure capital would issue a variety of securities that would be acquired by a financial institution. The financial institution would then provide the borrower with the needed funds by issuing its own debt. Thus, financial institutions intermediated the flow of funds from final lenders to final borrowers. This form of securing funds indirectly, rather than directly on capital markets, was the dominant form of finance in Japan.

Overborrowing: The capital structure of borrowers, primarily corporations, was based on an exceedingly small amount of equity capital and an excess of borrowed capital. This was at a level unheard of in the United States.

Overloan: Financial institutions, particularly the major banking firms, were continually dependent on borrowings from the Bank of Japan. Stated another way, leading Japanese financial institutions were exceedingly illiquid.

Uneven endowment of funds availability: Large financial institutions (e.g., the city banks) were perpetually short on reserves and had to borrow from other financial institutions (e.g., call money, Bank of Japan borrowings) to make up the difference. Smaller or medium-size banks—regional banks, mutual banks (i.e., Sogo Banks), and credit associations (i.e., Shinkin Banks)—on the other hand, often had an excess of funds available relative to their opportunity to extend loans and make investments and could therefore place their risk capital in call loans.

These issues are examined in greater detail in Yoshio Suzuki, *Money and Banking in Contemporary Japan* (New Haven: Yale University Press, 1980).

[2]An analysis of the effects of a policy of artificially low interest rates on capital allocation can be found in Juro Teranishi, *Nihon no keizai hatten to kinyu* (Finance and the Economic Development of Japan), (Tokyo: Iwanami Shoten, 1982), chap. 8. When considering the effect of artificially low interest rates on the distribution of funds, one must not fail to take industrial policies into account. The reverse is also true: when discussing industrial policies, one must consider artificially low interest rates as a means of organizing capital allocation.

[3]Henry Wallich and Mabel Wallich, "Banking and Finance," in Hugh Patrick and Henry Rosovsky, eds., *Asia's New Giant* (Washington, D.C.: Brookings Institution, 1976), 315.

[4]Let me expand on my previous definition of indirect financing. By examining various documents, we can determine that indirect financing and its opposite, direct financing, have taken on three different meanings in Japan. The first, which I have already elucidated, concerns the manner in which funds flow from lenders to borrowers. In this case, the term points to the process by which debt issued by the borrower is accepted by a financial institution, which then issues its own debt that is acquired as an asset by the lender. Second, the term is used to distinguish the manner by which borrowers (e.g., corporations) procure capital. If on capital markets (by issuing stock or bonds), the process is called direct financing; if through financial institutions, it is called indirect financing. Third, the term is employed to differentiate whether a party involved in a financial transaction is a bank (i.e., indirect financing) or a securities house (i.e., direct financing). Those wishing to pursue the matter further may refer to Mikiya Higano, *Kinyu kikan no shinsa noryoku* (The Inspection Capacities of Financial Institutions), (Tokyo: Tokyo University Press, 1986), chap. 5; and Shoichi Royama, *Kinyu jiyuka* (Financial Liberalization), (Tokyo: Tokyo University Press, 1986), chap. 11.

Here I will use *indirect finance* according to its first sense. This is most faithful to the manner in which the term was used by John Gurley and Edward Shaw, who popularized the use of direct and indirect finance as concepts for analyzing financial systems. According to Gurley and Shaw, debt (i.e., primary securities) issued by the final borrower that is acquired by a financial institution is indirect financing, while that directly purchased by the ultimate lender is direct financing. They called the flow of funds based on indirect financing financial intermediation and the institutions that issue indirect securities to acquire primary securities (or those who transform the latter securities into the former) financial intermediaries. See John G. Gurley and Edward E. Shaw, *Money in a Theory of Finance* (Washington, D.C.: Brookings Institution, 1960).

[5]See Royama or Thomas F. Cargill and Shoichi Royama, *The Transition of Finance in Japan and the United States: A Comparative Perspective* (Stanford: Hoover Institution, 1988).

[6]See endnote 4.

The Showa Economic Experience

Edward J. Lincoln

***E**conomists have been striving for years to explain the spectacular success of the postwar Japanese economy. Japan's household savings rate, corporate structure, governmental guidance, and import policies have all been cited. It is only in identifying what separates Japan from the other industrialized nations recovering from the war, and in examining the Showa period as a whole, including the years before World War II, that a partial picture of this uniquely non-Western advanced economy emerges.*

At the core of the Showa experience lies a story of tremendous economic achievement: the transformation of Japan from a developing country into an advanced industrial nation. At the beginning of Showa in 1926, Japan was a middle-income industrializing nation with pretensions of being a great power; by the end of Showa in 1989, Japan was a great economic power with doubts about the role it should play in the world. It had caught up with the West and become a major international creditor. No longer could it assume that its actions had no impact on the world.

Modernization is a complex process which transforms society as well as the economy, and Japan has been no exception. But as in other nations, economic growth and industrial success have provided the means or incentive to alter social behavior. The shift of population from farm to city, the rise of complex economic organizations, and the expansion of human horizons through enormous increases in

Edward Lincoln is Senior Fellow at The Brookings Institution in Washington, D.C.

income, as well as a revolution in transportation, all characterize this period. The difference between Japan and other successful economies has been the speed with which these changes have occurred and the remarkable adaptability of the population in embracing change.

How and why development accelerated during the Showa years has engaged economists and political scientists for many years, although they have focused mostly on a prewar-postwar dichotomy rather than treat the Showa era as a whole.[1] Among specialists, disagreement abounds about why industrialization succeeded in Japan but at least some broad areas of agreement exist. The following discussion is a review of the magnitude of Japan's achievement and the areas of agreement and disagreement. It would be only fair to say that we remain quite far from a deep understanding of why Japan succeeded where others did not, and why the Showa era brought an acceleration of industrialization.

THE CENTRAL FACTS

When the Showa era opened in 1926, most U.S. urban and suburban dwellers had running water, flush toilets, and central heating in their houses or apartments. Japan, despite almost six decades of modernization and industrialization had few of these amenities; people relied on public baths, cooked their meals with charcoal, and used small space heaters for warmth. Few had ever seen flush toilets. By international standards life remained harsh and adult mortality remained high.[2]

But important changes were occurring which would vastly improve the lives of all Japanese. The Showa era did not begin at a propitious time. In the 1920s Japan had a major shake-out in the financial sector and a rather depressed agricultural sector affected by falling prices for rice and silk. Nevertheless, it is important to note that Japan did not participate in the wrenching depression which gripped the United States and Europe in the 1930s. "Mild recession" would be a better term to describe what happened to Japan at the beginning of the 1930s, characterized by a small one-year drop in GNP in real terms. Aided by currency devaluation and Keynesian fiscal policies, and then by military demand, the economy performed well for the rest of the 1930s. Real economic growth from 1925 to 1938 averaged 4 percent per annum, even with the brief stagnation at the beginning of the decade, and was considerably higher than in the first decades of the century.[3]

The war years are often ignored by economists, for the simple reasons that many statistics are unreliable or nonexistent and the final outcome was great destruction. By 1945, GNP had fallen by half, much of the capital stock of the nation was in disrepair, and severe shortages of food and other basic materials gripped the nation. Out of these ashes Japan reemerged with a tremendous burst of sustained high-speed economic growth.

War destruction, a determination to rebuild, and a restructuring of the institutional framework also characterized European nations after the Second World War, and much of what the Japanese believe is distinctive about their experience bears strong resemblance to the European experience. Nevertheless, the magnitude of Japan's postwar success exceeds that of European countries. From the early 1950s to 1971, Japan's economy grew at an annual real rate of 9.3 percent, compared with 5.5 percent in West Germany and somewhat less in other major European countries.[4] By the early 1970s, Japan could lay claim to being an advanced industrial nation, with a level of per capita income half that of the United States and ahead of those of some European countries.

The oil shock of 1973 marked the end of this period of extraordinary economic growth, and the following year brought the first and only recession which Japan has experienced since the end of the war. Subsequent economic growth has been at a much lower pace, but it has still been above that of other industrialized countries. From 1974 to 1985, Japan's average annual real GNP growth was 3.8 percent. It was 2.2 percent for the United States, 1.8 percent for West Germany, and 2.1 percent for France.[5] The disparity between Japan and the others is much smaller than in the years of rapid growth, but Japan does remain ahead. Industrial maturity did not deny Japan the vitality to continue progressing; it has been a remarkably successful advanced industrial society.

INVESTMENT-DRIVEN GROWTH

For economic growth to take place, some portion of the output of the nation must be invested in the construction of productive plant and equipment, as well as in economic infrastructure (such as transportation and the communication network). The relationship is not linear; as economic growth rises, investment levels rise proportionately more. Explaining Japan's rapid development becomes an exploration of why investment levels were high. In addition, successful development requires that these investments be redirected away from traditional agriculture or handicrafts and toward modern manufacturing, incorporating new technologies as well as factory production.

As a latecomer to industrialization, Japan was confronted with a pool of Western technology far more advanced than its own. But borrowing and adapting technology for domestic use is no easy matter; if it were, all nations would be fully developed. Putting together an institutional framework conducive to private-sector-based industrial development took some time. Tinkering with commercial codes, banking laws, and mandatory education occupied much of the time from the Meiji Restoration in 1868 until the turn of the century. Even with a framework in place, knowledge of the rest of the world was limited and Japan made an effort to learn, both through the importation of foreigner teachers and engineers and through education abroad. Economic growth in these early years remained centered on agriculture and traditional industries because the modern manufacturing sector was minuscule even though it was expanding quickly.

Adapting Western technology to domestic factories produced leaps in labor productivity. Because Japan possessed a large pool of labor relatively willing to leave agriculture and work in the modern manufacturing sector, the expansion of employment did not put much upward pressure on wages. Thus, manufacturers could expand production and productivity through new investment without having to share all of that increase with the workers in the form of rising wages.[6] By the time the Showa era began, this process had already brought rapid expansion to the modern textile sector and was beginning to stimulate chemicals, steel, and other industries characterized by greater complexity and large investment units.[7] The institutional and learning base for these industries had finally been completed and they were beginning to take off. What the Japanese often call the heavy and chemical industrialization of the 1950s and 1960s was actually a major structural shift which dates back to the beginning of Showa.

As the 1930s progressed, economic output was affected increasingly by the demands of the military and war. From the standpoint of industrialization, however, an equally important impact was the isolation of Japan from the West, which lasted for roughly the decade of the 1940s because contact with the rest of the world was greatly limited even after the war until at least 1947. This isolation widened the gap in technology between Japan and the industrial nations, and thereby increased the potential gains from borrowing and adapting foreign technology.

Increased potential gains, coupled with enhanced ability to absorb technology stemming from better education and technical training programs during the war, opened the way for the extremely high economic growth of the years of the 1950s and 1960s. Entrepreneurs held optimistic expectations about profits from investing in new facilities incorporating borrowed technologies; actual results confirmed their expectations; and the process fed upon itself. Investment was extremely high as a share of total economic activity, exceeding the share in other major nations. As a percentage of gross domestic product, gross fixed capital formation in Japan over the very high growth years from 1960 to 1967 was 31 percent, whereas in West Germany it was 25 percent and in the United States only 18 percent.[8]

Rapid growth based on borrowed technology has its own logical conclusion imposed by successfully catching up with the world's technological frontier. Japan appears to have reached that point in the 1970s when its growth rate moderated after the 1973 oil shock, an event which conveniently demarcates the transition to lower growth. The final decade and a half of the Showa era was a time of adjustment to being a mature, advanced industrial nation.

AN INCOMPLETE EXPLANATION

Investment-driven growth stemming from technological catch-up is an incomplete and unsatisfying explanation of Japanese economic history during the Showa era, and the remaining parts of the explanation bring us to areas of disagreement and insufficient knowledge. Investment must be the central focus; nations grow because they invest, and capitalist investment must be motivated by profit expectations. But the existence of a technological lag and ample labor supplies are insufficient explanations by themselves of why investment occurred. Many other features of the economic system fed into the creation of high profit expectations and motivated high levels of investment. Let us consider several of the salient factors.

• The money for investment in plant and equipment must come from somewhere in the economic system in the form of savings. To say that Japan was characterized by a high share of fixed capital formation in GDP implies that either Japan generated a large share of domestic savings or borrowed extensively from the rest of the world. Japan did not borrow heavily from international capital markets, a feature that was reinforced by government policy in the high-growth years after the war (which essentially prohibited the private sector from borrowing abroad). Therefore, high investment was funded by high domestic savings. Some of those savings came from the retained profits and depreciation allowances of corporations which were reinvested in new plant and equipment. However, one of the key features of Japan's growth experience was a high level of household savings, much of which was reallocated by the financial system to investment in the corporate sector (rather than being used to finance housing investment or consumer durable purchases).

Japan is not alone in having high levels of household savings, but it has been (and remains) on the upper end of the spectrum. In 1960, net household savings as a percentage of disposable (after-tax) household investment was 17 percent. It was 16 percent in Italy, 12 percent in France, 8.6 percent in West Germany, and only 7 percent in the United States. Italy (and from the 1970s to the present, Greece) come very close to resembling Japan in terms of high household savings.[9] But savings alone do not produce economic growth; they provide a pool of funds which has the potential of providing growth when invested efficiently in infrastructure, plant, and equipment. Japan not only produced high savings; it carried out high levels of productive investment.

What remains poorly understood is why households in Japan have engaged in such high levels of savings. Economists have tried a number of theories: a lag in consumption as incomes rose rapidly, a bonus system which provided large lump-sum payments twice a year (an easy means to save), a poorly developed social security system and private pension system, a lack of consumer finance (pushing households to do their saving prior to major purchases rather than after), or incentives which exempted interest income on certain forms of savings accounts from taxes until 1988.[10] Other features that cannot be ignored are the vast destruction of housing which occurred in the final year of the war and the high inflation in the late 1940s which devastated the value of personal financial assets. Rebuilding a desired level of household wealth, involving unusually high savings out of current income until reaching that level, could be another motive for high savings levels. Each of these concepts has its adherents, and yet none has provided a fully satisfying answer.

Household saving involves features of social behavior which may be difficult or impossible to capture in economic models. For example, throughout the postwar years households have usually placed savings in bank accounts with controlled interest rates at generally low rates of return. Even the rather high inflation of the mid-1970s brought only moderate modification of this pattern. Considering the remarkable increase in prices on the Japanese stock market, and the absence of a capital gains tax on individual long-term holdings of corporate equity, this is an astounding financial conservatism. Frugality and conservatism remained strong features of household savings behavior until the end of the Showa era.

• Occupation of Japan after the war brought major institutional reforms which affected economic activity, and controversy remains over the impact of these changes on postwar economic performance. To put these changes into the context of investment-driven growth, Occupation reforms may have raised profit expectations and increased investment by transferring land ownership to tenants (who could now reap the fruits of their own investment) and by adding competition in the industrial sector through disbanding the large *zaibatsu* (industrial combines) which dominated much of modern industry in the prewar years of the Showa era. A small number of *zaibatsu*, which competed with one another in many markets and which were characterized by centralized control over investment decisions, were less likely to engage in aggressive investment out of fear of upsetting competitive relationships. The postwar history has been one of more fluid competition, and the ferocious competition over market share may have motivated some of the high level of investment which has characterized Japan.[11]

Opponents of this view adopt one of two approaches. First, the changes which occurred during the Occupation were significant, but they grew out of domestic pressures which were already building during the war years, so that the existence of American demands were neither necessary nor significant in determining the outcomes. Second, the changes themselves were not important in altering the competitive environment or fostering investment. To some extent, the desire to downplay the significance of the reforms comes from a Japanese desire to deny that the United States (as the leading actor in the Occupation) had a major positive impact on Japanese economic development. National pride and a determination to demonstrate that Japan was capable of generating sensible economic policies on its own leads to this revisionist approach.[12]

Economic studies of agriculture yield ambiguous results about whether reform led to rapid productivity change.[13] Even here, though, one could note that land reform eliminated the rural protest that characterized the 1930s and that provided a convenient platform for the radical military officers of that era. Political stability is beneficial for economic growth, and land reform certainly contributed to that stability. Industrial reform is more difficult to quantify, but the fact remains that the *zaibatsu* were eliminated and have not reappeared in the same form. The industrial groupings that re-emerged after the Occupation around roughly the same set of firms are far looser and lack centralized control over investment decisions of member firms—distinctions that may be crucial for encouraging more vigorous investment.

• Economists tend to treat corporations as black boxes, and yet these are the units which borrow and adapt foreign technology, make investment decisions, hire labor, provide training, and produce economic growth and industrial transformation. Economists studying Japanese economic history have rarely looked inside companies to ask why they have behaved as they have or how they have managed to succeed in using foreign technology. This aspect of Japan's experience became more important during the late Showa years, when Japan had caught up technologically but still had economic growth rates above those of other industrial countries. The continued superior performance of Japan must have something to do with the internal workings of the corporation.

Indeed, historians looking back at the Showa era may see the forging of a new set of corporate behavior patterns as the outstanding economic legacy of the era. In the early years of the era, the Japanese were still learning about corporate forms and factory organization. What is often called "lifetime employment," in which employees have implicit job guarantees until they reach mandatory retirement age, was just beginning in the 1920s as large firms sought to cope with the costs imposed by high labor turnover rates. The *zaibatsu* were largely family-owned organizations and were just beginning to seek wider equity participation as their scale increased. Quality control was not a high priority in Japanese factories.

Experimentation and response to the problems of production inside the factory from that time through the 1970s produced what could well be labeled an indigenous revolution in production processes. Management of the flow of parts through the factory; organization and tight control over inventory; engagement of blue-collar workers in the design of production and quality control processes; cooperative interaction among engineers, marketing people, financial officers, and factory managers; new concepts in plant maintenance to reduce downtime and increase product quality; and aggressive reduction of the variety of parts in products were all elements of the revolution created within Japanese firms.[14] Management consultants and business schools are responsible for most of what we know about the internal features of Japanese firms, and the subject deserves broader scholarly investigation.

The dilemma involved in investigating the nature of this revolution in manufacturing is to separate those features which are bound up in distinctive Japanese social behavior patterns and those which are not. A frequent refrain among Japanese manufacturers in the past has been the belief that their ability to produce at low cost and high quality cannot be transferred overseas, justifying a relative lack of foreign direct investment. The rapid appreciation of the yen since 1985 pushed more manufacturers in the direction of overseas investment, challenging the belief in Japanese uniqueness, but important questions remain concerning what or how much of the organizational innovations in domestic manufacturing will be transferred with these operations.

• Governments in all countries interact extensively with the private sector and thereby affect profit levels, the allocation of investment, the direction of research and development, and competition from imports. Relative to the United States, though, Japan has had an articulated industrial policy as part of this interaction, in which the government recognizes and acts upon a belief that it has a legitimate microeconomic role to play in guiding the nation on a path of economic advance. This is not unusual for a latecomer to industrial development, and most European nations have a more coherent government involvement in industry than does the United States. Great controversy surrounds the question of the extent to which the Japanese government involvement with the economy created or influenced the economic success of the Showa era.

According to Chalmers Johnson, a central proponent of this position, the institutions and policies that guided economic development were worked out over many years. Initial mistakes involving excess control during the 1930s and the war years were corrected during the late 1940s and resulted in the emergence of a successful industrial policy. It involved a variety of direct and indirect incentives for the private sector which reduced risk perceptions, increased profits, and thereby contributed to the high level of investment.[15] Industrial policy was most visible during the 1950s, when control over the allocation of foreign exchange to buy imports gave the Ministry of International Trade and Industry enormous power to influence corporate decisions. Many of the policy tools of that era, however, disappeared over time. Today the main tools consist of informal means to deny market access for imports (allowing domestic industries to develop a secure home market and volume production scales without foreign competition), research and development support aimed at key industrial technologies, and a generally cooperative attitude in setting other regulatory conditions (such as standards) or providing government procurement to foster industrial development.

Objections to the importance of industrial policy come in a variety of forms. Believing that under most conditions markets provide superior performance, economists have traditionally been suspicious of substituting bureaucrats for market forces. The existence of a Japanese government industrial policy in support of a given industry does not necessarily mean that it is the critical element in the industry's success. Furthermore, Japan has given much of its overt support to declining industries (such as agriculture, coal mining, and forest products) for the very same political reasons other nations have.[16]

Proponents argue that industrial policy enabled or encouraged the private sector to invest in industries which would become important in the future but which did not seem justified under comparative advantage when labor was abundant (such as capital-intensive steel) or where the size and strength of foreign competition would preclude new domestic firms from entering. In their view, faith in the market is overdone in American thinking; market failure is more widespread than economists believe, or market outcomes in many important industries are biased against the emergence of new competition in advanced developing countries.[17]

This argument remains far from resolution and has important implications for the United States. Should Japan be praised for policy innovations during the Showa years which the United States should adapt? Or should Japan be punished for pursuit of policies which are intrinsically unfair in a world system that espouses liberal trade ideals? In many cases, the key element to Japanese industrial policy has been explicit or implicit import barriers, denying or limiting the entry of competing foreign products until such time as domestic manufacturers have sufficient market power to limit foreign penetration even when barriers are removed.

It is worth noting that in general Japan's industrial policy has been quite different from Europe's. Japan has eschewed government ownership or sponsorship of "national champions." The more common pattern is encouragement of industrial structures with a relatively small number of firms which may be forced to share technology (to prevent a single firm from gaining an overwhelming position) and in which quasi-cartel arrangements keep domestic prices high, but fully permit ferocious competition over product development. Competition over market share through product innovation seems to be sufficient to drive a process in which investment is active and production costs are driven down to yield industries that become formidable international competitors.

Active industrial policy may have a role to play in developing economies, such as Japan in the 1950s, where economic growth is very rapid, but may be neither necessary nor desirable in mature economies at the technological frontier. Although Japanese industrial policy has discarded many of the strong tools of the past, it is still very much in existence and actively shaping future industries in Japan—new industrial materials, superconductors, supercomputers, biotechnology, and high-definition television. The debate over the desirability of this behavior will continue, and it will continue to have important consequences for American and other foreign firms competing with the Japanese.

• The nature of economic development from the beginning of Showa until at least the 1970s was heavily biased away from the public (households, consumers, or labor) and toward corporations. Housing investment, sidewalks, sewers, residential telephones, paved residential streets, libraries, and other elements of social infrastructure suffered at the expense of industrially useful infrastructure investment such as harbors and railroads. On the regulatory side, the public suffered from a rapid and severe degradation of the environment in the 1950s and 1960s, workers suffered from a notable lack of government concern for workplace safety and worker compensation, and consumers suffered from food prices kept far above world levels by stiff import barriers. Some of these skewed policies may have accelerated the measured level of economic growth by allocating more resources toward industrial expansion; a new factory has a larger and longer impact on increasing GNP than does a new sidewalk. But the cost in terms of health, safety, and stunted human aspirations was considerable.

For a brief time in the late 1960s and early 1970s public protest and shifting political support brought a burst of changes, including aggressive pollution-control measures and new or increased social welfare programs. However, even at the end of Showa, public welfare lagged far behind what one would expect for the high level of per capita income. Housing units remained small compared with those in other industrial countries; sewer systems remained appallingly limited in coverage; working hours remained at the upper end in comparison with other industrial countries'; prices for both food and manufactured goods were astonishingly high in international comparison, and the penetration of imported manufactured goods remained the lowest among industrial nations.

A standard response to foreigners who raise these points in Japan is that the differences represent "cultural" differences; the Japanese have always lived in small houses, men like to center their lives on the workplace rather than the family, and domestic agriculture (and especially rice) must be protected because it is at the core of

"Japaneseness." However, at every point there is deliberate government policy rather than free choice underlying the results. Even if differences in social behavior, consumer taste, or availability of land imply that Japanese consumption patterns would not be identical to those in other industrial countries, the existing pattern in Japan cannot be considered a natural outcome.

DILEMMAS FOR JAPAN AT THE END OF SHOWA

Achievement of advanced industrial status by the early 1970s set in train important macroeconomic shifts which brought Japan to a new position in the world by the end of the Showa era. Saving is an important virtue, and the conservative social values that appear to have contributed to the high savings levels in Japan during the Showa era were useful for industrialization by enabling a high level of investment without depending on foreign capital. But that virtue was less obvious in the 1970s and 1980s. The slower growth resulting from the completion of industrial catch-up implied less demand for investment. Savings, however, continued at a high level. When the households and corporations of a nation desire to save more than they desire to invest, three outcomes are possible: a depression occurs to push savings and investment back toward equality; the government can run an expansionary fiscal policy (increase government deficit spending) to absorb the excess savings of the private sector; or the nation can export its excess savings to the rest of the world. Japan has not experienced a depression since the early 1970s, and, quite to the contrary, has maintained an average growth at the upper end among OECD-member countries. Therefore, one or more of the other two possibilities must have occurred.

During the 1970s, the government absorbed the excess through a much larger government deficit. During the 1980s, on the other hand, the government deficit shrank and Japan began exporting its savings to the rest of the world. The size of that new flow in 1987 and 1988 was on the order of $90 billion, and since 1984 the level has ranged between 2 and 4 percent of GNP, a high level for this sort of flow.

The mechanisms by which surplus private-sector savings generate a net capital outflow are complex. But the process can be explained in at least outline form in this manner: Japan produces more goods and services than it desires to consume at home, so that the excess flows overseas (in the form of a current-account surplus). The current-account surplus represents net income; Japan receives more foreign currency for its exports than it must pay for its imports. That money could be spent on more imports, but the existence of the surplus implies that the Japanese have chosen not to do so. Therefore, the Japanese could either hold the foreign currency received or invest it. Even if held in the form of currency, this action would constitute a capital flow to the rest of the world (since currency represents non-interest-bearing debt instruments of government). Most of the money accumulated from the current-account surplus, however, is invested; the Japanese have invested their dollars, for example, in dollar-denominated financial assets in the Eurodollar market and the United States, as well as in the form of direct investment in corporate subsidiaries abroad and in foreign real estate. These large financial flows during the 1980s have pushed Japan into the position of being the largest net creditor in the world. Because the Japanese financial sector was well established (unlike those in the Mideast during the 1970s when the OPEC countries were faced with the need to invest abroad), much of the financial flow from Japan to the rest of the world has been through the hands of Japanese financial institutions. These institutions are now important players in some segments of the New York and London markets.

During much of the Showa period, government regulation and private-sector behavior eschewed financial management in favor of real investment in productive resources. People saved rather than borrowed and put their money in low-return bank accounts; corporations used these monies to expand factories at home; and the government concentrated on providing industrially useful infrastructure. The stock and bond markets remained poorly developed for many years, and government regulation and corporate behavior discouraged unfriendly takeovers or the exercise of stockholder power. The focus of the nation was not on financial manipulation, but on increasing production. How ironic that a nation of financial conservatives should become major international financiers!

But these shifts are more than ironic; they challenge many of the basic premises of Showa economic development. Japan remained an insular nation for much of the Showa era, and not just during the war and Occupation. Building a domestic manufacturing base and exporting to the world as a major component of economic strategy, as well as imposing restrictions on manufactured imports from abroad, and the limited personal exposure to the rest of the world caused by low personal incomes all meant that Japan remained relatively isolated from the world. Statistical data on the share of manufactured imports as a share of GNP, on the number of travelers going abroad, or on the level of foreign direct investment all show Japan to have been more insular than other industrial nations until the end of Showa.

That insularity cannot continue; rapidly rising foreign assets, swiftly expanding foreign aid, exploding numbers of people traveling and living abroad, rising numbers of people from Asian developing countries seeking employment inside Japan, and the greater incentives to import manufactured goods because of the strengthening of the yen have all put enormous pressure for change on the economic and social fabric of Japan. These are revolutionary changes and the Showa experience provides little guidance for the future. Japan attempted to behave in the international manner of the day in the early Showa years, pursuing imperialism in Korea and Taiwan, and extending its reach into Manchuria and China. But this foray into "internationalization" turned out to be an abject failure, marked by a sense of ethnic superiority and arrogance, as well as by a narrow view of economic benefit to Japan. After the war, economic development at home gained the exclusive attention of the nation, with the government managing to keep the nation away from any direct involvement in most of the contentious international problems.

In the final Showa years of the 1980s, the newly emerging international outreach continued to exhibit many of the features of the past. Economic success bred a renewed sense of superiority and arrogance toward the rest of the world that ill suits an international power. Foreign aid expanded rapidly in quantity, but the motivation appeared to be one of impressing other industrial nations that Japan was a "good citizen" rather than with truly helping developing countries; the structure of Japanese foreign aid continued to demonstrate a mercantilist bias toward aiding Japanese firms operating in developing countries. Factories built overseas are criticized for failing to provide a significant technology flow from Japan and for reserving a high number of managerial slots for Japanese expatriates. Inroads in foreign financial markets have brought strong complaints of unfairness because of the lack of reciprocal access for foreign firms in Japanese markets.

CONCLUSION

The Showa economic story was one of epic success. Japan "got it right," putting together the magical combination of government policy, aggressive entrepreneurship, education, social behavior norms, labor-management relations, and dedicated hard work that produces swift industrialization. Its record of becoming the only non-Western nation to achieve advanced industrial status is one of which all Japanese can be justifiably proud and which Westerners must respect.

Not only did Japan catch up; it appears to have created something of its own in the form of new production technologies which will continue to have an important impact on manufacturing around the world for years to come. Furthermore, in putting together an economic and social organization that suited industrialization, Japan has built a domestic system that remains well suited to continued success. The low rates of crime, high educational achievement, and ability to work well in the large group settings that characterize modern economic organizations all suggest that Japan will perform well in the future. Both the revolution in manufacturing processes and the general success in organizing an industrial society are major achievements of the Showa era. The distortions in the economy which damage consumer welfare detract from but cannot completely offset the respect which Japan deserves for its stunning industrial achievement.

But the death of the Showa emperor in 1989 also rang down the curtain on this economic era; the transition to advanced industrial status was over. Just because Japan has a domestic system that continues to work well in comparison with other industrial nations does not mean that Japan will necessarily do well in facing the demands of being an international power. Shifts in attitudes, behavior patterns, and government policies in the direction of a greater openness to the world remain urgently necessary. These shifts will not be easy and pose a challenge to the Heisei era as daunting as those which faced Japan at the beginning of Showa.

ENDNOTES

[1]Among the sources available in English are Hugh Patrick and Henry Rosovsky, eds., *Asia's New Giant: How the Japanese Economy Works* (Washington: Brookings Institution, 1975), which focuses on the period from the end of the war to the early 1970s; Kozo Yamamura and Yasukichi Yasuba, eds., *The Domestic Transformation,* vol. 1 of *The Political Economy of Japan* (Stanford: Stanford University Press, 1987), which analyzes the late Showa years of the 1970s and 1980s; and Kazushi Ohkawa and Henry Rosovsky, *Japanese Economic Growth: Trend Acceleration in the Twentieth Century* (Stanford: Stanford University Press, 1973), which is a more technical book looking at the years from 1900 to the beginning of the 1970s. A more institutional approach, as well as a somewhat more idiosyncratic view, is contained in two works by Takafusa Nakamura: *Economic Growth in Prewar Japan* (New Haven: Yale University Press, 1971) and *The Postwar Japanese Economy: Its Development and Structure* (Tokyo: University of Tokyo Press, 1981).

[2]William W. Lockwood, *The Economic Development of Japan: Growth and Structural Change 1868–1938* (Princeton: Princeton University Press, 1968), 147–50. Lockwood quotes a source placing Japan's overall per capita consumption in the mid-1930s at 28 percent of that of the United States, just slightly ahead of the Soviet Union's.

[3]Kazushi Ohkawa, Nobukiyo Takamatsu, Yuzo Yamamoto, *National Income,* vol.1 of *Estimates of Long-Term Economic Statistics of Japan since 1868* (Tokyo: Toyo Keizai Shimposha, 1974), 249.

[4]Edward F. Denison, *How Japan's Economy Grew So Fast* (Washington: Brookings Institution, 1975), 45. This particular comparison is based on net national product, which yields slightly different results than gross national product or gross domestic product do.

[5]Edward J. Lincoln, *Japan: Facing Economic Maturity* (Washington: Brookings Institution, 1988), 3.

[6]This statement is intentionally vague here. Enormous controversy has swirled around the supply conditions for labor during Japanese economic development and whether (or when) it was characterized by "surplus labor" conditions as developed in the theoretical development models of John Lewis and refined by John Fei and Gustav Ranis. For our purposes, it is sufficient to say that expanding manufacturing employment did not put undue pressure on wages.

[7]Yuichi Shionoya, "Patterns of Industrial Development," in Lawrence Klein and Kazushi Ohkawa, eds., *Economic Growth: The Japanese Experience since the Meiji Era* (Homewood, Ill.: Richard D. Irwin, 1968), 73–75. Shionoya notes that manufacturing growth as a whole accelerated from roughly the beginning of Showa through the 1930s, with textiles slowing down while chemicals and metals accelerated.

[8]Organization of Economic Cooperation and Development, *OECD Economic Outlook: Historical Statistics, 1960–1984* (Paris: OECD, 1986), 65. Several smaller European nations had investment shares in GDP that exceeded West Germany's, including Austria (26 percent), Finland (27 percent), Ireland

(28 percent), Luxembourg (27 percent), Norway (29 percent), and Switzerland (28 percent), but none as high as Japan's.

[9]Organization of Economic Cooperation and Development, 70.

[10]Henry C. Wallich and Mabel I. Wallich, "Banking and Finance," in Hugh Patrick and Henry Rosovsky, eds., *Asia's New Giant: How the Japanese Economy Works* (Washington: Brookings Institution, 1975), 256–61, review the many theories of high savings.

[11]A primary advocate of this view is Eleanor Hadley, in *Antitrust in Japan* (Princeton: Princeton University Press, 1970), 205–56, 408–53.

[12]Takafusa Nakamura, *The Postwar Japanese Economy: Its Development and Structure* (Tokyo: University of Tokyo Press, 1981), 14–48. Nakamura is a major proponent of this position.

[13]Hiromitsu Kaneda, "Structural Change and Policy Response in Japanese Agriculture After the Land Reform," in Lawrence H. Redford, ed., *The Occupation of Japan: Economic Policy and Reform* (Norfolk: McArthur Memorial, 1980), 133–46.

[14]*Kaisha: The Japanese Corporation, How Marketing, Money and Manpower Strategy, Not Management Style, Make the Japanese World Pace-Setters,* by James C. Abegglen and George Stalk, Jr. (New York: Basic Books, Inc., 1985) is one of the best-known examples of the writing on this topic. There is now a rising volume of literature in English written by some of the engineers who were intimately involved in these developments, such as Taiichi Ohno (a former production engineer at Toyota Motor Corporation), *Workplace Management* (Cambridge, Mass.: Productivity Press, 1988), and Ryuji Fukuda (formerly of Meidensha), *Managerial Engineering: Techniques for Improving Quality and Productivity in the Workplace* (Cambridge, Mass.: Productivity Press, 1984).

[15]Chalmers Johnson, *MITI and the Japanese Miracle* (Stanford: Stanford University Press, 1982), 83–197.

[16]Such skepticism is voiced by Philip H. Trezise and Yukio Suzuki in "Politics, Government and Economic Growth in Japan," in Hugh Patrick and Henry Rosovsky, eds., *Asia's New Giant: How the Japanese Economy Works* (Washington: Brookings Institution, 1975), 792–811.

[17]Miyohei Shinohara, *Industrial Growth, Trade, and Dynamic Patterns in the Japanese Economy* (Tokyo: University of Tokyo Press, 1982), 21–35.

Regional Japan: The Price of Prosperity and the Benefits of Dependency

William W. Kelly

No longer does Japan have agrarian communities where full-time farmers labor in pastoral tranquillity. There are only regions, the necessary reserves of metropolitan Japan. A look at one rural Japanese family reveals the vast changes that took place in these regions during the Showa period, as urban middle-class values and agricultural subsidies influenced farming areas.

The corrugated landscape of the Japanese archipelago has given a distinct imprint to patterns of habitation and conceptions of regions. Mountainous topography has divided the islands into about a hundred small plains, either intermontane basins or coastal flatlands, which have come to frame political units, economic activity, and cultural identity. The settlement form of these small regions is generally a hinterland of hundreds of nucleated villages and a handful of small towns all now within an hour or so drive of the one to three cities at the plain's center.

One such region of course stands above the rest: the densely packed Kanto Plain—Japan's largest, though only 100 kilometers at its widest, across which sprawls the metropolis of Tokyo. Devastated by the Great Earthquake of 1923, Tokyo recovered to become the highly concentrated core of Showa Japan. Within a 50-kilometer radius (3.6 percent of the country's land area) live 30 million people, or 25 percent of the Japanese population. It is the world's most populous metropolitan area, and for half a century, it has been the capital of politics and administration, the headquarters of corporate

William Kelly is Professor of Anthropology at Yale University.

life and financial capital, the center of mass media and cultural institutions, and the pinnacle of the educational hierarchy. It is Japan's core, to which all other regions are peripheral.

Three generations of the Sato family live together in a rambling house in one of these peripheral regions, the northern plain of Shonai. Save for the home-grown rice and a few of the vegetables and fruits, all the foods on their dining table are national-brand supermarket items. The Sony television in the kitchen that broadcasts during most meals is tuned to NHK public television. Their mealtimes must conform to three different timetables: the mother's job as an accountant at the local factory of a Tokyo-based prefab door manufacturer; the father's three-season job as a salesman for a small printing firm in the nearby city; and the busy civic schedule of the grandfather, including his meetings as head of the town education committee. Only the grandmother is (reluctantly) housebound, having quit a part-time factory job to care full-time for her five-year-old granddaughter and three-year-old grandson until they enter the town kindergarten.

The three outside jobs explain the three vehicles in the driveway: a compact Celica, a subcompact Daihatsu, and a Nissan light truck. The truck is a concession to the family "farm"—three hectares of paddy land and 100 persimmon trees, which require the fourth season of the father's labor and occasional assistance from the grandparents. Almost every evening during my several months with the family, the father raced home to exchange his business suit for either a casual sweater or a loose winter kimono. In the former attire, he drove off to sample area restaurants that featured regional Shonai cuisine—research toward a local public relations pamphlet he had been commissioned by a friend to write. Kimonoed, he settled by the stove to practice Noh drama, drumming under his father's stern direction in preparation for the annual, and nationally famous, village festival.

The net return on the farming contributes only about 25 to 30 percent to the Satos' combined household income, and requires even less of their total work life. Nonetheless, by self-description, they are a resolutely proper—if somewhat nervous—*noka,* a "farm family," and the representativeness of their profile is a measure of both the depths of the farm crisis and the basis of the prosperity that now characterizes rural Japan. The son's balancing of his roles as office worker, farmer, amateur journalist, and Noh drummer suggests the multiple ways in which life in regional Japan has been drawn into and held apart from society's mainstream.

To be sure, declining agriculture, migrations to the cities, and the "modernization" of rural life are staple, if hackneyed, characterizations of the countryside in all industrial societies. Yet in generalizing from Shonai and the Satos to the regional dynamics of Showa Japan, it is better to avoid a framework of lagging development and "catch-up" linear progress, of rural-urban moves and agrarian-industrial sectoralization. Shifting the usual rubric for talking about the Japanese countryside from "agrarian" to "regional" is not only analytically productive but also historically resonant with changes during the Showa period in the public debate about rural Japan.

One may find in this public debate at least four themes that have come to mark rural Japan as more "regional" than "agrarian": the "rice price problems" besetting Japanese agriculture, the consequences of a particular pattern of "local development," the spread of "mainstream consciousness" across the countryside, and the faddish sentimentalism of "rural nostalgia." Neither their selection nor their order is random. The largely unintended farm crisis has contributed substantially to the subsidized nature of rural prosperity, which permitted and promoted the penetration of institutions and ideologies of the metropolitan center, which in turn has contributed to the romantic backlash of nostalgia for a countryside that, to complete the circle, no longer exists. The four themes thus highlight the contradictory pressures that define regional lifeways and the continuing tensions in the position of Japanese regions as peripheries of a national state and metropolitan culture.

CREATING A FARM CRISIS

In little more than a century, Japanese agriculture has undergone a threefold transformation. At midnineteenth century, the countryside was populated with tenants and peasant smallholders, much of whose surplus production was appropriated by the Tokugawa warrior elite and absentee merchants. By the early twentieth century, innovating landlords had seized the initiative in promoting new labor-intensive practices that were profitable to them if onerous to tenant cultivators. Now, in the late twentieth century, further agricultural change has produced a countryside of weekday workers and weekend farmers, whose highly mechanized overproduction of rice is reluctantly subsidized by the state at considerable economic cost for partisan political gain and, perhaps, more general social welfare. At international forums, national policy circles, and local farmer gatherings, "rice price problems" *(beika mondai)* are the focal issues.

Put simply, the farm crisis in rural Japan today is how it has come to pass that Japanese agriculture, which contributed mightily to the country's early industrialization, has become one of the most technologically advanced and economically inefficient farming systems in the world. That is, how have Japanese rice farmers become world leaders in rice crop yields and yet a substantial drag on their national economy? Ironically, the present-day difficulties are in large part a product of past success—unintended, unanticipated, but related nonetheless. Having restored the productivity levels of agriculture in the 1950s, policy planners through the 1960s and 1970s fervently hoped that their programs and subsidies would produce a core of (a) full-time, (b) cooperating, and (c) diversified farmers. They have been frustrated on all counts. What we find instead is a countryside of noncooperating, part-time farmers concentrating on the one crop for which there is an unmarketable surplus, rice.

The prevailing image of this part-time farming is captured in the popular phrase *sanchan nogyo,* or "farming by grandpa, grandma, and mom." In fact, we can parse this stereotype into two actual patterns. The first is what may be called *toshiyori nogyo,* that is to say, "senior citizen farming" by the elderly grandparents of the household, while the commuter adults and the student children spend their days in the workplaces and schools of the town. In contrast, in the real rice bowls like Shonai, young adult males such as Mr. Sato are the sole (though still seasonal) farmer of the household, and the other adults find nonagricultural jobs. The Ministry of Agriculture calls this *kokeisha nogyo,* or "successor agriculture," which the locals render colloquially as *segare nogyo.* Curiously, postwar mechanization has produced both outcomes. In marginal areas and on small holdings, rototillers, chainsaws, portable sprayers, and small trucks enable an elderly couple to handle most of the tasks of vegetable garden, orchard, and woodlot maintenance. In regions like Shonai, tractors, transplanters, combines, and gas dryers allow the young males to perform most of the rice work as solitary, independent farmers.

This suggests a further point about the current crisis. Most part-time farming is *rice* farming, because of the structure of the subsidies and the direction of postwar technological innovation. Perhaps that is why the government now believes that by reconfiguring the subsidies and redirecting the technology, it can induce the part-timers away from rice to something else, anything else. Thus, for two decades it has pursued a carrot-and-stick program known as "diversification."[1] For all their exhortations to diversify, however, neither the government extension service nor the agricultural cooperative can offer much guidance. People in Shonai were perhaps exaggerating when they complained to me that coop technicians couldn't tell the difference between lettuce and cabbage or between a pea and a soybean, but it certainly is true that their expertise does not extend much beyond rice.

It is worth remembering that while rice has always had a central place in Japanese farming systems, even those on the broad river plains have been "rice plus"—rice in conjunction with other crops. The trend toward rice monoculture, even monovariety cultivation, is quite recent and government-induced. *Purasu arufa* (plus alpha), as the young Shonai farmers say now, or as Ronald Dore put it so felicitously, "the search for the alchemist's secret," is a deeply felt concern among farmers, but it is proving discouragingly elusive.[2] Young Mr. Sato often pointed wistfully to a small plot in front of his house on which he intended to construct a greenhouse and begin growing herbs to sell in a university classmate's specialty shop in the prefectural capital. However, he was vague about his timetable and ignorant of herb cultivation and retail market conditions. It is not cultural conservatism but economic good sense and political cynicism toward the "latest variety" *(shinhatsumei)* that extension agents are touting that keeps the rice surpluses mounting.

It must be quickly added, however, that there is more than greed and cynicism behind the continuing salience of a *noka* identity for households like the Satos'. One must understand the reluctance to abandon such an identity in cultural and political terms. The resonance of *noka* is rich, suggesting *jikyu jisoku, komyunichii, inasaku, furusato*. That is, "self-support and communal membership, providing food for the country and folk for the nation." Growing rice makes more sense culturally than it does agriculturally.

Moreover, in the postwar period, most employment has been effectively *de*politicized; the enticements and idioms of public service and corporate employment are economic growth, job security, and organizational loyalty. Even the Confucian familial metaphor of the workplace has been sanitized of its imperial referents. The farmer stands as a striking exception. Agricultural work, the subject of protracted prewar tenancy disputes, was effectively *re*politicized: by the Land Reform, which linked it prominently to democratic principles; by the Agricultural Cooperative Law, which emphasized a democratic association of independent proprietors; and by political party reorganization, which linked it to a party machine, the Liberal Democratic Party (LDP). Under such circumstances, one can appreciate the resistance to yielding such an identity.

SUBSIDIZING RURAL PROSPERITY

Nonetheless, however perplexed is agricultural policy and however dire is agricultural practice, one cannot be unrelievedly pessimistic about this farm crisis. Perhaps the political scientist Kato Eiichi exaggerates in contrasting "urban poverty and rural affluence," but the fact of regional prosperity, both as improvement over the postwar decades and in comparison with urban areas, is remarkable and undeniable.[3] By a number of indicators—house ownership, car ownership, per capita disposable income, per capita domestic space, air quality, and so on—rural regions offer better living circumstances than major urban centers. In part, this is a function of personal income, which is enhanced by agricultural price supports, multiple-worker households in rural regions, and lower tax payments due to income-reporting practices of many self-employed.

More significantly, it results from a net outflow of state resources from urban to rural regions. In calculating the pattern of revenue sharing and direct project grants by the central government in 1980, for instance, Kato found that the ratio of tax burden to revenue benefit reveals a striking deficit for urban prefectures and a large surplus for predominantly rural prefectures.[4] What has happened has been that the same government programs that have produced agricultural crisis have also brought enormous infrastructure improvements to rural society; road networks, telephone lines, community centers, and other public service facilities are constructed with subsidies from the basic agricultural assistance programs or from ancillary programs. Like the rice price supports, this more general state subsidization of regional prosperity has broad parallels but important differences with European and North American government policies.[5] In Japan, this generosity has been stimulated by, and has in turn sustained, a vibrant local politics, national party brokerage by the dominant conservative LDP, and government ministry intentions. To appreciate both the real benefits and the substantial costs of such a pattern of "local development" *(chiiki kaihatsu),* one must consider each of those three elements.

Amalgamating local units of government has been a crucial administrative transformation of the countryside for 100 years. Since the 1880s, the Interior Ministry and its descendant, the present Home Affairs Ministry, have been as intent upon increasing the scale of local governmental bodies as has the Ministry of Agriculture with increasing farm scale. However, as often as not, this ongoing incorporation of villages into towns and towns into cities has energized rather than paralyzed political process at the local level. One cannot overemphasize the political activity it has generated over the last 40 years and the community consciousness and redefinitions of identity it has engendered. This "amalgamation drive" *(gappei)* has presented opportunities not only for effective top-down administration but also for viable local autonomy.

Jackson Bailey, for example, has described the instructive case of the remote Iwate village of Tanohata. Here, after successfully avoiding amalgamation with adjacent villages, an activist mayor mobilized residents to promote international educational cooperation as a slogan for distinctive local identity, as a platform for town initiatives, and as an attractive ploy for national recognition and government assistance. Likewise, another Iwate village, Sawauchi, made itself nationally famous in the 1970s as the "Village of Nature and Health" because of a program of pensions, comprehensive health care, and preventive health examinations, which had been initiated by a dynamic, energetic mayor in the late 1950s and early 1960s and expanded by later local leaders.[6]

Revitalized local administration has both contributed to the current farm crisis and helped to deflect its worst effects. That is, together with the land-improvement district and the agricultural cooperative, the town office has been one of the key units through which many of the postwar agricultural programs have been channeled. At the same time, though, these local governments have lobbied effectively for an extensive restructuring of regional infrastructure concomitant with agricultural projects—roads and communications improvements; school, clinic, and other public facility construction; and so on. In this way, local government efforts have exacerbated the contradictions of farming even as they have greatly enhanced the material conditions of life in the countryside.

Yet, one must be careful not to exaggerate the scope of local initiative or the extent to which material prosperity has politically empowered the regions. Perhaps the most repeated stereotype of the postwar Japanese political system has been the mutually beneficial linkage of the LDP and the rural farmers that keeps the former in power and the latter overrepresented—to the disadvantage of the urban voter and the urban consumer. It does not require apologetics to see that it is doubly glib to speak of an alliance of LDP and farmers.

First, rather than an "alliance" of LDP and farmers, it is more accurate to talk about the critical intermediary role that the LDP has played between the national bureaucracy and the regional populace. On the one hand, major LDP factions are beholden to rural regions for electoral support, but they also share with the state bureaucrats a commitment to what one might call a managerial pattern of state governance. The plan rationality that for Chalmers Johnson characterizes economic policy may be taken to be even more broadly descriptive of the logic of the postwar Japanese state.[7] Both ministry bureaucrats and LDP politicians share an ideological commitment to the centralization of policy planning, program design, and resource allocation and to the delegation of policy execution and program accountability.

Second, since at least the late 1960s, rural support for the LDP has come not from the increasingly endangered species of full-time farmers, but from the far more numerous part-timers, whose interests in employment, consumption, and local services are quite different. If anything, full-time farmers have done rather poorly by LDP agricultural policies. It is the support for price subsidies to part-time rice farmers and for services and public works for the regions that better explains LDP electoral success and political action.[8]

Thus, both ideological disposition and electoral interests reinforce a pattern of regional development through extensive subsidies. There are real benefits—the transfer of wealth and expertise and the stimulus to local politics—but there is also an ultimate price, and that is a multidimensional subordination. The dispersion of state resources has, if anything, doubly reinforced the hierarchies of education and of private and public employment. That is, it has secured both ideological compliance and institutional efficiency. The Satos are resentful but sanguine about the slim chances that a local graduate could gain entrance to a leading national university, and yet the grandparents had fretted and calculated to insure that their children passed into the best possible local high school. A frequent slogan of recent local conferences and workshops in Shonai has been *jinzai-zukuri:* "how to foster and retain people of talent in the region?" Its popularity speaks more to crisis than opportunity, to the ever more extensive and efficient culling of the best regional talent for the national center.

Employment works as education does to draw the rural population more tightly into the national economy. A symbiosis of farm and factory is not surprising; family farming frequently serves as a reserve labor pool for manufacturing, and present-day Japan is no exception. As a number of scholars have argued[9] and as the Satos know from their own work careers, there is a vital connection between part-time farming and the subcontracting sector of Japanese industry, which itself is a required cushion around the corporate core. It is a necessary mutualism that is not without benefit to rural households, but which is constructed largely on industry's terms.

Finally, the enormous government investment in infrastructure has enhanced significantly the state's ability to *force* certain changes, when it deems necessary. In Shonai as elsewhere, for example, the extensive irrigation-drainage projects for rice growing have been predicated on redefining agricultural water rights. Longstanding, vaguely defined, but legally guaranteed water use practices have been converted to fixed-term, fixed-quantity permits, issued and renewed through the Ministry of Construction. This ministry, which has long lobbied for greater municipal and industrial access to agricultural water quantities, now has direct authority for regional water resource allocation. Another example of the loss of control entailed by subsidy dependency has been the success of the Home Affairs Ministry in imposing a retrenchment of local government employees through legislative mandate and budgetary squeezes during the 1980s. These are precisely the jobs most desired by many of the younger locals for their security and status.

METROPOLITANIZING REGIONAL LIFEWAYS

If farming occupies little of the daily lives of the Sato "farm family," what does? Many of their concerns and routines of work, schooling, and family are indistinguishable from those of their many relatives and acquaintances who have moved to metropolitan Tokyo. Life chances in contemporary Japan are not equal, nor have lifeways become homogenized, but they have become more standardized. Regional Japan has become more closely synchronized with the metropolitan center, and "mainstream consciousness" *(churyu ishiki)* is a term frequently used to characterize the consequences of the institutional and ideological articulations I suggested in the previous section.

Mention of mainstream consciousness immediately calls to mind what is perhaps the most notorious public opinion survey in postwar Japan. This is the Survey on the People's Life-style *(Kokumin seikatsu chosa),* which the Prime Minister's Office has conducted annually since the late 1960s.[10] It asks a large sample of respondents to rank their present circumstances as well above, just above, right about, just below, or well below some felt average life situation. For over 20 years, about 90 percent of the respondents have avoided the two extremes and placed themselves at, just above, or just below average, and it is this which commentators have seized upon as evidence for a 90-percent middle-class society.

Critics of this interpretation rightly point to objective dimensions of continuing stratification,[11] but I think it would miss the significance of the self-assessments to dismiss the survey as fanciful interpretation or false consciousness. The link between the "New Middle Class" professions of the survey and the private lives of ordinary Japanese is neither direct nor transparent. It lies in the emergence, since the 1950s, of powerful typifications of the ideal organization of family, school, and work. It is only when accosted by opinion polltakers (and perhaps inquiring anthropologists) that most people lapse into general talk about "middle-class consciousness." The dilemmas and decisions of everyday life are framed in more concrete language, but my point is that this language, which organizes much of daily experience, owes a great deal to the institutional interests that shape that public discourse.

In the last four decades, both official policy and public opinion have idealized career employment in large organizations, meritocratic educational credentialing, and a nuclear household division of labor between the outside "working" husband and the inside domestic wife. This configuration may fly in the face of the realities of life for many Japanese. Nonetheless, by the 1970s and early 1980s, this New Middle Class ideology had come to effectively define standards of achievement, images of the desirable, and limits of the feasible.[12]

Three of the most prescient studies of Showa Japan have been ethnographies of everyday life that reveal this process. In her journal of life in the mid-1930s in the Kyushu village of Suye-mura, Ella Wiswell noted the first intrusions of state promotion of a female ideal of "good wife and wise mother," a growing sense of "propriety" that she felt even more strongly in the decorum of her brief return visit in 1950. Settling into the town of Mamachi on the outskirts of Tokyo in the late 1950s, Ezra Vogel witnessed both population displacement and life-style displacement. A "new middle class" of white-collar employees was emerging amidst the shopkeepers, small business-people, and professionals of the old middle class, and this was changing the character of Mamachi from urban fringe town to metropolitan bedburb. At the same time, David Plath was out in the countryside around Nagano Prefecture's Matsumoto City, where he documented the prevailing regional lifeways of the farmer, the shopkeeper, and the white-collar "salaryman" but also demonstrated the growing attractiveness, across the region, of the life and leisure of the salaryman.[13]

There is as much danger in misreading these observations as in misinterpreting the Prime Minister's Office survey. It was not so much the reality of the white-collar salaryman that they saw or predicted. Ninety percent of the residents of Suye-mura, Mamachi, Matsumoto—and Shonai—have not become salarymen. Rather, the residents have come to widely accept certain cultural constructs as the terms which give meaning and value to their actions. Visions of the nuclear family, meritocratic schooling, and large organization workplaces have narrowed the preferred meanings of support in family, success in school, and security in work.

The process continues throughout regional Japan. In few ways do such New Middle Class idealizations accurately describe the realities of family, school, and work for the Satos or most other residents of Shonai Plain. Like many married women, the young Mrs. Sato continues her full-time accounting job and must accommodate that to her domestic ambitions as wife and mother. Yet she does have such ambitions, which differ from those held by her mother and mother-in-law. Her husband is one of the very few of his generation in Kurokawa who have gone on to university and returned; almost all of his neighbor peers found work after graduating from one of the area's less competitive high schools. He has recently bought a used portable computer from his print-shop boss to bring home for his children's use with (he hopes) educational software. And while no one in the Sato family enjoys the full security of white-collar employment, it is precisely this security that is a central concern in their assessments of alternative work opportunities.

Certain New Middle Class routines as well as standards have come to characterize their lives. The individuation of their factory work and even their farm work, and its displacement from the home, has redrawn the boundaries between family and society as sharply for this part-time farm family as for more stereotypically white-collar families. The Satos remain a "three-generation family" *(san sedai kazoku),* seemingly at odds with the nuclear norm, and yet new spatial layouts, chore assignments, and leisure patterns reflect a middle-class sensitivity to privacy *within* the family as well as between family and society. The young couple, for example, in physical space (in their own cars and their own areas of the house) and in social time (after the evening bath and on "family" trips), has carved out a nuclear unit within the multigenerational residence group.

At the same time as new lines are drawn between home and society, institutions of that larger society—schools, public agencies, mass media—intrude upon family life with a force that regularizes the life-cycle experience across occupations and family forms. The young Mr. Sato's brother is a research professional for a prefectural forestry station; Mrs. Sato's siblings include a high school teacher and a nonworking housewife-mother. In their particulars, these life courses have diverged. But this generational set has been tightly synchronized in their timing of school leaving, work entrance, marriage, and childbearing. They illustrate how life-cycle transitions have become increasingly orderly and uniform, and how metropolitan rather than distinctly urban and rural standards often prevail.

CELEBRATING THE IMAGINARY COUNTRYSIDE

There is at least one element of my profile of young Mr. Sato, however, that may have struck the reader as hardly "metropolitan," and that is his diligent evening practice of Noh drumming. Every February 1 and 2, hundreds of people gather at the main shrine of the Satos' village for an annual festivity that includes Shinto ritual, youthful competitions, copious drinking, and all-night presentations of stately Noh drama. Like their ancestors, the Sato father and grandfather are both musicians, and they alternate in playing the small shoulder drum during the long Noh programs.

In 1989, the assembled included local parishioners of the shrine, friends and relatives, tourists and Noh scholars from Tokyo, Europe, and North America, and camera crews from NHK TV and the BBC. Indeed, this Kurokawa festival and its Noh drama have become one of rural Japan's most well-known "folk art performances"—the subject of television documentaries, scholarly dissertations, and tourist guidebooks.

While unusual in its notoriety, it is but one of hundreds of vibrant regional festivities that continue to draw throngs of locals and metropolitans alike. They are riding the crest of a "rural nostalgia" *(furusato bumu)* sentimentalism that has engaged the nation for almost 20 years.[14]

Several weeks after the festival, on a frigid February morning, I accompanied the grandfather to the opening ceremony for the new local elementary school. It is an imposing edifice of futuristic architectural lines, an art deco pastel exterior, modular classrooms, and well-appointed science labs. Following the predictable speeches, the ceremony closed with each grade presenting a special activity—tumbling and floor exercises, a recorder-percussion band, and so on. The fifth graders were led by one of the chief Kurokawa actors in chanting sections from several Noh plays, which he practices with them each Friday afternoon.

I seemed to be the only one in the audience disoriented by this juxtaposition of education for a high-tech future and heritage of a preindustrial past, but other discordancies are more keenly felt. These include especially the shifting regard for rural life by the metropolitan center. That urban imaginations of the countryside oscillate between snobbish condescension and rhapsodizing sentimentality is of course a recurring theme of all nation-states.[15] Showa Japan has certainly been no exception. In the interwar decades of the 1920s and 1930s, the countryside figured prominently in a "national folklore," which gained academic and popular recognition around three overlapping fields of research: the collection and classification of folk customs of the agrarian countryside by Yanagita and Origuchi; the discovery and promotion of folk arts of pottery, weaving, and handicrafts by Yanagi Muneyoshi; and Honda Yasuji's exhaustive recordings of and writings about folk performances of ritual festival dances. It was in fact Honda's visits to Kurokawa Noh in the 1930s that first brought it national attention.

In the decade following defeat in World War II, metropolitan views of the countryside turned to denigration. It was now suspect, the bastion of residual "semifeudal" elements and superstitious customs that were antithetical to that which was "modern" and "democratic" and desirable. An enthusiasm for "rationalization" swept the rural regions as fervently as it reshaped society's center.[16] Yet even as society's center aimed to transform Shonai life through its programs of rationalization, it began again to appropriate Shonai's past as a nostalgic reassurance of its own idealized past. By the late 1960s, the chains of blind custom became the roots of authentic tradition, and the countryside was again upheld as a last preserve of noble virtues. In a flush of rural nostalgia, the cultural institutions and authorities at the society's center have come to fetishize countrysides like Shonai in travel posters, tourist itineraries, and television specials. Now it is the quaintness of farmhouses, the integrity of farm work, and the bonds of the village community that are celebrated and valorized as a moral counterweight to the industrial core of bureaucracy and corporation.

People in regions like Shonai are sensitive and even savvy about these shifting nuances, especially in their use of *noson,* "farming village," as both *furusato,* "the old homeplace," and *inaka,* "the hick boonies." Few of the hundreds of Shonai settlements have even a significant minority of full-time farmers, but *noson* (like *noka*) remains a common self-description. At least in part, this plays on the term's ambivalent connotations. As the backward *inaka,* the *noson* seems a most eligible and appropriate target for the state's generously subsidized rural development programs, including the block grant from the Ministry of Education to construct the Satos' new elementary school.

In other contexts—as the traditional *furusato—noson* life offers a rhetorical defense against the felt excesses of the national society its residents otherwise eagerly embrace. The same Ministry of Education has also designated Kurokawa Noh as a "national intangible living folk treasure," and has funded a new hall beside the village shrine, with a practice stage, exhibit space, and lecture rooms. This official designation is an important example of agrarian cultural heritage, although like the Satos, there isn't a full-time farmer among any of the core participants.

Thus, in Showa Japan there was no simple contest between an incorporating center and regions struggling to preserve autonomy. Prevailing typifications of life and structures of state power have had a directive force in regional lifeways, even as mass culture draws contradictory images of such regions and their residents. Japan's countrysides are now both its *inaka* and its *furusato*. As the backward "boonies," they must be assimilated into a modern society, but as the nation's "folk," they must be preserved as testimony to a moral society.

And yet we now know that these contradictory impulses mark transformations of private and civic life in the cities as much as in the regions.[17] One now finds modern kitchens and "traditional" festivals in the center and at the periphery. When the world's largest advertising agency, Dentsu, establishes a Regional Culture Development Division and engineers a festival campaign called "Shitamachi Live '85" for one of Tokyo's central wards, one can talk not only about the commercialization of culture (an overused notion anyway) but also about the "urbanization of nostalgia."[18] Perhaps even more appropriately, it marks the metropolitanization of nostalgia. As the drive to rationalize has moved from the state center outward to its regions, the urge to sentimentalize has insinuated itself from the peripheral countryside into the urban core.

DEVELOPING SHONAI FOR THE TWENTY-FIRST CENTURY

We have seen that beginning an analysis of contemporary rural Japan with rice and the rice crisis is at once necessary and misleading. It was the notably successful democratization and mechanization of rice farming in the first three postwar decades that radically transformed rural life and provided the basis of the fragile but real material prosperity of regions like Shonai. Yet the growing contradictions within agricultural policy and practice and the standardizing intrusions of state institutions into rural life have precipitated a reconfiguration of employment patterns, social relationships, cultural identity, and political allegiance. There are no agrarian countrysides in contemporary Japan, except in the (senti)mental imagery of *furusato* motifs. There *are* regions—the necessary, dependent reserves of metropolitan Japan, both favored and disadvantaged, valorized and stigmatized.

At community meetings and other gatherings in Shonai, there is usually little abstract policy debate about the "rice crisis" and about "dependent prosperity." Rather, people's concerns focus, naturally enough, on concrete issues of direct impact. Prominent in the late 1980s have been the following four proposals that both supporters and critics have claimed as representing the wave of the region's future.

1. Disposition of a new Epson/Seiko integrated-circuit manufacturing plant. In the mid-1980s, after controversial negotiations to acquire paddy land in the middle of Shonai Plain, the Epson/Seiko Corporation began construction of a new microelectronics assembly plant that was to provide several hundred factory jobs. Its opening was soon suspended, as the company increasingly shifted such manufacturing operations to its overseas plants. It became a local casualty of what is frequently and ominously labeled in the national press as the "hollowing" of industrial Japan.

2. Prospects for the new Shonai Regional Airport. Plans for the Seiko plant were an important element in the successful campaign, against some local opposition, to construct a regional airport, also in

the central plain. This is a local manifestation of a larger national debate about the desirable and feasible shape of a futuristic transportation network for northeastern Japan involving air links, high-speed rail lines, and superhighways. Airport supporters argue that it is a valuable first step, essential to attracting corporate investment and offering a new route for hydroponic flowers and fresh vegetables to the Tokyo markets. Critics fear it is an extravagant and frivolous alternative to much-needed but (given land acquisition costs) more expensive rail and road improvements.

3. Plans for metropolitan play and local work. Several national ministries and agencies are now actively promoting leisure resort industry for regions like Shonai. The Seibu Group has recently purchased a large tract on the slopes of Mt. Chokai, the local "Mt. Fuji," with plans for an "all-season" leisure resort. In addition to skiing, swimming, tennis, and other predictable offerings, it has plans for what it calls "tourist agriculture" and "cultural tourism." The employment of locals as cleaning women and groundskeepers by day and traditional carvers and authentic folk dancers by evening is a paradox not lost on Shonai residents, but willing to be overlooked by many of them.

4. The "rationalization" of the Faculty of Agriculture at the prefecture's national university. Among the Ministry of Education's worries about the nation's universities is the precipitous decline in applicants for faculties of agriculture. Each of the six national universities in northeastern Japan has such a faculty; Yamagata University's is located away from the main campus, in the Shonai city of Tsuruoka, where it sits proudly as the region's pinnacle of higher education. The ministry is hoping to eliminate the majority of these agriculture faculties and to repackage their departments as biotechnology, robotics engineering, leisure sociology, regional economics, and so on. Some would like to coordinate this with the regional "technopolis" proposals in the 1986 Fourth National Development Plan *(Yonzenso)*. In Yamagata, this would spell the closing of the Tsuruoka campus in favor of a consolidated campus at the interior prefectural capital. Shonai residents bitterly oppose this as a fatal blow to whatever educational prestige the region can presently lay claim to.

No region is alike in the particulars of its present concerns, but taken together, these four issues illustrate the more general paradoxes of regional Japan, which have been outlined here and which Shonai households like the Satos' enact in their everyday lives. *Prosperity* is not a word the Satos use to describe their nonetheless modestly comfortable lives, nor is a mood of impending crisis at all reflected in the guardedly optimistic manner in which they greet most days. And yet throughout the Showa decades, both conditions, in equal measure and in mutual determination, have characterized the shape of their lifeways and that of their region.

ENDNOTES

[1]Richard Moore, *Japanese Agriculture: Patterns of Rural Development* (Boulder: Westview Press, 1989).

[2]Ronald Dore, *Shinohata: A Portrait of a Japanese Village* (New York: Pantheon, 1978).

[3]Kato Eiichi, "Toshi no fukushu: Echigo daimyo Mejiro-dono no kozai," *Chuo koron* (June 1983): 72–89. A partial translation of this article appeared as "Urban Discontent Under Tanaka's Political Machine," *Japan Echo* 10 (4) (1983): 15–25. On postwar improvement, see Robert J. Smith, Jr., *Kurusu: The Price of Progress in a Japanese Village, 1951–1975* (Stanford: Stanford University Press, 1978), and Dore.

[4]See Kato, 78.

[5]See the discussion in Kent E. Calder, *Crisis and Compensation: Public Policy and Political Stability in Japan, 1949–1986* (Princeton: Princeton University Press), 234–44 and 277–85.

[6]Jackson Bailey, "Local Politics and Political Leadership in Rural Japan: Tanohata-mura, 1955–1980," unpublished paper presented at Association for Asian Studies Annual Meetings (Philadelphia, March 1985); on Sawauchi: Christie W. Kiefer, "Care of the Aged in Japan," in Edward Norbeck and Margaret Lock, eds., *Health, Illness, and Medical Care in Japan: Cultural and Social Dimensions* (Honolulu: University of Hawaii Press, 1987), 95–97.

[7]Chalmers Johnson, *MITI and the Japanese Miracle* (Stanford: Stanford University Press, 1982). Kent Calder (op. cit.) has recently proposed a provocative "crisis and compensation" dynamic to explain the political policies that have subsidized a wide range of domestic sectors and interest groups in postwar Japan.

[8]See, for example, Gerald L. Curtis, *The Japanese Way of Politics* (New York: Columbia University Press, 1989), 49–61.

[9]For example, Calder; Moore; and David Friedman, *The Misunderstood Miracle: Industrial Development and Political Change in Japan* (Ithaca: Cornell University Press, 1988).

[10]For English-language debate on this poll and its interpretations, see Aoki Shigeru, "Debunking the 90%-Middle-Class Myth," *Japan Echo* 6 (2) (1979): 29–33;

Taira Koji, "The Middle Class in Japan and the United States," *Japan Echo* 6 (2) (1979): 18–28; and Murakami Yasusuke, "The Age of New Middle Mass Politics: The Case of Japan," *Journal of Japanese Studies* 8 (1) (1982): 29–72.

[11]For example, Tominaga Kenichi, ed., *Nihon no kaiso kozo* (Tokyo: University of Tokyo Press, 1979).

[12]Although I talk here rather generally about a "New Middle Class" ideology, in fact public commentary on class and mass has shifted much in the course of the Showa period. In just the postwar period, it has moved through at least three broad stages. In the two decades of recovery and catch-up, 1945–1965, much of the debate focused on the significance and character of an emerging "mass society" *(taishu shakai)* and "mass culture" *(taishu bunka),* borrowing from American and European controversies of the time. The mid-1960s introduced a new rubric for public commentary—"mainstream consciousness" *(churyu ishiki)* or "the mass mainstream of 100 million people" *(ichiokunin sochuryu)*. It was this which prompted the boasts of a "90 percent middle class" society. By the end of Showa, in the 1980s, this class-mass discourse had taken another turn, toward what some have called a "consumer culture" debate. A uniform middle class with standard needs, many claim, has given way to a "diversified middle class" with multiple preferences. The advertising executive Fujioka Wakao, for example, uses the term *micromasses* in his *Sayonara taishu* (Tokyo: PHP Institute, 1984). The Hakuhodo Institute of Life and Living, prefers "fragmented groups" or *bunshu* in its *"Bunshu" no tanjo* (Tokyo: Nihon keizai shimbun, 1985). Thus, from *taishu* to *bunshu,* debate about a "New Middle Class" has been a shifting rather than a fixed ideological field during the postwar decades.

[13]Robert J. Smith, Jr., and Ella Lury Wiswell, *The Women of Suye Mura* (Chicago: University of Chicago Press, 1982); Ezra Vogel, *Japan's New Middle Class* (Berkeley: University of California Press, 1971); and David Plath *The After Hours: Modern Japan and the Search for Enjoyment* (Berkeley: University of California Press, 1964).

[14]William W. Kelly, "Rethinking Rural Festivals in Contemporary Japan," *Japan Foundation Newsletter* 15 (2) (1987): 12–15, and "Japanese No-Noh: The Crosstalk of Public Culture in a Rural Festivity," *Public Culture* 2 (2) (Spring 1990): 65–81.

[15]For an instructive example, see Susan Carol Rogers, "Good to Think: The 'Peasant' in Contemporary France," *Anthropological Quarterly* 60 (2) (1987): 56–63.

[16]William W. Kelly, "Rationalization and Nostalgia: Cultural Dynamics of New Middle Class Japan," *American Ethnologist* 13 (4) (1986): 603–18.

[17]For example, Theodore C. Bestor, "Tradition and Japanese Social Organization: Institutional Development in a Tokyo Neighborhood," *Ethnology* 24 (1985): 121–35; Jennifer Ellen Robertson, "The Making of Kodaira; Being an Ethnography of a Japanese City's Progress," Ph.D. dissertation, Department of Anthropology, Cornell University, 1985; and Sugiura Noriyuki, "The Urbanization of Nostalgia: The Changing Nature of Nostalgic Landscape in Postwar Japan," unpublished paper presented at the Association of American Geographers Annual Meetings (Portland, Oreg., 1987).

[18]Sugiura.

The Japanese conception of collective time is very distinctive. It is not historical; it does not look on the passing of events and of epochs as the unfolding of some plan or of forces leading in some specific direction. Rather, it is essentially mythic: the myth of the origins as constituted in the early period serves as the basic paradigm—even if nobody believes the myth now.

This conception is very closely related to the continuous formulation of the Japanese collective identity as a divine nation—Shinkoku—a nation under the protection of the deities. This conception was couched in terms of sacred particularity. It never had the connotation, as in monotheistic religions, of a chosen people called upon to perform a transcendental and universalistic mission. (This conception of sacred particularity usually held its own even when confronted with universalistic ideologies—whether Buddhist or Confucian, or in more recent times, liberal, constitutional, progressive, or Marxist—all of which called for a redefinition of the symbols of collective identity in universal or universalistic directions. Except for small groups of intellectuals, such redefinition never struck roots in the Japanese collective consciousness.)

In many paradoxical ways this conception is the mirror image of the American one in which collective consciousness and identity are seen as the almost timeless realization of a utopian vision.

Shmuel N. Eisenstadt
Professor, Committee on Social Thought
University of Chicago

My-Car-isma: Motorizing the Showa Self

David W. Plath

The Japanese media christened 1966 Year One of the My-Car era, when the number of automobiles surpassed 10 million. The automobile has transformed Japanese culture in ways having as much to do with self-expression as transportation. Despite a dependence on foreign oil and monumental traffic jams, the Japanese celebrate the car as a family unifier and as a metaphor for individualism in a corporate society.

When Allied troops invaded Normandy in June of 1944, their landing sites were code-named for places familiar back home: Omaha Beach, for example. When plans were drawn later that year for an invasion of Japan's main islands, the beaches were coded for something else familiar—American automobiles.[1]

Japan surrendered before the invasion could be mounted. Allied Occupation forces went ashore peaceably in September 1945, carrying orders to liberate the Japanese people from their military rulers and teach them the road to freedom via democratization. Already two decades earlier, however, by the beginning of the Showa period, American and European motorcars had established their own beachhead in Japan and were offering a road to liberation via auto mobility.

Cars were costly and roads were poor until the late 1950s. But in the second half of Showa, *motarizeshon* came to rival democratization as a force reshaping the environment, popular consciousness, and the textures of everyday life. At the beginning of Showa, the body of the Taisho emperor was transported to the Tama Mausoleum in

---

David Plath is Professor of Anthropology and Asian Studies at the University of Illinois in Urbana-Champaign.

an ornate, lacquered palanquin of ancient design. Motor hearses were already in use in Japan's cities by that time, but the nation's leaders were in a traditionalizing mood. Sixty-three years later, at the beginning of the Heisei era, the body of the Showa emperor rode to Tama in an unadorned black motor hearse manufactured by Nissan, a company whose name is an acronym for "made in Japan." By the end of the Showa period, car culture was taken for granted as part of Japanese core culture.

The world admires Japan's bullet trains and urban mass transit systems. They certainly are convenient—though often crowded—*if* you want to travel where and when they operate. Large numbers of Japanese would rather travel at *mai pesu* (my pace). Since the mid-1970s they have been logging more passenger miles per year by road than by rail, and most of those miles have been traveled in private automobiles.

The world also admires Japan's rigorous policing of weapons and narcotics. The addictive appeals of automobile use and possession, however, have been difficult to control. For every two thousand persons in Japan at the beginning of Showa, there was one motor vehicle (of any type); by the end of the era, the figure was one vehicle per person, or one automobile for every two persons. In the 1970s social critics came up with a new name for the car: *hashiru kyoki*, "the runaway weapon."[2]

Japan's mass media reckon the year 1966 to have been *maika gannen*, the first year of the My-Car era. That year the number of automobiles went past the 10 million mark (as it had in the United States in 1920). And the price of a new economy car dropped to where it was equivalent to the average annual per capita income.[3]

Gannen, or "base year," is the first in a new emperor's reign, when the calendar count is started over. In media whimsy the Showa throne was usurped in 1966 by the king of the road. (In Aldous Huxley's *Brave New World* the calendar is calibrated "in the year of our Ford.")

The word *maika* functions grammatically in Japanese as a unit noun. It would have to be back-translated into ordinary English phrasing as "own car" or "personal automobile" since one can refer in Japanese to his, her, your, or even my, *maika*. A whole lexicon of *mai* words was created in the years of rapid economic growth after 1955. Some other examples are *maikara* (my + color = television set), *maikura* (my + cooler = room air conditioner), and *maikon* (*kon* being short for *konpyuta,* my computer).[4]

These *mai* words suggest the individuating potential of owner-user mass technology, of machines that empower the mundane self to expand into new domains of action and imagination. By their linguistic form the *mai* words imply that this self-machine linkage is so novel it cannot be adequately communicated by conventional Japanese terms for personhood. In contrast to the persona of traditional Japanese morality, embedded in human relations, the *mai*-self has an English-seeming separateness and yet is bonded to a machine. The hardware individualism of *mai*-tech implies an alternative notion of personhood that crosscuts the web of Confucian interpersonalism, much as does, from another direction, the hard individualism of civil rights.

All around the twentieth-century world the automobile as a self-propelling entity has become a master metaphor for personal freedom within an industrial order. "The automobile put Everyman in the driver's seat and let him choose his destination," writes Phil Patton in *Open Road*, "and the social and moral implications of that system were revolutionary."[5] Received ideologies, established systems of status and prestige, all have had to come to terms with this new engine of individual empowerment.

By 1920 the American ethos of individual liberty, fed by cheap oil from Texas and Oklahoma and by ever-cheaper supplies of model-T Fords, had become hopelessly auto centric. *Motorization* and *auto mobility* became buzzwords for America's mass-production answer to the problem of sluggish social mobility and the threat of class warfare. A 1924 advertisement for Chevrolet put it this way:

> The once poor laborer and mechanic now drives to the building operation or construction job in his own car. He is now a capitalist—the owner of a taxable asset. . . . How can Bolshevism flourish in a motorized country?[6]

In the view of automobile historians such as James Flink, the United States overspent recklessly on car culture in the 1920s, and as a result the Great Depression was more severe than it need have been.[7] But by that time the dream of Everyman-in-the-driver's-seat had captivated the rest of the world. Other industrial nations encouraged the production of their own "people's car"—the famed

Volkswagen of Nazi Germany, the less well-known *kokuminsha* of Japan—as evidence that their economic systems, too, could deliver a measure of my-car-isma to the masses.

Might Japan have become motorized by the early years of Showa? Such was the view, or at least the hope, of a man who in 1922 produced the earliest field report, in any language, on Japanese car culture. William Irvine was sent by the U.S. Department of Commerce to evaluate Japan's potential as an automotive market.[8] The economic boom of World War I had given rise in Japan to a new middle class, which was evolving a suburban life-style built around electrical appliances and indoor plumbing and other consumer hardware. Irvine believed that this new class was ready to buy automobiles—if certain barriers could be removed. His phrasing echoes in the free-market rhetoric of American industry sixty years later.

Tariffs were one barrier. As part of its campaign to reduce its persisting deficit in international trade, Japan laid heavy import duties on already assembled automobiles. Knocked-down vehicles incurred a much smaller duty. So Ford and Chevrolet in the 1920s built assembly plants in Japan—technicians being sent from Detroit to train and supervise the Japanese workers—and the two U.S. makers dominated the market until Nissan and Toyota began mass production a decade later.

Irvine was more concerned, though, about what today's rhetoric refers to as nontariff barriers. Police regulations, by his American yardstick, were too severe. Drivers and vehicles both were subjected to excessively rigorous testing. And there were peculiar requirements such as a set of mudguards, available only in Japan, that had to be hung over the wheels before one could legally drive in the rain.

Another barrier was conceptual. Irvine called it "the chauffeur evil": the assumption that the automobile is so complicated a machine it must be operated by a specialist. He urged car dealers in Japan to propagate enthusiastically the Detroit gospel of the owner-driver.

The barrier of barriers, however, was the road system. Few rural roads were motorable and most city side streets were so narrow that two vehicles could not pass. Modern motor roads were under construction between Tokyo and Yokohama, and between Osaka and Kobe—a few executives already were commuting between those cities by car—and Irvine hoped that these projects would inspire larger ones.

Boulevards were being widened and paved for mass transit by the end of the Meiji period, but until early Showa the narrow side streets and lanes gave rickshaws a time-and-cost advantage for short-distance travel. One hundred thousand rickshaws were still in use in 1930, the year that automobiles first began to outnumber them. A national highway improvement program was launched in 1919, and short stretches of model roadway were in use by early Showa. But an American who rode rear-seat on a motorcycle from Tokyo to Osaka in the late 1920s reported that the 300-mile journey covered only one short strip of paving, outside of Tokyo, and a few miles of graveled surface, south of Kyoto.[9]

Documentary writers in the United States during the Great Depression bragged of having driven thousands of miles around the nation in order to meet the real American people. Their contemporaries in Japan, students of folklore and popular culture, boasted instead of having personally traversed the length of the archipelago, from Hokkaido to Kyushu, on foot.

In the retrospect of a half century the early Showa leaders drove Japan into the automobile age with one foot on the accelerator and the other on the brake pedal. They fostered a domestic auto industry, and by 1940 its output had reached 50,000 units per year. On the other hand they channeled revenues that might have been used for highway construction into military adventuring instead. A 1935 government survey found only 20 percent of the national and prefectural roads suitable for motor traffic. The criterion was not whether they had been surfaced but whether they were at least 3.7 meters wide. A Tokyo motorist writing a year later griped that he was unable to obtain a reliable civilian road map for any area of the country.[10]

By the beginning of World War II, though, the automobile had become well established in Japanese popular consciousness. A driver's license was not yet essential equipment for ordinary daily living nor a necessary badge of personal maturity. But the *takushii* (taxi) and the *haiya* (hire, i.e. limousine) were familiar everyday-use objects. And the affordable personal car had moved over the horizon from fantasy into possibility.

People knew what cars are good for and had acquired a vocabulary to use in talking about them. Much of the vocabulary came from American, and sometimes British, English. It included words for types of vehicles, such as *torakku* (truck) and *basu* (bus); words for vehicle parts, such as *bureki* (brake) and *taiya* (tire) and *kurakuson* (Klaxon; "horn" in present-day U.S. idiom); and operating commands such as *sutato* (Start!) and *sutoppu* (Stop!) and *orai-orai* (All right! All right!—i.e., it's safe to continue backing up).

Whether people who had grown up in the Showa years thought of these as foreign words is arguable. When the state prohibited the uttering of "enemy words" in the wartime passion of the 1940s, and replaced them with bureaucratically devised, tongue-twisting "pure Japanese" terms, people had difficulty making the switch. Imperial Army veterans have told me of being beaten by their sergeants for lapsing into linguistic disloyalty. By the time of World War II, cars had become almost culturally "ours."

Before the war Japanese studied the United States example of motorization from a distance, through print media, newsreels, and especially Hollywood movies. After 1945 they were subjected to a free home demonstration of it, one that continued for a decade through the Occupation period and the Korean War. The Allied forces brought in hundreds of staff cars, thousands of trucks and jeeps. The image of the GIs in their versatile jeeps driving everywhere—on and off the roads—and obviously enjoying it—is burned into the memory of every Japanese I have ever talked to about those early postwar years.[11]

Resident American civilians were just as auto dependent, and families could be observed taking weekend trips and going for *sande doraibu* (Sunday drives). During the Korean War, freshly commissioned in the U.S. Naval Reserve, I was assigned as a deck officer on an amphibious ship. I had to revise my vision of warfare as heroic combat when I watched supplies being loaded for our first voyage across the Pacific. Our cargo holds were filled with personal automobiles consigned to U.S. officers and their families living in Japan. Used jeeps and civilian cars were a major source of supply for Japanese buyers until the early 1950s, when domestic output of automobiles climbed beyond prewar levels.

The decade of the 1950s saw the arrival of the *pepa doraiba* (paper driver) who had obtained a license even though he had not yet been able to buy a car. For the majority of people, more important than the availability of automobiles was the affordability of motorbikes, motor scooters, and three-wheeled light trucks. These were the training wheels that first inducted vast numbers of Japanese into the habits of everyday driving and the liberating pleasures of travel at *mai pesu.*

National and local governments poured revenues into motor-road construction with an enthusiasm like that of their United States counterparts. Another decade would pass before a full infrastructure was in place everywhere, with paved roads, parking lots, superhighways, scenic routes, and strip cities of roadside businesses. But during the 1950s owner driving became experience-near. By the time of the 1964 Tokyo Olympics Japanese mental inscapes had been motorized and people were ready, even eager, for the bulldozers to rearrange the outer landscapes across the countryside.

Japan continues to tax the automobile as a luxury: current rates are twice those in Europe and four times that in the United States. But by the latter half of Showa the car had become, to ordinary citizens, a necessity: as essential to civilized living as having telephones, television, or flush toilets. Of all industrial nations, postwar Japan has had the lowest rate of increase in population but the highest rate of increase in cars.

As *maika* rolled into arena after arena of Showa society, it triggered a remapping of not just transportation routes but also the lines of human sociability. The promise of a freewheeling self had to be brought to terms with Japan's heritage of ethical and aesthetic "assumptions about the conduct of life."[12] And the premise of hardware individualism—equal opportunity of access to limited roads—had to be reconciled with affluent Japan's great poverty of space, on the roads or off.

As in other motorized countries the family became a team of social-space raiders with home as their launchpad. Ever since early Taisho the new-middle-class house has featured a Western parlor in addition to the traditional Japanese parlor, which has tatami floors and a tokonoma. The Western parlor is carpeted and contains upholstered furniture (plus a stereo system these days: evidence of involvement in the cosmopolitan world of Western music).

These days the house also offers a private room to the family car. If other space must be sacrificed, the veranda or part of the garden or the Japanese parlor may be eliminated but not the Western parlor.

The family car is a Western parlor on wheels. Its interior is kept as meticulously clean as that of its fixed-base counterpart. Both are decorated according to family taste, with the same kitsch dolls and antimacassars. A New Year's ornament of oranges and green branches, traditionally put on display in the tokonoma, may also be draped across the hood of the car. And some families remove their street shoes before ascending into the car, as into the house. When parked, the family car can be used as an emergency private room, as in the 1983 film *Family Game*, where the husband and wife, having momentous matters to discuss, lock themselves in the car so that the children can't overhear.

A line that was popular early in the My-Car era described the ideal bridegroom as one who comes "with house, with car, and without Granny." By late Showa the idea was less and less humorous. With housing space continuing to shrink and the number of widowed grandmothers continuing to expand, many Japanese in the Heisei period will confront the dilemmas of Confucian filial piety in their motorized mode. Families may be forced to choose between offering a private room to Grandma or excluding her in favor of the Grand Car.

Today as in the past, the Buddhist altar inside the house, holding memorial tablets to deceased members of the family, emblemizes the line of succession that binds together the living and the dead. But the automobile has become the chapel of togetherness for the living, who reaffirm their unity in periodic Sunday drives.

On weekdays all members of the family may be in the same room at the same time only episodically. In an earlier day when commensal eating was more frequent and meals were taken in the Japanese parlor, Alpha Male sat at the head of the table, facing the others. His back was to the tokonoma or the Buddhist altar, which framed and made visible his authority over them. In new houses, however, any collective meals are as likely to be eaten while family members sit on chairs in the modernized kitchen, the domain of Alpha Female. The room is monitored from the corner by the authoritative eye of the television set, its remote-control device in the hands of the children. The room cooler on the wall is set for the comfort of the grandparents. The head of the house no longer commands a fixed seat of visible authority.[13]

The family car puts him in the driver's seat. Others may use it during the week, especially Mama on her errands. But on weekends

Dad will rebaptize it to remove the smut of practicality and prepare it for a sabbath of reunion. For a period of hours on Sunday it will encapsulate the family, protecting them against the public corruptions of traffic as two-meter-high concrete-block walls shield the house from the gaze of passersby. They will dine together at a roadside *fuamiri resutoran* (family restaurant). Blurred on weekdays while members are pursuing their purposes separately, family power structure is made visible in Sunday communions of auto mobility.

The metaphor of the car as family unifier, driving its members together at a moment of rupture, appears in a memorable scene from the 1987 Itami Juzo film *The Funeral*. Grandfather has just died. His daughter and son-in-law must hurry to the hospital to arrange for his funeral. We see them speeding in their car, two little sons safely asleep in the rear seat. Mama, copiloting from the front, offers Dad a sandwich and helps him navigate the cosmic gloom of a cloudburst that blots from view everything except the roadway a few meters ahead.

The car in Itami's film binds a family together so it can drive against the darkness of death. In recent television dramas the car may instead serve to transport the family into death. So-called family suicide occurs in actual life about as frequently as does *hara-kiri*. But suicide, as Ruth Benedict commented years ago, is Japan's most-favored "flagrant case" for projecting an ethical dilemma.[14] Until the My-Car era the usual technique for depicting the self-destruction of a modern family was for it to turn on the gas inside the house. The new method of choice, in media visualizing, is for everybody to assemble in the family car, run a hose to the exhaust pipe, and die from the poisonous wastes of modernization.

An automobile may divide as well as unite, symbolically. Is *maika* "mine" or "ours"? This is the dilemma of the owner-driver portrayed in *Hashiru Kazoku* (Runaway Family), Kuroi Senji's 1971 fugue-like novella about a family that ends up on the road to nowhere.[15]

Proud of his new car, the head of the house refuses to contaminate it by driving it to work; he preserves it for private travel. Driving it brings out his real self, a self that must be suppressed while performing the pedestrian duties of his job. Tonight his wife and children are in the car with him, as are his aged parents, whom he is taking home from their Sunday visit. But what if the family were not with him? . . .

He imagines a drive with that seductive young woman from the office.

His wife is disturbed by his reckless speed, as if—she muses to herself—he were on a journey of escape rather than delivery. His mother thinks he is acting like a child with a new toy, but she is pleased that he did not send her and Grandfather home by train. All she wants out of life anymore is to live where her son lives, and he comes alive in this car. She doesn't really care where it is going, or how fast.

Normally the trip takes about thirty-five minutes. Tonight they have been on the road for two hours but have not yet arrived. The car speeds on. Its driver no longer knows where he is, and yet he does not feel lost. Driving has become pure activity.

Following classical precedent, the tensions become reconciled in an æsthetic self-centering: self fuses with implement. To call it a zen of driving would be to overmystify the pathways to liberation found in Japan's heritage of arts and martial arts as well as in sedentary meditation. One strives to go beyond technical skill to that plane of expertness where one can act from pure motives unsoiled by moral obligation or calculated intent. Like a traditional calligrapher composing his text by "following the brush" as "it" writes, the driver follows his car, merged into its ongoingness.

For every Japanese who composes his or her life in the time-honored manner by following a soft brush across paper, there are, I suspect, a thousand others trying to compose their autobiographies instead using hard rubber on concrete, following their cars along the narrow roads to the interior.

I should modify that statement to say that the others would do life writing with their *maika* if only the roads were not so crowded, if blank stretches of paving were as easy to find as blank sheets of paper. By the end of the Showa era Japan had so many vehicles that if all of them had lined up bumper-to-bumper, the great motorcade would have been longer by one-fifth than all the highways in the country. If every family went for a drive on the same Sunday, they would all end up on the road to gridlock. Motorization no longer is, as in early Showa, a problem of the economics of supply or the ergonomics of design: cars are easy to own and easy to operate. The problem is the ecology of operation: cars may be user friendly, but roads are not. Having learned to drive at *mai pesu* in the 1950s,

Japanese subsequently have had to learn where and when *not* to drive, or else to go along with the pace of traffic.

To become streetwise in a My-Car era means to master complicated configurations of time-and-space niches in the road network, and to know how to diagnose traffic paralysis. In a case brought to the Supreme Court of Japan in 1975, one issue was whether the police had acted lawfully when they halted a political demonstration because it was disrupting the flow of traffic. In deciding in favor of the police, the court applied a kind of reasonable-person test. Any ordinary citizen, said the court, is capable of judging whether traffic is moving at its normal pace.[16]

Acquiring Geertzian "local knowledge" of road culture involves one in extensive information gathering and social networking. One has to learn the alternative routes around points of congestion, needs to know which byways and alleys are wide enough to accommodate the size of the vehicle one is driving, and not least, needs a network of acquaintances who have parking spaces that one can borrow while in their neighborhoods on errands. When people were asked, in a 1986 survey, what information they wanted so that they could better plan their weekend trips to the seacoast, they responded by calling first for better weather reports and second for better traffic reports.[17]

Special measures have had to be taken to preserve the endangered species known as the pedestrian, the semiotic Other needed to define the motorized Self. In the United States two out of ten traffic casualties are persons who were outside the vehicle; in Japan, as in Europe the number is five out of ten. In the 1960s guardrails and overbridges were put up to protect the ambulatory along busy roadways and intersections. In the 1970s Sundays became *no ka de* (No Car Day) on numerous center-city streets, euphemistically decreed to be "pedestrian paradises." The runaway weapon was banned from them, temporarily, as the Shogunate banned guns—permanently—from entering its capital in Edo. And by the 1980s a campaign urging the citizenry to *Disukaba Japan* (Discover Japan) urged them to leave their cars at home and rediscover their feet. One of the campaign's slogans was *Aruku, miru, kiku,* "Walk, look, and ask."

The automobile has been one of the great totems of the twentieth century: an object good to think about as well as consume. But by the last years of Showa its flavors were bittersweet. The commercial and technical success of *Nihonsha,* the Japanese Car, on the world scene was a source of justifiable pride and sweet revenge at home. Once subjected to invasion by American and European automobiles, Japan was colonizing all continents and humbling the Detroit *daimyo*. *Nihonsha* had taken up and would complete the crusade begun by the model-T Ford: to liberate humanity from bunions. When Japanese automakers opened assembly plants in the United States and Western Europe, their executives diplomatically warned the television audience at home that "cars don't carry passports." But media anchors asserted on their own authority that foreign workers are simply incapable of producing a machine of *Nihonsha* quality.

Success overseas, however, only distracted attention from the domestic difficulties. Auto addiction had left the nation helplessly dependent on foreign oil. And the *maika* union of Self with machine was becoming a marriage of inconvenience, a partnership one cannot live without but finds more and more bothersome to put up with.

When unemployed coal miners in Fukuoka were told in 1984 to sell their cars or lose their welfare payments, some chose to live with their cars. When university students were asked what they would do during the Golden Week holidays of early May, they said they would get together with friends. "And then, if we feel like it, we'll drive around in our cars. . . . We just can't imagine a life without them."[18]

Others, however, were already imagining a Japan without automobiles, or with a new version of *maika* that would no longer be confined to cramped roadways. In the early decades of Showa there had been a popular legend about the First Car in Japan, a machine so dangerous that it had to be locked away.[19] But by the last years of the period the automobile had become low-tech, uncharismatic, offering little nourishment for fantasy in its normal models. A 1970s cartoon serial by Nagai Go centered on Mazinger Z, a humanoid robot that can be driven or flown into battle using carlike controls. And in the early 1980s Japan's runaway best-selling new toy was the combination robot *(gattai robotto)*, later marketed with great success in the United States as the Transformer. This is a miniature device whose parts can be manipulated until the assemblage takes on the form of either an automobile—or an automaton.[20]

Technovisionaries are sketching scenarios for the Information Society, the new moral order that will routinize the charisma of the automatons. Computer games on the *fuamikon* (family computer) already are able to keep the children occupied. A Filial Piety Robot (yet to be perfected) will take over the nettlesome chores of feeding and diapering Grandfather. This will make it possible for Dad as well as Mom to stay home all day at their electronic workstations, discharging their adult duty to produce and consume electronic data.

Maika will be obsolete, since personal travel will no longer be necessary either for work or for play. In the breathy forecasts of Ito Toshiharu,

> Human society will eventually be transformed into a single integrated media space. . . . With the help of advanced media our bodies will spread out into networks spanning the entire earth. . . . interactive television and satellite communications will allow us to travel anywhere in the world without taking a single step. Robots will travel in our stead, transmitting data moment by moment via communications satellite. . . . Scenes of distant lands will unfold before us on our video screen, just as the outside world appears through the windshield of a car.[21]

Software individualism, it seems, will be the moral challenge of the Heisei era, and information flow rather than traffic flow the totemic circulation that will demonstrate the robustness of the social system.

The scenario also is being retrojected into history. Tokugawa Japan is said to have been the world's first information society already 300 years ago, well before the Industrial Revolution in the West. Foreign examples and imported technology were not involved as they were in the automobile age. (Motorization's legendary First Car arrived in Japan in 1900 as a gift to the crown prince from Japanese who had emigrated to the United States.) Tokugawa Japan had automatons in the form of spring-powered dolls that could carry objects: the first robots. And its system of social control consisted of a network of castle towns linked by roads along which dispatch runners sustained a high rate—by world standards up until that time—of information flow.

By the time the Showa emperor went for his last ride in a motor vehicle, some Japanese seemed ready to send the king of the road along with him.

ACKNOWLEDGMENTS

Many people helped me find materials on car culture in Japan and alerted me to patterns in those materials. My chief consultants have been Professor Okuno Takuji and Mr. Yoshida Masanori. Professor Okuno shared his collection of materials on the culture of technology in modern Japan and struggled to correct my outsider's misperception of the subject. Mr. Yoshida, my research assistant for the 1988–1989 academic year, is a superlative library sleuth who also, drawing on his personal experience, helped me sense what it is like to grow up in *maika* Japan.

A number of persons sent articles, books, newspaper clippings, and videotapes I would otherwise not have known about. I particularly thank Ms. Kusumoto Wakako and Professors Jeff Hanes, Robert J. Smith, Takada Masatoshi, Joseph Tobin, Ronald Toby, and Paul Zito.

The Research Board, University of Illinois at Urbana-Champaign, provided money for hiring assistants for this project.

I presented versions of this report to several audiences; their questions and comments helped me hone the argument. The occasions were: the Regional Seminar on Japan, University of California at Berkeley, May 1988; the session on "domestic material culture of contemporary Japan" at the annual meetings of the American Anthropological Association in November 1988; a public lecture at Konan University, Kobe, in June 1989; the Northern Thailand Seminar at Chiang Mai in July 1989; and the Japan-America Society of Honolulu in August 1989.

ENDNOTES

[1]"Elapsed Time: 100 Years of Motorcars," *TWA Ambassador* (July 1985): 58–59.

[2]Basic sources on the history of car culture in Japan published in Japanese are: Kaneki Shozo, *Gendai kuruma shakai* (Tokyo: Sankei Shimbunsha, 1984); Ozaki Masahisa, *Jidosha Nihonshi* (Tokyo: Jikensha, 1955); and Takada Masatoshi, *Jidosha to ningen no hyaku-nen shi* (Tokyo: Shinchosha, 1987).

Sources published in English focus upon the automobile industry—for example, David Halberstam's *The Reckoning* (New York: William Morrow, 1986)—and only occasionally shed light on Japanese car culture. The most informative items I have found are Takada's summary of his 1987 book, "The Japanese Meet the Automobile," *The Wheel Extended* 17 (3) (1987): 19–25; Yoneyama Toshinao, "The Motorization of Japan," in Umesao Tadao, ed., *Seventy-Seven Keys to the Civilization of Japan* (Osaka: Sogensha, 1985): 257–60; and Marco Ruiz, *The Complete History of the Japanese Car, 1907 to the Present* (New York: Portland House, 1986).

[3]For a historical table of the My-Car era see "Shashiteki seso zukai: motarizeshon imeji mappu," *Jidosha to sono sekai* (183) (1981): 59–62.

[4]For other examples of the *mai* lexicon see Herbert Passin, "My Story," in his *Japanese and The Japanese, Language and Culture Change* (Tokyo: Kinseido, 1980), 24–29.

[5]Phil Patton, *Open Road: A Celebration of the American Highway* (New York: Simon & Schuster, 1986), 60.

[6]The Chevrolet ad is quoted in Patton, 61.

[7]James Flink, "Three Stages of American Automobile Consciousness," *American Quarterly* 24 (4) (October 1972): 451–73; and *The Car Culture* (Cambridge: M.I.T. Press, 1975).

[8]William Irvine, *Japan as an Automotive Market,* Department of Commerce, Special Agent Series No. 217 (Washington: U.S. Government Printing Office, 1922).

[9]Glenn Shaw, *Osaka Sketches* (Tokyo: Hokuseido Press, 1928), 145–49.

[10]Otaguro Motoo, "Jidosha zakki," *Seruban* (February 1936), as reprinted in *Dokyumento Showa sesoshi, senzen-hen,* vol. 1 (Tokyo: Heibonsha, 1975), 236–40.

[11]For a recent instance of memories of meeting the jeep see Tessa Morris-Suzuki, *Showa, An Inside History of Hirohito's Japan* (New York: Schocken Books, 1985), 197.

[12]Ruth Benedict's definition of a culture, given in her book *The Chrysanthemum and the Sword: Patterns of Japanese Culture* (Boston: Houghton Mifflin, 1946), 13.

[13]I am elaborating here on an idea first suggested to me by Professor William Kelly.

[14]Benedict, 167.

[15]Kuroi Senji, "Hashiru kazoku," in his *Kuroi Senji shu* (Tokyo: Kawade Shobo Shinsha, 1972), 159–212.

[16]Lawrence Beer mentions the case on pages 20–21 of his "Japan's Constitutional System and Its Judicial Interpretation," in John O. Haley, ed., *Law and Society in Contemporary Japan: American Perspectives* (Dubuque: Kendall/Hunt Publishing Company, 1988), 7–35.

[17]Sorifu Kohoshitsu, "Umibe niizu," *Yoron Chosa* (July 1986): 2–35.

[18]"Fukuoka Miners," *Japan Times,* 28 August 1984; and "University Students and Driving," *Asahi Evening News,* 30 April 1985.

[19]According to the legend, the First Car came to Japan in May 1900, as a wedding gift for the crown prince, the future Taisho emperor, from loyal Japanese emigrants in California. Since nobody in Japan knew how to operate such a machine, the state railways were ordered to send out their best engine driver. Unfortunately, he backed the car into the palace moat. The horrified grand chamberlain ordered it locked away permanently in an empty stable.

Such a gift was actually sent, and the car was seen for some months sliding around hilly streets outside the palace. What became of it is unknown. What is known now, on the basis of recent research, is that it was not the first car to be landed in Japan. The first verified instance was a Panhard & Levasoir phaeton brought to Japan in 1898 by a commercial agent, who advertised it for sale as "the only car in Japan."

See Osuka Kazumi, "Nihon jidosha shi no shiryo-teki kenkyu #4," *Naka-Nihon Jidosha Daigaku Ronso* 10 (1980): 35–43; and Saito Toshihiko, "Beru o nuida maboroshii dai-ichi-go sha: kuruma machi ni arawareta hi," *Jidosha to sono sekai* (a magazine from Toyota Motors), issue no. 222. I am grateful to Mr. Saito, of the Reference Bureau, Japan Broadcasting Corporation, for sending me copies of his personal file of newspaper reports on the first automobiles in Japan.

[20]The information on robots appears in Frederik L. Schodt, *Inside the Robot Kingdom: Japan, Mechatronics, and the Coming Robotopia* (Tokyo and New York: Kodansha International, 1988), 82–86, 92–98.

[21]Ito Toshiharu, "Media and Metamorphosis," *Japan Echo* 14 (1) (November 1987): 69–72.

The Intellectual Community of the Showa Era

Masakazu Yamazaki

The divided intelligentsia of the early Showa period fell prey to the anti-intellectual rise of militarism; indeed, many intellectuals were swept up in the nationalist fervor. The postwar era saw a brief rise in left-wing populism that replaced right-wing nationalism, but the economic boom effectively ended Marxism on Japanese campuses. What is needed at the close of Showa is a new global vision, interdisciplinary and broad.

I

The Showa era can be said to have begun in 1921, when Crown Prince Hirohito became regent for the bedridden Emperor Taisho, five years prior to the prince's succession to the throne as Emperor Showa. The death in 1922 of the two Meiji giants Aritomo Yamagata and Ogai Mori was symbolic of the endogenous change that Japan's intellectual community was undergoing at that time. Yamagata was a soldier-politician; Mori was a natural scientist and man of letters. The two, each in his own way, were typical of the first-generation leaders of the Meiji era. They had not been born and raised in an established order but were themselves architects of modern Japanese organizations, institutions, and the state itself. They did not absorb alien cultures in translation, but had to translate foreign sources themselves before they could begin to absorb them. First-generation intellectuals of Meiji had their own fields of specialization but had also to develop all-around insight as a foundation for their specialized knowledge.

Masakazu Yamazaki is a playwright and Professor of Theatre Studies in the Department of Aesthetics at Osaka University.

Half a century after the Meiji Restoration of 1868, these first-generation leaders were gradually replaced by a different breed. The new generation were initiated into learning by their first-generation mentors, climbing the institutional ladders erected by their predecessors to become professionals in the specialized disciplines already established in the academic community. The school system, in place for more than thirty years, provided an environment for nurturing the intellectual elite. The educational progression leading from primary, junior high, and senior high school to university, essentially established by the School Ordinance of 1886, remained substantially intact until after the end of the Second World War.

The strong government interest in education during and after Meiji was shared by the people, who had faith in the hierarchical system of education, at whose pinnacle was the imperial university. With modernization perceived as the *sine qua non* for the survival of the nation, there was tacit but unanimous agreement to give priority to the acquisition of new knowledge and technology. There was no opposition between "gown" and "town," as in other modernizing societies; senior high school and college students won the respect of the populace.

These second-generation intellectuals, on the rise since the last years of the Meiji era, encountered a dramatic shift in climate in the early Showa years. This was caused, first and foremost, by their sheer numbers. In 1918, the Ministry of Education promulgated the University Ordinance and the High School Ordinance, embarking on an ambitious program to expand institutions of higher education. In the decade between 1910 and 1920, enrollment at high schools and professional schools expanded from 29,000 to 58,000, and the university student population jumped from 7,000 to 22,000. The next decade, ending in 1930, saw a doubling of the former figure to 110,000 and a tripling of the latter to 69,000.

The numerical change reduced the scarcity value of intellectuals; it gnawed at the self-awareness and self-pride of prospective intellectuals. Demand in intellectual employment showed no substantial growth; second-generation intellectuals had now to learn to live as members of the unemployed. In 1929, Yasujiro Ozu's early box-office success "I Graduated, But . . ." immediately captured the popular fancy and made that movie's title a popular phrase of self-scorn.

Another wave that engulfed these second-generation intellectuals was the rise of mass culture, exemplified in the progress of media technology, radio and movies. The first radio station opened in Atagoyama, Tokyo, with full-scale broadcasting in 1925. It proved so popular that nearly every household had a receiving set by 1930. Beginning in the late 1890s motion picture production made rapid progress; the first talkie, "The Neighbor's Wife and Mine," produced in 1931, was a watershed in the history of popular media.

The print media also changed. Newspapers and magazines became extremely popular; major publishers based in Tokyo and Osaka competed fiercely with the local press. The destruction of the Great Kanto Earthquake of 1923 caused the Tokyo-based papers to lose ground, succumbing to their Osaka-based rivals. The mergers that resulted gave birth to "nationwide papers," such as the *Asahi* and the *Mainichi*. Their circulation jumped from tens and hundreds of thousands to millions. In their content, these newly amalgamated large newspapers obliterated the traditional distinction between papers of good quality and the popular press, eschewing a class orientation by catering to a middlebrow readership.

As for magazines, in 1923 the famous novelist Kikuchi Kan founded the monthly *Bungei-Shunju*. Its relatively short essays and commentaries, edited for readability, were designed for the new middle-intellectual reader. The publication was an instant success; the size and diversity of its readership made it one of the best-known monthlies in Japan, which it still is today. The monthly *King* followed as a more popular version of this same format, as did a number of weekly magazines like the *Asahi Weekly* and the *Sunday Mainichi*.

The most symbolic event in the evolution of the intellectual climate of early Showa was the 1927 genesis of the *Iwanami Bunko* series. These pocket-size paperbacks, modeled on the *Reklame Bibliothek* of Germany, offered a wide range of good literature, from Japanese classics to Kant, Marx, and others in translation. In terms of quality, quantity, and low price, *Iwanami Bunko* paperbacks were designed to open the ivory tower to the common people. The project reflected the *zeitgeist* of enlightened thought prevalent in those days. Earlier, in 1926, Kaizosha Publishing Company marketed its *Collection of Japanese Literature* series at the attractive price of ¥1 per volume. Such cheap editions, enthusiastically received and quickly known as "¥1 books," triggered a rush of competing collections by rival publishing houses, encompassing titles from classical Japanese literature, world literature, and the history of ideas.

These editions sold extremely well. The Kaizosha editions attracted 600,000 subscriptions; the thirty-eight-volume Shinchosha *World Literature* series garnered 580,000 subscriptions. During the five-year period preceding 1929, more than 300 series of ¥1 books were published, contributing to an overall average of well over 10,000 new titles published every year. Indeed, the boom represented a drastic change from the final years of Meiji when a book of serious literature averaged 700 copies, and few titles ever sold more than 1,000 copies.[1] Translation, annotation, and commentary in cheap editions made once-esoteric sources of knowledge and enlightened thought widely accessible to millions of readers across the nation.

II

The Japanese intellectual community from the Meiji through the mid-Taisho years was structured in a dichotomy, between a handful of elite and the great majority. Ironically, the rapid expansion of the intellectual community in the late Taisho years and the progressive blurring of hierarchical distinctions tended to encourage intellectuals to be more aware of their partial status.

The year 1917 disclosed the presence of an anti-establishment "intelligentsia." Borrowed and shortened to *interi* in Japanese, the word proved a felicitous neologism with which the newly rising middle class could identify itself. The intellectual community of early Showa found itself split between research scholars in the academic world and *interi*, chiefly active in the world of journalism. The latter's sense of self-assurance was mixed with hostility toward academics, eloquently stated in the *Iwanami Bunko* manifesto of July 1927:

> Truth longs to be pursued by all people and art yearns to be loved by all people. Art and science were once closeted and jealously guarded in order to perpetuate the ignorance of the masses. It is now the ardent desire of aspiring and progressive people to win back Knowledge and Beauty from the monopoly of the privileged class. The *Iwanami Bunko* is designed to promote the aspirations of progressive people and to seek their support. The project will liberate living and immortal books from the private libraries and studies of the select few, and make them easily accessible to the man on the street . . . .[2]

The drafter of the manifesto, availing himself of the then fashionable vocabulary of socialism, identified the "private libraries and studies of the select few" as the arch-enemies of the masses. Whatever their social status, they were a small coterie who had no need for cheap *Iwanami* paperbacks. The real opposition was between those seeking knowledge through translations, annotations, and commentaries and those providing such guidance from their specific expertise. The irony, of course, is that the writer of the manifesto, while ostensibly taking sides with the intellectually hungry "masses," was on the producing side, working to enlighten the masses. The academics and the *interi* differed not so much in terms of objectively measurable capabilities as in their understanding of what knowledge was and how it should be used.

But the writer of the manifesto was in part correct. A small coterie of elite intellectuals was jealously guarding its "private libraries and studies." The great majority of university and high school professors and teachers, and some renowned writers and artists, wished to conserve the traditions of the first-generation intellectuals of the Meiji era. Their pride and self-assurance rested on their firsthand knowledge of modern Occidental civilization, of classical literature of both the East and the West, which they had mastered the hard way through reading original texts. Generally versatile in one or two foreign languages and in classical Chinese and/or Japanese, many had studied abroad, an exclusive privilege in those days. While university professors would sometimes deign to translate foreign literature for the benefit of the new middle intellectuals, they despised those who had to depend on such secondhand sources of knowledge. The avowed faith of the academic elite was the pursuit of truth; their code of ethics emphasized self-discipline through scientific research. Their life-style was marked by an aloofness from mundane concerns, a complete disinterest in and disdain for contemporary politics.

In this respect, they differed from their mentors, the first-generation intellectual elite of the Meiji period. Surgeon General Ogai Mori, Keio University president Yukichi Fukuzawa, Waseda University president Shigenobu Okuma, and Tokyo College of Arts president Tenshin Okakura had no qualms about involving themselves in political affairs. Writers like Soseki Natsume, Kanzo Uchimura, Sakuzo Yoshino, and other members of the elite used journalism to air their views. While the pioneering giants of the Meiji era had a generalist slant over and beyond their respective fields of specialization, their would-be followers of the Showa era were consciously committed to narrowly defined specialties.

Given such a stance on the part of the academic elite, the obvious strategy for the new rising middle intellectuals was to justify their existence by doing exactly the reverse. As their adversaries professed disinterest in current affairs and faith in eternal and universal truth, the *interi* professed faith in progress and reform. Because they wished to change present realities, they kept themselves informed of the latest trends in general knowledge. As the privileged class sought haven in individual aloofness, the middle intellectuals derived strength from their group affiliation, with their code of ethics dictated by organizational discipline. Staunch supporters of the new information media, they were the most visible defenders of the fashionable vehicles of mass culture—radio broadcasts, movies, photography, art reproduction.

The new middle intellectuals represented a legitimate product of modern industrial society; they supported anything they thought would contribute to industrial development. Viewing modernism as the cultural symbol of industrialization, they sympathized with socialism as the ideal form of industrialization. From either perspective, they were opposed to anything that was antiquarian or outmoded. Their Janus-faced stance reflected their position in the intellectual hierarchy: above them were their arch-enemies, the transcendental few who were detached from the currents of history; below, and far outnumbering them, were the premodern grass roots.

As of 1920, when the educational reform was set in motion, the total working population of Japan of 27,270,000 is said to have been composed of 3,900,000 modern industrial workers, 15,110,000 farmers and fishermen, and 8,950,000 merchants and tradesmen.[3] While the masses had received a primary education in the modern sense, achieving literacy, their occupations were limited. The intellectual motivation of the masses was limited to the orally and manually transmitted craftmanship and technology of the trades; their ethical discipline was dictated by deep-rooted traditional mores and rites. Neither detached individualists nor organized collectivists, they were members of communities of kinfolk, villagers, or tradesmen.

The expansion of industrialization would gradually erode the stratum of the grass roots, some of whom rose from the ranks and became incorporated in the *interi*. The government encouraged this, in addition to the normal sequence from primary to secondary school, it opened an additional path leading to trade or professional training schools. Such institutional incentives contributed to a leveling of intellectual standards and further promotion of industrialization. This gave rise, then, to awareness of a delicate distinction between two strata, *interi* and *semi-interi*. For the more that distinct strata are equalized, the more keen is the awareness of their distinctiveness.

III

This three-tiered stratification of an intellectual hierarchy had more to do with people's modes of awareness than with any tangibly definable terms, as in an economic hierarchy. The middle *interi* included a wide range of people, some close to the grass roots below, others close to the academics above. The legitimacy of the word *interi* made for cohesion and collective awareness. The presence of this ideational frame of reference made a number of otherwise inexplicable social phenomena comprehensible. Take, for instance, the closed structure of the Japanese military, particularly in the Showa years, which reflected strains in the intellectual hierarchy. The military leaders of Meiji were indisputably of the elite; many had studied abroad or cultivated a classical sophistication on their own. Given the dearth of information in general, their level of knowledge and skill in organizational management and technological operation in military matters was as high as that common in any field. In the absence of a sizable class of middle intellectuals, they had no cause to feel inferior.

The younger leadership of the Showa military, in contrast, included those who had risen from the ranks of the grass roots, having been professionally trained in military academies. Compared with the university degrees of their peers, the education of these young military leaders was limited, their qualifications less versatile. Conversely, the authority of the university was allowed to assert itself within the military, with college students eligible for deferment and college graduates for reserve officer status. The intellectual prestige of military officers was sharply reduced, in form as well as in substance. And those eager to achieve success and recognition, whether outside or inside the military, sought involvement and influence in political affairs. Their unspoken sense of resentment against the intelligentsia became palpable, allowing an anti-intellectualist psychology to prevail, particularly in the army.

In the world of literature, the *interi* manifested their sense of self-identity. Modern Japanese writers identified themselves with "pure" or "popular" literature, meticulously distinguishing one from the other. This again reflected the ideas of the middle *interi*; pure literature catered neither to the exoteric tastes of the masses nor to the esoteric fancies of the academics.

The anti-grass-roots nature of pure literature manifested itself in its rejection of entertainment in literature and, more specifically, in its avoidance of all decoration in storytelling. Pure literature in Japan dates back to the last years of Meiji and the rise of naturalism *à la japonaise,* with its central theme consistently sought in the realities of daily life and its mode of expression in the confessions of the writer. The most favored literature for the Showa *interi* was the uniquely Japanese form of *Ich-Roman,* in which the "I," the first-person protagonist, was the obscure man in the street. Agonizing over poverty and discord in the family, afflicted with a nagging self-torture and sense of self-pity, he found solace in meticulously recording the minutiae of daily life. Showing no interest in adventure, crime, or history, he had nothing to do with heroism or tragic passion.

Such a stance, meshed with the anti-elitist position of pure literature, was perhaps a corollary to its avoidance of all philosophical and religious matters. Heroism and tragic passion, products of abstract idealism, were not conceivable in the absence of philosophical interest. The most telling phrase in Japanese literary criticism of the times was "a solid sense of the reality of life." All idealistic abstractions were rejected as so many lies. Abstract concepts, classical quotations, and clever figures of speech were shunned; intellectual dialogue played little part in characterization.

The pure literati were mostly university graduates, but as writers and critics they had a pronounced anti-academic stance. In the last years of Meiji, Soseki Natsume, Shoyo Tsubouchi, Bin Ueda, Kafu Nagai, and other renowned writers readily accepted university appointments. Once these men were gone, the literary and academic worlds were severed, and remained so well into the 1950s. Professors considered studies in modern literature to be unworthy of their attention; literary critics spoke of "classroom esthetics" with disdain.

Imbued with the spirit of enterprise and admiring action, the intelligentsia suffered from insecurity. Most had abandoned their extended families in rural areas to become urbanites; they were nagged by a sense of rootlessness. Disenchanted with traditional modes of action, deprived of reliable social conventions to fall back on, they tried to overcome their anxiety by attuning themselves to whatever happened to be in fashion. Forced to realize that their aspirations for reform were pipe dreams in the face of the inexorable status quo, they had no alternative but to become "impassioned men" in Eric Hoffer's sense. In their eagerness to seek general knowledge as opposed to the narrow specialization of the academics, they often found themselves attracted to ideological doctrinairism. The almost endless political oscillations of the Showa intellectual community, together with the rising confrontations between left and right, may be ascribed largely to this deep-rooted sense of anxiety.

This distressed class of *interi* replaced the Meiji elite. They helped create the new wave of enlightened thought in the highbrow press, typified by the *Iwanami Pocket Library* and by other intellectual magazines. During the early Showa years the panel of contributors to highbrow publications was rapidly reshuffled, making room for the new elite with middle-intellectual dispositions.

For example, in eight years, from its first appearance in 1921, followed by a temporary suspension and resumption of publication in 1929, the prestigious monthly *Shiso* (*Thought*) changed entirely. In its "Inaugural Statement," the magazine said that it would "not curry favor with the crowd but . . . address eternal problems," and that it would "print distinguished articles in the service of Truth, Beauty, and Virtue . . . for the benefit of the general education of the national readership." Eight years later, the "Editor's Postscript" opined that the magazine had been regarded as a "specialized academic journal," irrelevant to the "general intellectual class." The "Republication Statement" promised that the magazine would provide "universal viewpoints and general perspectives as requested by the readers," reserving ample space as well for "commentaries on current affairs" to address "matters of the greatest concern to the modern man." The change in editorial policy was quickly evident in the increased feature-length coverage of current affairs, and in the shift in its panel of regular contributors from Nosei Abe, Horyu Komiya, Jiro Abe, and other contemporaries of Soseki Natsume to Kiyoshi Miki,

Tatsuo Hayashi, Goro Hani, Junzo Karaki, Hideo Kobayashi, and other polemicists typical of the Showa breed.[4] The latter, esteemed as top intellectuals of their day, for all their ideological differences, shared a common distaste for the academic world, rejecting university positions.

The Showa "enlightenment," characterized by its anti-establishment bent, was influenced, in particular, by Marxism. This was understandable, given the widespread poverty in Japan at the time, and the worldwide credibility of Marxism as the one ideology that directly addressed the problem. However, if poverty alone accounted for the intellectual climate of the day, Marxism was not the only solution available. Ample adumbrations of more effective prescriptions were proposed by others, including Korekiyo Takahashi and Tanzan Ishibashi. Their alternatives, however, never captured the attention of the Showa intellectual community.

For Showa intellectuals, Marxism provided psychological leverage. As a system of metaphysics, it offered an all-inclusive sort of general knowledge, ranging from ontology and the philosophy of natural science to the theory of art. Less arcane than other philosophical systems of the day, it was attractive because it prescribed a drastic cure for all problems. To the middle intellectuals, no other theoretical apparatus appeared so effective a weapon in their fight with the unrealistic specialist elite, entrenched in its ivory tower. As a theory of social classes and social movement, Marxism gave a sense of ideological solidarity to urbanites severed from their traditional community affiliations. The *interi* could at least feel absolved of the guilt of cultural rootlessness, and at last be given a positive code of conduct.

Along with the grass roots, the *interi* were also the harbingers of populism in Japan. The early Showa version of Japanese populism generally had a right-wing slant; the hard-core populists, of grass-roots descent with middle-class aspirations, were typified by professional soldiers of rural origins educated in military academies. When they joined hands with civilian intellectuals, excluded from the highbrow press, their ideological orientation reversed that of the enlightenment group. Under circumstances of general poverty, the coalition between the middle intellectuals and the grass roots rose in the name of nationalism, advocating direct rule by the emperor, as demonstrated in the abortive coup of February 26, 1936.

The process of Japan's industrialization, motivated in the first instance by national aspirations to modern statehood on a level equivalent to that of the Western Powers, reflected from the outset two contradictory orientations. One sought universal principles of modernization; the other leaned toward exclusionist nationalism. To the extent that a delicate balance is maintained between the two, such strange bedfellows may work together. More often, however, such a coalition will split, with each running to ideological extremes. In the case of Japan in the early Showa years, the first radicalized itself into Marxism, which in turn stimulated the second to become radicalized into right-wing populism. The ideal system of imperial rule it envisioned had nothing to do with the traditional institution of emperorship in Japan.

Japanese emperors had, for the most part, been similar to English sovereigns, who "reign but do not rule." The nationalists, whether they knew it or not, were trying in effect to transplant the image of the Russian tsar or the German kaiser to Japanese soil. To the great mass of urban dwellers, haunted by a gnawing sense of lost affiliation, the nationalists' advocacy of national identity proved as tempting as the Marxist alternative of class solidarity. The appeal for a revival of the traditional moral order had a ring of simplicity not only to the grass roots but to the college-educated *interi* as well.

Another kind of alliance involved elitist academics and the grass roots. It represented what may be called conservatism of the Eric Hoffer type, in which the elite, sick of the tawdriness and frivolity of the *interi*, went out of their way to identify with the grass roots, seeing them as the last spiritual resort of their idealism. Looking askance at the frenzy of industrialization, they remained cynically detached from the alleged reforms that came in its wake, instituted by both left and right. But the idealized grass roots, bound to disappear sooner or later, meant that this brand of conservatism was promoted by only a small minority of transcendental intellectuals. Kunio Yanagita, a former high-ranking bureaucrat, and founding father of folklore studies in Japan, was typical of this persuasion. He tried all his life to create an idealized image of farmers as the "folk," to establish them as the prototype of the Japanese nation.

In the same vein, the world of literature had Kafu Nagai. Born into the wealthy family of a successful bureaucrat-turned-entrepreneur, Nagai repudiated his father's infatuation with modernization, deliberately took an ex-*geisha* as his wife, and rolled in defiant debauchery in the red-light district. He provided a precedent of respectable escapism for the *interi* when they wearied of the futile ideological battle between the left and the right. In the meantime, critics of the pure-literature tradition, such as Hideo Kobayashi for one, held it as an article of faith that commonsense conventions were closer to the truth than fashionable ideologies, that common people were better judges of the realities of life than academics.

IV

The steady process of industrialization and popularization was thus accompanied by a structural malaise in the intellectual community, which adds another dimension to the more obvious causes of the deplorable disruptions of the Second World War. Of particular relevance is the role of the press, which loudly argued for an unrestrained military, and at times gratuitously goaded the nation to military adventurism. Intensive competition in the fourth estate led highbrow newspapers with limited circulation to be absorbed by burgeoning popular papers. These mass organs catered to the numerically overwhelming coalition of middle-class and grass-roots readership, both susceptible and prone to sensationalism and nationalism. The best way for the press to appeal to its readers' contradictory desires to see the government attacked and patriotism praised was to propagandize in favor of hawkish options in foreign policy. The liberal lineage represented by such distinguished journalists as Nyozekan Hasegawa, Kiyoshi Kiyosawa, and Shigenharu Matsumoto was overshadowed, powerless to stop this nationalism. The belligerent posture of the popular press became more pronounced during the early Showa years, and the outbreak of the Manchurian Incident in 1931 pitted the *Asahi* against its arch-rival *Mainichi* in an unprecedented newsgathering spree. Though motivated by naked commercialism, fueled more by sensationalism than militarism, the frenzied competition of the two leading popular papers undeniably whipped up the war spirit in the nation.

In addition to the influence of the sensational press, the Japanese perception of the United States was also deeply affected by the changed climate in the intellectual community. The United States and its ever-growing presence represented a symbol of modernization to the Japanese, who readily projected their modernization complex on the global power across the Pacific. American influence on Japan manifested itself in movies, jazz, dance, and other forms of popular culture, but also in automobiles and mass-production factories, indicative of the progress of mass society. To the Japanese, the Europeans more than the Americans appeared to provide the models of modernization in philosophy, literature, art, classical music, and even the natural sciences. The American model seemed representative of the sound and fury, the hustle and bustle, of modernization.

The United States provoked antipathy among both conservative academics and the grass roots. Their anti-American sentiments meshed spontaneously with a shared fear of the rapidly growing *interi*. The academics found the ephemeral character of American culture an insult to their belief in eternal truth, a threat to their position of authority in the intellectual community. The grass roots, not riding the waves of modernization, found the U.S. a symbol of a bandwagon behind which they felt themselves struggling in obsolescence.

The *interi*, wishing to ride the waves of modernization and enjoying American ways, did not feel they could openly defend their new-found values without a guilty conscience. In the vanguard of popular modernization, they had an uneasy feeling that the waves of popularization would sooner or later drown them. The three tiers of the Showa intellectual community each had reason to look askance at the *mobo* or "modern boys," and the *moga* or "modern girls," who wasted their time with jazz, dancing, and the movies.

In July 1942, soon after the outbreak of the Pacific War, the monthly *Bungakukai* sponsored a panel discussion, "Overcoming Modernity." The distinguished panel included Professors Keiji Nishitani and Shigetaka Suzuki of Kyoto Imperial University, who represented the academic stratum, writers like Hideo Kobayashi and Fusao Hayashi, and movie critic Hideo Tsumura, who spoke for the *interi*. At this gathering, designed to provide ideological justification for Japan's involvement in the war, the participants agreed that modern Western civilization was biased toward individualism and rationalism, that the Western nations were trying to propagate their values as universal principles, that the Japanese act of war represented a justifiable reaction to such hubris. There was a subtle difference in the way the university professors and the journalist critics addressed the nature of intellectuality. The former dwelled on the evolution of Western thought, defined the modern ages in historical perspective, and tried to identify the dialectical possibility of both denying and overcoming the modern ages so defined. In contrast, the latter cast doubt on the validity of such analysis and interpretation; they tried to reject historical attempts to understand civilization as so many fallacies of the modern mind.

Such fine intellectual divisions, however, did not prevent the participants from unanimously denouncing American culture. The literary critic Katsuichiro Kamei spoke for the *interi* when he attacked the elite for their "specialization" and "scholasticism." While he advocated the general knowledge of the "intellectually whole man," Kamei vilified the popularization of culture. He condemned movies, photography, rapid transit systems, the popular press, and other products of American functionalism.

Finding himself in the unenviable position of having to defend the newfangled art form of motion pictures, which came under general attack, the movie critic Hideo Tsumura went out of his way to denounce the adverse effects of delinquent "Americanism." Movies, he argued, were a mechanical convenience, like electric lamps, radios, and the wireless telegraph; the genre could serve in time as an artistic medium for overcoming the modern age. In his view, it was the American way of life since the 1920s that had contaminated an otherwise promising form of artistic expression. His argument was intended to take possession of the movies away from Hollywood, just as Nazi Germany had done in appropriating radio.

Deeply influenced by modern Western culture, the participating intellectuals were in no position to turn their backs wholly on the entire spectrum of modern civilization, ranging from rationalism to more tangible mechanical conveniences. Of all the salient aspects of modernization, they rejected excessive individualism, which they feared would erode social affiliation. The "rebellion of the masses" would jeopardize the intellectual legitimacy of traditional culture. In arguing this, however, they were not being barbarously and narrow-mindedly fascistic.

A moment's reflection should make it clear that the rise of individualism and mass society has always been contradictory. The self-centered modern individual and the "other-directed" populace, in David Riesman's sense, are fundamentally heterogeneous, their interests overlapping only in their pursuit of material affluence. To attack the two together would have been an exercise in sophisticated logic, making use of an elaborately constructed theoretical apparatus, for which the early Showa intellectuals were unprepared. Shaken emotionally by the avalanche of modernization, they tried to strike down individualism and mass society with a single stroke, finding contemporary American society the best available straw man.

During the years following the end of World War I, the United States had risen to material affluence, physically demonstrating its individualistic self-expansionism. Self-expansion, in physical and material terms, was the easiest way to realize individualism; it had the additional attraction of being open to anyone. In those years the United States offered the best environment for the spirit of individual enterprise, blurring the distinction between the individual and the masses. By condemning the United States as the epitome of rampant individualism and vulgar populism, the early Showa intellectuals found a scapegoat to salve their own guilty consciences, basking in modernization's benefits, remaining silent about its ills.

Such emotional and ideological simplification was the hallmark of the popular press at the start of the war, and presented an irresistible appeal to the popular psyche. The *interi* could identify with the grass roots in their blatant anti-American sentiments, and on this common ground of solidarity they could regain their sense of social affiliation, getting even with the academics for whom they shared a mutual contempt.

V

Viewed in this perspective, the postwar history of the intellectual community in Japan is nearly self-explanatory as a process by which the expanded class of intelligentsia steadily absorbed academics above and the grass roots below. In doing so, the middle stratum helped obliterate its own distinctiveness. In the course of the forty-odd years that have followed the war, the term *interi* has completely disappeared in journalistic as well as in daily parlance.

In 1948, three years after the end of the war, the government reformed the system of higher education. By the time the transition was completed in 1954, the number of universities and enrolled students increased fivefold over the figures at the end of the war, to 227 institutions having an aggregate student enrollment of 490,000. These figures kept rising steadily so that by 1986 there were 465 four-year universities as well as 610 two-year junior colleges and three-year senior professional high schools. These institutions boasted a combined enrollment of 2,330,000, of which 1,880,000 were university students. Thus, in forty years, the number of institutions of higher education jumped by a factor of 10; that of students, by a factor of 20! Translated into the aggregate number of university graduates for the period, the factor would be close to 400!

The once-prestigious status of the old imperial universities was officially denied, but the new universities were unable to rise to the old standards of authority and excellence. The scarcity value of university teachers was substantially depreciated; their once-privileged income level was relatively reduced. The most decisive change, however, was the drastically curtailed power of the university elite as the source of information for setting the course of social affairs.

The immediate postwar years saw the revival of Marxism and the rise of left-wing populism to replace the right-wing nationalism of the prewar years. The "impassioned men" of the *interi* class did not change their disposition with the end of the war. They simply replaced one ideology with another as they came to exercise leadership in the progressive political parties, trade unions, farmers' cooperatives, students' associations, and the press. Postwar left-wing ideology was espoused by the *interi* in coalition with the grass roots. It thus took over the role of a now defunct right-wing populism. Many young wartime militarists went through a conversion, becoming fervent revolutionaries. The thread of anti-American sentiment, held in abeyance for five or so years following the end of the war, was eagerly picked up by left-wing activists. American individualism was branded as the enemy of collective solidarity; popular culture was the sign of capitalist degeneration; American Occupation policies manifested the imperialist oppression of a defeated nation. Ignorant of Stalinist despotism, of the Sino-Soviet confrontation, of the realities of the Spanish Civil War, the Japanese had little ideological immunity to Marxist rhetoric. Marxism, for a time, spread across campuses like wildfire, particularly in fields like history, politics, economics, and philosophy.

It should be noted that Marxism was characterized by its ethical nature, by its emphasis on political practice rather than by its concern with theory and knowledge. To the extent that the motto "Mingle with the masses and learn from the masses" was widely accepted, the authority of the academic elite was bound to be restricted. With the vanguard party and its cadre mandated to interpret the world, the intellectual asset of having read Karl Marx in the original paled in significance when compared with the attributes of more practically experienced activists. The right to interpret Marxist orthodoxy rested with the Cominform; and the domestic mission to spread its message, with the national party leadership. The role of university dons as creators of the *Zeitgeist* was decisively affected; their authority began to be invisibly but inexorably eroded.

Marxism in postwar Japan gradually lost its influence; by around 1955 it virtually ceased to be accepted as the guiding principle of the intellectual community. The cause of its decline was partly internally generated, owing to Sino-Soviet ideological disputes, anti-Stalinist criticism within the Soviet Union, and factional splits in the national revolutionary movement. However, by far the most significant factor in Marxism's steady decline was Japan's economic growth. Accepted in the first place for its purported boldness in confronting and resolving the problems of poverty, the reality of an affluent society led a once-impoverished nation to question the Marxist prescription.

A Marxism now in disgrace, however, did not help the old academic elite to regain its superior status; rather, it accelerated the fall of an already damaged prestige. The source of authoritative information for determining the course of social affairs was now securely in the hands of government economists, engineers, corporate managers, and intellectuals of a different strain. The new breed was not tormented by the inferiority complexes, resentments, and guilty consciences of the old. Having the language skills to read foreign books and newspapers in the original, they had greater opportunities to travel abroad than did university professors. Their pragmatic expertise in business led them to feel no awe for general knowledge or metaphysics; they were not at all intimidated by ivory-tower specialization.

The new intelligentsia enjoyed a solid sense of getting things done; they found the gap between the ideal and the real narrow enough so as not to become "impassioned" in the Hofferian sense. Both the business and the government sectors were expanded and consolidated, complete with lifetime employment systems and seniority wage scales. The intelligentsia's fear of solitude and of rootlessness, living in an urban desert, was effectively mitigated by a sense of job security and corporate affiliation. With the urban population rapidly outstripping the rural, intellectuals had less cause to feel guilty.

Economic growth effectively dealt a fatal blow to the traditional pattern of community life in the country. The dislocated grass roots rushed in great numbers to join the ranks of the urban middle class, shedding whatever vestiges remained of their once-typical mores and ethics. The expanded middle class found itself free of any threat from below; its sense of having lost a distinctive identity was largely relieved by a feeling of security in material matters.

Social realignment was accelerated by the "information revolution" set in motion in midcentury. Television broadcasting, which began in 1953, proved an instant success, catching the popular fancy more rapidly and widely than radio in early Showa. Comprehensive television coverage, ranging from international news to art, contributed to a leveling of the nation's intellectual standards.

Building on its legacy from the prewar years, the film industry came into full bloom, producing such distinguished directors as Akira Kurosawa, Yasujiro Ozu, and Keisuke Kinoshita. This cultural genre, in stark contrast to pure literature, drew support from the nation at large, without regard to intellectual stratification. The cinema was the one art form in relation to which the *interi* did not have to develop emotional complications with other classes. Under no compulsion to limit themselves to the first-person confessions of the I-novel, moviemakers delighted in storytelling, drawing liberally from a rich variety of sources, from epic history to sensational crime. The rich reserve of know-how was transplanted to the new world of television, which produced a whole series of excellent video dramas from the mid-1950s to the mid-1960s.

The print media also found themselves prosperous and growing, both in types of publication and in circulation. A few highbrow general monthlies sold by the hundreds of thousands; new series of pocket books and deluxe collections of literature, philosophy, and the arts were successfully marketed. A single combined volume of Nietzsche's *Birth of Tragedy* and *Thus Spoke Zarathustra* in a *History of Ideas* collection is reputed to have sold 400,000 copies. In the meantime, beginning in the mid-1950s and continuing until today, a new dimension was added, the proliferating subgenres of critical commentary and counsel, covering every sort of private interest and social concern. New pundits and old, genuine and spurious, realized that they could pen and mouth their way to respectable comfort, and could earn, if they tried hard enough, more than professors, with all their academic qualifications, could ever hope to. With a growing number of professors becoming columnists for extra income, the barrier between "the rostrum" and "the press" crumbled, and the image of "the privileged few monopolizing Beauty and Knowledge" disappeared.

The world of literary art, which traditionally was an important forum of self-expression for the *interi*, also changed as both exclusive "pure" literature and the power of literary circles dominated by elder masters declined steadily. Publishers and editors came to have a greater say in literary affairs than ever before, offering a variety of contests and other opportunities for aspiring new writers. In fiction as in drama, ideational themes and supernatural plots, which had little to do with the descriptive realism of I-novels, came to be accepted and appreciated. The subgenre of popular entertainment literature also attained respectability as high-quality detective stories and historical novels began to attract a sizable readership.

Changes created by sprawling urbanization, industrial restructuring, and an aging population combined to usher in "the age of the learning society." Industrial restructuring proved a mixed blessing; while it gave workers additional leisure time, it required them to catch up with an ever-changing technology. Many city dwellers today, comfortably adjusted to urban conditions, having liberated themselves from the nagging sense of rootlessness that plagued their predecessors, are groping toward an individualized way of life. Members of the younger generation, in particular, beginning to establish their identity, are "doing their own thing" in respect to taste, knowledge, and skill; they are little concerned with collective corporate affiliation. Those in the senior age brackets, eager to learn, seek material comfort, mental security, or something to keep them busy in their final years. Since the mid-1970s, this trend has become so pronounced that the government is now involved in extension education, and the private sector is beginning to cash in on this learning boom. In both business organizations and government agencies interest is growing in keeping abreast of the shifting currents of the information age, and general education is sometimes encouraged in on-the-job retraining curricula for the managerial class.

Intellectual currents in Japan today seem to be channeled in two directions, each affecting the rostrum and the press, and posing unsettling problems. One is individualization, or the desire to look over and beyond the facile indoctrination of past middle-class ideology for more advanced and specialized knowledge and sophistication. So-called synthetic monthlies are slipping from the peak of popularity they had twenty years ago, and are being replaced by a large number of highly specialized magazines targeted at narrowly defined groups of readers. Collections in literary art and the history of ideas are no longer in fashion, and books in general are losing in circulation what they are gaining in titles. This trend is in evidence also in other genres of intellectual entertainment. Box-office successes of astronomical proportions are now rare; modest productions, for stage and screen, together with small concerts and exhibits, are doing quite well. Contemporary Japanese are not wholly content with such individualized offerings, and are trying to live down their doctrinairism of the past with some sort of universal perspective. What is needed is a new *Weltanschauung*, something more general and more fundamental than the compartmentalized specialties and technologies that are rapidly outdated by the ongoing process of industrial restructuring and attendant social change.

What is being called for, in short, is an interdisciplinary knowledge, a common perception created by dialogue between advanced specialties, for which Japanese society is not fully prepared. Academic research is getting more compartmentalized, and successful interdisciplinary departments and programs are few and far between. Intellectual salons of the West and their counterparts in Japan in the seventeenth and eighteenth centuries would fit the bill, and their revival might help develop new forums for uninstitutionalized joint research. Only faint random adumbrations are as yet in sight, however.

ENDNOTES

[1]*Iwanami* launched a twelve-volume series, *Philosophical Books,* in the fourth year of Taisho (1915), which attracted only 800 subscriptions.

[2]Advertisement copy for Kaizosha's *Collection of Contemporary Japanese Literature*, published in October 1926, similarly spoke of the new series as being designed to "liberate for the entire people the art of the privileged class." (Quoted by Kazutami Watanabe in his *Hayashi Tatsuo to sono jidai* [Hayashi Tatsuo and His Times], [Tokyo: Iwanami Shoten, 1988]).

[3]After Takahide Nakamura, *Showa keizaishi* (Economic History of Showa), Iwanami Seminar Book No. 17 (Tokyo: Iwanami Shoten, 1986).

[4]After Watanabe, ibid.

High Culture in the Showa Period

J. Thomas Rimer

The dominant foreign model for Japanese aesthetics in the Showa era was European, both avant-garde and traditional. Japanese arts remained strong, but their significance fluctuated greatly as the nation experienced periods of nationalism, war, and defeat. In the current era of economic renewal, the threat to a distinctive Japanese culture is not Western dominance per se but international pop aesthetics and commercialism.

In some ways the Showa period, which began in 1926, may seem an arbitrary moment at which to begin an examination of the development of Japanese ideas, ideals, and institutions. In the realm that might be defined as "high culture," however, the beginning of this period of sixty-odd years does provide a propitious moment. By the beginning of Showa, most if not all of the cultural institutions common to a modern society were in place and prepared to function in terms of a public that had already shown both an enthusiasm and an increasing knowledge concerning the worlds of ideas, arts, and letters. In one sense, the record of accomplishments in high culture during the Showa period serves as a chronicle of how these institutions, and the men and women who used them, came to function together.

I

In 1868, Emperor Meiji opened his nation from its long period of seclusion and instructed the young generation of his country to go

J. Thomas Rimer is Chair of the Department of Hebrew and East Asian Languages and Literatures at the University of Maryland.

forth and learn from the world. The Japanese society he addressed, however, possessed a high level of artistic and scholarly culture, and one that had already come to include a considerable intellectual momentum toward Western learning. Nevertheless, the free play of Japanese intellectual and artistic life was cordoned off by a social structure established during the Tokugawa period (1600–1868) that, because of sharply defined social categories, limited both expectations and artistic techniques in a different fashion for each social group.

By the 1920s, however, through extraordinary efforts in both public and, increasingly, private sectors of society, institutions had been created capable of responding to the interests of a new and far more broadly based public that, because of the new and comparatively democratic educational system that had been created toward the end of the nineteenth century, was to develop wider and more general cultural interests than had ever been possible in the preceding period. In the field of the visual arts, for example, the Tokyo National Museum, first established as early as 1882, was fully reorganized in its present extensive scale in 1928. The Kyoto National Museum was opened in 1897. The government-sponsored contemporary Japanese art exhibitions, usually referred to as *Bunten,* were begun in 1907 and by five or six years later were attracting upward of 160,000 viewers each year.

The best Japanese universities, which were often based on the German model, provided instruction in a variety of intellectual fields at an often surprisingly sophisticated level. In particular, the centrality given the humanities in the German intellectual world during this period continued to provide a powerful influence in the Japanese milieu. Graduates of the best Japanese universities were reading, as a matter of course, Nietzsche, Kant, Hegel, and other of the German philosophical masters. By the 1920s, distinguished young Japanese intellectuals were able to find mentors directly in Europe. Watsuji Tetsuro (1889–1960), for example, whose work *Fudo* (Climate), published in 1935, still stands as a monument in modern Japanese intellectual history, went to Germany to study philosophy. The cultural Marxist Miki Kyoshi (1897–1945), a few years later, repeated the same process. Kuki Shuzo (1888–1941), one of the great modern writers on Japanese aesthetics, studied with Rickert and

Heidegger in Germany and, while in France, shared a youthful friendship with Jean-Paul Sartre.

Nor were these intellectual encounters restricted to a small group of elite specialists. Through the efforts of such shrewd publishers as Iwanami Shigeo (1881–1946), good translations of Western philosophy and literature were made widely available at reasonable prices, and they sold well. A hunger for contemporary European thought assured the rapid availability of such works in Japanese versions, which often saw print in Tokyo even before they were translated into English. National newspapers, notably the *Asahi,* disseminated popular articles on such material, often commissioned from leading Japanese intellectuals, novelists, and social critics. Such commentaries quickly became a common feature of the urban intellectual landscape. Even the Tokyo earthquake of 1923, as devastating in its way to the capital as were to be the firebombings of 1945, had a certain positive effect on the internationalization of the city. Many old sections of the city were destroyed, allowing for the construction by the beginning of Showa of new and up-to-date cultural facilities, among them the Tsukiji Little Theatre, where the newest stage and lighting equipment allowed for the rapid development of modern and avant-garde stage productions.

From that time on, there developed in the Showa period a curve of deepening interest in the development of the sort of Japanese high culture that was to be, at least to some extent, created in consonance with the ideals of contemporary Europe. Such a development is not surprising. In the areas of high culture, Japan, like France, has always been at her best when at her most cosmopolitan. In a sense, the war period, those years from the late 1930s through the American Occupation in the late 1940s, the decade that, spiritually as well as in every other way, was to break the Showa period in two, subdued the steady growth of that culture but did not stop it. While it is true that close ties with Europe were to some extent cut off during this time, the momentum already created was such that little permanent damage was done to those connections; indeed, the energies pent up during that decade spilled out in 1946 in a burst of literary and artistic creativity. From the perspective of forty years later, the war seems at most an interruption in the steady development of high culture. The recent ascendancy of commercial popular culture in

Japan has had, in my opinion, a far stronger inhibiting effect on the high culture in that country than the darkness of the war years.

II

Effective mechanisms to create, sustain, and make available an authentic high culture, even when linked to profound convictions on the part of the intelligentsia and a large public of the need for such a culture, cannot in and of themselves guarantee the quality of the results. The history of high culture in modern Japan shows a number of stresses and strains that indicate the difficult, sometimes intractable, challenges that were to be undertaken. These matters are extremely complex; I will try to sketch out three issues that strike me as suggestive of the larger problems involved.

Culture on the European Model

In the first place, as a whole generation or two of creative personalities continued to pay homage to Western, international ideals, there was bound to develop a sense of constraint among those participating. The psychic distance, in both form and ideal, between Western imported ideas and the older traditional ideologies and methodologies was often simply too great to permit the development of the sort of flexible attitudes adequate to undertake all the shifts involved. In fact, this distance helped to create a curious kind of dual track of cultural production. Therefore, for example, avant-garde poets wrote in a sort of free-verse form that opened up remarkably evocative verbal possibilities; yet in the shade of their accomplishments, other writers continued to compose thirty-one-syllable traditional *waka* and seventeen-syllable *haiku* poems. By the first years of this century, young Japanese painters had already absorbed the styles created by impressionist and postimpressionist European painters and were creating their own authentic pictures in consonance with developments in France and elsewhere; yet others had developed a so-called *Nihonga* style of painting that kept stubbornly closer to older Japanese ideals. These two sets of writers and artists tended to work separately, although some so-called Western-style painters and writers occasionally dabbled in these more traditional forms. On the whole, however, in terms of perceived attitudes, the arts and literature created in the Western mode retained pride of place for the

Japanese intelligentsia. There was during much of the Showa period, and to some extent there still is, a double creative track in the high culture of Japan. Thus, rather than a generalized vision of a modern Japanese high culture, the parameters of which would be more or less generally agreed upon, there appear, at least from our Western point of view, to have existed instead a series of overlapping convictions, as well as overlapping audiences, that only in the aggregate can be said to constitute the domain of high culture in Showa Japan. It would appear that artistic forms and techniques may achieve a high state of development within such a loose linkage, but the artistic and intellectual content expressed in those forms, particularly in terms of their social and political implications, was not to be embedded as firmly as it might most usefully have been. Tighter connections were not pursued. High culture did not always bite deep enough into the realities of the society that created it.

The method of absorbing ideas of Western culture revealed certain patterns already deeply engraved in Japanese historical behavior. In previous periods, the models adapted from international culture had largely been Chinese. Borrowing took on roughly the following sequence: the Japanese, often at great personal risk, sometimes on their own, sometimes sponsored by an organization (the Japanese ruling house, or the Buddhist hierarchy), went to China to learn new ideas and techniques. Such persons usually then returned to Japan to serve as privileged and prestigious advocates of a new cultural point of view which they promulgated, one which would slowly be understood, accepted, and assimilated. Sometimes the process was quickly accomplished; sometimes it took many decades. So it was that Buddhist learning and the texts of the sacred Sutras themselves came to Japan, and so it was that T'ang dynasty poetry and Sung dynasty ink painting came to enter the Japanese artistic canon. By such methods of transmission, new cultural possibilities entered Japan at a pace slow enough to stimulate without throwing the indigenous culture off balance.

In the modern period, however, a number of new factors altered the relatively smooth functioning of these methods of transmission. Some of these changes caused severe problems of assimilation. By the time Japanese and European culture came into meaningful proximity at the end of the nineteenth century, the Japanese found themselves face to face not merely, as in the case of China, with another imposing high cultural tradition itself strong and stable, but with a European high culture, that, while confident in the midnineteenth century, would soon give pride of place to a restless avant-garde bent on altering, if not destroying, those traditional European conceptions. The Japanese, in other words, came to learn from the West just at a time when, in some areas at least, their new partners were trying to rid themselves of the very received opinions and traditions that the Japanese, newcomers to the circle, were of necessity still trying to do their best to understand and assimilate.

In some areas, of course, such rapid changes caused, at least in the long view, relatively few problems. A number of outstanding young Japanese novelists and poets, for example, were quick to experiment, and successfully, along the lines laid down by the European writers, artists, and intellectuals they came to so much admire. In fact, the Showa writers of fiction, in the aggregate, represent the greatest flowering of literary talent since the time of Lady Muraski and *The Tale of Genji* in the eleventh-century Heian period. In the great universities, developing trends in such important fields as continental philosophy could be studied by young Japanese who had begun at the end of the nineteenth century with Kant and Hegel and moved even by the beginning of Showa to a study of Marx, Von Hartmann, then Kierkegaard, Husserl, and Heidegger.

In those areas of high cultural production that require a tradition of specific tactile skills, however, such as in painting or sculpture, the necessary time required to learn and master new techniques caused more complex difficulties. Nowhere was this problem more evident than in the area of Western-style painting. Japanese artists traveling to Paris and elsewhere were still learning the requisite skills through the kind of academic training now scoffed at by their advanced European contemporaries. Japanese painters, like their American colleagues, were turning out extremely respectable works of art in the sort of conservative style available to them, just at a time when the Picassos and Kandinskys set out to destroy the very assumptions on which such training rested. The same problem was faced by Japanese composers who sought out the requisite technical training in Europe only to find that their mentors in the musical academies there were often as bewildered as they by the work of the Bartoks, Stravinskys, and Schoenbergs. It was really not until the 1960s that a truly sufficient understanding of the freewheeling, often nihilistic attitudes that had become a part of high culture in Europe were to be fully and comfortably integrated into the Japanese mentality. The fact of the war, of course, helped delay the date of that presumably fruitful level of assimilation; by the same token, the war helped create a generation of new mentalities more open to the kind of spiritual emptiness that Europeans had come to identify after their own terrible experiences in World War I, thirty years before.

In sum, it would seem that, in the musical and visual arts at least, it is impossible to learn a tradition while destroying it at the same time; a basis for sympathy must be established before it can be questioned. No one but a rare genius indeed could be expected to take on successfully such a double burden. It was only when these new Western traditions were firmly internalized and respected in Japan that an authentic avant-garde could come into being. The creation of a viable internationalized modern tradition in Japanese poetry, for example, provided a sufficient context for the reception in Japan of the astonishingly effective surrealist poetry of Nishiwaki Junzaburo (1894–1982), who because of his linguistic skills and deep interest in European literature, could sojourn in Europe in the 1920s and come to create his works in a kind of free, internationalist mode that he, at least, could take for granted.

To put the problem another way, it would seem that not only the ideas and ideals of Western culture but the creative context had to be imported as well into Japan. This is surely one reason that a prodigious translation industry developed, that theatre companies devoted to presenting Western drama were created, and that symphony orchestras were established by the early years of Showa. Indeed, it is a remarkable—and from a Western point of view, a sobering—thought that the first full-length recording of a work now as popular as Mahler's Fourth Symphony was made, not in Berlin or Vienna, but in Tokyo in 1930 by Parlophone, using a Japanese conductor and a Japanese soprano (both trained in Europe), as well as a Japanese orchestra. It is difficult to create such effective institutions, but possible; and indeed, in matters of artistic execution, they can be brought to a high degree of perfection. Perhaps that fact is miracle enough. Still, the existence of such musicians does not suggest, by the same token, that a Japanese composer of Mahler's talents will inevitably appear as well. The means may well need to precede the ends, but they cannot replace them.

Then too, there is still an additional problem related to issues of international cultural attitudes. Even if a Japanese Mahler should appear, problems of authenticity in the creative aspects of modern high culture as perceived in the West would have made the acceptance around the world of a Japanese Stravinsky, Matisse, or T.S. Eliot most problematic during these interwar years, perhaps even later. The difficulties inherent in maintaining a Japanese point of view while making use of artistic or intellectual stances and techniques developed in the West have posed and continue to pose delicate problems of judgment. In the field of art, for example, a painter like Fujita Tsuguji (1886–1968), well known and patronized in France and elsewhere as a member of the Ecole de Paris has always been regarded by the Japanese modern-art establishment as a bit of a renegade, one who simply sold out by adopting Western values for his own ends. The Japanese much prefer the paintings of his older contemporary Umehara Ryuzaburo (1888–1986), until his death long the doyen of the art establishment. Umehara maintained close and productive ties with France, but, for his viewers in Tokyo and elsewhere, his essential Japaneseness has never been in doubt. Foreign enthusiasts for modern Japanese art, however, have consistently chosen Fujita.

In the context of traditional Japan, Chinese artists and intellectuals were able to see or read very little concerning what had become of their traditions when they were borrowed by those to whom Japan was simply a small, far-off island country. In this century, on the other hand, quick scrutiny from all sides and at all times makes any slow, deliberate artistic and intellectual development increasingly problematic. It is one thing, say, for a contemporary French playwright to take an avant-garde stand vis-à-vis the work of his own contemporaries; it is a difficult and far more ambiguous task for a Japanese playwright who, by imposed self-definition is responding to the developments centered in another culture, to proceed quickly while still remaining authentically himself. Again, certain fields of scholarly inquiry and literary expression had had more time to develop smoothly. Ironically, one reason for this relatively healthy maturation may lie in the fact that, because of the awesome language barrier involved, most of such work is kept away, except on an occasional and fragmentary basis, from immediate comparison with any putative European models. The Japanese language remains the one wall as yet unbreached in our century, which has seen so many others fall in Japan. In fields of high cultural expression such as the visual arts, theatre, and music, however, where the impact can be far more immediate, those working in such forms may well feel themselves too quickly exposed to European, and often Eurocentric, standards.

The Past in the Present

However internationally centered the high culture of the Showa period was intended to be in the minds of many of its creators, two problems soon arose that were, and to some degree still remain, difficult to resolve. Both are related to earlier attitudes of mind inherited from a nexus of traditional Japanese values.

The first of these problems involves the relationship between high culture and more broadly based cultural attitudes in the population at large. In one sense, this relationship involves the relation between culture and politics, but the shifting context of popular attitudes during the Showa period makes any simple or definitive explanation of these issues elusive. Perhaps a brief comment on the nature of the interconnections, or lack of them, between high cultural attitudes and political power might serve, however, as one means to examine the question briefly. In the prewar period, writers and intellectuals, at least through the 1920s, felt that their sometimes close alliances to the highly educated men who often held important positions in the various government bureaucracies, the press, and the Foreign Office, should provide a context in which more universalist ideas could develop, and perhaps gain hegemony. With the rise of the military in the 1930s, however, which brought to power a group of men who tended to come from rural areas and be less well educated, less worldly, and more spontaneous in their expression of traditional Japanese values, the presumed persuasive power of a high and Westernized culture in guiding Japan's practical destinies was revealed as impotent; indeed, the force of unhappy political events spawned a whole new grouping of intellectuals who often committed themselves to new nationalistic ideals. In this onslaught of ideas that at first may have appeared reactionary to many, it was only the Marxist intellectuals in the universities and in certain artistic circles who retained the sufficient psychological power to resist.

Ironically, in the postwar period many of those same Marxist intellectuals, seen in the late 1940s with some justification as heroic figures, were eventually revealed as too rigid in their own beliefs to appeal to any majority of the Japanese public in the face of the economic advances that followed that last great internal political upheaval in the Showa period, the widespread demonstrations against the renewal of Japan's security treaty with the United States in the 1960s. In terms of wielding any real political influence, proponents of high culture were forced to learn, then relearn, their limitations.

In terms of artistic form as well, long-held assumptions about the etiquette of possibilities (and concomitant limitations) appropriate within the accepted Japanese canons of artistic creation placed certain implicit limitations on the creation of any authentic art or literature sensitive to the need to articulate directly social and political relationships in modern Japan. The very greatness of the older aesthetic traditions, long assumed in the culture, made these patterns, which so often privileged lyric introspection, very difficult to break, submerged as they were at a deep level of consciousness in writers, artists, and readers alike, whatever the shifting nature of the surface, or of the fashionable modes of contemporary expression. After all, the greatest early documents of Japanese literary expression, which go back to the sixth century and before, were poetic, creating lyric impulses binding poet and reader together, often through a shared symbolic use of nature images. This deep lyrical mode of exchange, and of understanding, later metamorphosed into prose in a work such as the eleventh-century *Tale of Genji,* continued into the modern period to inform structure, style, and content even in such new forms as the modern novel. The masteries of Tanizaki Junichiro and Kawabata Yasunari probe the poetic and erotic depths of the relationships portrayed with a high poetry of narrative skill, but in such a linguistic and emotional landscape, there remained little room for ruminations on politics and history. Even in such a powerful novel of war as Ooka Shohei's *Nobi* (Fires on the Plain), the inward, lyrical thrust informs the mental constructs of the narrator. It is perhaps only in the forms furthest removed from those traditions that trenchant political and social commentary could find adequate means of expression, notably in the *shingeki* (Modern Theatre) movement. *Shingeki* dramatists seized altogether foreign models, beginning early in the century with Ibsen and Chekhov. This theatre produced in both its prewar and its postwar phases a succession of gifted playwrights who, however differing in their political persuasions and stylistic affinities, were able to bear witness to the dangers and complexities of the times in which they lived. Often their personal points of view drew on outside, universalistic value systems, notably Marxism and Christianity, which were able to provide a more universal and critical framework with which to construct such critiques. By the same token, such frameworks were perceived as somehow "foreign" by many readers and spectators.

Geography

Those who inhabited the world of high Japanese culture have remained relatively unsuccessful in addressing themselves to questions of cultural and political geography. In the earlier years of Showa, the Japanese may have dreamt of Europe, but they conducted their most meaningful foreign relations, and sometimes very badly, in Asia. From the time that the Chinese lost to Japan in the Sino-Japanese War of 1894–1895, the advocates for an internationalized cultural matrix turned from China, so long a model of excellence, to embrace the West. Thus, on the whole, the Japanese artistic and intellectual world did little during the interwar years to come to terms with any necessary understanding of the progressively darkening relationships in which the Japanese nation found itself involved during its Asian wars, which by the broadest definition might be said to have begun with the annexation of Korea in 1910 and certainly were paramount in shaping the nation's destiny by the 1930s. In some ways, that vacuum of sympathy and understanding for Asia still exists. While some writers of the postwar period, such as the novelist Takeda Taijun, have attempted to address and assess the ambiguous role of Japan in Asia during the earlier years of Showa, a truly rigorous examination and a genuine understanding of these complex attitudes by Japanese intellectuals remain incomplete. All the wounds inflicted on Japan's Asian neighbors have therefore yet to heal in a satisfactory manner. The proponents of high culture in Japan may well have stressed the possibility of a Japanese culture able to function in a larger contemporary world, but not perhaps in the *whole* world.

Indeed, it might well be argued that even the United States did not enter the Japanese framework of high culture in any meaningful way until the Occupation in 1945 made this rapprochement inevitable. Even then, it has been the more popular elements of American culture that have continued to find an appeal, rather than the accomplishments of American high culture. Films, not Faulkner, cartoons and not Jackson Pollack, continue to fascinate the larger Japanese public. Europe remains the focus, and the classical ideas (of Goethe, Stendhal, Mozart, down to Sartre) remain important in the Japanese pantheon; most cultivated Japanese know little if anything about, say, Henry James, Henry Adams, William Carlos Williams, or John Dewey. It is perfectly true, by the same token, that America in her own cultural past has always turned to Europe. The fact that, in the past, both civilizations have been attracted to Europe, and for many of the same reasons, suggests certain congruences of aspiration running parallel in both societies that have not on the whole been much commented upon by the Japanese intellectual establishment.

III

The accomplishments of high culture in the Showa period—and they have been many—have in the end played a central part in leading Japanese society through the complex political, social, and moral vicissitudes of this sixty-four year period. Some of the ways in which high culture has played out this role have been unexpected.

Japanese intellectuals educated to appreciate and occasionally to appropriate Western methodologies and points of view had by the beginning of the Showa period begun to look at their own culture from a cosmopolitan point of view. The writing of a succession of novelists such as Tanizaki Juniichiro, Dazai Osamu, and Oe Kenzaburo shows the nature of a sort of modern self-awareness that can capture authentic assumptions that lie behind much of modern Japanese intellectual, indeed spiritual, life. Couched in an idiom relatively approachable for Western readers, such modern works of high culture can also function as points of access for outsiders seeking to understand Japan. Such works were, of course, never written for such a purpose, but they provide articulate examples of the shifting distances that govern the borders of Japanese and Western cultural suppositions.

Indeed, by the 1960s, both artistic and intellectual works were being produced in Japan that bore powerful witness to the ways in which the West and Japan had come to develop a vocabulary in common (although I would be the first to agree that much more is needed on the side of the West to bring a sense of mutuality to the exchange). Yamazaki Masakazu, for example, in such powerful theatrical works as *Zeami* (1963) or *Sanetomo shuppan* (1973) chooses for his protagonists Hamlet-like figures who are perceived as such by his audiences, which have by now assimilated the work of the greatest English playwright into their culture just as we have into ours. A perceived ambiguity and emptiness of modern life have produced such figures as the playwrights Samuel Beckett and Edward Albee in the West, Abe Kobo and Betsuyaku Minoru in Japan; and if there appears to be a certain generic resemblance between the work of all four, that fact has more to do with the commonality of contemporary sensibilities than it does with matters of superficial literary or intellectual influence. Indeed, in the arts at least, a number of significant projects in recent years have been openly cross-cultural. Miki Minoru, one of Japan's most stimulating younger composers, has written operas, using both Western and Japanese modes and musical instruments, that have been performed with real success both in and out of Japan. Suzuki Tadashi, arguably the greatest director in contemporary Japanese theatre circles, has found genuine success with his troupe in his American and European performances; indeed, so many foreign actors have worked with him that in 1987, Suzuki was able to create, and in his own wholly authentic style, a version of *King Lear* with an all-American cast, which evoked a highly successful response in both Japan and the United States. Thus, the promise of a kind of authentic cultural amalgamation with the rest of the world that sparked so many hopes at the beginning of the Showa era is, in a few areas at least, coming to fruition.

What are the problems that Japanese high culture must face now, and in the future? Ironically, the problem is a transcultural one as well, one common to the United States, Europe, and Japan. It is the overwhelming pressure from an internationalized popular culture that is establishing a new hegemony. Even in a country like Japan, with old and aristocratic traditions, the onslaught is a powerful one: comic books now replace the inexpensive paperback editions of Tolstoy, Dostoyevski, Hegel, and Flaubert read and devoured by earlier generations of Japanese students. It is not altogether clear how those who believe in the high traditions of modern Japanese culture will frame new attitudes capable of coping with these rampant energies. There is a sense in Tokyo, as in New York, London, Berlin, and Paris, that an era has come to an end. Still, loyalties and commitments have always been strong in Japanese culture, and those who respect and love her modern accomplishments—be they in music, the fine arts, literature, or in intellectual life in general—will undoubtedly remain loyal. Nevertheless, the next generations, those brought up out of Showa, may develop other enthusiasms that could finally break ties to the past that still give Japanese modern culture a resonance of continuity. Whether that sense of continuity will ultimately come to be identified as a last peculiarity of the Showa period must await the assessments of other generations on both sides of the Pacific.

FURTHER READINGS

I have provided no endnotes in this article, since, despite the copious information available in Japanese, there exist as yet few systematic studies in English of the kind of modern Japanese cultural history sketched here, with the exception of the concluding sections of H. Paul Varley's *Japanese Culture, A Short History* (Honolulu: University of Hawaii Press, 1974). Donald Keene's sympathetic and complex *Dawn to the West, Japanese Literature in the Modern Era* (New York: Holt, Rinehart & Winston, 1984) gives a nuanced account of the development of fiction, poetry, drama, and literary criticism. Those wishing information on the development of modern Japanese art may seek, for the prewar period, the volume *Modern Currents in Japanese Art*, by Michiaki Kawakita, in the Heibonsha Series (Tokyo: Kodansha International, 1974) and the catalogue for the exhibition *Paris in Japan* (St. Louis: Washington University and the Japan Foundation, 1987), which concentrates on painting in the Western style. Postwar currents are sketched in another Heibonsha volume, *Japanese Art in World Perspective*, by Toru Terada (Tokyo: Kodansha International, 1976). Vol. 6 of the new *Cambridge History of Japan* (Cambridge: Cambridge University Press, 1988) contains a probing analysis of modern Japanese intellectual attitudes, including a discussion of Watsuji Tetsuro. There is virtually nothing available on modern Japanese concert and operatic music. The only book-length treatment of modern Japanese theatre, which concentrates on the prewar period, is my own *Toward a Modern Japanese Theatre: Kishida Kunio* (Princeton: Princeton University Press, 1974). Anthologies of translations of postwar plays may also prove helpful, in particular those of Ted Takaya, *Modern Japanese Drama* (New York: Columbia University Press, 1979) and David Goodman, *Japanese Drama and Culture in the 1960s* (Armonk, N.Y.: M. E. Sharpe, 1988) and *After Apocalypse* (New York: Columbia University Press, 1986). All three contain useful and provocative essays on the development of postwar Japanese theatre. The two plays by Yamazaki Masakazu are available in *Mask and Sword* (New York: Columbia University Press, 1980).

How They Have Looked to Us

Edward Seidensticker

Japan and the Japanese are on America's mind as never before. In the war years America's concern was to beat the Japanese, not to study or understand them. Today, America is told that it has much to learn from the society and culture of the island nation. America's view of Japan during Hirohito's reign, as enemy, ally, and rival, has been as turbulent as Showa itself.

The Japanese view of the United States is more homogeneous, more of a piece, than the American view of Japan. The latter is sometimes in better focus than at other times, but it has tended to be rather diffuse and absent-minded. Though regional differences are to be detected in Japanese opinion,[1] Tokyo may be held to speak for Japan as New York and Washington cannot always speak for the rest of the United States. New York and San Francisco sometimes agree, and often they do not. There are times when a general American view of Japan may be averred, and times when one must make note of several Americas; and through it all a certain inattention prevails. If societies may broadly be divided into the convergent and the divergent, or the centripetal and the centrifugal, then Japan is surely the former and the United States the latter. The Japanese view of the American view of Japan also tends to be clearer than its reverse.

The Japanese saw the American view of Japan at the beginning of Showa as hostile. Shortly after the earthquake of 1906, San Francisco discovered that it did not have enough schoolrooms for all its children. So it excluded, among others, the Japanese, who were fewer than a hundred in number. The Japanese government protested, the children were readmitted, and the Gentlemen's Agreement of 1908

Edward Seidensticker is Professor Emeritus of Japanese at Columbia University.

went into effect. Japan agreed to issue no more passports to laborers and to be careful about other categories as well, including even students.

There seemed no reason to believe that the agreement was not working as well as imprecisely worded agreements usually do, and serving its essential purpose; and then in 1924 the United States unilaterally abrogated it, with the Japanese Exclusion Act. On July 7, 1924, the day the act went into effect, there were anti-American demonstrations all across Japan. Ten thousand people gathered in Shiba Park in Tokyo. These were not the first "demos" in which hostility to the United States was an element, but they were perhaps the first of a most imposing series in which it has been the only element.

Such is the Japanese view of the American view, which was blurrier. Only on the West Coast did people think much at all about Japan. The 1924 act was an act of the American Congress, to be sure, but it would probably not have come into being except for the California lobby. Japanese immigrants suffered many an indignity in California. Haru Reischauer's interesting biography of her American grandfather, as we may call him, informs us that things were more gentlemanly in New York.[2] (Though he was Japanese, he spent most of his life in and near New York.) If New York too had had a surge of Japanese laborers such as poured in upon California after the annexation of Hawaii, matters might have been different. The important point is that California knew its mind very well, and the rest of the country paid little heed to the matter.

Yet something like a unified view was emerging. Japanese popularity in the United States had been distinctly on the wane since the Russo-Japanese War. The Anglo-Japanese Alliance, the Russo-Japanese War, and (small matter though it may seem beside the others) the San Francisco school incident all came in the first decade of this century. There was sympathy for the Japanese in the war with the Russians, never a popular people, but Japan was coming to seem an intrusive presence. Among the purposes of the Washington treaties of 1921 was to supplant the alliance, which was held by the American government to accord ill with Anglo-American friendship. The treaties gave Japan more liberty to do what it wished in China, and what it chose to do was coming to seem aggressive.

This was the view of a widely read piece of fiction, a futuristic one, predicting how the Japanese would exploit the new liberty—*The Great Pacific War,* written in 1925 by Hector C. Bywater, a British journalist and specialist in naval affairs. The book is not sensational, nor does it contain, as futuristic novels often do, speciously dramatic passages.

The war begins in 1931, not with an air attack on Pearl Harbor but with sabotage against the Panama Canal. This occurs before the declaration of war. It ends not with Hiroshima, which not many futurists of the day can have foreseen, but with something similarly improbable, a rain of propaganda bombs on Tokyo that brings the war-weary Japanese to their senses. The Showa emperor, so controversial a figure today in the matter of what he might have done to keep Japan out of the mess, does not figure in the story at all. There is an Admiral MacArthur, but no general by that name. The winning of the war—the United States does win it, after recovering from the initial shock—is not of course in every detail what happened in the forties, but the process of moving up through the islands is essentially the same.

What is most interesting for our purposes is the view of the Japanese. They are hostile, and not to be trusted:

> To appreciate what followed it is necessary to emphasize the fact that Guam, in Japanese eyes, was something more than a lonely islet in the broad Pacific. It had stood to them as a symbol of alien power in the Far East, a fortress which sooner or later might become an impregnable stronghold, from which an American fleet could dominate their own waters and menace the very threshold of Dai Nippon itself. True, the Washington Treaty had bound the United States not to fortify Guam or otherwise exploit it as a naval base, but to the Oriental mind paper guarantees have always counted for little. For these reasons the conquest of the island in the first month of war had evoked enthusiasm out of all proportion to the actual achievement.[3]

It may be unfortunate for our purposes that Bywater was English and not American, and then again it may in some ways be a good thing. For all the coolness and martial erudition apparent throughout, the book is prejudiced. It carries a strongly pro-American bias, which could weaken it if the author were American. The point is in any event a small one. Such Japanese as are aware today of Bywater and his work seem to think that he was American, or to assume that English and American can be lumped together (as Anglo-American beasts, in the jargon of a later day).[4]

He was widely read, and contributed much to the image that was forming. There were new editions of the book in 1930 and 1942. Nothing else quite like it exists in English, to my knowledge,[5] but in Japan such books made a thriving industry, at the hands of now almost forgotten writers, which lasted into the thirties.

It was a time when almost no Americans really knew much about Japan. A few diplomats and missionaries and an occasional businessman and professor were the full count of the knowledgeable. Before Showa, Japanese studies scarcely existed in American universities. So there was no sudden burst of interest in and erudition about Japan. Yet the view was becoming general that Japan had grown too big for its britches. People like Bywater contributed something, and events in North China in the first decade of Showa contributed a great deal. In 1932 the League of Nations condemned the Japanese occupation of Manchuria, and in 1933 Japan withdrew from the league. The image of Japan was becoming aggressive and pushy.

Nitobe Inazo, the most prominent in his day among the liaison persons, the explainers that modern Japan has always had as buffers between itself and the world, set off once more for North America, to explain things. Commonly listed in the biographic dictionaries as an educator, Nitobe is so highly regarded in his own land that his picture is on the new five-thousand-yen note. (Fukuzawa Yukichi, one of the other two persons on the new banknotes, is also usually listed as an educator. Education is important in Japan.) Nitobe gave a series of lectures at the University of California in 1932. Later collected under the title *Lectures On Japan,* they are rather elegant, and they are impassioned:

> That Manchukuo was established with the help of Japan, no one denies. It is a common experience of new countries to be founded with the help of others. . . . Does the new dispensation provide that if a new state is born, it must receive no help from a midwife? Certainly the help which the Japanese army gave to Manchukuo was conspicuous, because it was not given clandestinely, as has so often been the case under similar circumstances. The chaotic conditions under which the new state came into existence . . . lend to it an appearance of being a mere puppet of the Japanese army. I can very well understand how

> such things can be, because I have heard of similar instances in other places. Where similar conditions prevail, similar methods are adopted and similar results follow. Rarely is man original. East and West, under similar circumstances, he thinks and acts much the same, and will continue to do so.[6]

This tells us with some clarity what was on the American mind—what Nitobe had to explain. Released not quite two months before the lecture was delivered, the Lytton Report to the League of Nations had rejected all of the Japanese claims, including the one here offered by Nitobe, that all the birth of Manchukuo needed was a bit of friendly nursing on the part of Japan. The report provided the immediate occasion for the Japanese withdrawal from the league.

Mrs. Nitobe's foreword to the lectures, which were published posthumously, tells us that the mood of the nation, whatever may have been that of Berkeley, was not friendly:

> Those were, indeed, dark days for Japan and for us personally, when my husband and I set forth in 1932 on his mission of interpretation for his Country. America was hostile in thought—even friends there often did not understand. Many thought that he had come as propagandist and protagonist for what he could not endorse—a part which Nitobe never did and never would play.[7]

We are now at a time when personal memory begins. I remember Arbor Day, 1932, very well. We children in a rural public school on the western edge of the Mississippi basin were indignant as we went out on the lawn to plant our tree. Word had come in that Tokyo was about to expand and become the second largest city in the world. It even seemed by way of overtaking New York and becoming the largest. We did not like Easterners and we did not like New York, but we did want New York to go on being the largest. We were particularly indignant at the way this was happening, a characteristically Japanese way, underhanded and deceitful. A good honest city grew gradually as it accumulated people. A dishonest one expanded its city limits and announced that its population had doubled overnight. It is a tiny scene, but revealing of the times. We schoolchildren in one of the most isolated and isolationist parts of the United States were acquiring an image of Japan. I believe that there were a few calls that day that we go to war immediately, and show them.

Yet even in this day when schoolchildren were learning to dislike Japan (I do not remember that we were ever taught to, but dislike was in the air), regional differences prevailed.

In Honolulu plenty of people knew that the Japanese were coming long before Pearl Harbor. I have an acquaintance whose mother would say, whenever by some coincidence numbers of ships were approaching the harbor simultaneously: "Well, here they are."

The Pacific Coast, being farther away, was less panicky, but here too anti-Japanese sentiment ran high. When Eugene V. Rostow wrote his famous article on the transporting of Japanese and Japanese-Americans inland,[8] he got many letters opposing and supporting his position, which was that it was a tragic mistake. I was privileged to read them one summer in New Haven. The ones that remain most vivid in memory argued that the relocation was necessary to protect the people relocated. They were not safe on the Pacific Coast. The doctrine that the potential victim of assault should be forcibly removed from the potential setting is a most dubious one morally and legally, but it was held by not unintelligent people. Such was the mood on the Pacific Coast.

In the great Mississippi basin, on the fringes of which I was growing up, there was a dull and uninformed hostility. I do not remember that after the one moment of fervor much was said in school about Japanese-American relations. Indifference prevailed, and isolationism. One summer an eminence from abroad came to town.[9] He said that all we had to do was give the Germans and Japanese enough rope and they would hang themselves. I joined in the murmurs of approval. It was what we wanted to hear. War would be a bother, and probably unnecessary.

And in New York the gentlemen's club of which Mrs. Reischauer's grandfather was a member continued to assemble. Dr. Tsunoda's peaceful life at Columbia was disturbed briefly when Pearl Harbor was attacked and he was taken off to Ellis Island, and resumed once more. The peaceful life was possible at Berkeley until early 1942, when the great rupture came. Whether or not the relocation would have occurred had there not been strong anti-Japanese sentiment on the Pacific Coast we will never know; but there is no question that it played a very important part. In the events leading up to the relocation was a repetition of 1924 and the Japanese Exclusion Act. Noise from California was the catalyst.

The only considerable treatment of American opinion during those years, *Japan in American Public Opinion,* by Eleanor Tupper and George E. McReynolds,[10] is based largely on newspaper columns and editorials. It makes the interesting point that Americans might on the whole have remained indifferent had the disturbances been confined to Manchuria. It took the attack on Shanghai to arouse general hostility:

> When the Sino-Japanese war began, September 18, 1931, the average American knew little about the Far East or the issues involved. Opinion in the newspapers in the United States during the first few months revealed clearly that there was no basic, inherent dislike of the Japanese people in this country; Japan had many defenders and apologists then, and even the attacks directed against it were mainly centered on the Japanese military. As the war continued, however, especially with the brutal Japanese attack on Shanghai, American public opinion changed rapidly.[11]

The book makes the equally interesting point that academic types were the slowest to turn against Japan. It ends in the summer of 1937, short of the Japanese invasion of China proper. Even in that summer the United States did not seem quite to know its own mind. "All the old suspicion of Japan's motives and policy in the Far East was reawakened" by the Amau statement of April 1934, to the effect that China was the business of Japan and Japan alone. Even as the incident at the Marco Polo Bridge approached, however, "the trend of opinion in the United States seemed overwhelmingly in favor of a policy of isolation. Americans in the past three years had given increasing evidence of their belief that the United States should uphold its treaty rights and interests by all possible diplomatic means but do nothing that might involve us in a war in the Far East."[12]

In Japan a single, concentrated orthodoxy prevailed. "The curs are yelping," said Sir George Sansom. "I've never known anything like this atmosphere."[13] They who disagreed kept their own counsels, lest the curs snap. The American view of Japan may presently have become similarly monolithic, but it was less intense and consistent—a pebblier monolith, perhaps. Humor prevailed, albeit frequently bitter humor. An eloquent statement of the American mood is in a little poem by Ogden Nash:

> How courteous is the Japanese;
> He always says, "Excuse it, please."

He climbs into his neighbor's garden,
And smiles, and says, "I beg your pardon."
He bows and grins a friendly grin,
And calls his hungry family in;
He grins and bows a friendly bow;
"So sorry, this my garden now."[14]

The attack came. On that Sunday morning when the isolationist dream was shattered and we of the masculine gender knew that we would all soon be off to war, someone who knew a deal more about the Orient than I did said: "It is the Year of the Snake. *Their* year." And indeed 1941 was the Year of the Snake, the sixth in the Chinese cycle of a dozen. Nineteen eighty-nine was again the Year of the Snake, and so we have come four complete cycles since the day expected to live in infamy. Like the Ogden Nash poem, the remark about the snake expresses the mood of the times eloquently.

The propaganda in the newsreels and over the radio was full of the word *yellow,* in at least two senses. Sheila K. Johnson, in her 1975 monograph on American attitudes toward Japan, quotes a statement by two officials of the Office of War Information to the effect that the image of the Japanese was during the war years less pleasing than that of the Germans:

> Hollywood had a distinct view of each of the enemies. Germans were gentlemen with whom it was possible to deal as equals. As soldiers they were efficient, disciplined, and patriotic; the bureau was unable to find a scene in which the Germans were morally corrupt or delighted in cruelty. . . . Japanese soldiers were pictured as less military than their German counterparts, and were almost universally cruel and ruthless. Japanese were short, thin, and wore spectacles. They were tough but devoid of scruples. In almost every film showing American-Japanese battles, the enemy broke the rules of civilized warfare.[15]

I may say that this runs against my own recollections, which inform me that we thought the Germans far more fiendish than the Japanese. Hirohito had to bear the burden of symbolizing the Japanese; and the Germans had Hitler.

Turning to the possibility, often averred, that there was racism in the dropping of the bomb on Hiroshima, Dr. Johnson introduces a view which may in some measure contradict that of the O.W.I.:

> Interestingly enough, in 1955 the head of the Manhattan Project, General Leslie R. Groves, revealed that precisely the opposite motiva-

tion was at work among some of his scientists. The only group at the project that objected to the use of the bomb, he observed, "did not object until after V-E Day. That group was mostly centered around people who were bitterly anti-German and did not appear to feel the same way towards Japan."[16]

There was a certain margin, as there cannot have been in Japan. Some entities, such as the *Denver Post,* went on being venomous even as propaganda in general softened and the barrages of "yellow" let up a bit. The *Post* was unrelenting in its attacks on the people in the relocation center nearest at hand, Hart Mountain in Wyoming. They had bananas for breakfast. Could the housewives of Colorado say as much for themselves? The wife of a student in the Navy Language School in Boulder canceled her subscription to the *Post* in protest. The *Post* printed her note on its front page, along with an open letter answering it. We all waited to see whether the navy would take disciplinary action against the spouse of this person who had, in the view of the *Post,* indicated sympathy with the enemy. Nothing happened. The incident passed.

One may speculate for a moment on what would have been the case with a Japanese naval officer whose wife protested to the *Asahi* about its more strident views, having to do with Anglo-American beasts and the like, and had her letter printed on its front page, along with an open letter answering it. The point is not to congratulate the United States, and of course oneself while one is about it, on liberality in time of crisis. It is to repeat a point already made: that the Japanese image of the United States is generally more consistent, less diffuse, than the American image of Japan. These were years when this last was as nearly in focus as it ever is, and yet a modicum of pluralism remained. The United States continued to be somewhat divergent and centrifugal.

In 1945 the United States changed its mind about Japan, which was once again what it had been in 1867, the eager student, this time learning about democracy. It was a quick change. And how long did the new image remain fairly whole? That it is now going to pieces (probably to come together in somewhat different form) seems clear enough. It was there through the Olympics of 1964, certainly, when the Japanese staged such a masterly show of competence and amiability ("cuddliness" might do as well); but in the decade of the seventies, when the dollar began to slide and the slide did not have the effect it should have had if all had been true to the principles of market economics, the image of a somewhat greedy and deceitful Japan began to come back.

Not everyone agreed about the postwar democratic revolution, and agreement in substance did not necessarily mean agreement in detail. Academic specialists were, many of them, cautious. Here is Professor Hugh Borton, writing in 1957 and looking back to the end of the American Occupation, five years before:

> Certain important gains remained unchallenged. Rural indebtedness and tenancy had been largely eliminated by the land reform program and by inflation, and farmers were developing a new feeling of independence and well-being. In education, both students and faculty members had now experienced the exhilaration of thinking for themselves and of being free to say and write what they believed. Freedom of the press had, for the first time, taken on a real meaning. While it was far from complete, the emancipation of women was taking place in practically all strata of society and Japanese women were beginning to cherish their new position. People everywhere no longer feared the police, nor were they willing to stand by and submissively follow the lead of the government. In fine, much of the postwar exposure to democracy was bearing fruit.[17]

It is a sober, guarded statement. Yet it is essentially a sunny one, sunnier than some of us would have made at the time and many of us would make today. Applause for the land reform was in those days almost universal. It had created the sturdy yeoman, we were told, even as in England, his independence and his demands for equality being among the more reliable of democratic pillars. The years since have produced increasingly strong evidence that the farm lobby is profoundly antidemocratic—and, incidentally, one that has contributed more than its share to friction between Japan and the United States.

In his next paragraph Professor Borton dwells upon the regressive tendencies of Prime Minister Yoshida, with regard to such matters as the police system, labor law, and economic decentralization. The paragraph concludes with this sentence:

> Since Yoshida had been at the head of the government during most of the previous five years and his party had for three years had an absolute

> majority in the House of Representatives, he was presumably reflecting the view of the majority of the people.[18]

The "presumably" suggests that Professor Borton is not so sure, and certainly he does not accept the notion, which has had some currency, that the revolution of 1945 was not as astonishing as it might have seemed to be, since Japan had already had experience of democracy, in "the Taisho democracy" of the years just after the First World War. "Through no fault of his own, the pre–World War II Japanese had little opportunity to participate in any phase of democracy at work."[19]

Despite reservations, his view is essentially sunny, holding that Japan did indeed undergo profound changes in and after 1945.

The official view is sunnier. Here is Ambassador William J. Sebald, who was in charge of the State Department enclave in General MacArthur's headquarters:

> I believe that the Japanese people are endowed with the unity of purpose which will enable Japan to become a respected, free, independent, and self-supporting member of the Free World. I believe that Japan will add its strength to the growing forces of freedom. And, finally, I believe that as Japan again becomes capable of contributing its just share to the forces of Freedom, it will never again dissipate its strength in aggressive venture, but will find its greatest satisfaction within the principles of the United Nations Charter.
>
> We have ahead of us an unparalleled opportunity to witness here in the Pacific area a great experiment of two sovereign and free nations sharing their energies in the interests of peace and security. We shall learn from you as you shall learn from us. The times are too critical, the forces of evil are too great, to allow of petty suspicions or want of mutual faith and trust. To stand still is to invite disaster. We must go forward in the interest of world peace.[20]

The ambassador is here quoting himself, in his memoirs of the Occupation, a decade and a half later, from an address he delivered to the America-Japan Society of Tokyo, in 1951, the last full year of the Occupation. A single sentence follows the quotation from himself, and the memoirs are at an end:

> Today, thirteen years later, I know of no words which would more clearly express the present-day hopes and aspirations of what I believe is the United States foreign policy for the far reaches of the Pacific.[21]

This final sentence is ambiguous. The ambassador does not come out and say that the view is his own. Yet the official position is important enough to him that he gives it a particularly conspicuous place in his book. Most striking is the almost casual use of the word *freedom*. It has the casualness of dogma: anyone who does not see the self-evident or God-given truth in it had better go back to school.

I can think of no way to establish whether it was the cautious academic view or the more exuberant official one which ruled the mind of America. One thing does seem fairly certain, that knowledge of Japan on the part of the general public was not a great deal more profound than it had been. It is true that ignorance of Japan has not since the war been quite what it was before. Thousands of Americans served in the Occupation, and the age of the airplane brings Americans to Japan in numbers many times larger than the passenger ship was capable of. Japanese studies in American universities really got started during the war. Before the war students often chose to go to Europe for their advanced training. The number of American universities with well-developed Japanese programs is now perhaps ten, perhaps a dozen. Many graduates of the army and navy language schools and the smaller specialized schools happily forgot Japan and the Japanese once the latter had seen them safely through the war, but the many who did not forget included most of the professors who have dominated Japanese studies in the decades since the war. The time has come for them to depart, but it is not as if their departure meant the end of anything. They have produced gifted successors. None of this means, unfortunately, that the general level of American understanding of Japan is much higher.

Another thing seems certain: that on the whole the mood of the country was friendly toward Japan. It seems most likely that friendly but essentially uneducated opinion was more accepting of the official view than of the carefully qualified academic view.

Awareness of the bombing of Hiroshima had something to do with the new friendliness. John Hersey's *Hiroshima* came out almost exactly a year after the end of the war. Occupying a whole issue of the *New Yorker* in August 1946, it made immediate and almost personal what had been distant and abstract. I remember that the announcement of the bombing brought delight that the war would soon be over, and apprehensions about the new age into which we were being pulled; it took the Hersey book to arouse horror and sympathy. In

1955 Norman Cousins began bringing his "Hiroshima maidens" to the United States for treatment. Sympathy grew, and perhaps guilt. It is surely a mistake to say that all Americans feel or have felt guilty about Hiroshima, but American acts of contrition on August 6 (and less conspicuously, on almost any other day of the year) have become routine. Americans became willing to give the Japanese the benefit of many doubts. In 1954 a Japanese fishing boat received a nuclear dusting because it approached too close to tests at Bikini. That too created a stir.

Yet Americans went on thinking that the bombing had been necessary. An opinion poll in 1971 showed that almost two-thirds did. In 1985 more than half still did.[22] Since one need not feel guilt for what cannot be avoided, the image of a uniformly guilt-ridden America is surely exaggerated. Yet awareness of Hiroshima did contribute to the friendliness. The rights and wrongs were not as simple as they had seemed during the war. People had died in a most appalling fashion.

We may note that a kind of see-saw has been in operation. When China is up Japan is down, and when Japan is up China is down. The direction of optimistic, hopeful America has always been westward. Having moved by land as far as we can in that direction, we seem yet to keep our eyes on the western horizon, in search of realms not for political or military but for evangelical conquest. China was under a cloud after Harry Truman lost it. Now it is emergent once more. This is true despite the happenings at the Tien-an Gate. It is by no means the only reason for Japanese who worry about such things to pay uneasy attention to the American view, but it is certainly among them. Nor is it the only element in the official view; but it is among them.

We have come to the age of Zen. The Japanese, perhaps by way of consoling themselves for not being a military power and not yet an economic power, kept telling us that they were a spiritual one, and many Americans, perhaps most Americans, were inclined to believe them. Those of us who lived in Japan during these years—in a general way the years between the San Francisco Treaty of 1952 and the Olympics of 1964—saw a stream of refugees from the noise and bustle and materialism of America in search of the quiet of old Japan. The wonder was not that they came searching for it, but that they found it, a Japan unconcerned about the thing of the moment, reposing in the calm of the centuries. Zen was the ideal object, because of its contributions to the rusticity thought to be the essence of Japanese culture, and because of the insouciance with which it ignores intellectual preoccupations:

> The next morning during tea with the Jikijitsu, a college professor who rents a room in one of the Sodo buildings came in and talked of *koans*. "When you understand Zen you know that the tree is really *there*"—the only time anyone said anything of Zen philosophy or experience the whole week.

This is from Gary Snyder's description of *sesshin,* a sort of Zen retreat, in Kyoto.[23] It is a very interesting account, not the least interesting for the absence of the intellect and of arguable doctrine from the regimen. Sutras were read, to be sure, but it is most unlikely that anyone understood them. They were part of the mood.

Zen was not everything in those years. For the Japanese, who adore booms, they were the years of the first big Japan boom in foreign regions, by which is meant chiefly western Europe and North America. Japan seemed to be attracting serious attention as never before, in all manner of lines and fields, from religion to judo. But Zen may after all provide the best rubric. It catches the essential mindlessness of the "boom," and the fact that not all lines and fields received equal attention.

We cannot of course reasonably expect that they would be so treated, but there was a pattern to the emphasis and the neglect. It was a day when Japanese fiction was being translated as never before, but, alas, not a great many people bought it and read it, very few indeed compared with those who bought art books. It takes some trouble to sit down and understand a work of fiction from a distant culture, and a huge amount of trouble to learn the language and read it in the original, as should be done if it is really to be understood. (Translation is a coarse net, allowing much to slip through.) Publishers such as Kodansha, which started out with a high sense of mission in the matter of showing the world the best of Japanese culture, and the best certainly includes literature, presently found themselves making such money as they made from coffee-table books. An interest in religion could have been ethereally intellectual, but for most people it was not. It was Zen.

The popularity of the martial arts seems a bit curious, a bit difficult to reconcile with the repose of the centuries. The theoretical foundations had been well laid, however. A great genius at organizing and at disseminating an idiosyncratic view had changed a technique into a way, jujutsu into judo. This was Kano Jigoro, who is also listed in the biographical dictionaries as an educator. He was the founder of judo, and judo is "the pliant way," and the way, a mystic thing, is a regimen of complete submission and dedication, monklike or nunlike if followed to its conclusion.

There was another way in which judo went well with the image of the new, quiet Japan, a nonfighting partner in the fight for freedom. In theory it is mostly passive. Wait for an adversary to come, and use his poundage to throw him effortlessly over your shoulder. The more weight the better. The bigger they come, the harder they fall. One may have trouble believing that all the thugs who are good at judo are strong on spiritual training, but then the image of Japan the spiritual, the land of Zen, wore a certain air of unreality. It may be argued that the element of unreality is the more considerable in the American image of Japan the more clearly it is focused. Ogden Nash's description of the Japanese leaves many things out of consideration, but it speaks eloquently of the times in which it was written. Large numbers of Japanese may have been living in tents and caves in the summer of 1945, but that did not keep them from being among the more urbanized people in the world, or remove them from all the modern bother. The clearly focused image can be in some degree illusory.

The day when we were supposed to learn from Japan came somewhat later, as Japanese successes at fabricating and selling began to make us lose confidence in our own. Works on Japanese business practices and how to understand the Japanese business mind came to sell better than anything, including serious literature, translated from Japanese. William Ouchi's *Theory Z* probably did the best. It urges American companies to find a response to Japanese methods without merely imitating the Japanese and discarding American methods that have worked well for a long while. It was published in 1981. Ezra Vogel's *Japan as Number One* (1979) sold more copies, but most of them were in Japanese. It is a dreamier book than Ouchi's and as if written for a Japanese readership, which the Ouchi book is not. One translation from Japanese, *The Book of Five Rings,* sold well at about the time the Ouchi book was most in vogue. It is attributed to Miyamoto Musashi, an accomplished swordsman and painter of the early seventeenth century. Musashi's theories about the martial arts were deemed applicable to the world of business. Indeed, business was reaching an intensity not far from war.

The high tide of eager learning from the Japanese (even as the Japanese had eagerly learned from America a hundred years before) came when the "positive" image of Japan as the good peaceful friend was beginning to break down. Japan no longer seemed the best possible place to go in search of quiet (and with the advent of the Yuppies, America was no longer so interested in that sort of thing), but it was a place to go and learn a thing or two. Some of the people who came back from Japan having learned a lesson seemed as out of touch with reality as the people who went off to escape from the twentieth century. The worst, perhaps, were the environmentalists. I would not wish to be understood as suggesting that concern for the environment is silly, but the idea that we have something to learn from the Japanese in that regard does seem a touch silly.

The point to be remembered is not a trivial one. Through perhaps a quarter of the Showa period, perhaps as much as a third, Americans had a fairly clear, coherent, and balanced notion of Japan. For perhaps the quarter preceding this one there had been a similarly coherent image, and it was an unfriendly one. Now we seem to be headed back toward our starting point. The favorable image has not gone utterly to pieces. It is not in tatters and fragments. But that it no longer has the acceptance it once had, and that they whom Japan delights unconditionally are ever fewer in number, seems beyond denying. Suspicion and doubt are in the air. Pockets of hostility emerge. The fear is that they will widen.

The source of it all, as everyone knows, is the Japanese reemergence as a power. It is easy to assign simple and generally rather base motives for the change in American feelings. Mere jealousy is averred. The United States does not like being Number Two. The minister of trade and industry recently accused the American Congress of racism for passing certain rather mild measures adverse to Japanese exports. It is a harsh charge, easy to make, very difficult either to prove or to disprove.

The truth of the matter is that the problem of Japanese economic power and what to do about it is a devilishly complicated one. Experts are ranged on both sides in every issue of detail; plausible arguments are offered in support of every implausible assertion.

This sort of exchange is always taking place:

"My but the Japanese banks do seem to be making great heaps of money."

"Are you speaking in terms of capitalization, or assets, or accretion as against amortization, or perhaps the Watanabe quotient?"

"Well, I just mean all those big bright buildings all over the city. Such slickness, such lucre. No New York bank could possibly match it."

"Tokyo, of course (do you not agree?) is not New York. You may have let Robinson's ratio momentarily slip your mind, and then there is always of course the Suzuki factor to be considered."

And, quickly and smoothly, the expert has demonstrated that the Japanese banks are in fact impoverished, and that they are keeping their doors open out of affection for their customers, and at great sacrifice. The nonexpert is easily stunned.

Many Japanese claim racism, even as did the minister, in attempts to tighten the American market a bit against Japanese imports. Many also claim it in the case of Hiroshima. If they are right, and who can tell whether they are or not, then at least Japan is being paid attention to; and so the complaint is inconsistent with that other common one, that Americans pay little attention at all. The latter complaint is probably the more valid, or at any rate the more easily argued. Running all through our treatment of the Japanese image has been an invariable: indifference and nescience. It is relative, of course. Some Americans know rather a good deal about Japan; more Japanese know a good deal about the United States.

The Japanese image of America continues to be clearer than the American image of Japan. We hear a great deal about "Japan bashing" in the United States. "America bashing" in Japan is every bit as thorough, and probably has greater force behind it because the country comes nearer being unified. The common Japanese view is that America must put its house in order, that there is nothing wrong with selling superior products to an America that cannot make them for itself and taking scarcely anything in return, that the Japanese are victims of racism, and more generally that they are victims. This last takes us back to the prewar notion of the ABCD powers—the Americans, the British, the Chinese, and the Dutch—consciously plotting to encircle and strangle tiny Japan.

It pains the Japanese that they occupy a smaller portion of American attention than America does of theirs. Polls consistently show that this is the case. A recent poll by the *Yomiuri Shimbun* has the United States first among nations the Japanese most rely on, while Japan is eleventh on the American list.[24] There are reasons why the Japanese need not fret. Eleventh is not a bad position to occupy when all the preceding ten are either English-speaking countries or countries of western Europe, and include places like Sweden and New Zealand, which it seems a bit unrealistic to put much reliance on. We need not be shocked, moreover, that the larger entity worries less about the smaller entity than the reverse. The Koreans make the complaint about Japan that Japan does about the United States. When Country A has only itself to rely on and must look for scatterings of friendship where it can find them, and Country B is utterly dependent on that country, it seems neither surprising nor unjust that Country B should pay more attention to Country A than Country A does to Country B.

Yet the complaint is valid. The United States is relatively indifferent to Japan even in this day when it seems impossible to run a household without Japanese appliances or to service the national debt without the assistance of Japanese savings.

The experts say everything possible about the Japan problem, by which is meant the trade problem. Some, it is true, worry about a newly militarized and politically expansive Japan, but they do not seem numerous, important, or realistic. A new image does seem to be emerging all the same, of a Japan which does not play fair, of a Japan which eats its cake and has it, of a Japan which says that it is going to do one thing and does another—and of a Japan which thinks it can buy its way out of any predicament.

Economic problems are seldom precisely separable from political ones, but a problem in which the dominant note was economic is becoming a predominantly political one. The contradictory arguments of the economists matter less and less, and what does matter is a growing sense that things cannot go on this way much longer. If we are returning, willy-nilly, to the Ogden Nash view of the Japanese, then we are returning to something which we had hoped would be forever in the past.

ENDNOTES

[1]See for instance Douglas H. Mendel, Jr., *The Japanese People and Foreign Policy* (Berkeley and Los Angeles: University of California Press, 1961).

[2]*Samurai and Silk* (Cambridge: Harvard University Press, 1986).

[3]The quotation is from the 1942 edition (Boston: Houghton Mifflin), 253 and 254.

[4]See for instance "Futuristic Theories of a Japanese-American War" (*Nichibei Mirai Sensoron*), in Japanese Foreign Ministry, ed., *Dictionary of the History of Japanese Foreign Affairs* (*Nihon Gaikoshi Jiten*), (Tokyo: Printing Office of the Japanese Finance Ministry, 1979).

[5]In 1909 there had appeared a piece not of futuristic fiction but of prophesy, by an American, Homer Lea. It too foresees war, but it is far wider of what actually happened than the Bywater book. Lea has a sleepy, decadent America losing Hawaii and the Pacific Coast to Japan. In his preface he says that the book, *The Valor of Ignorance* (New York: Harper and Brothers), was "partially completed" immediately after the Portsmouth Treaty, which ended the Russo-Japanese War.

[6]*The Works of Inazo Nitobe*, vol. 4 (Tokyo: University of Tokyo Press, 1972, first edition 1936), 249 and 250.

[7]Ibid., 5.

[8]"Our Worst Wartime Mistake," *Harper's* 191 (September 1945): 193–201.

[9]It was James Dillon, a member of the Irish parliament and later a Cabinet minister.

[10]*Japan in American Public Opinion* (New York: Macmillan, 1937).

[11]Ibid., 444.

[12]Ibid., 446–447.

[13]From a letter written to Lady Sansom in 1940. Katherine Sansom, *Sir George Sansom and Japan* (Tallahassee: The Diplomatic Press, 1972), 115.

[14]From *The Face Is Familiar* (Boston: Little, Brown, 1940), 233.

[15]*The Japanese through American Eyes* (Stanford: Stanford University Press, 1988), 20. The officials are Gregory D. Black and Clayton R. Koppes. The statement first appeared in *Foreign Service Journal* (August 1974).

[16]Ibid., 42. The Groves quotation is from *New York Times Magazine,* 31 July 1955.

[17]*Japan between East and West* (New York: Harper and Brothers for the Council on Foreign Relations, 1957), 4.

[18]Ibid., 5.

[19]Ibid., 3.

[20]*With MacArthur in Japan, A Personal History of the Occupation,* written with Russell Brines (New York: W. W. Norton, 1965), 299 and 300.

[21]Ibid., 300.

[22]Johnson, 53.

[23]"Spring Sesshin at Shokokuji," in Nancy Wilson Ross, ed., *The World of Zen* (New York: Vintage Books, 1960), 329 and 330. *Jikijitsu* means something like "chief preceptor." The other two Japanese words refer respectively to the meditation hall and the conundrums or questions that are the subject of meditation.

[24]The *Honolulu Star-Bulletin and Advertiser,* 11 December 1988, carries an account from the *Chicago Tribune.*

Index